Losing Control is an important bo
Kammer explains why a liberal r
in the national interest. Democra
eral restrictionists; they wanted t
migrants to protect similar US workers. Kammer explains how foundations, employers, activists on the left and right, and editorial writers pushed for the expansionist policy that now prevails in the Democratic Party. He also provides a perceptive account of the evolution of the backlash that found its hero in the 2016 election of Donald Trump.

—Philip Martin, Professor Emeritus of Agricultural and Resource Economics, University of California-Davis; economist, Select Commission on Immigration and Refugee Policy, 1979-1980; editor of *Rural Migration News*

Our country's failure to manage immigration has most affected working-class Americans and set the stage for Donald Trump's politically opportunistic xenophobia. The fault is not in the immigrants, whom Kammer views with empathy, but in our ourselves. You may not agree with his criticism of those who promote fewer restrictions or take advantage of cheap labor, But his straight-shooting, fair-mindedness, knowledge of history and politics, and rejection of the nativism that pollutes the immigration debate make this an important book for anyone who wants to understand how we reached our current state of paralysis and what it will take to repair the system with sustainable reform.

—Jeffrey Davidow, U.S. Ambassador to Mexico, 1998-2002; author of *The Bear and the Porcupine: The U.S.and Mexico;* career Foreign Service officer

If, like me, you consider the current anti-immigrant fever a toxic assault on fundamental American values, then you must read Jerry Kammer's *Losing Control.* No one in the immigration restriction camp makes its case as clearly as Kammer does, and he does so without any taint of racial or ethnic bias. This book may not change your mind, but it will certainly open it.

—Daniel Okrent, author of *The Guarded Gate*

Want more equality and inclusion in the United States? A better deal for working people and a stronger social safety net? Jerry Kammer revives the progressive case for immigration enforcement. An original and important contribution to an urgent national debate.

—David Frum, *The Atlantic*

For decades the overwhelming majority of the American people have opposed illegal immigration. Yet an unholy alliance of business leaders, libertarian and conservative ideologues, liberal activists, and politicians of all stripes have consistently colluded to ensure open borders. Jerry Kammer, an old-fashioned shoe-leather reporter, liberal but scrupulously objective, nuanced and thorough, has written a masterful history of illegal immigration from the early 20th century to the present. As a long-time observer of immigration politics, I suggest that this is simply the best analysis of illegal immigration to date bar none.

—John Fonte, Senior Fellow, the Hudson Institute

For those of us on-the-scene in the old INS, enactment of the Immigration Reform and Control Act of 1986 (IRCA)was reason for optimism. But a flawed worker verification process was vulnerable to massive fraud. Special interests who profited from the illegal influx worked their will in Washington, leading to the demoralization of the enforcers and the rapid growth of the illegal immigrant population. With vivid writing based on meticulous research and on-the-ground reporting, Jerry Kammer does a wonderful job telling the story of how immigration policy was rigged to make a mockery of the original goal of deactivating the jobs magnet.

—Gregory Bednarz, former Deputy Assistant Commissioner,
Immigration and Naturalization Service

Kammer is terrific at putting a human face to both sides of the immigration debate and explaining why comprehensive US immigration reform has proved so elusive. He shows that although most Americans want a pragmatic solution, both Democrats and Republicans have polarized the debate, rousing raw emotions to advance their partisan interests. Eschewing the noise and confusion that has characterized America's recent debate on immigration policy, *Losing Control* neither panders to political interest nor peddles easy solutions. Instead, it presents a thoughtful examination of how we arrived at this point and how we can move forward. For those seeking respite from the echo chamber, this book is a must read.

—Armand Peschard-Sverdrup, CEO of Peschard-Sverdrup
International (PSI) and Senior Associate (Non-Resident) at the
Center for Strategic and International Studies (CSIS)

LOSING CONTROL

Also by Jerry Kammer

What Happened to Worksite Enforcement?: A Cautionary Tale of Failed Immigration Reform (2017)

The Wrong Stuff: The Extraordinary Saga of Randy "Duke" Cunningham, the Most Corrupt Congressman Ever Caught (2007)

The Second Long Walk: The Navajo-Hopi Land Dispute (1980)

LOSING CONTROL

How a Left-Right Coalition Blocked Immigration Reform and Provoked the Backlash That Elected Trump

JERRY KAMMER

The Center for Immigration Studies
Washington, DC

Losing Control: How a Left-Right Coalition Blocked Immigration Reform and Provoked the Backlash That Elected Trump

Published by The Center for Immigration Studies, Washington, DC
CIS.org

ISBN 978-1-881290-03-2 (paperback)
ISBN 978-1-881290-04-9 (eBook)

Publishing consultant: David Wogahn, AuthorImprints.com

America in general has deep affection for immigrants, knows they are part of the dynamic, a part of our growth and our endless coming-into-being. But when your heart is soft, and America's is, your head must be hard. We are a sovereign nation operating under the rule of law. That, in fact, is why many immigrants come here. They come from places where the law, such as it is, is corrupt, malleable, limiting. Does it make sense to subvert our own laws to facilitate the entrance of those in pursuit of government by law?

— *Peggy Noonan,* The Wall Street Journal, *April 13, 2006*

We need to get between employers addicted to an endless flow of cheap labor and unauthorized immigrants for whom a substandard job here is a step up. We have the technology to implement a reliable system that tells employers whether they're hiring an illegal worker. What we have lacked thus far is the political guts to mete out serious punishment to those employers who ignore the law. Without that true immigration reform will never occur.

—Jared Bernstein, Economic Policy Institute and former adviser to Vice President Joe Biden

Populist campaigns and parties often function as warning signs of a political crisis. In both Europe and the US, populist movements have been most successful at times when people see the prevailing political norms—which are preserved and defended by the existing establishment—as being at odds with their own hopes, fears, and concerns. The populists express these neglected concerns and frame them in a politics that pits the people against an intransigent elite.

—John Judis, The Populist Explosion, 2016

Contents

A FEW WORDS ON THE LANGUAGE OF IMMIGRATION

The immigration debate raises compelling questions on many fronts: law, politics, morality, economics, national identity, culture, ethics, demography, and international relations, to name those that come immediately to mind. Another dimension, one worth mentioning at the very beginning of this book, is the language of immigration, i.e., the terms of the debate. Consider the 2012-2013 controversy at the Associated Press over the term *illegal immigrant.*

Tom Kent, the AP's deputy managing editor declared that *illegal immigrant* was the appropriate term for those in the country illegally. He deemed *undocumented,* the term most favored by immigrant advocates, to be misleading. "Many illegal immigrants aren't 'undocumented' at all," Kent observed. "They may have a birth certificate and passport from their home country, plus a U.S. driver's license, Social Security card or school ID. What they lack is the fundamental right to be in the United States."

Kent undoubtedly thought he was advocating accuracy, precision, and common sense. But a year later, as the national debate intensified during Senate's consideration of reform legislation, the A.P. withdrew the imprimatur for *illegal immigrant.* The A.P. Stylebook, considered a Bible in newsrooms, was amended to read: "Except in direct quotes essential to the story, use illegal only to refer to an action, not a person: illegal immigration, but not illegal immigrant."

In 2015, a respected legal journal, *Law360,* was involved in a related skirmish when its editors declined to publish an article by two retired U.S. Immigration Court judges unless they removed *illegal alien,* a term they considered derogatory. The judges refused. They complained that the Obama administration, along with "a compliant media and the 'political correctness' word police have taken control of the immigration debate with an agenda of deception, doublespeak and censorship."

My reporting on immigration made me aware of the sensibilities around these issues. In the heat of the moment, *illegal alien* and *illegal immigrant* are often interpreted as signals of aggression. At the same time, *undocumented immigrant* can provoke resentment from those who consider it a dodge, a calculated evasion. I think there is legitimacy on both sides of this semantic tussle, though I think *undocumented* obscures the reality that those who are in the U.S. illegally frequently have multiple sets of bogus documents. In an effort to invoke the wisdom of Solomon, I use both *illegal* and *unauthorized* in this book.

On a personal note, I am uncomfortable with the term *restrictionist* to describe those of us who want to stop illegal immigration and limit legal immigration. Some immigrant-rights activists tend to dramatize their disapproval by pounding that second syllable, or even hissing it. The term not only *sounds* harsh; it also suffers from its connection to the *Immigration Restriction League,* the xenophobic organization founded in 1894 by three graduates of Harvard. As someone who finds that history repugnant, I would prefer to claim another name, one that would make clear my desire for immigration that is firmly and humanely *regulated.* But *regulationist* is a nonstarter, and no other term seems available.

So, I have accepted my semantic discomfort. I am a restrictionist. But just as I accept that as fact, I assert this: To be a restrictionist is not to be anti-immigrant, any more than those who want to regulate Wall Street are anti-capitalist or those who believe in careful diets are anti-food. Let's can the cant. Let's have an open, probing debate of this endlessly fascinating issue of such vital importance to our country.

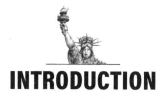

INTRODUCTION

When Donald Trump was running for the 2016 Republican presidential nomination, *New York Times* columnist David Brooks decried the bombastic New York developer's "vast narcissism" and called him "ethically unprepared" to lead the country. Nevertheless, Brooks acknowledged that Trump had illuminated a crisis that many Americans had failed to understand or even recognize. "People across America have been falling through the cracks.... Trump, to his credit, made them visible," he wrote. Another Trump critic, George Packer, writing in *The New Yorker*, credited him with understanding an emergent fact of American life in an era when the political establishment of both the Democratic and Republican parties endorsed free trade, loose borders, and expansive immigration. "The middle-aged white working class has suffered at least as much as any demographic group because of globalization, low-wage immigrant labor, and free trade," Packer wrote. "Trump sensed the rage that flared from this pain and made it the fuel of his campaign."

Trump drove his campaign with the accelerator of his nationalist and nativist grievances slammed to the floor. He started with a contemptuous assessment of Mexican immigrants. "They're bringing drugs; they're bringing crime; they're rapists," he said, before adding the condescending admission that "some, I assume, are good people." The campaign's first television ad promised: "He'll stop illegal immigration by building a wall on our southern border that Mexico will pay for." He attacked Hillary Clinton as part of a corrupt elite who had betrayed the American people, exposing workers to the perils of free trade and open borders while accepting six-figure speaking fees from Wall Street banks that had nearly wrecked the economy with their wild risk-taking and self-dealing,

Trump understood that much of the fury of his white working-class base stemmed from the federal government's failure to meet its responsibility to control immigration, as Washington had promised decades earlier when Congress passed and President Reagan signed the Immigration Reform and Control Act of 1986. At the White House signing ceremony Reagan predicted, "Future generations of Americans will be thankful for our efforts to humanely regain control of our borders." Almost exactly thirty years later, the election of Donald Trump was a consequence of the colossal failure of that prediction and the accumulated fury of those who felt betrayed and abandoned. "We've defended other nations' borders while refusing to defend our own," Trump said in his inaugural address. He vowed, "From this moment on, it's going to be America First. Every decision on trade, on taxes, on immigration, on foreign affairs, will be made to benefit American workers and American families."

In 1986, IRCA (ER-kuh), as the immigration reform law is known, was touted as "a grand bargain," a hard-won compromise that coupled an amnesty for illegal immigrants with a promise to stop future waves of illegal immigration by ensuring that employers hired only authorized workers. The amnesty was delivered. But as Doris Meissner, Commissioner of the Immigration and Naturalization Service during the Clinton administration, would acknowledge years later, "We never did in any serious way the enforcement that was to accompany the legalization of the people who were here illegally."

And so, by the second decade of the new millennium stories were being told across the country like the one from North Dakota that was told to C-SPAN host Greta Wodele in 2013. A caller named Phil, who identified himself as the owner of a construction business in Minot, gave an accounting of IRCA's failed enforcement. He spoke in a tone of anguished bewilderment, with the wounded spirit of a man who had played by the rules, only to be trampled by those who either profited financially from illegal immigration or were enthralled by the opportunity to demonstrate their commitment to inclusiveness, diversity, and equality.

Said Phil: "You have people in this country trying to run their businesses legally. They pay their taxes. They pay their workers' compensation. They pay their insurance. And you have other businesses hiring illegal immigrants. They hire them. They know they can't cover them with insurance. They pay them less money and they don't cover them with workers comp. They don't cover them with liability insurance. So, they can bid the job way cheaper than anybody running their business legally. If you're running your business legally, you're not hiring illegal immigrants. So, I don't hire illegal immigrants....So, I have to bid my job to cover my expenses in this country. So, I am going out of business because you guys are allowing people to hire illegal immigrants.... And they're really damaging this country. I don't understand how people cannot see this. I mean they are putting me out of business because I won't work illegal immigrants."

ONE OF THE MOST CONSEQUENTIAL FAILURES OF GOVERNANCE

Phil's predicament was produced by the forces that are the subject of this book. Worksite enforcement failed because it was not allowed to succeed. A strange-bedfellows, left-right coalition of ethnic politicians, open-borders advocates, business interests, and others rigged the worksite enforcement rules so that illegal immigrants could find work by presenting phony documents. Although IRCA required employers to verify that new hires were authorized, it provided no secure means to verify the authenticity of documents workers presented for the Employment Eligibility Form, commonly known as Form I-9. And so the process of completing the I-9 became an administrative Potemkin village, an elaborate façade of legality. In 2006, David Martin, a former general counsel to the INS, wrote that fraud had reduced the process to "an empty ceremony."

IRCA's flaws meant that workers could pretend to be legal, and unscrupulous employers could pretend to believe them. In effect, Congress had established a system that said, "Don't come without authorization, but if you can get past the border patrol, you'll be able to work." Far from coming to a halt, illegal immigration accelerated. During the 1990s, the population of unauthorized immigrants soared at an average annual rate of 500,000, despite repeated declarations from the Clinton administration that it was committed to establishing "a seamless web" of enforcement from the border to the workplace. The presidential candidacies of right-wing firebrand Pat Buchanan in 1992 and 1996 were an early warning signal of the burgeoning populist discontent that would become so dramatically evident with the election of Donald Trump.

Because IRCA's failure has had such profound political, economic, and cultural effects, it has proved to be one of the most consequential failures of governance in American history. This book is a history of that failure. It is an examination of the forces that asserted themselves against IRCA's promise of control. It also examines the emergence of opposition to the more recent proposals for "comprehensive immigration reform." That opposition comes primarily from those who say another amnesty would be a magnet for more illegal immigration. With a won't-fool-us-twice skepticism, they say immigrant-rights activists would resist any future enforcement as a form of oppression.

THE PLAN OF THE BOOK

This book is structured in Three Parts. Part One is the backstory of the Immigration Reform and Control Act. It charts the political and cultural cross-currents of a national debate that ultimately produced the legislation. Part Two is the story of the institutions and organizations—in the media, liberal foundations and the immigration activist groups they funded, and in the labor, civil-rights, and environmental movements—that became part of the left-right coalition to loosen borders and unravel enforcement. The Southern

Poverty Law Center joined in, labeling some restrictionist organizations as "hate groups," in what it acknowledged was an attempt to drive them from the public forum. The SPLC injected the what we now know as the cancel culture into the national debate.

One of the groups that received the corrosive designation of the SPLC's Scarlet H was the Center for Immigration Studies, where I have been a research fellow since 2009. Ever since the SPLC's Heidi Beirich, whose militant ideology and unscrupulous tactics we'll examine in Chapter Six, applied the tag to the Center for Immigration Studies in 2017, immigrant-rights activists have used it to admonish Congress and the public to shun us. A prime example presented itself in early 2020, when I wrote an op-ed column that appeared in *The New York Times* under the headline, "I'm a Liberal Who Thinks Immigration Must Be Restricted." The subhead neatly condensed the message: "Immigration can invigorate the country. But when it is poorly managed, it can cause social division — just as it's doing right now." A chorus of howls arose on the left, with especially shrill commentary from *Huffington Post* and Media Matters for America. *Huffpo*'s headline and subhead teamed up to tell the tale: "New York Times Runs Anti-Immigration Op-Ed by Noted Hate Group," read the head. This was followed by what the activists considered to be evidence: "The Center for Immigration Studies, an anti-immigration think tank, is categorized as a hate group by the Southern Poverty Law Center." After reading those attacks, whose authors didn't bother to consider what I wrote because they were setting their hair on fire about where I worked, I was almost grateful to read the *Slate* column, which was headlined: "Times Taps White Nationalist Organization for Thought Provoking Perspective on Immigration."*

---

* It was encouraging to see many positive reviews among the 975 reader comments on the website. Said one, "I am so afraid of being called a racist, because I agree with everything in this piece. And I am a Democrat." Another reader, while saying he rejected President Trump "on almost every level," admonished Democrats that Trump had "tapped into a very real insecurity/anxiety among the US electorate.... Some of it's racism,

One of the reasons I came to CIS was that I wanted to examine the immigration advocacy of the Southern Poverty Law Center. I admired the work SPLC attorneys did on behalf of some migrants, particularly those who had been exploited by employers. But I felt a strong dislike for the attempt by Heidi Beirich and her colleagues to vilify the restrictionist movement, which sought enforcement against illegal immigration and restraints on legal immigration, both of which grew rapidly during the final third of the 20th century.

Guilt-by-association tactics have long been used by immigrant expansionists to muddle the debate. Way back in 1980 Lance Morrow of *Time* magazine wrote: "Ku Klux Klansmen have paraded around Florida lately, dispensing their old nativist bile and giving a bad name to an argument that has more thoughtful and respectable proponents." This effort to raise suspicions about the basic decency of restrictionists also features prominently in Chapter Nine, the story of the civil war over immigration that shook the Sierra Club. It will explain why a typical environmental activist in 1990 was likely to favor limits, while a similar person a decade later probably would oppose restrictionist proposals.

THE LONG UNRAVELING

Part Three is the story of IRCA's long unraveling during the five presidential administrations between 1988 and 2017. It shows how the law enforcement agencies and members of Congress who sought to implement worksite enforcement were thwarted by the coalition, allowing the steady expansion of illegal immigration, fueling both calls for comprehensive immigration reform and the backlash that elected Trump. The epilogue examines the immigration politics of the Trump era, as the president's draconian policies radicalized a liberal resistance against all enforcement. This confrontation set the stage for the 2020 election campaign, in which Trump's strategy is to discredit the Democrats as recklessly leftist on immigration and

---

some of it's a sense of fairness, some of it's cultural unease, some of it's economics, or a mix of these. No matter, it will matter."

other issues, including climate change, health care, college tuition, and loyalty to the country.

This book is an effort of explanatory journalism. Most is straightforward reporting. But there is also a great deal of opinion, reflecting the judgments I have formed and the sensibility I have developed since 1986, when I became a correspondent in Mexico for the *Arizona Republic* two months before President Reagan signed IRCA into law. I've been fascinated by the story ever since, drawn to its complexity and moral ambiguity, its cast of compelling characters, and its importance for our fractious society's effort to find a modus vivendi as we become ever more diverse.

This book reflects my perspective as a liberal restrictionist. This means that while I favor clear limits and enforcement that is both humane and firm, I celebrate immigrants as a vital part of our national story, and I abhor demonization of migrants, regardless of their legal status. Moreover, I support a comprehensive immigration reform that includes a generous amnesty if—and this is a big if—Congress ensures that it will not repeat the failure of IRCA. This time both ends of the deal—amnesty and enforcement—must have bipartisan buy-in. To make the compromise hold, both sides must nurture the spirit of reconciliation. Hardline restrictionists will have to foreswear their insistence that amnesty is an intolerable capitulation to illegality. And true-believer expansionists will have to abjure the utopian notion that a green card is a universal human right. The expansionists will have to lay down the banners that declare, "No human is illegal," just as the restrictionists will have to stop chanting, "What part of illegal don't you understand?!"

As these controversies suggest, a fundamental challenge facing immigration policy makers is to resolve, or at least manage, the tension between competing American values that is inherent in the debate. A pluralistic, democratic nation that was built by immigrants cannot be indifferent to the pathos of uniformed agents pursuing those who come or stay in defiance of the law. But a diverse and pluralistic society that depends on a broad commitment to play by the rules cannot defy the necessity of limiting access to the world's most coveted document: the green card that represents a path to citizenship in the United States.

A MOMENT OF REVELATION AT THE MAYFLOWER HOTEL

I learned a great deal about immigration at the street level when I lived in Mexico and Arizona in the 1980s and 1990s. But my education in the nitty gritty of immigration politics at the national level began when I moved to Washington in 2000. Shortly after the election of George W. Bush, I became the *Arizona Republic*'s Washington correspondent. One particularly salient moment of illumination took place at the National Immigration Forum's "Keepers of the American Dream" dinner at the Mayflower Hotel.

The NIF, one of the most prominent immigration advocacy organizations, is a forum for the left-right coalition of expansionists. Over the years, its board of directors has included representatives of the National Council of La Raza, the National Restaurant Association, the American Nursery and Landscape Association, and the Service Employees International Union. Reporter Jonathan Tilove, a hard-nosed veteran of Washington political reporting, laconically observed that NIF held "events where those who exploit immigrant labor break bread with those who labor against that exploitation."

At the dinner, NIF Executive Director Frank Sharry, the master of ceremonies, made a pitch to business allies who wanted Congress to allow them unfettered access to foreign workers. Looking over the crowded room, he said: "I've got a proposal, a negotiating proposal. You guys in business get all the workers you want, whenever you want them—no bureaucracy." Sharry was an immigrant-rights activist with a background helping Central Americans who had fled to the United States. But his business-friendly proposal drew an enthusiastic response from one of the tables. "Sold!" shouted John Gay, a lobbyist for the American Hotel and Lodging Association. Sharry countered that the deal would have to include a concession to his side. He puckishly called it "a small catch," saying it required "three little, tiny pieces of paper: a green card, a union card, and a voter registration card."

For me, a Washington novice from the borderlands, the moment was a revelation about the politics of immigration in Washington. Business lobbyists like Gay—conservatives who seek loose labor markets so employers can keep wages down—align themselves with liberal activists like Sharry to pursue policies that serve the interests of both their groups.†

Who, I wondered, was lobbying for the American workers competing with the new arrivals? The answer, I learned, was no one. As the former labor secretary Robert Reich once put it, "There's no National Association of Working Poor." This mismatch of political influence, combined with the social and fiscal consequences of a wave of low-skilled immigrants, led me to believe that immigration should be restricted so that its power to invigorate our country is not eclipsed by its potential to harm workers. I think immigration, like capitalism itself, should be regulated in the national interest, not shaped to serve the free-market libertarianism of the right or the post-national humanitarianism of the left.

THE MIGHTY IMMIGRATION LOBBY

John Gay was part of the veritable army of lobbyists who flock to congressional offices and fundraising venues to assert their constitutionally guaranteed right to seek the redress of their grievances about insufficiently loose labor markets.

The non-partisan Sunlight Foundation, doing work that reporters failed to do, would report that between 2007 and 2012, a total of 678 lobbying groups had sought to shape various immigration bills. The most active lobbyists represented minority ethnic groups, educational institutions, chambers of commerce, computer software

† Gay would later become a lobbyist at the American Restaurant Association, which opposed efforts to raise the federal minimum wage.

organizations, and the dairy industry. Their cumulative outlay for lobbying alone was a mountainous $1.5 billion.

The immigration lobby is so large because many ethnic groups, politicians, and corporate chiefs have a stake in immigration policy. Ethnic groups enjoy a boost in political clout with the arrival of countrymen. Employers push for labor markets jammed with eager job-seekers. Businesses profit from the increased demand for everything from groceries to housing to automobiles. Libertarians and cosmopolitans delight in the elimination of borders. Humanitarians take moral satisfaction in embracing illegal immigrants. Far from acknowledging that there are legitimate reasons to oppose those who come illegally and in large numbers, many warm-hearted liberals regard such an influx as an opportunity to demonstrate their commitment to diversity and inclusion.

As I watched the *sturm und drang* of Capitol Hill lobbying on immigration I was struck by the realization that the movement to loosen borders had something in common with a far different story I had covered in Arizona. As a member of the Republic's investigative team, I had dug into the financial empire of Charles Keating, the Phoenix financier who became the national poster boy of the political and financial scandal involving the collapse of the savings and loan industry in the late 1980s. Keating, a high-rolling real estate developer, had bought Lincoln Savings and Loan Association in 1984, shortly after Congress deregulated the industry. The rationale for deregulation, which lobbyists spread with the same thoroughness they applied to their distribution of checks to finance the election campaigns of members of Congress, was that deregulation would take the government off the backs of the industry so that the industry could create wealth that would benefit the entire economy. Keating led the new gang of buccaneering S&L owners who converted "thrifts" from mom-and-pop mortgage shops into casinos of rip-snorting, anything-goes finance. With outrageous risk-taking, blatantly fraudulent deal-making, and bogus bookkeeping, they soared into the wild blue yonder of deregulation, only to crash and burn in a flaming, federally insured wreck. Deregulation was a hustler's dream because it privatized profit and socialized loss.

The effort to loosen borders and unravel enforcement is a movement for deregulation. For reasons that range from the nobly unselfish to the greedily irresponsible, it seeks to get governments off the backs of would-be immigrants and the panoply of special interests that profit from immigration. In Washington, I was fascinated by the interest groups' distribution across the traditional-liberal-left-to-conservative-right axis of American politics. Latino activists at the National Council of La Raza (later renamed UnidosUS) and the Mexican American Legal Defense and Education Fund joined Cato Institute libertarians, the Chamber of Commerce, the Service Employees International Union, and the *Wall Street Journal* editorial page in envisioning a future of unimpeded movement and opportunity. Meanwhile, labor unionists in the skilled trades, social conservatives like those at *National Review* magazine, and the environmentally oriented NumbersUSA warned of downside risks and threats to social cohesion.

AN OPPORTUNITY TO DIG INTO THE STORY

President Bush's efforts to pass a comprehensive reform bill were part of his advocacy of "compassionate conservatism." They were also part of the impossibly large agenda of Arizona-related stories that were part of my beat. I was frustrated by the lack of time to dig deep into important stories. Immigration was the story that interested me most. It grabbed me by the shoulders, demanding my attention and provoking the restless curiosity that fuels the urge to question and learn. It was the same bug that had made me spend four years on a book about a bitter land dispute between the Navajos and Hopis over high-desert rangeland east of the Grand Canyon. The same fever that woke me up at three in the morning with a hunger to unravel Charles Keating's fraudulent sales of thousands of acres of desert so that he could book phony profits and fabricate the illusion of profitability. This time, I was drawn by the vast, fascinating, frustrating dimensions of immigration in all its political, moral, cultural, economic, ethical, and historical complexity.

So, in 2002, when George Condon and Marcus Stern, editors in the Washington bureau of the Copley News service, offered me the immigration and border beat, I jumped at the opportunity. The bureau's principal job was to report for the largest paper in the Copley chain, the *San Diego Union Tribune*, where immigration and the border were as much a part of daily discussions as the naval base and the San Diego Padres.

From the Copley office in Washington's National Press Building, I traveled widely in the Southwest and across Mexico. I visited the home communities of Salvadoran immigrants who worked at the National Press Club, where I taught informal English classes to janitorial workers who dreamed of acquiring legal status. At towns named San Jorge, San Miguel, Intipuca, and Aguilares, nearly everyone I met had relatives in the U.S., and most of the young men talked of joining them. A young fisherman told me that the most he could earn was $20 a day. A shotgun-toting motel security guard told me he earned $180 a month working 24-hour shifts every other day. In the tiny Honduran border community of Guascaron, I visited a family that depended on the money sent home by two of its members, whom I had met when they were laying tile at the new food court at the National Press Building.

In an email from El Salvador, I wrote to Marc Stern, my editor. "If I were a 20-year-old Salvadoran, I'd be looking north, too. But as an American I'm thinking there's no way we can absorb all those who want to flee the misery and corruption and brutal inequalities of just about all of Latin America." A few months later, I had Sunday dinner in Washington's Maryland suburbs with a Mexican couple who had left their two children with family in Chiapas. Shortly after Becky served the chicken, she received a call from her manager at McDonald's, who was badly short of workers for the evening shift. Eager to earn the extra cash, she headed out the door. She and her husband were part of a diaspora from the small town of San Pedro

Buenavista that had taken root in the 1980s and sprouted in the 1990s. Most of them worked at a string of fast food restaurants—McDonald's, Wendy's, Burger King, Chick Fil-A—that stretched from the edge of Washington to the Baltimore suburb of Towson, where my family lived. It was a diaspora story that was being repeated countless times in both countries. Mexican demographers reported that 96 percent of Mexico's 2,420 county-sized *municipios* sent immigrants to the United States, producing the human equivalent of a downpour that suddenly floods a river with the flow of a thousand new streams.

LEAVING JOURNALISM, MOVING TO THE CENTER FOR IMMIGRATION STUDIES

In 2008, sizing up the Internet-driven weakening of the newspaper business model that had sustained the in-depth reporting that I loved, I decided to take a buyout from Copley. About a year later, when I was freelancing, I accepted an offer to become a research fellow at the Center for Immigration Studies, whose researchers I had interviewed for my stories. While I thought some of CIS's positions were too hard line, I respected its work, which featured reports from a wide range of experts, including several who identified as liberal restrictionists. I believed that CIS played a valuable role as immigration skeptic, pointing to the costs and strains imposed by mass immigration, especially illegal immigration. I also thought that like NumbersUSA and the Federation for American Immigration Reform, it provided a valuable counterweight to the enormously bigger expansionist lobby. Mark Krikorian, the executive director of CIS, has unfailingly honored his pledge that I would be able to report on immigration under the same standards of fairness and rigorous reporting I had followed as a newspaperman.

Over my ten years at CIS, I have developed a great respect for Mark's integrity and his tenacity in the face of the brutal attacks from self-styled defenders of tolerance whose work we will examine in Chapters Five and Six. And I felt a special kinship with CIS founding chairman Otis Graham, a history professor and a former Marine officer whose contrarian instincts made him a critic of the Vietnam War. Otis was a lifelong liberal. But he was alarmed at the work of the intolerant and hyperventilating wing of American liberalism that smears every effort to limit immigration as racist.

In his 2008 memoir, *Immigration Reform and America's Unchosen Future*, Graham reflected poignantly on his commitment to studying immigration "without disparaging immigrants or their cultures, reserving condemnation for our own incompetent and shortsighted public officials and ethnocentric lobbyists." He died in 2017, at the age of 82.

Like Otis Graham. I believe that immigration needs to be limited—a.k.a. restricted—so that its power to build is not eclipsed by its potential to disrupt. I believe that unchecked immigration is a threat to our ability to hold together as a people, our ability to maintain the *Unum* while honoring the *Pluribus*. My appreciation for this spirit—for its soaring poetry but also its fragility—was solidified by my travels to immigrant-sending communities in Mexico and Central America. No place is more memorable in that regard than the small town of Pahuatlan in the Mexican state of Puebla.

Pahuatlan is a placid community in the lush, misty beauty of a sierra, where waterfalls came tumbling down through the coffee farms that were the major source of employment. When I visited in 2004, it had four *tortillerias* but no bank. There a was a lively outdoor market and a shop that specialized in the sale and repair of machetes. There were cars with American license plates, street-level evidence that coffee's role as the biggest economic engine had been eclipsed by remittances from the United States.

I met a young man who had worked illegally in construction in "Carolina del Norte"—North Carolina. He was enthusiastic about his experience and planned to return. "I like the United States," he solemnly explained, extending his right hand in a smooth horizontal plane as he said with a smile, "It moves on wheels." I forget his name. But I will never forget that observation. When I asked what he meant, he said he had been impressed that American police were honest and the rules of the social road were clear in the U.S. It wasn't like Mexico, where *caciquismo* —the authoritarian, arbitrary and often brutal rule of the local strongman--still prevailed. He liked the ethic of waiting in line, of deference to the rules, of appreciation for civility, stability, and predictability in daily life. He was discouraged by his country's inability to overcome a problem that was described by former Mexican Foreign Minister Jorge Castaneda.

A FUNDAMENTAL CONTRAST BETWEEN MEXICO AND THE U.S.

Castaneda, now a professor at New York University, has written that Mexico is "a society terribly riven by class, race, gender, age, region, and future, where a middle- and upper-class minority segregates and discriminates against the vast majority of the population." Castaneda also understands a fact of American life that explains the intensity of the backlash in the United States against illegal immigration. Noting the visceral connection that many Americans have to playing by the rules, he said large-scale illegal immigration "runs counter to the legalistic nature of a society that has little else to hold it together beyond the belief in and devotion to the rule of law."

Castaneda's insight into American civic culture is key to understanding not just the differences between our countries but also the resentment many Americans feel about our government's failure to control immigration. They want immigration laws to work for the same reason they want our traffic lights to work and our police to be honest. These things provide a framework for cooperation, for confidence in our ability to lead orderly lives, to make plans, to build dreams through a spirit of hard work and cooperation that brings coherence not only to our lives as individuals but to the lives of our communities. In Mexico, traffic signals are sometimes dismissed as mere suggestions and cops are widely assumed to be corrupt. Mexicans have a saying that encapsulates the pervasive, quotidian cynicism that saps the vitality and creativity of its citizens: *Un politico pobre es un pobre politico*—A politician who is poor is a poor politician.

I fear that our country is headed in Mexico's direction. The ties of social equality and solidarity across class lines have been fraying for decades. In his 1987 book, *The End of Equality*, Mickey Kaus, an editor of *The New Republic*, reported on the estrangement between working-class Americans and affluent professionals, including those who harbored a "smug contempt for the demographically inferior." We Americans are cloistering ourselves in like-minded communities along lines of class, income, and ideologies. Immigration is one of the most contentious dividing lines. As we will see, this social chasm has been pried ever wider in the 34 years since IRCA was passed, as Americans have clashed over multiculturalism, the politics of identity, globalization and free trade, and the rising tide of immigration that is destined to render whites a minority well before the middle of this century. The Internet and social media allow for incessant pounding of our tribal drums.

While a minority of Republicans have supported comprehensive immigration reform, most members of the GOP have long been averse to what they regard as CIR's magnetic attraction to ever more illegal immigration. This tendency has become more pronounced during the Trump presidency. As Trump has sought to consolidate his base behind harsh and inflexible policies, he has provoked an equal and opposite reaction from Democrats who now march under the banner of resistance, opposing nearly all enforcement and even calling for the abolition of Immigration and Customs Enforcement.

THE LIBERAL DRIFT TOWARD LOOSE BORDERS

This book's epilogue will provide a synopsis of immigration politics and policy in the era of Trump. But the primary purpose of this book is to explain the movement in the opposite direction—away from IRCA's promised enforcement—that unfolded in the 30 years between enactment of IRCA and the election of Trump. During this period, Democrats have undergone a shift—incremental until the

Obama administration and more rapid since then—away from the conviction that illegal immigration must be checked and toward the belief that it must be welcomed. A few bullet points illustrate the zig-zag course of the transformation.

- In his 1995 State of the Union address President Bill Clinton said Americans "are rightly disturbed by the large numbers of illegal aliens entering our country." He pledged "to better identify illegal aliens in the workplace." But after Clinton won a second term in 1996, worksite enforcement fizzled.
- In 2006, liberal economist Paul Krugman cited the negative labor-market and fiscal effects of the large influx of low-skilled immigrants from Mexico. First, they "drive down the wages for the worst-paid Americans," he wrote. And because they didn't earn enough for their taxes to cover the cost of the public benefits they received, they "threaten to unravel" the social safety net. The bottom line, he concluded, is that "many of the worst-off native-born Americans are hurt by immigration." But in 2007, the *New York Times* editorial board dismissed not only such concerns but also the distinction between legal and illegal immigration. From the lofty height of the *Times* editorial boardroom, it proclaimed: "It is the nation's duty to welcome immigrants, to treat them decently and give them the opportunity to assimilate." Krugman's column described an economic reality that shaped public concerns. The editorial was an edict that dismissed such concerns as the work of narrow minds.
- In 2006, as he was preparing to seek the presidency, Senator Barack Obama wrote: "[T]here's no denying that many blacks share the same anxieties as many whites about the wave of illegal immigration flooding our Southern border.": But as Obama sought a second term, he pledged support for reform legislation that would not just provide a generous amnesty

for illegal immigrants but also vastly expand the flows of legal immigration.
- In 2007 Sen. Charles Schumer wrote, "Democrats should become the party that aggressively stanches the flow of illegal immigrants....Ending illegal immigration is not about closing our doors. It's about enforcing the law and protecting the rights that working Americans have spent more than a hundred years fighting to win."

As we will see in Part Three, President Obama faced a dilemma. Seeking to demonstrate his commitment to enforcing immigration limits, he oversaw a vigorous program to deport illegal immigrants, focusing primarily on those who had recently crossed the border or who had committed serious crimes. But when a Senate-passed comprehensive reform bill bogged down in the House, and when Latino leaders blasted him as the "deporter-in-chief," the president sought to placate critics with executive orders that created a program (known as DACA) to provide protections for those who had crossed the border illegally as children—usually because they were brought here by their parents. As immigrant-rights advocates gained strength within the Democratic coalition, their new electoral might and the momentum of the immigrant-rights movement became apparent when former Secretary of State Hillary Clinton and Sen. Bernie Sanders competed for the Democratic presidential nomination in the 2016 election to succeed Obama.

BERNIE SANDERS CONDEMNS "A KOCH BROTHERS PROPOSAL"

Sanders, who had long demanded that immigration policy protect American workers, made his last stand in 2015, with a thunderous declaration to Ezra Klein of *Vox*. Klein, an immigrant-rights partisan and a woke citizen of the world, suggested that in order to demonstrate solidarity in the fight against global poverty the U.S. should commit to "sharply raising the level of immigration we permit, even up to a level of open borders."

Sanders was incredulous. "Open borders?!!" he replied. Invoking the names of the industrialist billionaires who bankrolled the libertarian Cato Institute, he said, "That's a Koch brothers proposal. What right-wing people in this country would love is an open-borders policy. Bring in all kinds of people, work for $2 or $3 an hour, that would be great for them." In the ensuing tsunami of immigrant-rights outrage, *Vox* huffed that "Bernie Sanders's fear of immigrant labor is ugly."

And so, in their fervor for unrestricted immigration, woke liberals had slid so far to the social-justice left that they came out on the libertarian right. Their influence in the Democratic Party became so great that Sanders, in order to keep the wind in his campaign sails, had to change course. Instead of holding to his 2007 commitment to "stopping illegal immigrants" in the name of American workers, he spoke warmly of "the undocumented," who, he said, should be granted legal status so they could demand better pay. As the Sanders-Clinton competition grew more intense, they seemed to be competing for the title of most welcoming of the undocumented. Four years later, contenders for the Democratic presidential nomination said they wanted free health care for the undocumented. Some wanted to minimize the misdemeanor offense of crossing the border illegally, saying it should be reduced to a civil offense, like speeding on a highway.

As the Democrats have shifted leftward in recent decades, I have found myself increasingly estranged from their open-borders or loose-borders ideology. At the Center for Immigration Studies, which makes far more room for centrists than does any activist expansionist group, I have tried to mediate between extremes. I am dismayed at the insistence of hard core restrictionists like Steve Bannon who have persuaded President Trump that amnesty would destroy the Republican Party. I have been equally disappointed with the rigidity of activists like Joshua Hoyt, of the Illinois Coalition for Immigrants and Refugees. When Josh and I spoke at a seminar in Oklahoma, I asked him if he could accept any principle of legal restraint on immigration. He responded instantaneously, not conceding a second to consider such a possibility. "My job is to help immigrants," he said tersely. "it isn't to help you hurt immigrants." I think Hoyt illustrates the aggressive idealism that is the liberals' Achilles heel in the immigration wars.

An excellent assessment of the problem comes from another contrarian liberal, NYU professor Jonathan Haidt, whose work as a moral psychologist led him to the conclusion that liberals tend "to overreach, change too many things too quickly." In their impatience for social justice, Haidt believes, liberals can degrade society's "moral capital"—the traditions, mores, and structures that preserve a society's ability to cooperate, cohere, and maintain solidarity. But Bannon exemplifies the other half of the great left-right divide as described by Haidt, who laments the conservative tendency "to fail to notice certain classes of victims, fail to limit the predations of certain powerful interests, and fail to see the need to change or update institutions as times change."

RECOGNIZING JOHN HIGHAM

This book will draw on the experiences and the beliefs of many liberals who insisted on the need of limiting immigration. I call them contrarian liberals because they dissented from the loose- borders inclinations of many on the left. We will examine how the debate was shaped by such figures as U.S. Rep. Barbara Jordan, the Rev. Theodore Hesburgh, labor leader Cesar Chavez, Earth Day founder Gaylord Nelson, and Sierra Club leader David Brower. But no one is more important in this story and in the evolution of my own views than historian John Higham, the Johns Hopkins University history professor who was known as the dean of immigration historians. His story is itself a fitting introduction to the story of this book.

Over a long career that extended from the middle of the 20th century until his death in 2003, Higham's brilliant scholarship and graceful writing illuminated the story of immigration to the U.S. in all its complexity and moral ambiguity. He was prescient in warning of the risks of losing a sense of common national identity within the "more and more kaleidoscopic culture" of the United States.

Higham is best known as the author of *Strangers in the Land: Patterns of American Nativism, 1860–1925*. Still widely read long after it was first published in 1955, the book is a masterful history of nativism, which Hingham described as "an inflamed and nationalistic type of ethnocentrism." Historian Ray Allen Bollington hailed the book as "an exciting volume, a tightly knit narrative that progresses with all the momentum of adventure fiction." Its influence has been lasting, especially among immigrant-rights activists. In 2007, immigration scholars Peter Skerry and Noah Pickus said the book "continues to be widely and approvingly cited by those concerned with underscoring the history of prejudice and intolerance toward newcomers in the United States."

Remarkably, Higham dissented from his book's popularity. He confessed that his good intentions and the tense political climate of the post-World War II years had caused him to exaggerate the influence of nativism. "Repelled as I was not only by the xenophobia of the past but the nationalist delusions of the Cold War that were all around me, I had highlighted the most inflammatory aspects of ethnic conflict," he wrote.

In the preface to a later edition of *Strangers in the Land*, Higham wrote that he should have given more consideration to "aspects of the immigration restriction movement that cannot be sufficiently explained in terms of nativism." He called for a more nuanced perspective, one that would recognize immigration concerns rooted not in virulent ideology but in quotidian matters involving status rivalries that were inevitable in a complex society, for example in the jostling for influence in such institutions as school boards, police forces, and fire departments.

Higham was critical of excesses on both sides in the immigration debate. On the one hand, he complained that "the restrictionists claimed to be the hard-boiled realists, though their 'realism' was seldom free of prejudice or hysteria." But on the other hand, he wrote, "Antirestrictionists tended to gloss over the dilemmas that immigration posed." He was an advocate for the immigration limits that Congress enacted in 1986, and in a letter to a Japanese scholar of American culture, he complained about the "knee-jerk liberals" who opposed those limits. As historian Michael Kammen, a longtime Higham friend, told me, "Whenever John thought the pendulum had swung too far, he would always push back."

Higham accepted cognitive and moral dissonance as inherent in the immigration debate. As an idealist, he understood that restriction would "not square easily with the belief that this is a land of opportunity for all." As a realist, he believed that the U.S. should enforce immigration limits because: "In the modern world free migration would result in excessive population displacement toward countries with high wages or political stability." As I pored over the Higham archives at Johns Hopkins, I learned that he described himself to the editor of one academic journal as "a mild restrictionist."

Higham's life immersed him for decades in the unfolding drama of immigration as it was lived in communities and debated in intellectual and political circles. Born in 1920, he grew up in Queens, New York, where he came to see assimilation as a catalyst of American dynamism. "At a wonderfully multiethnic New York City high school in the mid-1930s I shared the joyous esprit and interactions of many second-generation-American classmates," he wrote. "All of us learned together to see beyond our respective provincialisms."

Believing that nationalism was essential to Americans' ability to cohere as a nation, Higham prescribed a form of nationalism that he saw as a healthy alternative to nativism. He called it "liberal nationalism" and "American universalism," a concept "that stressed the diversity of the nation's origins, the egalitarian dimension of its self-image, and the universality of its founding principles." In the 1980s, as multiculturalism asserted the value of diversity and group identity, he dissented from the ethos that prevailed in the academy. "Because the scholars who specialize in ethnic studies generally see nations as oppressive and captive, the relations of ethnic groups to a core culture do not interest them," he wrote. And because postmodernism rejected an overarching theory of national identity, he wrote, "It encouraged every emergent group to pursue its own oppositional microhistory."

At the end of the millennium, as Higham neared the end of his life and surveyed the troubled landscape of the nation's immigration debate, he felt a sense of foreboding about what it might portend. "Are we experiencing, basically, an increasing indifference of people to one another, both within and between ethnic groups?" he asked in an essay. "If so, immigration may prove to be just an aspect of a wider social fragmentation." That fragmentation has come in the era of Donald Trump, who exploited it to win election and who has made it clear that immigration will be key in his 2020 campaign. I hope this book, by showing how we got here, will help inform discussion of where we go as a nation.

Part 1
THE SEARCH FOR LIMITS

Chapter 1:

From Harry Truman to Ronald Reagan

The Rough Road to the Immigration Reform and Control Act of 1986

> **[The reform bill before Congress] substantially reduces a growing underclass of persons increasingly identified by ethnicity; and it inaugurates a national policy of curtailing illegal migration and visa abuse through a system of employer sanctions.** —Washington Post *editorial,*[1] *1984*

> **If we fail to act, I fear the American people will not forever tolerate the "revolving door" on our Southwest border. How many more years of millions of undocumented entering at will will our people accept before demanding a repressive response?** —*Rep. Hamilton Fish, R-NY*[2]

> **We ethnic minorities in this country remember what our history is, and therefore will never forget and we will forever stand up and fight against any kind of identification system or anything that would approach what those cruel and evil people have done in Eastern Europe and other places.**
> — *Rep. Mickey Leland, D-TX*[3]

A 1913 editorial in *The Fresno Republican* provided a sarcastic description of the ideal field hand, according to fruit and vegetable farmers in California's vast Central Valley. "The supreme qualities of the laborer are that he shall work cheap and hard, eat little and drink nothing, belong to no union, have no ambitions and present no human problems," the editorial read. "Particularly, he should appear from nowhere, when we need him, put up with what accommodations he finds, provide his own food, and then disappear... until the busy season comes around again."[4]

Cold-hearted indifference to human need was an occupational hazard among growers, as the big farmers were known. It was induced by the variability of their need for labor, which was shaped by the vagaries of climate and the duration of a crop's growing season. Hundreds of workers might be needed at peak harvest, far fewer once the crop was in. They were a factor of production that had to be managed, like land and a loan from the bank. In the Rio Grande Valley of Texas, another major producer of perishable crops, one of the growers told a congressional committee in 1920 why he preferred to hire Mexicans: "The whites want more water, etcetera, and are troublemakers. If there is a labor shortage, they want exorbitant [wages]... You can handle the Mexicans better. They're more subservient, if that's the word."[5]

In the first half of the 20th century, California growers cycled through waves of hungry field hands. In the early years they came from China, Japan, and the Philippines. Then came the "Okies" fleeing the suffocation of drought and dust and the Depression in Oklahoma, Texas, Kansas, Colorado, and New Mexico. By 1950, the workforce was largely Mexican, and the preference for illegal migrant labor from Mexico was stirring controversy along lines of class, race, and nationality.

In a letter to President Harry Truman, Jesús Clemente of Mission, Texas, wrote that his area just north of the Rio Grande River "is full of wetbacks... working in all kinds of jobs" and displacing Americans from many sectors of the economy. Roy Wilkins of the National Association for the Advancement of Colored People wrote to the president to complain that Mexicans had been imported to break a strike in California cotton fields that had employed blacks. "The use of citizens of another country to wreck the economic hopes of Americans is a practice which our government must actively oppose," said Wilkins, in an appeal for national solidarity.

Against this turbulent background, the Truman administration was negotiating with Mexico to extend a program that since early in World War II had imported Mexican workers known as braceros. That term, adapted from the Spanish *brazo*—for "arm"—indicated the strenuous nature of field work. Mexican government officials, responding to their employers' alarm that workers were abandoning their jobs to cross the border illegally and earn dollars, threatened to terminate the bracero agreement if the U.S. did not stop the hiring of "wetbacks," as unauthorized workers were commonly known in the borderlands. The Mexicans were also indignant at the abuse their countrymen suffered from American farmers who provided miserable pay and working conditions.

Responding to such concerns, Truman established the presidential Commission on Migratory Labor to investigate. At a hearing in the Rio Grande Valley, Dr. George Sanchez of the University of Texas said Mexican-American families were being uprooted because of the "scandalous, disgraceful exploitation of illegal labor." Ernesto Galarza, an organizer for the United Farm Laborers Union of the AFL, described the epic displacement: "There were no caravans of refugees in dramatic flight, but a steady withdrawal of families from border areas where they could not compete for a living."[6]

The commission also heard from a Mexican-American man who said that in California the "wetbacks... don't care what the wages are... sometimes they don't get wages at all, only beans, coffee and tortillas." The wage-depressing effects were widespread. An African-American man from Arkansas said that when Mexican workers appeared at local cotton farms, the American workers were fired. The presidential commission expressed alarm at the intensity of the influx, reporting that, "In its newly achieved proportions, it is virtually an invasion."

THE DISPLACEMENT OF AMERICAN WORKERS

Truman called on Congress to take action. "Thousands of our own citizens, particularly those of Latin descent, are displaced from employment or forced to work under substandard conditions, because of the competition of these illegal immigrants," he said. "Illegal immigration must be stopped, and the use of our domestic labor force must be improved." Truman also expressed concern for the treatment of the unauthorized workers from Mexico. "They live always under the threat of exposure or deportation," he said. "They are unable, therefore, to protest or to protect themselves." A front-page story in *The New York Times*, published under the headline "'Wetbacks' Curbs Sought by Truman," was an indication of how uncontroversial the term "wetbacks" was at the time.*

Despite Truman's insistence on reform, agribusiness sought to protect the status quo, asserting the power it had accumulated at every level of government. Some of the growers were themselves politicians, well connected and well protected. *Texas Monthly* reported that Texas Gov. Allan Shivers, who "had managed to ride his father-in-law's grapefruit empire all the way to the Governor's Mansion," was heavily engaged in hiring illegal labor in the Rio Grande Valley. A similar story in California's Imperial Valley involved a 1,750-acre vegetable farm owned by the brother of the U.S. ambassador to Mexico, William O'Dwyer. Union organizer Ernesto Galarza wrote that in Washington the Labor Department was "less an advocate of workers than a sensitive barometer of the powerful forces in the national capital. ... It was continuously exposed to the ever-present lobbies of farm employers."[7] At a 1951 congressional hearing, three officials of the Immigration and Naturalization Service complained that a powerful "pressure group" of farmers was forcing suspension of law enforcement against illegal Mexican immigrants in order to get cheap labor.[8]

* Ruben Salazar, a Mexican-American columnist for the *Los Angeles Times* used *wetbacks* matter-of-factly as he wrote sympathetically of their plight. In his column of April 24, 1970, for example, he wrote, "There is no law against hiring wetbacks. There is only a law against being a wetback."

THE TEXAS PROVISO

Perhaps the most remarkable metric of the growers' political might was that under U.S. law, it was not illegal to hire an illegal immigrant. The only guilty party in such a transaction was the worker. In 1952, after the Senate passed a bill to outlaw the employers' part in the arrangement, the Texas delegation in the House of Representatives saddled up and cut it off at the pass. Riding in the lead was Rep. Lloyd M. Bentsen, a Democrat from the Rio Grande Valley. Bentsen, whose father had built a fortune by buying and selling farmland, rigged the legislation to shield the growers from legal risk. While the new law outlawed "harboring or concealing an illegal immigrant," it specifically provided that hiring was not to be confused with harboring and concealing. This legislative sleight of hand became known as the Texas Proviso.

The Texas Proviso was a borderlands version of Catch 22. Just as Joseph Heller's satirical 1961 novel by that name centered on a paradox that ensured generals an ample supply of airmen for suicidally dangerous missions, so the Texas Proviso enacted an absurdity that assured growers of a dependable supply of exploitable field hands. It made Bentsen a hero in the Rio Grande Valley. The president of the local Agricultural Council told the *McAllen Monitor:* "I know personally that Bentsen did everything humanly possible to get the legislation we wanted."[9]

In 1953, the year Dwight Eisenhower succeeded President Truman in the White House, Attorney General Herbert Brownell, Jr., renewed the call for congressional action. After a visit to the California-Mexico border, Brownell said the illegal influx from Mexico presented "a serious and thoroughly unsatisfactory situation." He learned that the entire Mexican border was patrolled by 750 agents, who had arrested 480,000 illegal border crossers the previous year, while about three times that many had made it through. According to the *New York Times* story on the visit, they "work for as little as 20 cents an hour," presenting what Kern County officials called a "menace to the wage security" of the area's workers."[10]

Brownell said that while he favored adjusting the bracero arrangement with Mexico to permit the entry of more workers, the government needed to "be careful that American workers are not displaced and the wage level is not depressed."[11]

OPERATION WETBACK

In 1954, as the borderlands turbulence continued, Brownell approved a massive enforcement campaign. Dubbed "Operation Wetback," it was led by INS commissioner General Joseph Swing, who had been an Eisenhower classmate in the West Point class of 1915. As a young officer he participated in General John Pershing's punitive 1916 expedition into Mexico in retaliation for Pancho Villa's raid on the New Mexico border town of Columbus.

Swing mobilized a special force of nearly 800 federal agents to conduct roadblocks and arrests, initially in California and Arizona. Trains filled with deportees began a long journey southward from the border town of Nogales. Two ships ferried deportees from Port Isabel, Texas, to the Mexican port city of Veracruz. Hundreds of thousands of people were apprehended. In addition, many Mexicans decided to avoid arrest by returning to Mexico on their own.

Mexican-American scholar Armando Navarro would write that: "Operation Wetback became one of the most traumatic experiences endured by Mexicanos in the United States in their dealings with the federal government." But the Mexican government willingly cooperated in the effort to control the border. Mexico City had long demanded that the U.S. stop the exodus of workers who had not been enrolled in the bracero program. UCLA historian Kelly Lytle Hernandez has written that: "Agribusinessmen along Mexico's northern border were particularly vocal in their protests that cotton was rotting in the fields because Mexican laborers chose to cross the border for higher wages rather than work within Mexico."

Mexican-Americans responded to Operation Wetback with a multilayered ambivalence that has been noted by professor David G. Gutierrez, a historian at the University of California at San Diego.

Relating the views of a man who became a bracero in 1944 and later acquired a green card, Gutierrez said that while the man expressed sympathy for the recent arrivals, "I also know that when the braceros come in, the wages stay very low; that's pretty bad for people who have to earn their whole year's income just during the harvest season." However, Gutierrez went on to report that the "dragnets not only were affecting putative illegal aliens but also were devastating Mexican American families, disrupting businesses in Mexican neighborhoods, and fanning interethnic animosities throughout the border region."

POPULATION BOOM IN MEXICO

In the 1960s, demography would cause the Mexican government's response to the illegal exodus to shift from alarm to relief. In the 1950s, Mexico was in the early stages of a baby boom that would see its population soar from 28 million in 1950 to 53 million in 1970, 86 million in 1990, and 118 million in 2010. Between 1970 and 2010, the number of people born in Mexico who were living in the United States jumped from 700,000 to 10 million. Instead of being condemned as a threat to the country's economic development, illegal migration was welcomed as a "valvula de escape," a safety valve to relieve the pressure and frustration generated by the country's vast inequality. Disillusionment with the country's systemically dysfunctional leadership has been a chronic feature of Mexican life, and a propellant for emigration. In 2017, a survey by the Pew Research Center found that 85 percent of Mexicans were dissatisfied with the course of their country, pointing to concerns about such problems as corruption, crime, and drug-related violence. Pew also found that one-third of Mexicans would move to the U.S. if they could and that 13 percent would be willing to do so illegally.[12]

THE END OF THE BRACERO ERA

In the 1960s, a Mexican-American Navy veteran and labor leader named Cesar Chavez surged to national prominence with his charismatic determination to improve the lives of farmworkers. Chavez founded a union that would become known as the United Farm Workers, or UFW. He was part of the effort that in 1964 persuaded Congress to terminate the bracero program, and he led a strike of California grape pickers with tactics that included a remarkably successful consumer boycott. In 1969, a portrait of Chavez occupied the cover of *Time* magazine, introducing a story titled "The Grapes of Wrath, 1969: Mexican Americans on the March." By the late 1970s, farm wages would rise to nearly 60 percent of manufacturing wages, up from less than half of manufacturing wages in 1965.[13] But the new center did not hold. The end of the braceros turned out to be the beginning of a new era of illegal immigration that frustrated Chavez and depressed wages.

Democrats aligned with the labor movement wanted to stem the influx. "My basic complaint is that we have a massive poverty population coming into the country virtually every day from Mexico," Democratic Sen. Fritz Mondale of Minnesota said at a 1970 hearing of the Senate Subcommittee on Migratory Labor.[14] A year later, an official of the Immigration and Naturalization Service warned of "dramatic changes" in the employment patterns of illegal immigrants since the 1950s, when they clustered close to the Mexican border. "We now have aliens moving into all of the United States," said INS regional commissioner Leonard W. Gilman.[15]

Illegal immigration was a major concern for Peter Rodino, a New Jersey Democrat with close ties to labor. In 1971, an immigration subcommittee headed by Rodino reported that "illegal aliens" were having a serious negative effect on American labor markets, and the problem had become national in scope. In 1972 and 1973, Rodino won House passage of legislation to penalize employers who knowingly hired illegal immigrants. He faced resistance from Hispanic critics who said sanctions would cause employers to discriminate against job-seekers with foreign accents. But he received support from the National Association for the Advancement of Colored

People, which complained that the current system guaranteed impunity to employers who hired illegal immigrants.

While Rodino's employer sanctions bill moved easily through the House, it ran into a Senate stone wall in the form of James Eastland, a classic figure of the old Democratic South. Born in 1904, he was the son of a prominent politician whose family farm eventually sprawled over nearly nine square miles of rich Mississippi Delta land, much of it planted in cotton that for decades had been picked by Mexican field hands. Eastland, who chaired the Judiciary Committee for 22 years, became known primarily for his resistance to civil rights legislation. But he was also known for blocking immigration reform bills sponsored by Rodino and others simply by refusing to hold hearings. Eastland exercised the pocket veto, committee-chairman style. Such was the power of seniority. Such was the clout of agriculture.

THE POWER OF DEMOGRAPHIC CHANGE

Another powerful policy measure was the Immigration and Nationality Act of 1965, which abolished the blatantly discriminatory system that distributed green cards through a quota system based on national origin. That system, established in 1924, was intended to stem the influx of Southern European Catholics and Eastern European Jews. The 1965 legislation mandated that green cards be distributed primarily on the basis of family connections. While Congress had anticipated that it would perpetuate the status quo of European-dominated immigration, the law had the unintended consequence of stimulating new waves of immigration from other parts of the world, as small groups of immigrants exercised their right to bring in relatives in ever-lengthening strands of chain migration. Immigration soared from an annual average of about 322,000 in the decade of the sixties to 734,000 in the eighties, 901,000 in the nineties, and more than a million in the new millennium. As a result, the immigrant population of the U.S. grew from 9.6 million in 1965 to 14 million in 1980, 31 million in 2000, and about 47 million in 2020. The largest-foreign born group came from Mexico, totaling 11 million, followed by China, India, the Philippines, Vietnam, and El Salvador.

While restrictionists have questioned the wisdom of this rate of legal immigration, the greatest concern has long focused on illegal immigration, which also grew rapidly. One metric of the influx is the number of arrests by the Border Patrol along the Mexican border. From 202,000 in 1970, the arrest figure swelled to 733,000 in 1977, the first year of the Jimmy Carter presidency. A cover story in the popular weekly magazine *U.S. News and World Report* was titled "Border Chaos: Illegal Aliens Out of Control."[16] The story quoted Labor Secretary Ray Marshall tying illegal immigration to the national unemployment problem. It also cited the complaint of Mexican-American labor leaders in El Paso that "wetbacks are eating our lunch." Having provoked what it called "a flood of mail on a hot issue," the magazine soon published another cover story titled "Time Bomb in Mexico: Why There'll Be No End to the Invasion by 'Illegals.'" Reporting on Mexico's rapidly growing population, it noted, "Each year, 800,000 young people pour into the labor market, and the flood of job seekers will swell as the present population doubles by the year 2000."[17]

In the summer of 1977, President Jimmy Carter called on Congress to pass legislation to combine amnesty and a prohibition on hiring unauthorized immigrants. Carter's engagement on the issue drew an inflammatory response from David Duke of the Ku Klux Klan. "Our government does absolutely nothing; therefore, the Klan will," Duke said. His concerns were explicitly racial. He announced mobilization of a border watch for "the single most important racial problem faced by white America."[18] His involvement would shadow the restrictionist movement for decades, as immigrant-rights activists claimed he demonstrated the bigotry underlying efforts to limit immigration.

Guilt by association, however tenuous the association, is one of the ugliest features of the immigration debate for those who believe that immigration must be limited. In 1993, *Phoenix Gazette* editorial writer Richard DeUriarte observed, "Hispanics have learned to manipulate the alternatively insensitive [and] guilt-ridden media." DeUriarte quoted an acknowledgement of the tactic's utility by Alfredo Gutierrez, a former Arizona state senator who was then a political consultant known for candor. "We call things racism just to get attention," Gutierrez said. "We reduce complicated problems to racism, not because it is racism, but because it works."[19] In the era of social media it works like gasoline on a fire.

Lawrence Fuchs, a renowned Brandeis University professor and immigration scholar, observed that Carter's proposal was problematic for congressional Democrats, who were increasingly attuned to "a growing constituency of Mexican-American leaders." Fuchs identified the divide between the Mexican-American political class, which resisted limits as it sought political influence, and the concerns of ordinary Mexican-Americans, many of whom were unhappy about illegal immigration. Fuchs wrote that Democrats looked for a way to "duck the issue and be high-minded and statesmanlike about it."[20] That aim was accomplished through the time-honored Washington tactic of appointing a committee to study a problem. In this case Congress established the Select Commission on Immigration and Refugee Policy.

SCIRP, as the commission was known, would have considerable clout. It was a 16-member blue-ribbon panel, composed of four members of the presidential Cabinet, four members of Congress, and four members representing the public, including a Mexican-American judge from California, a Cuban-American official of the AFL-CIO, and a Japanese-American assistant to the mayor of Los Angeles. The chairman was the Rev. Theodore Hesburgh, president of the University of Notre Dame and a former chairman of the U.S. Commission on Civil Rights. Guided by Hesburgh and executive director Lawrence Fuchs, the commission held hearings across the country, commissioned a host of studies, and prepared comprehensive reports and recommendations for reform legislation.

Of the commission's four congressional members, the most engaged was Sen. Alan Simpson, a Republican from Wyoming who got the assignment because he was a junior member of the Judiciary Committee and no one else wanted it. "I tried to get out of the job," Simpson said later with characteristic wry humor, "but I was stuck."[21] Known both for amiability and irascibility, the slender, six-foot-seven-inch Simpson was part Jimmy Stewart and part Yosemite Sam. He became troubled by what he saw as troubling conflicts between the national interest and the political and economic forces that sought to shape immigration policy. He was particularly alarmed at the power of "the greedy growers" of agribusiness. He won friends across Washington by telling stories like the one about answering his office phone when a caller demanded, "Where is that skinny bastard?" Simpson replied, "Speaking." As Washington commentator and political insider David Gergen wrote, "His personal friendships and his humor were part of the glue that kept the place together."[22]

"THIS NATION HAS A RESPONSIBILITY TO ITS PEOPLE"

SCIRP chairman Theodore Hesburgh had been a formidable figure on the national stage for years before becoming involved in immigration policy. In 1964, when President Lyndon Johnson awarded him the Presidential Medal of Freedom, he said Hesburgh had "inspired a generation of students and given of his wisdom in the struggle for the rights of man."[23] Hesburgh served on the U.S. Commission on Civil Rights for 15 years until President Richard Nixon replaced him in 1972 after he criticized the administration's record on civil rights.

In 1981, as Hesburgh presented SCIRP's final report to Congress, he endorsed the notion that immigration needed to be limited in the national interest. "As important as immigration has been and remains to our country, it is no longer possible to say as George Washington did that we welcome all of the oppressed of the world, or as did the poet, Emma Lazarus, that we should take all of the huddled masses yearning to be free," he said. He sought to temper romantic myth with pragmatic necessity. While he expansively hailed immigrants as representing "a portion of the world's most ambitious and creative men and women," he added a restrictionist caveat: "This nation has a responsibility to its people—citizens and resident aliens—and failure to enforce immigration law means not living up to that responsibility."[24]

The core of the commission's recommendations was a call for compromise: amnesty for illegal immigrants who had become established in the U.S. combined with measures to demagnetize the worksite by outlawing the hiring of illegal immigrants. The commissioners had voted 14–2 in favor of employer sanctions. But consensus broke down over the devilish issue of a worker identification regime to make employer sanctions work. The vote in favor of implementing a new form of worker identification was tight, with eight in favor and seven against. But Hesburgh failed in his effort to forge a consensus in favor of a fraud-resistant Social Security card. Convinced that the absence of such a verification system was essential, he would speak regretfully of that failure for the rest of his life.[†]

CIVIL LIBERTARIANS PUSH AGAINST NATIONAL IDENTIFICATION

SCIRP commissioner Patricia Roberts Harris resisted Hesburgh's push for worker identification. Expressing a concern that was held by critics on the civil-liberties left and libertarian right, she protested that a fortified Social Security card would be a step toward a national identification card. Harris became the first African-American woman to hold a Cabinet position when President Carter named her to be Secretary of Housing and Urban Development. The daughter of a Pullman railroad car waiter, she was famously determined and strong-willed, qualities that she brought to bear on immigration policy. "I am against identity cards absolutely and

† The failure would also be a lasting concern for a young SCIRP staff member named Rob Portman. In 2013, as a Republican senator from Ohio, Portman would join Montana Democratic senator John Tester in an effort to bolster verification. More of that in Part Three of this book.

unalterably," she said. "It is a historic reversal of a quality of independence and of lack of central government control of individual activities."[25] She was unmoved by Hesburgh's insistence that without a secure means of verifying that a worker was authorized, a law mandating worksite enforcement and employer sanctions would be meaningless.

THE CONFLICTING VIEWS OF MALDEF AND CESAR CHAVEZ

The Select Commission's effort to build a national consensus on immigration reform was complicated by the conflicting views of prominent Mexican-Americans. In late 1978, when SCIRP began its work, the Mexican American Legal Defense and Education Fund (MALDEF) was developing a reputation for hard-nosed pursuit of political power. Its Washington counsel, Al Perez, was blunt in explaining the organization's conviction that employer sanctions must be resisted because they would threaten not just employment opportunities but also the accumulation of Mexican-American political power that would flow from unchecked immigration. As an article in *The Atlantic* magazine put it, "Perez says that even if there were an equitable way to control access to the labor market—perhaps through a work permit required of all persons on being hired—he would not support such a deterrent to illegal immigration." Perez explained his cool calculation of risk and reward: "More Mexican-Americans mean more political power for us. Time is on our side. Yes, we fear the backlash which may come as a result of illegal immigration, but we believe that on balance the migration is in our interest."[26] Such calculation by Latino activists has had enormous influence in blocking attempts to keep unauthorized workers out of the American workplace. It has been a major reason for the failure of efforts to manage immigration in the national interest.

Cesar Chavez, of course, disagreed with MALDEF's advocacy for illegal immigrants. In 1974 his United Farm Workers union, on strike against lettuce farmers near the Mexican border in California's Imperial Valley, stationed "wet lines" along the border to block unauthorized Mexican workers from breaking the strike. The effort had limited success, and Chavez's frustration grew. In a speech at the National Press Club in Washington, Chavez complained bitterly that the Immigration and Naturalization Service was largely ignoring the growers' importation of strike breakers. Chavez demanded action from the Carter administration. "This kind of strike-breaking, condoned by the federal government, condoned by supposedly our friends at the White House, is breaking our union," he said. "And it's taking the only possible hope that workers have to be able to make a decent living."

It was a cry from the heart from Chavez, a call for understanding of the stakes for the workers he represented. But the second question off the Press Club floor came from a reporter who suggested that Chavez had become an ally of David Duke and other bigots. The reporter, who is not identified in the Press Club's transcript, asked, "Do you feel uneasy being allied with the reactionary groups like the Ku Klux Klan in calling for stricter enforcement of immigration laws?"

That question, loaded with piety and arrogance, did more to illustrate the reporter's ignorance than it did to identify a dilemma for Chavez, whose charismatic leadership had made him a national figure. Chavez's exasperation was palpable. He replied that he would want strikebreakers arrested even if his mother were among them. "It's a union, and people are being hurt and being destroyed—and with the complicity and with the help of the federal government."

Chavez's concerns about illegal immigration were widely shared. A 1980 Gallup poll showed that 90 percent of Americans wanted the federal government to go "all out" to stop it. In 1984, researchers at Pan American University in the Rio Grande Valley of Texas reported that 85 percent of first- and second-generation Mexican-Americans there said job competition from undocumented immigrants was a "major problem."[27]

A SENSE OF PUBLIC UNEASE AND URGENCY

Congress received the SCIRP report shortly after the inauguration of Ronald Reagan, whose overwhelming victory had also given Republicans control of the Senate. Simpson then became chairman of the Immigration Subcommittee of the Judiciary Committee. He joined forces with Democratic Congressman Romano Mazzoli of Kentucky in sponsoring legislation to enact the compromise reforms recommended by the commission. It became known as *Simpson-Mazzoli*.

The national mood was conducive to congressional action. The public had become alarmed about the influx not only of illegal immigrants from Mexico but also from Cubans fleeing Castro and refugees from Southeast Asia. As a *Washington Post* editorial put it, "The massive flow of illegal aliens across the Mexican border and successive flotillas of 'boat people' have produced in the public a sharp sense that the United States has lost control over this vital and sensitive area of its national life."[28]

Jack Rosenthal of the *New York Times* would win the Pulitzer Prize for editorial writing with a selection of 1981 essays, including one that endorsed Hesburgh's position and echoed his themes. Rosenthal likened the need for a reliable system of worker identification to the proverbial nail whose absence led to the loss of a horse in a string of events that led the loss of a battle and ultimately of a kingdom. Asserting a need to constrain immigration, he cautioned, "The more the system spins out of control, the more Americans lose patience with Government —and perhaps with any immigration at all."[29] We will see more of Rosenthal's work in Chapter Five as we examine *The New York Times'* later conversion to impassioned advocacy on behalf of illegal immigrants.

EDWARD ROYBAL'S GUERRILLA WAR AGAINST THE REFORM BILL

First introduced in 1982, Simpson-Mazzoli defined the battlefield for nearly five years of legislative struggle. One of the most determined combatants was Edward Roybal, a Mexican-American congressman from Los Angeles. Roybal would emerge as a historic figure in the cause of winning political power and social recognition for his people. In 1963, he became the first Latino elected to Congress from California in the 20th century. He was a founding member of the Congressional Hispanic Caucus and co-founder of the National Association of Latino Elected and Appointed Officials. In 2014, when President Obama posthumously awarded Roybal the Presidential Medal of Freedom, he saluted him for "opening doors for a new generation of Latino leaders."[30]

Roybal told stories of bitter experiences with prejudice. One involved his encounter with a Los Angeles policeman in the 1940s, when Roybal was on a date with his future wife. The policeman approached him, demanded identification, and then contemptuously dropped it on the sidewalk.[31] He never forgot the bitter taste of humiliation. He used it as motivation, as fuel. Forty years later, as Congress debated immigration reform, Roybal's sense of grievance against abusive authority primed him to resist legislation that would require workers to prove they were legitimate.

Like many other Mexican-American political leaders, Roybal said the Simpson-Mazzoli effort to keep unauthorized workers out of the labor market would invite discrimination. He believed that employers, fearful of getting on the wrong side of the law, would avoid hiring anyone who looked or sounded "foreign." Said Roybal: "Placing a stigma upon millions of American citizens is an unacceptable solution to the problem of illegal immigration."[32]

The identification card controversy placed Roybal in opposition to Lawrence Fuchs, who also had impressive liberal credentials. Fuchs had been an adviser to President John F. Kennedy on ethnic issues. He had served on the board of MALDEF and he had been active in the civil rights movement of the 1960s. Political scientist Gary Gerstle would later describe Fuchs as an eloquent advocate of "soft multiculturalism," a term Gerstle used to describe the ideology of those who "believe in diversity but also continue to value the nation, as long as the nation allows for a wide range of ethnic and racial difference." But Fuchs was also attuned to the widespread public anxiety about unchecked immigration, and he warned that a failure to control the influx could provoke a "xenophobic, racist reaction." With their contrasting views on worksite enforcement and employer sanctions, Fuchs and Roybal represented a defining dichotomy of the national immigration debate.

ROYBAL'S ATTACK ON SIMPSON-MAZZOLI

In 1982, after the Senate passed Simpson-Mazzoli, Roybal began a campaign of guerrilla warfare, smothering the bill with amendments, 200 of which he himself proposed. In 1983, when the bill came up again, Roybal misled House Speaker Tip O'Neill into canceling a vote on the bill, falsely claiming that Reagan intended to veto the bill in order to gain Latino support. Roybal took the fight to the Democratic National Convention, where he helped persuade all three leading candidates–Vice President Walter Mondale, Sen. Gary Hart, and the Rev. Jesse Jackson–to condemn the bill as discriminatory. Jackson even called it "racist." He claimed, falsely, that the bill would require non-citizens to carry passbooks like those that South African blacks were forced to carry. Roybal added that the bill would make legal immigrants wear dog tags around their necks. He said Simpson-Mazzoli's mandate for eventual development of a worker identification system would be the first step toward totalitarian oppression. "We may face the danger of ending up like Nazi Germany," he warned.

A *Washington Post* editorial condemned the "ugly misrepresentations" from Jackson and Roybal. "The fact is that Simpson-Mazzoli specifically repudiates a national identification card as a means of establishing employee eligibility for lawful resident aliens and citizens," the *Post* said.[33] "One can understand Roybal's anxieties, given the history of discrimination against Hispanics in the Southwest. It is also understandable that Mexican-American leaders oppose the inauguration of a national policy that would eventually curtail the flow of undocumented workers, with whom they empathize. But that does not justify Roybal's misrepresentation of the bill." An editorial in *The New York Times* blasted Jackson, Roybal, and Hart, saying their opposition to the reform bill amounted to "pandering to Hispanic leaders."[34]

Years later, Simpson would still recall Roybal's tactics with exasperation, saying they had a chilling effect on the search for a secure identifier. "When you're playing with emotion, it's a fearful thing," he said. "Talk about a means of identification and [people bring up] Hitler and tattoos and concentration camps. And that's that."[35] He was equally frustrated with Simpson-Mazzoli antagonists at the *Wall Street Journal* editorial board, which favored open borders in the name of free markets and individual liberty. In his 1997 memoir, titled *Right in the Old Gazoo*, Simpson wrote that the *Journal* wanted "a national immigration policy that allows fat-cat businesspeople—that is, many *Wall Street Journal* readers–to import, exploit, and then casually discard wasted illegal aliens."[36]

THE FORMIDABLE VILMA MARTINEZ

One of the most outspoken critics of Simpson-Mazzoli was MALDEF's Vilma Martinez, whose convictions drew power from the long history of discrimination against Mexican-Americans. She was a woman of penetrating intellect and personal magnetism who graduated from Columbia Law School and became MALDEF's general counsel and president, then U.S. ambassador to Argentina in the administration of President Barack Obama.

Born in San Antonio in 1943, the daughter of a construction worker, Martinez didn't learn English until she entered school, a circumstance that would help shape her character and her politics. "One time, some kids were putting me down in school because I was Mexican-American... I went to my mother crying, but she did not comfort me," she recalled years later. "She took me to a mirror and she forced me to look at myself... Tears were all over my face, and then she said, 'I want you to take a good, hard look and see what you have let them do to you.' And I decided, little girl that I was, that they would never do that to me, or to other little girls or boys, again." Indelible memories of such malice fueled her conviction that Simpson-Mazzoli should be defeated. At a congressional hearing she testified that although an identification requirement might seem benign to some, for others it would cause difficulties. "People will hassle you," she said, speaking on behalf of Latinos she hoped to shield from that humiliation.

Rep. Romano Mazzoli, whose father was an Italian tile setter who emigrated to the U.S. early in the century, understood the sting of xenophobic discrimination. But he was a Democrat from conservative Kentucky, inclined by personality and sensibility to build bridges and forge compromise. A graduate of Notre Dame, he formed immigration views that meshed with Hesburgh's. So, when Martinez told her story at a congressional hearing, he responded with gentle frustration to her opposition to any form of identification. "It would be so much more helpful to us if you could give some wisdom, instead of just simply saying that everything that has been presented... you cannot go along with," he said.[37]

No one was more frustrated at the resistance to employer sanctions than Hesburgh, who spoke of employer sanctions as one of three legs of the stool of reform. The other two were amnesty and tightened border security. "It seems to me that stool can only stand on three legs," Hesburgh said at a Senate hearing. "You're going to get all three of them or you're going to get none at all."

THE POWER OF AGRIBUSINESS

While the influence of Latino political leaders has grown tremendously since the 1970s, the single most powerful interest group in the debate that preceded enactment of IRCA was Western agribusiness.[‡] Growers from California, where federal irrigation projects had made possible the evolution of gigantic "factories on the fields," were

‡ The term "agribusiness" is appropriate because large farm businesses account for the bulk of agricultural production. A landmark 1990 study by economist Don Villarejo reported that the 3.4 percent of California

particularly potent. Their critics, particularly those who represented workers, argued that if the growers offered better pay and working conditions, they would find authorized workers in rural communities with an agricultural heritage and unemployment rates double the national average.[38] As the growers pressed their demands in 1985, Willard Wirtz, labor secretary under Presidents Kennedy and Johnson, lamented "the cynicism and greed that has characterized the actions of so many growers for so many years."[39]

In their determination to maintain access to the workforce needed to harvest their perishable crops, the growers could count on the support of influential Republicans like Sen. Pete Wilson of California and Democrats like Leon Panetta, whose district along the Central California coast was home to producers of lettuce, artichokes, and nuts, as well as processing plants in Salinas. For added influence with House Democrats, they hired the powerhouse lobbying and law firm Akin, Gump, Strauss, Hauer and Feld. The firm's co-founder was legendary Washington power-broker Robert Strauss, who famously explained that Washington's lobbying industry had proliferated "because there's just so damn much money in it... It's a company town, and the business is lobbying."

Strauss apparently took no direct role in the firm's lobbying on immigration. He left that work primarily to another member of the firm, former Agriculture Department lawyer Ruth Harkin, whose husband was Rep. Tom Harkin, a Democrat from Iowa.

For influence with Republicans, the growers contracted the services of lobbyist James H. Lake, who had worked for President Reagan as a campaign adviser, communications director, and press secretary. Their most important advocate was Sen. Wilson, who was determined to mitigate the risk that workers who received legal status would leave the fields for better work. Wilson won Senate passage of an amendment for a program to import 350,000 guest workers for up to nine months. The idea infuriated American labor.

---

farms whose sales were $1 million or more accounted for 60 percent of the state's agricultural production.

"No other industry in America is guaranteed an oversupply of labor in order to assure a ready supply," said a lobbyist for the AFL-CIO.[40] *The New York Times* called the Wilson amendment "a blazing example of special interest politics."[41]

CHARLES SCHUMER'S EXTRAVAGANT COMPROMISE

The Senate passed Simpson-Mazzoli again in 1985, sending it on to the House for a debate that would carry over into the next year's congressional session. The principal antagonists would be the representatives of agribusiness, who wanted lots of workers, and the advocates of labor, who wanted the best possible deal for field hands. The task of reconciling them fell to IRCA's geographically and culturally unlikely broker, Rep. Charles Schumer of Brooklyn. Schumer was an inveterate dealmaker, eager to make his mark as a legislative craftsman. In 1986, when it looked as if the two sides had irreconcilable differences, Schumer engineered a plan to give both sides what they most wanted.

Schumer's centerpiece was called the Special Agricultural Worker (SAW) program. It provided a path to citizenship for unauthorized migrants who had worked a mere 90 days in the fields in 1985–1986. That was a big sweetener for immigrant-rights activists. The deal also featured a massive insurance policy for the growers. It provided that when newly legalized workers left the fields to find work elsewhere, the growers would be able to hire "replenishment workers" who–in another stroke of generosity–would also be put on a path to citizenship. Schumer, who assembled the package without a single congressional hearing to gauge its dimensions or anticipate its effects, hailed it as a compromise. *The Washington Post* called it ridiculously generous to both growers and workers. "It looks like a cave-in to us," said the *Post*. "By giving agricultural lobbyists all they could possibly have dreamed of and by offering incredibly generous benefits to illegal agricultural workers, the congressmen have won the support of these groups."[42]

On the other side of the compromise, IRCA offered restrictionists the abolition of the Texas Proviso and a program to cut off the jobs magnet. The *Houston Chronicle* identified Schumer, a Democrat from Brooklyn, as the man who held the deal together. In a reference to the host of the "Let's Make a Deal" television game show, it reported that Schumer was "so determined to forge enough compromises to pass a bill that some lobbyists dubbed him 'the Monty Hall of Immigration.'" Schumer called the legislative struggle "a test of governance." He would recall that the compromise was propelled by the conviction that "we've done so much work; we've got to work something out."[43] Schumer was like a strike negotiator who keeps all sides at the table for as long as it takes to get them to accept a deal. His effort was sincere. The product may have been the best he could achieve under the circumstances.

Lawrence Fuchs, in recognition of the multiple instances when negotiations collapsed, only to be revived again, called IRCA "the corpse that would not die." But the determination of sponsors to achieve real reform was so battered by those who wanted to kill it and by the sheer complexity of the issues that they were eventually reduced to a willingness to accept what they could get. "It's a monstrous s.o.b.," said Alan Simpson, "But it will be sure as hell a lot better than anything we've got now."[44]

IRCA became law almost by default. Some in Congress decided that it was time to pass a bill, declare victory, and move on. Rep. Dan Lungren (R-CA) observed that "some people were just exhausted."[45] Rep. Bill Richardson (D-NM), dissenting from Roybal's last-ditch resistance, had concluded that employer sanctions were inevitable and that Hispanic legislators needed to move beyond obstructionism. "The time has come to bite the bullet on immigration reform," said Richardson.[46] He was willing to accept employer sanctions as the price for amnesty, a prize that was worth protecting against the Republicans, who protested that it would reward illegal immigration and encourage more of it.

Indeed, an amendment to strip amnesty, proposed by Florida Republican Bill McCollum, was just barely defeated by a vote of 192–199. In the end, even McCollum voted for the final version of the bill as it emerged from a conference to resolve differences between the House and Senate versions. McCollum reluctantly concluded that IRCA was acceptable because employer sanctions and worksite enforcement presented "an opportunity to close our borders" to future illegal immigration.[47] The urgency of that need had been underlined by the news that during the 1986 fiscal year, the Border Patrol had made a record 1.8 million arrests of illegal border crossers.

The contrasting views of Peter Rodino and fellow Democrat Patricia Schroeder encapsulated the divide between the 168 Democrats who voted for the bill and the 61 Democrats who opposed it. Rodino thought the bill would reduce migratory pressure from Latin America. "When we consider the economic conditions and political turmoil in the countries to the south of us, the problem of illegal crossing will continue to mount unless action is taken," he said on the House floor. He warned that if Congress didn't act and illegal immigration continued, "there will be a backlash against all immigrants."

Schroeder's greatest concern was the plight of illegal immigrants. True to her liberal value of compassion for the vulnerable, she disputed the concerns of those who wanted to stop illegal immigrants. "I heard from proponents of this legislation that we must control our borders, we must secure our borders for national defense purposes," she said. "From whom? From some peon from El Salvador? A little Indian from Guanajuato, Mexico. We in this country are the last beacon of democracy, liberty, and justice. That is why they want to come."

SEEKING TO MAKE THE SYSTEM "REASONABLE, FAIR, ORDERLY, AND SECURE"

President Reagan's sunny optimism brightened the IRCA signing ceremony at the White House as he predicted that "future generations of Americans will be thankful" for the new legislation and its "critically important reforms." He called the provisions for employer sanctions "the keystone and major element." And he declared that the purpose of the legislation was "to establish a reasonable, fair, orderly, and secure system of immigration."

Reagan's speech was, of course, a political performance, staged to present the federal government as resolute and capable. But beyond the realm of ceremony and symbolism, IRCA would fail in large part because Congress and successive administrations, responding to pressures from the strange bedfellows coalition for loose borders, have not been committed to fixing its flaws and making it work. That problem, a contradiction if not an hypocrisy, has been present from the beginning, despite rhetorical flourishes at the White House over the years. IRCA was a pledge of reform and control to which Reagan himself was never committed. As the administration worked on its first budget of the post-IRCA era, it requested far less money for the Immigration and Naturalization Service than Congress had authorized to administer and enforce the law. "I was always worried that parts of the administration were ambivalent about the immigration bill," said Charles Schumer. "Now they may succeed in killing the law by starving it."

Meanwhile, Schumer had many allies on the immigrant-rights left who had their own reasons for wanting the bill to fail. Some were so convinced of the righteousness of their cause that they felt justified in launching campaigns of smear and character assassination against those who wanted the law to be enforced. And, of course, the growers would continue to pursue their own peculiar interests, beckoning an ongoing flow of illegal immigration into their endless rows of lettuce and strawberries. Observers of Congress sometimes say controversial legislation that makes it to the president's desk has been "successfully passed," but IRCA can be described as having been *unsuccessfully passed.* The weakness built into it fulfilled the prediction of *The Economist* magazine, which during the 1985 debate, advised its readers, "Experience suggests that immigration reform cannot get through Congress without a covered wagon first being driven through it by the Californian farm interests, rich, voracious and brilliantly led."[48] But big agriculture was only one of the interests that worked to thwart effective immigration control.

IRCA'S IRONIC LEGACY: STIMULUS FOR ILLEGAL IMMIGRATION

Philip Martin, an immigration scholar and agricultural economist at the University of California at Davis, concluded that IRCA's effect was exactly the opposite of what Congress and the president had promised. In his book *Promise Unfulfilled,* Martin wrote: "Perhaps the most important effect of immigration reform was to spread unauthorized workers from the Southwest to the rest of the country."[49]

Those who were granted legal status were able to move freely around the country. When they found work and pleasant surroundings, they put out the word to friends and relatives back home. Then, many more crossed the border illegally to join them. The growth of immigrant communities in the United States had a mirror image on the other side of the border. The "source" communities spread across Mexico and ever deeper into Latin America countries—and then around a world bedeviled by hunger, conflict, natural disaster, and corruption. By 2002 Mexico's National Population Commission (CONAPO) was reporting that residents of 96 percent of the country's 2,350 county-sized *municipios* had migrated to the U.S. I learned the dynamics of the process through my reporting. For example, the immigration of a single man from the Chiapas village of San Pedro Buenavista to Washington, D.C.'s Maryland suburbs in the 1980s led to the migration of dozens of his relatives and former neighbors, who by 2005 were working primarily in fast food restaurants—McDonald's, Burger King, Chick-fil-A—that extended more than 30 miles to the north. At a McDonald's in Towson, near my old high school, I was surprised to learn that one of the women working on the grill was from San Pedro. But I wasn't as surprised as she was to learn that I had been there, visiting some of her former neighbors.

GAMING THE SYSTEM: AMNESTY AND FRAUD

The Special Agricultural Worker program devised by Schumer was a fraud magnet. Because it was common for field workers to be paid in cash, they were allowed to establish eligibility for permanent legal residence by submitting letters from employers. The result was a new industry in which farmers and labor contractors collected $1,000 for one-page letters of attestation. *The New York Times* reported that it was "one of the most extensive immigration frauds ever perpetrated against the United States."

A fundamental supposition of Schumer's grand compromise was that employer sanctions would force the growers to improve wages and working conditions in order to keep newly legalized workers in the fields. But the enforcement never came and the flow of illegal immigration intensified. Researchers found that farm workers' wages, adjusted for inflation, fell by 8.7 percent during the 1980s, while non-agricultural wages rose by 11 percent. "We would argue that the price of agricultural labor has declined in the 1980s because there has been a substantial excess supply of agricultural labor,"[50] said Don Villarejo of the California Institute for Rural Studies at a 1990 conference

The failure of enforcement meant that the Immigration Reform and Control Act has never come close to living up to its name. Far from controlling illegal immigration, the law fueled it. Throughout the decade of the 1990s, in particular, IRCA enabled enormous demographic change of the sort that Al Perez had described to *The Atlantic*. The Latino population grew from 22 million in 1990 to 35.3 million in 2000. That growth rate was four times that of the overall U.S. population. It was fueled by a robust birth rate and major increases in both legal and illegal immigration. During the 1990s, while legal immigration continued at an average annual rate of about 900,000 illegal immigration rose by about 500,000 per year. SCIRP had warned Congress that this was possible. It had reported that without effective enforcement, "legalization could serve as a stimulus to further illegal entry." The commission went so far as to recommend that legalization begin only after "new enforcement measures have been instituted to make it clear that the US is determined to curtail a new flow of undocumented illegal aliens."

THE POLITICAL-PORK THEORY OF VISAS

In 2000, Harvard professor Christopher Jencks assessed the political calculation that encouraged politicians to support expansionist policies despite longstanding public opinion favoring less immigration. Noting that the green cards that signify the right to live permanently in the U.S. have great value, Jencks drew a lesson of immigration economics. "Since the 1970s, Congress has learned to treat these permits like other forms of political pork," he wrote. "Legislators who work to expand the number of green cards win friends. Legislators who work to reduce the number make enemies. Unless that changes, immigration will keep expanding no matter what the polls show."[51]

It may be that expansionist forces are simply more powerful than the forces of restriction. The expansionist lobby is certainly larger, more diverse, and vastly better funded. The watchdog Sunlight Foundation reported that between 2008 and 2012, lobbyists spent a whopping $1.5 billion to push for expansionist immigration policies. Beyond such financial interests, lobbying from ethnic groups grows as newcomers themselves seek to bring relatives to join them. Moreover, the generous allocation of green cards receives strong support from Americans who value inclusiveness and diversity or who join Speaker of the House Nancy Pelosi in affirming that, "Immigration is who we are."

The election of Donald Trump provided evidence of the enduring power of the restrictionist impulse. And one of the most salient features of the national immigration debate since the 1970s has been the persistent warnings that although immigration brings many benefits to our country, it also has a disruptive effect that makes a populist backlash unavoidable if the government fails to set limits and enforce them fairly, firmly, and coherently.

John Higham, the great chronicler of the nativist backlashes against Irish immigrants in the middle of the 19th century and Italian and Jewish immigrants in the first quarter of the 20th century, forcefully criticized anti-restrictionists in 1993 for thwarting what he regarded as reasonable and necessary efforts to control illegal immigration. He drew an analogy between that period and the era that incubated the nativist outbreak that followed World War I:

> *A fair policy of immigration restriction was becoming increasingly desirable in the early twentieth century as part of the responsible organization of an industrial society. But immigrants and their employers simply adopted an inflexible posture of defending the status quo. That kept the nation's doors wide open to everyone who could pass a simple physical examination or pay for cabin passage. The opportunity, between 1910 and 1917, to think out an immigration policy that might be both realistic and democratic was therefore lost. After the war the forces of ethnic self-interest and national hysteria took over .... Today a third major wave of immigration is building around us, and again it puts special strains on parts of the country where it is breaking. We are, I submit, at a moment analogous to the years between 1910 and 1917. Serious protective measures against unregulated (i.e.,undocumented) immigration are called for, and desired by the public at large, but influential groups do not wish to listen.*[52]

In 2017, a similarly forceful lament came from Andrew Sullivan, the British immigrant, conservative writer, and outspoken critic of

Donald Trump. Noting that backlashes against immigration were also underway in Britain, France, and Germany, Sullivan said this of the backlash in the United States:

> *You can call it racism in a way. But you can also say that it's simply an instinct, that they don't want their entire society to be radically changed overnight or over a couple decades. The America that they grew up with is not the America that they see winning. And I think combined with the rather aggressive—more than rather, extremely aggressive—attempts by the sort of social justice crowd, to implicate anybody with this discomfort as utter racists and bigots and fascists, has only entrenched their sense of cultural isolation and siege and made the resilience of the support for Trump even greater.*
>
> *We're in a bad, bad dynamic here. And I think it's perfectly legitimate to argue that in order for the wave of immigrants that we've had over the past couple of decades to be properly integrated and assimilated into this country, we could do with a pause. We could do with stronger enforcement against illegal immigration and we could do with, I think, a decline of legal immigration. That is simply a matter of digesting this kind of social change. It can't be done overnight without a backlash, a huge backlash. That's what we're dealing with.*[53]

We now turn our attention to the backlashes that developed in two frontline states of the immigration debate: California, where illegal immigration soared in the 1980s and 1990s, and Arizona, which experienced an intense influx that began in 1994 and continued well into the new millennium.

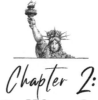

Chapter 2:
Backlash in California and Arizona

> An overwhelming majority of Californians say they are fed up with illegal immigration, with 86% describing it as a major or moderate problem and nearly three-quarters in favor of using the National Guard to patrol the southern border, a new Los Angeles Times Poll has found.
>
> —Los Angeles Times, *1993*[1]

> The reason Arizona and other states have deputized police as amateur immigration agents — and contemplated making enforcers out of school principals, emergency-room nurses and other civil servants — is that we have failed so utterly to fortify the most obvious line of defense. No, not the Mexican border. Employers. Jobs are, after all, the main magnet for illegal immigration. If we had a reliable way for employers to check the legal status of prospective workers, and held them strictly accountable for doing so, we would not feel the need for all these secondary checkpoints
>
> —New York Times, *2012*[2]

When Congress debated immigration reform in the 1980s, Pete Wilson was a U.S. senator from California. He was a forceful advocate of his state's agricultural industry and its demands for a large supply of low-cost labor. But he lost his enthusiasm for loose borders in the early 1990s, when he was governor and the state suffered a severe economic downturn. In a sense, his 1994 bid for reelection put Gov. Pete Wilson up against the record of Sen. Pete Wilson.

Wilson's Democratic challenger was California treasurer Kathleen Brown, whose father, Pat, and brother, Jerry, had been California governors. She took a big lead in the polls as she promised to lead the state out of what she called "the Wilson recession." But Wilson kept his eye on another poll, which, as the *Los Angeles Times* reported, showed that "an overwhelming majority of Californians say they are fed up with illegal immigration." Seventy-five percent were in favor of sending the National Guard to the Mexican border, and nearly 60 percent favored requiring job seekers to present tamper-proof identification to prove their legal status.

In other words, Californians wanted government to get serious about delivering IRCA's promise of worksite enforcement. The law's amnesty provisions had affected California more than any other state. Of the 2.7 million people who received legal status, some 800,000 settled in Los Angeles County alone. Many were from Mexico's impoverished countryside. About three-quarters of them lacked the Mexican equivalent of a high school education. Many were joined by relatives and friends, who often crossed the border illegally. The stress on schools and social services intensified. Meanwhile, new waves of illegal immigrants poured in from Central America and other regions of the world battered by civil war, social unrest, political turmoil, endemic corruption, and wretched poverty. California's population of unauthorized immigrants in 1994 was conservatively estimated at 1.6 million.

Against a background of rising public bewilderment and frustration, two former officials of the Immigration and Naturalization Service launched a populist uprising through an organization they named Save Our State. Cleverly dubbed "S.O.S.," it promoted an initiative to deny state services, including education and non-emergency health care, to illegal immigrants. After attracting the 385,000 signatures needed to qualify for the 1994 ballot, it was listed there as Proposition 187.

"California is in big trouble due to illegal immigration," said Harold Ezell, a former western regional chief of the INS who co-wrote Proposition 187 with Alan Nelson, the INS commissioner under Reagan. In 1994, Nelson was a lobbyist in Sacramento for the restrictionist Federation for American Immigration Reform. He hoped the proposition would pressure Washington to fix IRCA and make enforcement work. The pamphlet that accompanied the ballot included a prediction by supporters that "Proposition 187 will go down in history as the voice of the people against an arrogant bureaucracy."

Immigrant rights organizations and Hispanic leaders denounced Proposition 187 as anti-immigrant and anti-Mexican. The publisher of *La Opinion*, a Spanish-language newspaper published in Los Angeles, called it "a direct attack on the Latino community." The California State Teachers Association rejected it. Kathleen Brown denounced it as "mean-spirited and dangerous." But Brown was careful to say she understood the public's frustration. She called for a fortified worker-verification system and a crackdown on employers who hired unauthorized workers. In other words, she wanted IRCA's flaws to be fixed so the law could do what it was intended to do. She was caught on the horns of a dilemma that was characteristic of liberals who were alarmed both at the fiscal and civic implications of illegal immigration and at the humanitarian implications of enforcing the law against illegal immigrants.

Brown's measured approach lacked the populist, no-nonsense appeal of Wilson's campaign. At a time of extreme austerity in the California budget, Wilson argued that it wasn't right that the state was required to pay $1.5 billion a year to educate the 300,000 children who were brought illegally to the state. His campaign produced a television spot featuring grainy black-and-white video of migrants dashing through traffic at the port of entry on Interstate 5, between Tijuana and San Diego. Against the heavy beat of a drum, a narrator sounded the alarm: "They keep coming. Two million illegal immigrants in California. The federal government won't stop them at the border yet requires us to pay billions to take care of them." Wilson appeared on screen, looking stern and resolute as he declared: "I'm suing to force the federal government to control the border, and I'm working to deny state services to illegal immigrants. Enough is enough."

Despite the resentment that Wilson's ads stirred among Hispanics who said he was scapegoating all of them, Hispanic opinion on Proposition 187 was closely divided. A *Los Angeles Times* survey of registered Hispanic voters found that 52 percent favored Proposition 187 while 42 percent opposed it. This was not a surprise to anyone who knew that although Hispanics felt sympathy for the undocumented, many resented the swelling ranks of newcomers they regarded as a threat to their chance for a better life. It had been that way for decades. In 1966, Mexican-American scholar George I. Sanchez put it this way: "Time and again, just as we have been on the verge of cutting our bicultural problems to manageable proportions, uncontrolled mass migrations from Mexico have erased the gains and accentuated the cultural indigestion."[3]

In 1994, the cultural indigestion rippled across California society, aggravating tensions felt most acutely at the workplace. Journalist Daniel Ast reported on the declining fortunes of Southern California drywallers. "In the 1970s, installing gypsum wallboard there was highly paid union work," he wrote. "But at the end of that decade, contractors began using nonunion Mexican immigrants, many of them from a single village. By the early 1980s, union drywallers had been completely displaced, and wages had plummeted."

Another frustration stemmed from a sense of civic disorder and breakdown. An immigrant from Taiwan told *USA Today*: "I got into a car accident with a guy who didn't speak English, had no green card, no driver's license, no form of ID, and he walks away. I'm left holding the bag. It's those little trivial everyday experiences that got enough people really angry to vote to do something about it." A *Washington Post* story from the city of Santa Ana said the intense influx, both legal and illegal, had "turned disputes on such issues as regulation of street vendors or creation of job centers for day laborers into emotional ethnic conflicts." One longtime resident blamed illegal immigrants for the brisk drug-dealing in a parking lot. He complained that eight Mexican families were living in a single rental home. "And they change the oil in the gutter, and it just runs down the street," he said.[4]

To many Californians, it seemed that familiar patterns of order were unraveling and a way of life was being lost in an open-borders free-for-all. Claims that those who were angry were racist only compounded their resentment. Latinos wrestled with their own tangle of emotions. George Ramos of the *Los Angeles Times* wrote that although a large majority of Latinos opposed illegal immigration, they felt threatened by the emotionalism of the issue—and also felt a duty to help the newcomers. "Almost every Latino family I know, including my own, has someone in it who came to Los Angeles illegally," he wrote. "You tell them not to come, but you also know you'll help them once they get here. They are, after all, family."[5]

GOV. WILSON PROVOKES A COUNTER-BACKLASH

The debate over Proposition 187 made national news. In Washington, President Clinton kept a watchful eye on California's turbulent immigration politics. Clinton, who in 1992 had been the first Democratic presidential candidate to carry the state since Lyndon Johnson in 1964, was wary of a possible reelection challenge from Wilson. He wanted the INS to show toughness at the border. The result was a Border Patrol build-up called Operation Gatekeeper, which INS Commissioner Doris Meissner promoted as an effort "to restore the rule of law to the border after years of neglect." The tactic of deflecting blame to Clinton's Republican predecessors would be standard procedure in the administration's communications strategy all the way through his 1996 campaign for a second term.

Meanwhile, Proposition 187 passed with 59 percent of the vote and was instrumental in Wilson's come-from-behind victory over Kathleen Brown. But it would be thwarted on constitutional grounds by a federal district judge whose decision was based in part on a 1982 Supreme Court ruling that the state of Texas could not deny public school education to undocumented children. Delivering the court's 5–4 decision in the case of *Plyler v. Doe*, Justice William Brennan said it was both unconstitutional and unfair to inflict "the stigma of illiteracy" and "a lifetime of hardship" on children because of their parents' decision to bring them illegally to the United States. Some of the architects for Proposition 187, anticipating legal challenges, saw it as a strategy that could result in a reversal of *Plyler v. Doe* by a conservative Supreme Court.

Pete Wilson's hardline against illegal immigration made him a symbolic figure, a unifying villain for many Hispanics and others in his state. "He created an environment where anti-Latino sentiment was winked at and allowed to be expressed openly," said Arturo Vargas, a MALDEF leader in Los Angeles. Vargas said on the day after the election, a caller left this message on his answering machine: "Get out of town, bean dip. Your time is up. Go back to your homeland. This is a white man's country." For decades, California demographics and politics had been dominated by its white suburban middle class. But a dramatic change was underway. Art Torres, a longtime chairman of the California Democratic Party, thundered that 187 was "the last gasp of white America in California." Mario Obledo, the fiery MALDEF co-founder, caused an uproar when he declared that California was becoming "an Hispanic state" and that those who didn't like it should "go back to Europe."

Not many people went back to Europe. But many California residents have left for other states, voting with their feet and their rental trucks against the transformation of the state's demography, culture, politics, and schools. In 2014 the *New York Times* reported that although the state continued to attract large numbers of foreign immigrants, 6.8 million California natives were living elsewhere.[6] The demographic shift helped turn California's electoral map a deep and reliable blue.

CALIFORNIA BY THE NUMBERS

The California of 1994 was a very different place from the Golden State of 1962, when Gov. Pat Brown declared a holiday to celebrate the triumph of becoming the most populous state in the union. That was the year the Beach Boys released "Surfin' Safari," their debut album, and emerged as rock 'n' roll evangelists of endless summer. The state delighted in its allure, the magnetic attraction of its sun, its Hollywood magic, its start-over mythology. Brown marveled that the nation's "western rim.... which a century ago was as much legend as land to a handful of pioneers, now assumes the role of leader on that continent." There were some admonitions about such booster euphoria. "Mere numbers do not mean happiness," warned former Gov. Earl Warren, who was then Chief Justice of the Supreme Court. Then, in 1964, the Census Bureau made it official. It reported that California's population had reached 18,084,000, surpassing New York.[7]

At the beginning of the 1960s, California's population was 80 percent non-Hispanic and most of the growth was the result of a domestic baby boom and immigration from other states. Immigration reform that Congress passed in 1965 abolished the national-origins system that discriminated heavily in favor of northern and western Europe. Opportunity now beckoned newcomers from around the world. Legal immigration to the U.S. tripled from its 1960s pace of about 300,000 per year to more than 900,000 per year in the 1990s. About a third of the newcomers chose California.

The magnetic attraction was especially urgent in Mexico, whose population was booming from its 1960 level of 35 million, on its way to more than 100 million in 2000. Many came with green cards. Many came illegally. Their numbers grew rapidly in California. The census showed that in 1970 the 2.4 million Hispanics—mostly of Mexican heritage—accounted for 12 percent of the state's population of 20 million. By 2000, the Hispanic population totaled nearly 11 million, about a third of the state's residents.* By 2014, California's 15 million Hispanics were the state's largest ethnic or racial group.

California's Asian-American population, meanwhile, was growing from a much smaller base. In 1970, Asian-Americans represented less than 3 percent of the state's population. But as newcomers naturalized and exercised their right to sponsor family members, they grew steadily. They came primarily from the Philippines, China, Vietnam, India, and Korea. By 2010, they were 15 percent of the population.

Many Californians, like many Americans elsewhere, delighted in the demographic, cultural, culinary, and linguistic diversity that transformed the state. They welcomed immigrants without hesitation and without concern for country of origin or legal status. But diversity also provoked discontent. Harvard sociologist Robert Putnam, while an immigration enthusiast himself, reported that as diversity expanded, communal engagement declined. He documented a loss of *social capital*, his term for the networks of solidarity and cooperation that allowed a community to cohere and cooperate. As a matter of human nature, people tended to hunker down, to isolate themselves in a withdrawal he called *turtling*. "Diversity, at least in the short run, seems to bring out the turtle in all of us," he said.[8]

The sheer volume of the change was remarkable. The state's population of unauthorized immigrants grew from about 1,450,000 in 1990 to about 2,250,000 in 2000, an average annual increase of 80,000 persons. In 2014, the Migration Policy Institute estimated that California was home to 3,019,000 unauthorized immigrants, 70 percent of whom were from Mexico. Another 11 percent came from El Salvador and Guatemala. Filipinos accounted for 3 percent, and Chinese accounted for 2 percent. Other Asian countries added 11 percent. Much smaller numbers came from Canada, Europe, and Africa.[9]

* By 1990 Hispanics totaled 7,688,000, or 26 percent of the state's population of 29,760,000. By 2010, Hispanics were 37.6 percent of the state's population of more than 37 million.

THE STORY IN ARIZONA

For decades, the most active portals for illegal immigration were El Paso and San Diego, major cities paired with Juarez and Tijuana, respectively, on the Mexico side of the border. Those two areas accounted for about two-thirds of all Border Patrol arrests.

That changed abruptly in 1993 when Silvestre Reyes, Border Patrol chief in El Paso, adopted a strategy to deter illegal crossers rather than arresting them after they had crossed. He deployed agents about 100 yards apart along a 20-mile segment of the border, and he made sure they were there around the clock. Reyes called it "Operation Blockade." But then, to show respect for Mexican sensibilities, he changed the name to "Operation Hold the Line." It was an immediate success, befuddling illegal crossers and establishing order in El Paso streets long roiled by break-ins and car thefts. Despite protests from immigrant-rights activists on both sides of the border, Reyes became a local hero for his determined effort to deter illegal crossings. In 1995 he retired from the Border Patrol, and a year later he became El Paso's new Democratic congressman.

A year after Reyes initiated Hold the Line, "Operation Gatekeeper" brought relief to the border near San Diego, where local residents had long complained of chaotic conditions. Back in 1990, as the widow of a Border Patrol agent joined a group of hundreds who turned on their vehicle headlights to illuminate the nightly drama of men, women, and children massing on the border and then pouring into the U.S., she explained her motivation. "I just want the place lit up, and with that will come proper attention and proper law enforcement." That idealistic belief in public engagement and democratic governance has been sorely tested ever since.

Coming just before the overwhelming vote in favor of Proposition 187 and in the midst of Pete Wilson's campaign, Operation Gatekeeper was as much a reflection of national politics as it was a border strategy. Gatekeeper and Hold the Line certainly made illegal border crossings much more difficult. But rather than stopping the migratory stream, they redirected much of it into Arizona's deserts and mountains. There the migrants paid a price in rising smugglers' fees and exposure to the desert's blast-furnace heat. But the American worksite still beckoned. Failed worksite enforcement combined with the migrants' determination and employers' eagerness for workers kept the river of illegal immigration flowing northward.

I met migrants who said they were tired of Mexico's *salarios de hambre* – starvation wages. They often added the stoic declaration that it was "better to die of heat in the desert than of starvation at home." A Mexican ballad titled "Los Ilegales" was an anthem of migrant determination and perseverance:

> *If one day the Border Patrol*
> *Should take me by surprise*
> *It will take them longer to take me out*
> *Than for me to come back*

UPHEAVAL IN MEXICO AND A REVOLVING DOOR AT THE BORDER

At the end of 1994, a political and financial crisis in Mexico intensified the migratory push. When Mexican President Carlos Salinas de Gortari delivered his last major address, he condemned supporters of Proposition 187 as xenophobes and declared that Mexico would "continue to act in defense of...our migrant workers." But the Harvard-educated technocrat ended his six-year term amid allegations of corruption and a catastrophic collapse of the peso. The shock set off rampant inflation, huge job losses, and a new wave of illegal migration to the United States that highlighted another dynamic of Mexican migration. It functioned as a safety valve for public frustration that otherwise might have been directed at politicians whose endemic corruption inspired a cynical Mexican saying: "A politician who is poor is a poor politician." Emigration provided an outlet for the frustration of the people. But it also provided protection for a sclerotic political system.

Under U.S. law, illegally crossing the border is a misdemeanor known as "entry without inspection." It can be punished with time in prison, but the number of EWIs was so enormous that the Border Patrol's usual policy for Mexicans was to return them to the border and release them.† That turned the borderlands into a revolving door. The migrants were patient and persistent, confident that they would eventually elude the Border Patrol and move on to find work in the U.S., which they called *el otro lado*—the *other side*—of a border, beyond which lay a world of possibilities that were denied them at home. For long stretches that beckoning *linea*, that line, was marked by an incongruously meager three-strand barbed-wire fence. Sometimes Border Patrol agents acknowledged that for every person they arrested, three or four got away.

In early 1995, Clinton's immigration commissioner, Doris Meissner, came to the Arizona border town of Nogales to show resolve and provide political cover for President Clinton. That January, agents at the local Border Patrol station made 19,426 arrests, nearly double the number for the same period a year earlier. Meissner, combining her official role as INS commissioner with her unofficial job as spokesperson for the Clinton campaign, expressed confidence that with the new resources the president was directing to border enforcement, "The message will go out that this is no longer a place where you can cross."[10]

It was a familiar, politically necessary pose. It was a promise that had no chance as long as IRCA was so easy to evade at the worksite. The 357-mile Arizona border offered so many potential crossing points that the smugglers were able to adjust their routes rapidly

---

† The policy for illegal crossers who were "other than Mexican"—OTMs in Border Patrol parlance—was complicated by the fact that they couldn't be returned to Mexico. So the Border Patrol generally released them with an "order to appear" in immigration court on a date months in the future. That was a real morale killer for Border Patrol agents, who called it "an order to disappear." As I learned in 2005, the vast majority never showed up in court, preferring to try to disappear in the vastness of the United States.

to get their customers across. Sometimes they were guided by lookouts in the hills with radios. Sometimes they would send a small group deliberately into the hands of the Border Patrol. While the agents were occupied with the arrests, a much larger group would come through. Having penetrated the border, they would hike to the spot where they would rendezvous with a *load vehicle*—the borderlands term for a car, van, or truck sent by the smugglers. A few hours later they would reach Phoenix, the hub of a smuggling wheel whose spokes reached across the country. Meissner acknowledged the underlying problem when she said, "As long as there are jobs available, there will be pressure on the border. So that availability of jobs has to be addressed."[11]

And yet, as Meissner herself would later acknowledge, the availability of jobs was not addressed in any serious or consistent manner. The Clinton administration continued to mouth platitudes and feign toughness, especially when Clinton was in campaign mode, as he was in his 1995 State of the Union Address. "It is wrong and ultimately self-defeating for a nation of immigrants to permit the kind of abuse of our immigration laws we have seen in recent years," Clinton said, "and we must do more to stop it." But between 1996 and 1998, as the Border Patrol presence in Arizona grew by 400 agents, the INS team responsible for worksite enforcement in Arizona added only one investigator.

Such facts made a mockery of Clinton's bravado, which faded quickly after he was reelected in 1996. Demographer Jeffrey Passel found the political moral of the story in the cynicism and fecklessness of federal policy. Said Passel, "It's much easier to build more fences and put more people at the border and try to make life more difficult for illegals than to try to bring employers in line."

"HE WHO PAYS MORE WALKS LESS"

I knew the Arizona border well from my 1980s work as the *Arizona Republic*'s correspondent in northern Mexico. I returned often to the border in the 1990s, when I worked out of the paper's Phoenix headquarters and in the early 2000s, when I was the immigration reporter in the Washington bureau of Copley News Service. Most of the migrants I spoke with said they had been guided by smugglers, who were called "coyotes" because they tended to be lean, wily, and tough. Some said they had walked for hours after crossing the border. Some said they walked for days. The smuggling business operated according to a simple rule: *El que paga mas camina menos.* He who pays more walks less. The money usually was paid in installments, with some paid up front, some when the migrants reached Phoenix or Tucson, where they were held until relatives wired more. A final payment was generally due upon delivery at destinations across the country. The most brutal smugglers would jack up their fees and then beat up their customers while relatives listened in horror over the phone, waiting for word on how much it would cost to make the beatings stop.

The deluxe smuggling package required no walking at all. The well-heeled were driven through a border port of entry with counterfeit papers in hand. I learned of a top-drawer smuggler in the town of Agua Prieta, the border twin of Douglas, Arizona. He took his female clients to a dress shop and a beauty shop before driving them through the port with counterfeit visas in their hands and their best imitation of nonchalance on their faces. Agents at the ports of entry, where cars and trucks were often backed up for blocks, faced the contradictory tasks of screening for fraud and facilitating the flow of people and commerce. Some smugglers drugged their human cargo, attempting to calm the nerves of adults or put children to sleep. In one notorious incident a man was sewn, in a sitting position, into the seat of a van.

It was all trade craft in an industry that every year took in hundreds of millions of dollars and corrupted many on both sides of the border. Agents at ports of entry were occasionally charged with waving through a vehicle loaded with contraband. In 2004, Arizona Attorney General Terry Goddard announced the seizure of 11 Phoenix used-car lots. Goddard also announced the indictment of

21 people who knowingly sold vehicles to smugglers for cash, then put phony liens on the vehicles, which were used to transport illegal immigrants. "That way," said Goddard, "when the Border Patrol or other law enforcement seized the cars, they were dutifully towed back to the 'lien holder' car lot and the process started all over."[12]

A SHOOTOUT ON THE INTERSTATE AND DESTRUCTION IN THE DESERT

The car-lot scam demonstrated the sophistication of the smuggling trade. Brutality was its most salient feature. Probably the most brazen act in Arizona smuggling history took place on Interstate 10 south of Phoenix. It was a running shootout as smugglers in a van sought to retake possession of valuable human cargo—15 smuggled migrants who had been kidnapped by another outfit. Both sides saw the terrified migrants as accounts receivable. Their gunfire left four people dead and several others wounded. Phoenix reeled from a 45 percent jump in killings over the previous year, while violent crimes—including home invasions and kidnappings—rose by more than 400 percent.[13] ABC news reported that in 2008, Phoenix had become "the kidnapping capital of the U.S.A., with 370 cases, many of them involving Mexican "drug cartels" that had extended their brutal reach far across the border. It told of "horrific cases of chopped off hands, legs and heads when a victim's family doesn't pay up fast enough."[14]

The border landscape also took a beating. In the summer of 2003, a *Chicago Tribune* story began with this description of Arizona's Organ Pipe Cactus National Monument:

> *For a tract of desert wilderness that is supposed to be left alone by humans, this national park is a mess. Fragile ocotillo shrubs and saguaro cactuses lay lifeless where they were mowed down. Foot trails and car tracks scar the delicate sandy ground in all directions. Trash is everywhere. The problem is not neglect by the National Park Service. The park has been overrun by illegal immigrants and drug traffickers*

who use its remote valleys to elude and outrun the U.S. Border Patrol on their clandestine journeys from Mexico.[15]

Organ Pipe ranger John Young told me about the wreckage left behind by a single smuggler who had driven a stolen SUV through a hole in the flimsy, chain-link border fence. In his 20-mile, cross-country drive from the border to the spot where the vehicle bogged down in the sand, the smuggler slashed a new road littered by hundreds of destroyed creosote and sage brush plants, dozens of battered mesquite and palo verde trees, and several badly damaged saguaros, the magnificent cactus symbol of the Sonoran Desert. "With the kind of rain we get—or don't get – it will take 100 or 200 years to repair this damage," Young said.[16]

The violence wasn't just environmental. In the summer of 2002, one of Young's colleagues at Organ Pipe, Ranger Kris Eggle, was shot to death by an AK-47-toting Mexican criminal who had driven through a hole in the fence. That tragedy was the most dramatic in a series of confrontations that prompted the National Park Rangers Lodge of the Fraternal Order of Police to name Organ Pipe the most dangerous park in the country.[17]

A few miles to the east, the wreckage piled up on the Tohono O'odham Indian Reservation. Ned Norris, Jr., vice chairman of the Tohono O'odham Nation, told a congressional committee that from the beginning of 2003 to the middle of 2004, a total of 2,675 vehicles had been abandoned on reservation lands by smugglers who routinely stole trucks and cars in Phoenix and Tucson, drove them into Mexico, and loaded them with drugs or migrants for the return trip. Norris testified that the illicit traffic of immigrants and drugs was "causing a flood of crime, chaos, and environmental destruction on our reservation."[18]

National Geographic News reported that the migrants and smugglers crossing Organ Pipe "have cut hundreds of new trails, trampled plants, and strewn water jugs and other garbage through the once-pristine desert...(and) disrupted the habitat of the park's population of endangered Sonoran pronghorn antelope."[19] In 2006, *USA Today* columnist Bridget Johnson wrote in dismay: "The carnage makes one wonder why environmental groups aren't out lobbying for a sturdy border fence."[20]

The Sierra Club led a charge in the opposite direction. As we will see in Chapter Nine, the club was striving to diversify membership rolls long dominated by middle-class whites. And so, in an effort to appeal to Latino activists, it pledged solidarity with immigrant-rights advocates. The club paired opposition to the border fence with reversal of its long-standing position that immigration should be limited in order to minimize the environmental effects of population growth. The Arizona chapter called for removal of the fence there, declaring, "This reckless project has meant dire consequences for vast expanses of pristine wild lands, including wildlife refuges, wilderness areas, and national forest lands, among others."[21]

I heard a very different story from government officials who managed federal lands at the border. Michael Hawkes, manager of the Buenos Aires National Wildlife Refuge, welcomed the fence. He said that before it was built, "We were getting 250,000 (illegal immigrants) coming through here every year. We had all the damage done by the vehicles. We had banditos coming up, robbing, raping, murdering people. Our buildings were getting broken into, vehicles were getting stolen. It was a war zone down here. It was a real mess."[22]

After the fence went up, Hawkes said, illegal crossings were cut 80 percent as smugglers moved elsewhere. While Hawkes noted that the fence obstructed the movement of wildlife, he insisted that "overall, it has been a blessing." The Interior Department's Larry Parkinson told the *Los Angeles Times*, "You've got to give up a little to save a lot. If we don't help the Border Patrol improve their control over the border, we won't have anything left to save."[23]

JIMMY BRESLIN AT THE ARIZONA BORDER

Those who defend illegal immigrants, especially well-intentioned liberals who sympathize intensely with the plight of the world's poor, often ignore or trivialize concerns about the negative effects of the influx. When Jimmy Breslin, the legendary New York columnist, came to Arizona, his mission was to write a book about the senseless 1999 death of an illegal immigrant who fell three stories into wet cement at a negligently managed Brooklyn construction site. In *The Short Sweet Dream of Eduardo Gutierrez*, Breslin presents a poignant scene of a brief encounter between a man who approaches the border fence from the Mexican side while a woman carrying a baby walked toward him from the north. For Breslin, the scene in the border town of Douglas represented the cruel stupidity of enforcing an international border. "Our country spends billions for protection from these most dangerous enemy acts,"[24] he wrote in a note of sarcastic indignation that ended a chapter. Breslin read that passage aloud during an appearance at a New York bookstore. Then he added, "I don't know why people are so worried about them. They're only coming here to work. I mean, what's the danger?"[25]

In 2004, a year after Breslin's lyrical, compassionate story was published, the investigative reporting team of Donald Barlett and James Steele presented a hard-nosed investigative account of the embattled Arizona border. Barlett and Steele are legendary in journalism circles for the deep-dive reporting that won them Pulitzers in 1975 and 1986. In recent years they have written articles and books that assign much of the blame for the declining fortunes of American workers to government officials and business executives who, they say, have callously pursued reckless policies of free trade and outsourcing.[‡]

The Barlett and Steele 2004 cover story for *Time* magazine was titled "Illegal Aliens: Who Left the Door Open?" Their conclusion: "The problem is one of the U.S.'s own making. The government

‡ In their 2013 book *The Betrayal of the American Dream*, they express outrage at the spate of "rapacious job-killing strategies."

doesn't want to fix it, and politicians, as usual, are dodging the issue, even though public-opinion polls show that Americans overwhelmingly favor a crackdown on illegal immigration." Like a number of other journalists, Barlett and Steele said President George W. Bush had aggravated the situation at the border with his business-friendly proposals for guest workers. Bush had expressed admiration for illegal immigrants and their commitment to showing that "family values don't stop at the border." But a *Los Angeles Times* story, citing Border Patrol agents' accounts of discussions with illegal border crossers, said Bush's proposal had "created confusion throughout Latin America, raising widespread expectations of amnesty."

That was a familiar story to those of us who had covered the border. Optimistic reports about high-level discussions in Washington had long stirred the migratory impulse, often with the added stimulus of exaggeration by smugglers who wanted to attract customers. The result in the Arizona borderlands was heightened exasperation with the federal government, which was spending enormous sums to treat the symptoms of a problem that could only be solved by delivering on IRCA's promise to punish rogue employers.

Instead, Congress responded with promises to *secure the border*, a phrase that became a chant, a ritual incantation that diverted attention away from the worksite. Lawmakers heaved money at the Border Patrol. From about 5,000 agents in 1994, the agency doubled to more than 10,000 in 2002, on its way to surpassing the 20,000-agent mark. Meanwhile, Congress in 2004 approved $1 billion to reimburse border states for medical treatment provided to illegal immigrants. The plan called for Arizona to receive $40 million per year, about a quarter of the treatment's actual cost. Several borderland hospitals, including the Copper Queen Hospital up the road from Douglas, would be forced to seek protection in bankruptcy court.

In 2013, when I contacted Jim Steele to talk about immigration reporting, our conversation turned to the tendency of many elite journalists to adopt a point of view similar to Jimmy Breslin's. Steele pointed to two sentiments that he said were common in cosmopolitan environments: admiration for the courageous spirit and commitment to hard work that are common among migrants, and suspicion that those who want to restrict immigration are hard-hearted and probably bigoted. "Immigrants have long been seen as the fabric of New York City," said Steele. "The city is filled with illegal immigrants working their butts off. New Yorkers see someone working hard and they think 'That's the spirit of America.' And then they look at someone like [infamous Arizona Sheriff Joe] Arpaio or [hard-line Arizona legislator Russell] Pearce, who they think are despicable. And that makes them discount anyone who questions illegal immigration."[29]

SETTLING IN PHOENIX

Most of those who crossed illegally into Arizona had destinations far away, from Florida to the Pacific Northwest. Many stayed in the Grand Canyon State, where job prospects in the late 1990s were buoyed by one of its cyclical real-estate booms. Jobs aplenty—construction, restaurants, landscaping — were available. The Mexican newcomers provided the abundant and cheap labor that eased fulfillment of the real-estate developer's prayer: "Oh, Lord, grant me just one more boom!"

Once such boom was underway in the late 1990s, while I was living in Phoenix. I got to know a former teacher from Mexico who received amnesty through IRCA. He had worked for a while as a cross-country truck driver, and then started a popsicle business that employed dozens of Mexicans, many of them illegal immigrants. They sold multi-flavored *paletas*, Mexican popsicles, from push carts they trucked to neighborhoods across Phoenix. He was frustrated that contractors would drive up to his *palateros* in pickup trucks and hire them away on the spot. Another recipient of the IRCA amnesty said he came to Arizona from Los Angeles because there were so many Latino immigrants in California that the wages were depressed. He started out in Phoenix making piñatas. Then he started a landscaping business that attracted some of the newcomers.

I could see the effects in a neighborhood close to mine, a few miles from downtown Phoenix. Westwood Elementary School was trying to cope with the sudden arrival of several hundred Mexican children who spoke no English. Because I spoke Spanish, I volunteered to help. Newspaper hours— start in mid-morning and finish when the story allows—made it possible for me to assist one of the second-grade teachers for a few hours each week.

The children were part of the cohort that would become known as "Dreamers." They were in the country illegally because their parents had brought them. I admired the school's commitment to meet the children's needs, to help them adjust to their new home, to incorporate them fully into the life of the community. But as I made my small effort to help ease the transition for both sides, I thought it would be better for the community if the influx subsided. But, of course, it didn't. The tide of newcomers kept rising. There was steady churn as families moved from place to place in search of new opportunities. The special needs of the newcomers diverted attention and resources from native-born children, sometimes causing parents to complain or to enroll their children elsewhere. The explosion in the illegal immigrant population that was so beneficial to employers also strained hospitals, social service institutions, and neighborhoods. As it continued, it eroded trust in government, undermined public willingness to accept newcomers, and bred public resentment.

Through the school, I learned about the work of a volunteer organizer in the Westwood neighborhood, a 6-foot-tall, red-haired mother bear of a woman named Donna Neill. She and her husband, Jerry, organized campaigns against gangs, graffiti, and negligent landlords, and for a new park and play area for children.

By 2004, as the influx continued, the Neills were lining up against the Arizona establishment— its congressional delegation, top state officials, the mayors of its principal cities, and the leaders of its churches and chambers of commerce—by supporting a ballot initiative that targeted illegal immigration. It was called Proposition 200. Like California's Proposition 187, it was an attempt to deny public services to unauthorized immigrants.

"We're sending a message that it's time to pay attention to what this is doing to us," said Donna Neill, 58.[26] She recited a list of problems in Phoenix that she tied to the influx of poor, unskilled immigrants: overcrowded schools, houses, and apartment buildings where two or three families crammed into a space meant for one; garages converted to two-family apartments; home additions hastily improvised in violation of housing codes that went unenforced by an overwhelmed city bureaucracy; and a general feeling of disorder and instability.

I wrote a story about Neill for the *San Diego Union Tribune*. "We've got more problems than we can handle," Neill said. "There needs to be some rules. What we've got now is just chaos. We're losing the simple things that make a society a society, but no one wants to step forward because they're afraid of crossing some line and being called a racist."[27]

Proposition 200 passed with an overwhelming margin despite the well-funded campaign against it. And even though Mexican-American leaders denounced it as racist, exit polls showed that 47 percent of Latino voters had supported it. They, too, clearly thought that immigration had gotten out of hand. "It's an issue of competition," University of Arizona political science professor John Garcia told me. "People think they're driving down wages and taking jobs. It's an emotional issue."[28]

A JUMPING OFF POINT JUST SOUTH OF THE BORDER

The year 2004 marked the 10th anniversary of Operation Gatekeeper. That year agents in the Border Patrol's Tucson sector, which is responsible for 262 miles of the border and vast expanses north of that line, arrested 492,000 illegal immigrants. That figure was more than twice the totals recorded that year by the San Diego and El Paso sectors combined. It represented 43 percent of the 1,139,000 arrests the Border Patrol made that year on the Southwest border.

In October 2004, I crossed the border at Nogales and drove the two-and-a-half hours to the small town of Altar, a regional trading center and a gas stop on the highway that connected central Mexico to Tijuana. Over the previous 10 years, smuggling had transformed its economy and its character. It boomed as a jumping-off point for illegal immigration, taking on rough edges and an occasional hint of menace in the eyes of those who competed for the lucrative trade of contraband human beings.[29]

The town was crammed with $3-a-night dormitories that stacked the migrants in triple-decker bunks. Shops and street merchants did a bustling business selling backpacks that migrants loaded with cans of frijoles or tuna. Liter bottles of flavored electrolyte fluids, the Gatorade of the borderlands, flew off the shelves, as did amulets and prayer cards seeking the protection of the saints. Some of the migrants lit candles at the church of Nuestra Señora de Guadalupe Church, where posters on the walls warned of scorpions, rattlesnakes, and brutal heat. In the adjoining plaza, I talked with young men who had just arrived from the Mexican state of Chiapas. They said coffee prices back home had fallen so low that the pay for harvesting the beans had dipped to 30 pesos a day—about $3 dollars. I learned that from one small town near the Guatemala border, five buses set out every week, jammed with young people heading to the border. Rural Mexico seemed to be emptying out. A young woman from the state of Veracruz wanted to join her mother, who worked at a restaurant in Kokomo, Indiana. Some of the young men had hotel jobs lined up in Florida. Others had heard that work was available in *Carolina del Norte*, where the Hispanic population in the 1990s soared from 82,000 to 379,000.[30]

When the migrants were ready to leave Altar, their smugglers loaded them into battered vans or retired American school buses for the 50-mile, 100-peso ride on a dirt road to a spot just south of the Arizona border. The migrants, usually young and wide-eyed, were called *pollos*, or chickens. The smugglers were known as *polleros*, chicken farmers, or *coyotes*. About 12 miles south of the U.S. border they passed through an informal checkpoint operated by Grupo Beta, an agency established by the Mexican government to safeguard migrants on their way to the border. In the first six months of 2004, the checkpoint, which was staffed during daylight hours, recorded the passage of 201,000 migrants. From there the migrants fanned out toward the Tohono O'odham Indian Reservation to the west and the Buenos Aires National Wildlife Refuge to the east. The trails their boots would carve in the ground became visible in Google Earth photos. Border Patrol agents from the Vietnam War era dubbed one the Ho Chi Minh Trail, using the name of the storied path along which North Vietnamese soldiers, munitions, and supplies moved south.

North of the Arizona border, I encountered a group of about 50 young men. They were sitting in the sand on the side of the road, next to Border Patrol SUVs. Most said they were from Chiapas. Most were headed to Florida, hoping to work at farms, restaurants, or hotels. I asked them about their education. None had gone to school beyond sixth grade, the end of primary school in Mexico. Most had not gone further than third grade. In the custody of the Border Patrol, they would be photographed, fingerprinted and checked against criminal databases. If there were no red flags, mostly criminal convictions, they would be returned to the border and released. Many would cross the border again and again until they made it through. Later they would buy phony documents and look for work. Whatever pay they received would be an upgrade from what they had earned back home. They would be able to send money back to their families.

PUBLICITY-HUNGRY SHERIFF ARPAIO STIRS THE POT

Joe Arpaio began his long run as sheriff of Maricopa County, Arizona, in 1993. He had little interest in illegal immigration until he was elected to his fourth term in 2004. Until then, his appeal to voters in the county, which included Phoenix and was home to two-thirds of Arizona's population, was based largely on the "America's toughest sheriff" image he had cultivated with his relentless in-house publicity machine. Arpaio showed off his toughness by putting prisoners in pink underwear, feeding them the cheapest possible food, banning coffee and long hair, hanging a "Vacancy" sign above his notorious "Tent City" jail encampment, and shrugging off lawsuits that claimed he had imposed a culture of abuse and humiliation. The county paid tens of millions of dollars in court awards, settlements, and legal fees during Arpaio's tenure. When I was still at the *Republic* I wrote about the death of an inmate named Scott Norberg, who had been forced into a restraint chair after becoming unruly. The county medical examiner said he had died from "positional asphyxia" after detention officers violently pushed his chin down, onto his chest. The county paid Norberg's family $8.25 million to settle their wrongful-death lawsuit.

Arpaio's attitude about illegal immigrants hardened as he noted the growing public backlash against the influx that swelled Arizona's illegal immigrant population from an estimated 88,000 in 1990 to 330,000 in 2000, on its way to a peak of 560,000 in 2008. Much of the public was disturbed by the massive demonstrations that in 2006 and 2007 filled the streets of downtown Phoenix with demands for amnesty. *Republic* columnist Ed Montini wrote that the outpouring "shocked and frightened" many Arizonans who had previously paid little attention to the immigration issue. "Those people suddenly began to demand that politicians take action, by which they meant punitive action against anyone in the country illegally," Montini wrote.[31] The protest organizers had sought to awaken the Latino vote, which was often described as a sleeping giant. They succeeded. But by assembling more than 100,000 protesters in Phoenix they also stirred anxiety among Arizonans who feared that the state was being "Mexicanized."

At a time when the state's economy was strong and jobs were plentiful, especially in the thriving construction and tourism industries, the anxiety was cultural rather than economic. Newspaper and television images of protestors filling the streets created the appearance of a takeover. The demographics were dramatic. The Latino population had risen to 29 percent of the Arizona population that year, up from 19 percent in 1990. But the trend line was even more dramatic because Hispanics were 42 percent of the under-16 population. "When I was in the first grade in 1960, Phoenix was the same distance from the border," said Grant Woods, a prominent Republican and former Arizona attorney general. "Phoenix now feels much more like a border town than it did even 10 years ago."[32]

"GUILTY OF LOOKING LATINO"

Arpaio's hunger for notoriety was as relentless as the desert heat. A decade before Donald Trump tapped immigration anxiety to become president, Arpaio recognized its electoral potential. His most notorious enforcement tactic was the "saturation patrols" he sent into Latino neighborhoods of Phoenix. Sheriff's deputies and members of the sheriff's volunteer posse pulled over drivers for minor infractions like failure to use turn signals or a defective tail light. Then they looked for the major infraction of being in the country illegally. The patrols drew criticism from Robert Robb, a conservative *Republic* columnist and editorial board member, who wrote that "lawful residents who happen to be poor and Latino are being subjected to unwarranted attention from government… The fact that a few illegals are also found in the process doesn't justify the gross abuse of discretion."[33] The city's Democratic mayor, Phil Gordon, denounced the raids as "made for TV stunts." An *Arizona Republic* editorial said that although about two dozen of the 43 people arrested in one round of sweeps were suspected of being illegal immigrants, "the rest were guilty of looking Latino. That's not a crime, Sheriff."[34]

Arpaio, undeterred, pressed on. In addition to making arrests under federal law, his deputies arrested illegal immigrants under Arizona laws against identity theft and forgery. Leveraging a state law against the smuggling of humans, he pursued not only the smugglers but their illegal immigrant customers, accusing them of being co-conspirators in their own smuggling. "The people agree with what I'm doing, a very high percentage," Arpaio said. "So, I do know I'm doing the right thing for the people I serve. That's what I'm supposed to be doing, serving the people."[35]

In 2009, a year after Arpaio cruised to another election victory, reporters Paul Giblin and Ryan Gabrielson of the *East Valley Tribune* in suburban Phoenix won the Pulitzer Prize for local reporting with a series that revealed what was neglected as Arpaio focused on illegal immigration. They documented a severe worsening of emergency response times. They also quantified lax enforcement against serious criminals, including those involved in homicides, robberies, and rapes. Arpaio, defiant as ever, pointed to the thousands of illegal immigrants he had taken off the streets and to the thousands of prisoners who, during their time in detention, were identified as illegal and therefore subject to deportation.

Critics scorned Arpaio as a bully and a racist. Some likened him to the big-bellied Southern sheriffs who in the 1960s had tried to repress demonstrators for civil rights. Some, mocking his bluster, likened him to Yosemite Sam of Looney Tunes TV cartoon fame. But in some ways, he was a sad and lonely figure whose bluster concealed a desperate need for attention, even at the cost of vilification. Arpaio and Trump had that in common. But Arpaio's story was shadowed by the sadness of knowing that his mother had died giving birth to him.

Arpaio was hit with a massive class-action lawsuit that alleged he was denying Latinos constitutional rights by unfairly singling them out. The Obama administration's Justice Department pursued him relentlessly. In 2016, as many voters became weary of the Arpaio turmoil and as George Soros pumped $2 million into the campaign to defeat him, the 84-year-old sheriff was finally defeated. Among his last public events were appearances with Donald Trump, who celebrated his endorsement even as Hillary Clinton declared that Arpaio "just makes my heart sink."[36] Arpaio's successor, announcing the closure of Tent City, declared, "Starting today, that circus ends and these tents come down."[37] In 2017, Arpaio was convicted of defying a federal judge's order to stop the racial profiling on the neighborhood patrols. But Arpaio, who had become a symbol of the anti-illegal immigrant backlash that helped fuel the campaign of Donald Trump, was pardoned by the new president.

A SKEWED PBS DOCUMENTARY ON ARIZONA

One of the most egregious distortions of the situation there took shape in a PBS documentary titled "The State of Arizona." Filmmakers Carlos Sandoval and Catherine Tambini told the story of the plight of illegal immigrants with tremendous sympathy but sketched a shriveled caricature of those who opposed their demands for legal status. One of the documentary's first scenes was particularly poignant and effective. Set against the flashing lights of three sheriff's vehicles stopped for an arrest, it showed a young woman, her wrists handcuffed behind her back. Anguish was engraved on her face. Tears glistened on her cheeks. A viola solemnly underscored the pathos of the scene. It was a powerful statement of the suffering of those ensnared by the law. Public frustration with illegal immigration took shape in the documentary, primarily in the form of Arpaio, hardline state Sen. Russell Pearce, and an elderly woman named Kathryn Kobor. As the filmmakers showed her with her car full of "Support Sheriff Joe" signs, her American flags, and her fears of those she called "illegal Hispanics," they all but tattooed her as a silly old lady. In their eyes she was an anachronism, an oddity, fit for condescension and easy to dismiss.

A Mexican-American man in Phoenix made me aware of a more serious failing. Rudolf Pena, a plumber and an opponent of illegal immigration, told me he had spoken at length with the filmmakers. He said he had taken them on a tour of his West Phoenix neighborhood, showing them the crowding caused by the influx and talking of the depressing effect it had on the earnings of tradesmen like him. He said he wanted them to understand "how illegal immigration could disrupt an established way of life." He said he had spent considerable time in front of a camera and had been optimistic that the film would show his side of the story. Disappointed that nothing he said made it into the film, he said in an email that he thought his concerns had been left on the cutting room floor because of "the complications they potentially may have caused for the intended documented outcome." I think he was right. Pena had a credibility the filmmakers did not want to acknowledge. Kobor was a good fit for their story frame. So was the 60-ish man who is shown in the film shouting toward a group of protesters in a noisy street scene. "Go back to your country!" he shouted, according to the subtitle. But the filmmakers got that wrong, too. They acknowledged their error after I pointed out that the man had actually shouted, "Acclimate to the country!" It was a call for civic and cultural accommodation, not an insulting rejection. But it was the insult that was broadcast across the nation. It badly distorted the factual reality, but it confirmed the biases that the filmmakers were determined to validate.

In 2018, Tambini posted a picture on Facebook that provided at least a suggestion of her philosophy. It showed a quotation from Elie Wiesel's speech as he accepted the 1986 Nobel Prize: "We must take sides. Neutrality helps the oppressor, never the victim." Tambini's film, drawing acclaim from her peers, was nominated for an Emmy. Her empathy for the undocumented was certainly admirable. But her inability to play it straight as she pretended to acknowledge equities on the other side of the argument warped the story and misrepresented an entire state. Those flaws are commonplace in reporting and story-telling about the national immigration debate. The documentary revealed more about the state of PBS than it did about Arizona.

Now we'll see how that tendentious spirit became entrenched on the editorial page of *The New York Times.*

Part 2
INSTITUTIONAL FORCES

Chapter 3:
The New York Times Goes All-In for Diversity and Inclusion

> **It's no longer acceptable to mention race, but fretting about newcomers' education, poverty and assimilability is an effective substitute**
>
> —New York Times, *2011*[1]

> **The immigration issue today is not ethnicity but numbers. How much immigration will there be, how diluted will the labor market become, how large a percentage of the population will be poor, and how wide will be the gap between rich and poor? These are the questions that progressive liberal critics of high rates of immigration have asked from Frederick Douglass to the Rev. Theodore Hesburgh to Barbara Jordan.**
>
> —*Letter to the editor,* New York Times, *2009*

In the early 1970s, when Arthur Ochs Sulzberger Jr was a student at Tufts University outside Boston, he was arrested twice for civil disobedience during turbulent protests against the Vietnam War. After the second arrest, his father, *New York Times* publisher Arthur Ochs Sulzberger Sr., was so concerned that he came for a visit to learn his son's thinking about the war and the country. As they walked together through Boston Common, the father, a Marine Corps veteran, asked. "If a young American soldier comes upon a North Vietnamese soldier, which would you want to get shot?" The response was defiant. "I would want to see the American get shot," said the young Sulzberger "It's the other guy's country; we shouldn't be there." The elder Sulzberger was infuriated, according to the authors of a history of the *Times* titled *The Trust: The Private and Powerful Family Behind The New York Times.* They present it as a measure of the personality and political sensibility of the young Sulzberger, who in 1992 succeeded his father as publisher after a long apprenticeship on the news and business sides of the paper. The book was written by former *Times* reporter Alex Jones and his wife, former *Time* magazine reporter Susan Tifft. They reported that as a child Arthur was shy and insecure. But when he was a teenager, wilderness-survival training with Outward Bound had a transformational effect. He became a young man of "remarkable self-assurance…cocky and confrontational," they wrote, and those characteristics were lasting. "From the moment he became publisher, he was like a silversmith, noisily banging *The New York Times* into a shape that reflected his own values, beliefs, and personality."[2] He was brash and assertive and "gave the impression that he knew all the answers."

The younger Sulzberger applied that didactic certainty to the paper's culture on a host of social issues. In 1988, when he was deputy editor, he had said diversity was "the single most important issue" facing The Times.[3] He became deputy chairman of the Task Force for Minorities in the Newspaper Business, which encouraged workforce diversity. After becoming publisher in 1992, he was widely praised for placing women and members of minorities in positions of power and for ensuring that the newsroom culture was welcoming for gays and lesbians. He was committed to the fight for equality on behalf of those who suffered from discrimination, whether because of race, gender, or sexual orientation.

In the early years of the new millennium, as immigrant-rights advocates demanded legal status for illegal immigrants, it became clear that Sulzberger included illegal immigrants among those whose struggle for inclusion would be a righteous cause for *The New York Times.*

A COMMENCEMENT SPEECH FROM A DOGMATIC PUBLISHER

Sulzberger issued a notoriously overbearing call for inclusion in his first commencement speech, which he delivered to the class of 2006 at the State University of New York at New Paltz. It was a public demonstration of brash confidence in his own moral rectitude. It was also a maudlin show of generational remorse. Sulzberger lamented the sorry state of a world still beset by the inequality, corruption, and war that his generation had failed to purge. Surveying the cultural landscape, he found it strewn with failure. Then he issued an apology from on high. "You weren't supposed to be graduating into a world where we are still fighting for fundamental human rights, whether it's the rights of immigrants to start a new life, or the rights of gays to marry, or the rights of women to choose," he told the graduates. He solemnly advised them that at many points in their lives they would face fateful decisions involving a binary choice. "You will choose at each point whether to be bold or hesitant, inclusive or elitist, generous or stingy,"[4] he said.

Commentaries on the speech were merciless. Conservatives were particularly aghast. On Fox News, Morton Kondracke called it "a left-wing rant" and cited it as an example of why "I never read the *New York Times* any more for information; I read The New York Times only to find out what the left-wing slant on things is."[5] *Vanity Fair* called it "self-aggrandizing...a vapid political message about the glories and disappointments of the 1960s."[6] A columnist for the *Rocky Mountain News* ripped Sulzberger for "breathtaking arrogance" and "sheer childishness."[7] The consensus was that the address was obnoxious in its self-satisfied dismissal of those who didn't measure up.

A similar tone of moral certitude was characteristic of *Times* immigration editorials in the era of Arthur Sulzberger Jr. In 2007 the newspaper proclaimed that there was a "national duty to welcome immigrants,"[8] regardless of legal status. In 2012, it declared that "each and every one [of the more than 10 million illegal immigrants] deserves a chance to get right with the law."[9]

Times editorials pulsed with the provocative self-assurance and boldness that Sulzberger cultivated in himself. They preached the ethic of diversity, inclusiveness, and commitment to a borderless, globalized world. It was a worldview congenial to the well-educated, prosperous, and cosmopolitan—an elite demographic that was well represented among readers of the *Times*. They relished the availability of international cuisine and of a workforce, often undocumented, of newcomers who provided low-cost daycare, domestic services, and yardwork. Many saw no reason to distinguish illegal immigrants from Latin America or Asia from their own grandparents or great grandparents, who fled poverty or persecution in Europe. Jews who lost relatives who had been unable to escape the Holocaust were often particularly committed to protecting the undocumented. They saw their activism as a moral responsibility, a way of honoring those who had been targeted by Nazis pursuing the "final solution" to the problem of unwanted peoples. They superimposed the story of the Holocaust onto the story of immigration policy.

Against this background, *Times* editorials expressed the conviction that restrictionists were heartless nativists and xenophobes. Lawrence Downes, the lead editorial writer on immigration from 2004 to 2017, was outraged at the use of "illegal" to describe those who were in the U.S. illegally. "It pollutes the debate," he wrote in a signed opinion piece. "It blocks solutions. Used dispassionately and technically, there is nothing wrong with it. Used as an irreducible modifier for a large and largely decent group of people, it is badly damaging. And as a code word for racial and ethnic hatred, it is detestable."

Many Americans, of course, saw "illegal" as an appropriate term for those who had violated the law. Downes spoke for those who were determined to scrub "illegal" from all discussions of immigration. To them it was an insult, a denigration, an offense against inclusiveness, equality, and diversity. They became prominent in the Democratic Party, rooting out expressions of concern like the 2008 platform's declarations that, "We cannot continue to allow people to enter the United States undetected, undocumented, and unchecked" and that "those who enter our country's borders illegally and those who employ them disrespect the rule of law." Such thinking was verboten by 2016, when the platform lamented the "broken immigration system," but avoided mentioning the illegality of those who had broken it. While the 2008 platform referred three times to people entering the country "illegally," the 2016 platform omitted the word *illegal*, or any form of it.[10]

AN EDITORIAL OBSERVER GOES TO PHOENIX

At *The New York Times*, as at other newspapers, editorials are produced by an editorial board whose function is to present the paper's institutional voice, as decided by the publisher. They speak for the publisher. They are his voice. Kathleen Kingsbury, deputy editorial page editor, said that while Times reporters describe the world as it is, the job of editorial writers is to "describe the world as it should be." While the Times in early 2020 announced it was in the process of reorganizing its Opinion section, for decades its practice was to publish unsigned editorials that were attributed to the entire board though they were usually written by a single member who had expertise in the subject at hand.

Subject-matter experts also occasionally put their bylines on "editorial observer" essays that combine opinion with reporting from the field. Such was the case in 2007, when Lawrence Downes reported from Phoenix about a months-long series of protests and counter-protests in the parking lot of Pruitt's furniture store. Headlined "Showdown in Arizona, Where Mariachis and Minutemen Collide,"[11] the piece provides a vivid example of the *Times*'s hostility toward opponents of illegal immigration.

The controversy in Phoenix was more complex and textured than the morality play elaborated by Downes. It began after store owner Roger Sensing heard from female customers who said that as they drove into the parking lot they were being intimidated by groups of day laborers who ran up to their cars in hopes of being hired. Sensing responded by hiring off-duty Phoenix police to patrol the parking lot. When the city of Phoenix forbade such patrols, Sensing hired off-duty Maricopa County Sheriff's deputies. That led to appearances by the infamous Sheriff Joe Arpaio.

For perspective on Lawrence Downes' editorializing, it is useful to see how the controversy was described by *Arizona Republic* columnist Laurie Roberts. "Every Saturday, day-laborer activists come to Sensing's furniture store to protest the crackdown on illegal immigrants," Roberts reported. "And counter protesters come out to protest the day laborers. And Sheriff Joe comes out to get on TV. And reporters come out to record the angst."[12]

Reporter Michael Kiefer, also of the *Republic*, wrote that while one side carried banners that declared "No human being is illegal" or stamped "KKK" on Arpaio's face, the other side waved American flags and carried banners that read "Undocumented means illegal," and "We love you Sheriff Joe."

There was a standoff between two protesters that neatly encapsulated the contention. "We don't need racists in Phoenix," said one. "We don't need illegals in Phoenix," said the other.[13] A *Republic* editorial pointed to the underlying problem of failed governance: "Like the ranchers along the border in southern Arizona, these storeowners bear the burden, pay the price, of a broken immigration system and border." It also noted that "illegal workers fill thousands of jobs every day" and that "much of middle-class Arizona benefits from the supply of these workers, who clean, move furniture, dig trenches on construction sites, trim trees, and landscape lawns and gardens."[14]

When Downes went to Phoenix, he saw a different story. His account made no room for the moral complexity that roiled Arizona civic life as illegal immigration surged early in the new millennium. It illustrated why Daniel Okrent, the *Times'* first public editor and in-house critic, wrote in 2004 that the editorial page was "thoroughly saturated in liberal theology."[15]

Downes reduced the story at Pruitt's to a Manichean struggle between strumming Mariachis who represented the forces of light and snarling Minutemen who represented the forces of darkness. He drew a portrait of goodness beset by bigotry. He delighted in the children attired in Mexican folk costumes who danced in support of illegal immigrants. His central character was Salvador Reza, an immigration activist who hailed unauthorized workers as "people with a work ethic that would make the Puritans proud." Downes observed that Reza "can't understand why America accepts global flows of companies, money, and jobs but not workers"—as if American workers should be glad to lay down their livelihoods for the transcendent cause of loose labor markets and open borders.

In a single condescending sentence Downes shot down Sensing's claim to be protecting customers from harassment. "Mr. Reza calls that ridiculous," he approvingly reported. Downes found no reasonable frustration among those who supported Sensing. He found only ugliness. He described efforts to drown the music in angry shouts of "Born in the U.S.A! KKK! Viva la Migra!" Making no attempt to moderate his righteous contempt, he claimed that restrictionists yearned for a time when immigration laws were enforced and "the Mexicans disappear and everything gets pure and legal again." He observed no one like the man who caught the ear of Laurie Roberts with his defense of the protesters. "None of these people is against immigration," he said. "We have laws in this country, bud. There's a proper way to enter this country."

Roberts wrote with an appreciation for complexity and an understanding of ambiguity. Downes wrote with the swagger and certitude required by a publisher who liked boldness and despised ambiguity. On immigration, Downes was Sulzberger's muse.[16]

Like many culture warriors of the left, Sulzberger and Downes appeared to be convinced that resistance to mass immigration is uniquely and pathologically American. Mexican journalist Sergio Sarmiento disagreed. In his syndicated column in 2009, Sarmiento wrote of a similar tendency in his own country. Sarmiento pointed out that between 1970 and 2008, the number of Mexican natives living in the United States had grown from 760,000 to 12.7 million.

That meant that 11 percent of all living persons born in Mexico had migrated to the United States, he noted. "If Mexico had had an avalanche of foreigners so large in a period so short, the resistance, would without a doubt, have been greater," he wrote. "When we have had much smaller flows of foreigners—Argentines, Chileans, Central Americans—the reaction of Mexicans has been very negative." Sarmiento was noting a fact of human nature that many immigration enthusiasts, in their expansive optimism and naïveté, do not recognize. Resistance to sweeping demographic change is much more likely to be rooted in a desire for stability, continuity, and familiarity. It is not the artificial construct of an oppressive hierarchy.

ELOQUENCE AND INTOLERANCE IN THE CAUSE OF INCLUSION

Although Lawrence Downes had been a respected copy editor at the paper, he had no immigration expertise when he was named to the editorial board in 2004. But he had a moral certainty that matched Sulzberger's, and he was a fine writer. He was passionately committed to the cause of illegal immigrants. He wrote lyrically about them. However, he had no understanding of those who saw illegal immigration as destabilizing and who wanted immigration limits to be enforced. He wrote scornfully about them. His disgust was palpable.

Downes's sensibility was shaped by his experience growing up in in Hawaii as "Okinawan-Irish," as he put it. Downes was "hapa"—mixed race—an identity that he had struggled to understand and eventually to embrace. "Dwelling on it can tie a person in knots," he wrote. "It can be disorienting to feel forced to choose between identities when you are both and neither. It can be infuriating to be stared at by people trying to puzzle out what you are."[17]

Downes' writing was especially poignant when he took up the cause of day laborers who were in the U.S. illegally. He was their defender, their advocate. He called them "the quiet ones at the bottom ... the street-corner guys....the most visible, most vulnerable, and most hated."[18] His compassion, given voice by a lyrical grace and simmering outrage, reminded me of Woody Guthrie, who, as Downes wrote, was "always against the rich and on the side of the oppressed." In a similar vein, Downes wrote that protesters against the arrest of illegal immigrants in California "looked like poor people marching for a better life, the kind we root for in movies like 'The Grapes of Wrath.'"[19]

"In truth, our biggest domestic menace never was waiting outside Home Depot, hoping to clean your basement," Downes wrote.[20] "Unauthorized immigrants are not about to destroy anything, not even when they get angry and loud and march in large groups. On the contrary, they are inspiring. Their ethic of self-reliance and hard work is one that Americans should recognize and celebrate."

While Downes was often graceful and eloquent, he was also strident and relentless as he preached the Sulzberger gospel of inclusiveness. *Times* editorials declared that it is mean-spirited not to embrace illegal immigrants as "Americans in waiting."[21] When the Arizona legislature, expressing widespread public frustration with the failure of the federal government, passed a series of anti-illegal immigration laws, the *Times* denounced the state as "ground zero for a new nativism."[22] With good reason, editorials ripped the laws as harsh. But if the *Times* editorial vision had been less constricted by moral certitude and anger, its opinions would have shown some inkling of understanding that a backlash was inevitable in a state like Arizona, where the illegal immigrant population grew at an extraordinary rate for in the 1990s and the first decade of the new millennium.

"Those numbers are telling," said Kelefa Sanneh of *The New Yorker*, who wrote in 2012, "Arizona has sometimes been portrayed as a state besieged by unauthorized immigrants, and for good reason."[23] Added Sanneh, "It's not hard to understand why people were worried: the population of unauthorized immigrants went from 88,000 in 1990 to 560,000 in 2008—and in a state with about 7 million people. I think in most parts of the country, even most parts of the world, that kind of demographic shock would produce a counterreaction."[24]

For someone like me, Sanneh's reporting was a rare breeze of common sense from Manhattan, where the editorial board of the *New York Times* persisted in portraying immigration as an undiluted blessing and Arizona as a state of racists reminiscent of the South at the height of the struggle for civil rights.

New York Times editorials on immigration exemplify a type of moral reasoning illuminated by Jonathan Haidt, a social psychologist and author of *The Righteous Mind: Why Good People Are Divided by Politics and Religion*. Haidt writes that people are naturally inclined to form "tribal moral communities" around core values so strong that they not only bind the group, but blind it to evidence from others.

Haidt offers an explanation for the moral values that prevail in many sophisticated circles. He notes that, beginning in the 1960s, the left was galvanized by a series of "incredibly important battles" they fought on behalf of blacks, women, and gays. "If you sacralize these groups, it binds you together to fight for them," he writes. "Follow the sacredness," says Haidt. "Once you sacralize something, you become blind to evidence."[25] Not far behind the blindness, he says, is demonization of those who disagree. In recent years that moral vision has been extended to other marginalized groups, including unauthorized immigrants.

THE *TIMES* DISSENTS FROM COMPREHENSIVE REFORM

Six months before the Downes visit to Pruitt's furniture store, a *Times* editorial endorsed a comprehensive immigration reform bill in Congress that, like IRCA, would have provided legal status and a path to citizenship. The *Times* issued a decree that was typically Sulzberger-esque: "It is the nation's duty to welcome immigrants, to treat them decently and give them the opportunity to assimilate."[26] This, of course, was an effort to obliterate the bright-line differentiation between legal and illegal immigration that for decades had expressed a national consensus. The *Times* was now rejecting that distinction as an offense against inclusiveness, the twin of diversity, which was a sacred value at the *Times*.

Having sought to obliterate one line, the editorial proceeded to draw another one, this time to excoriate what it called the bill's "repugnant" provision to redesign the system of legal immigration, basing it more on skill and less on family connections than the current system. The bill would have left untouched the preference for immediate family members of citizens and permanent residents. It proposed to take visas that had long gone to extended-family members and give them to applicants whose education, training, and language skills would help them to assimilate into the U.S. culture and economy.

This was not a revolutionary concept. It already was the policy in Canada, Australia, and Britain. *Times* columnist David Brooks praised the idea as more equitable and coherent. "Under our current immigration system, most people get into the United States through criminality, nepotism, or luck," Brooks wrote. "The current system does almost nothing to encourage good behavior or maximize the nation's supply of human capital."[27]

But this concept sent the *Times* into an editorial tizzy. Its denunciation was so floridly over-written that it might have been inspired by a horror movie whose setting was the U.S. Botanic Garden, on the grounds of the Capitol. "The Senate bill is repellant in many ways," the editorial declared. It introduced the image of a toxic flower garden, describing the legalization proposal as "fragrant blossoms grafted to poisonous roots." Then came a predictable homage to the poem on the base of the Statue of Liberty. The editorial denounced "the repellent truth... that countless families will be split apart while we cherry pick the immigrants we consider brighter and better than the poor, tempest-tost ones we used to welcome without question."[28]

At *the Times*, the plan was repugnant. The newspaper demanded that the United States adopt a course rejected by all other major immigrant-receiving democracies. It insisted that the U.S. continue to offer green cards not just to individual immigrants and their immediate families, but also to their extended families in ever-lengthening links of in-laws and cousins known as "chain migration"—a phrase that advocates of unchecked immigration came to regard as a form of denigration.

But as *Times* reporter Linda Qiu noted in 2018, "Chain migration was originally a neutral, if not dry, phrase used by academics to describe the immigration process." She said the term, in use for decades, had been "eclipsed by the more recently established 'family reunification.'" What caused the eclipse was the celestial intrusion of an intrusion of those who took offense at the term, as if it were an attempt to revive the reviled "wetbacks."

Thus was begun a new mini-drama of protest and counter-protest. "Democrats and immigration advocates claim it is a pejorative phrase that demeans recent arrivals," Qiu wrote. "Republicans argue its useful shorthand for family sponsorship."[29] The story was headlined: "'Chain Migration' Has Become a Weaponized Phrase."

A TALE OF TWO SULZBERGERS

One of the most remarkable features of the era of Arthur Sulzberger, Jr., is the stark contrast in substance and tone between its editorials and the editorials that spoke for the paper when his father was publisher. The younger Sulzberger's *Times* produced a body of editorial work that was brash, self-righteous, and confrontational. The work that appeared during his father's era stands out for its moderation, moral modesty, and understanding that there were respectable reasons for opposing illegal immigration on the massive scale of the 1990s and early 2000s.

During the five-year congressional debate that preceded passage of the Immigration Reform and Control Act of 1986 the editorial board's compassion for illegal immigrants was coupled with recognition of the risks of mass illegal immigration, particularly of unskilled workers in low-paying jobs. In 1981, for example, a *Times* editorial observed: "Uncounted millions cross our porous borders in search of a better life. Like prior immigrants, many enrich our land with industry. But their numbers are so great that they also strain community resources and threaten the jobs and well-being of those who preceded them."[30]

A year later, an editorial criticized the left-right coalition against worker verification. Under the headline "Guerrilla War on Immigration," it observed, "Without effective verification, there can be no effective enforcement of the borders. Without effective enforcement, there can be no immigration reform worthy of the name. The choice for the House is clear: legislate or pretend."[31]

In 1983, an editorial made the case that it was naïve to expect the national fabric to stretch to accommodate all those who clamored for inclusion. "For reasons of vitality, humanity and history, America wants and needs immigrants," the editorial said. "What it does not need is such an uncontrollable flood of illegal migrants that it tries public patience and foments a backlash against all newcomers. That's the genuine danger." The editorial was headlined "Time to Turn the Illegal Tide."[32]

In 1984, the growing influence of the Latino vote prompted a *Times* editorial expressing frustration that the House Democratic leadership was stalling the bill. "That means America's immigration policy will continue to be a Big Wink," an editorial warned. "Illegal aliens will keep streaming in past the pitifully overworked Immigration Service. Americans will turn even more cynical and nativist, and sentiment to curtail all immigration will continue to rise. Slam the door, people will say."[33]

A 1985 editorial gave a concise description of the challenge before Congress. It, too, was prescient as it observed: "The ultimate test of any immigration reform can be stated in two words: employer sanctions. As long as employers can hire illegal aliens with impunity, illegal aliens will find a way to be hired." It opined that without worksite enforcement, "the migrants stream in to jobs like iron filings to a magnet."[34]

THE WISDOM OF JACK ROSENTHAL

The lead editorial writer at the *Times* was Jack Rosenthal, the son of a refugee from Nazi Germany. Rosenthal was himself an immigrant. He was born in Tel Aviv in 1935. He was three years old when his family came to the U.S. His name back then was Jacob, but he would change it to Jack because he thought it sounded more American. He graduated from Harvard, became a spokesman for Attorney General Robert F. Kennedy during the civil rights era of the 1960s, and then became a journalist.

In 1982, when Rosenthal was deputy editorial page editor, he won a Pulitzer Prize for a packet of 10 editorials on a range of topics. One was an appreciation of baseball and its offer of an escape from real-world crassness to "an amiable, ordered world contained within the neat geometry of a stadium." He loved the game's "constant potential for the heroic, the sly, and the unpredictable."[35] Another editorial, challenging Reagan administration proposals to trim the food-stamp program, said they were an effort to "cut holes in the bottom of the safety net."[36]

Rosenthal's Pulitzer entry included an editorial that, once again, was rooted in the conviction that limits were essential. It was a warning that the federal government must assert control over illegal immigration in the name of responsible governance, fairness, and diversity. Rosenthal wrote:

> *Who should decide which foreigners are allowed into the United States, the foreigners or the United States? In a responsible society, the question would answer itself. But that's not the way things now work in the United States.*
>
> *We are a rich and generous country given to bragging about our immigrant origins. When there is obvious need, we live up to the romantic images of Miss Liberty and the Golden Door, taking in waves of freedom fighters or boat people. But romance notwithstanding, there is no longer any such thing as unlimited immigration. A million people are*

> *waiting in line to enter the United States legally; millions more are eager to jump the line; and the nation must choose which to let through the door.*
>
> *Undocumented farm workers from Mexico, for instance, may be brave and industrious. But each takes a place that, if society were choosing fairly, might be assigned instead to a refugee from Somalia, a sister from Korea or a more deserving Mexican applicant.*[37]

The editorial not only encapsulated the pragmatism of that era at the *Times*; it also articulated a broader, vastly wiser, vision of diversity than Sulzberger Jr. and Downes could accept. For them, a commitment to diversity meant open arms for whoever made it across the border, regardless of how they came. In their moral universe, to establish limits was to sin against inclusiveness.

When Jack Rosenthal died in 2017, Max Frankel, a former *Times* editor, hailed him as a great talent "at every turn gave voice to our shared liberal values."[38] Rosenthal's greatest concern was to defend values that tied the nation together in a common enterprise of loyalty and mutual obligation. He was a pragmatic idealist. He was not inclined to thunderous certainty or utopian fantasy. He didn't think he was a Zeus heaving thunderbolts from on high.

LOOKING FOR LAWRENCE DOWNES

As I did my research for this chapter, I asked Lawrence Downes for an interview. I wanted to understand how someone so empathetic to the plight of the unauthorized had no understanding of, no feel for, the Americans on the other side of the story. His bias was so strong and so passionately felt that he looked upon restrictionists with a cold, contemptuous conviction of moral superiority. We talked once by phone, but he would not speak for the record. I told him that while many restrictionists would accept another amnesty as part of a compromise reform, this time the government must be held accountable for delivering the worksite enforcement that is the other side of the deal. I said advocates like him, who claim to understand the need for law enforcement but then oppose enforcement at every turn, are as big an obstacle to passing a law as Republican obstructionists who go to the opposite extreme in order to avert a primary-elect challenge.

Downes' sincerity was beyond question. He wrote from a deep well of feeling and conviction. At the same time, he tended to be overwrought. He was blind to the concerns and equities of American workers. Liberal journalist Michael Lind addressed that problem in a 1995 essay in which he wrote that among Democrats, any suggestion that the arrival of almost a million legal immigrants a year has any effect on job opportunities and wages in the United States is said to be sinister, racist "scapegoating."[39]

Lind wrote that essay for the op-ed page of *The New York Times*. He wrote it at the suggestion of a *Times* editor who thought Lind's contrarian liberalism deserved the space. But Lind learned that after the piece appeared in print, Sulzberger had registered his displeasure with the editor who, in the interest of balance, had requested it. "She got a phone call from the publisher, complaining, why she is running all these anti-immigration op-eds," Lind said.[40]

THE *TIMES* ON "THE BASIC REPUBLICAN MESSAGE"

Just before the 2016 Iowa Republican caucuses a *Times* editorial observed that at a candidates' forum, Senator Marco Rubio of Florida "tried to put a younger and more charming face on the basic Republican message of anger, xenophobia, fear and hate." It was a sweeping condemnation, voiced with a disdain for conservatives that would infect much of the *Times* coverage of that year's presidential campaign. Ironically, on the same day, the *Times* published an op-ed piece by R. R. Reno, editor of *First Things*, who criticized the leadership of both the Democratic and the Republican parties for failing to understand the cultural and economic anxieties of the middle class. Referring to the insurgent campaigns of Donald Trump and Bernie Sanders, he wrote, "The populism we're seeing stems entirely from the collision of whites who flourish in the global economy – and amid the cultural changes of the last 50 years – with those who don't."

After Donald Trump's stunning win in the 2016 race, the *Times* published a mea culpa for its dismissive coverage of the Trump campaign, which it had never been able to take seriously. Under a joint byline, publisher Arthur Sulzberger, Jr., and executive editor Dean Baquet wrote, "Did Donald Trump's sheer unconventionality lead us and other news outlets to underestimate his support among American voters? What forces and strains in America drove this divisive election and outcome?"

A CASE STUDY OF THE VIEW FROM THE BUBBLE

Dean Baquet and his staff would not have been so badly blind-sided by Trump if they had shown any understanding of the anger that many Americans felt at the rampant violation of immigration law. Times immigration reporter Liz Robbins provided a museum-quality demonstration of this incapacity with her fawning review of the polemical autobiography *Undocumented: A Dominican Boy's Odyssey from a Homeless Shelter to the Ivy League*. The book is the story of Dan-el Padilla Peralta, whose middle-class family comes to New York on a tourist visa. But while his father returns home, his mother decides to stay, becoming eligible for a variety of public assistance programs after giving birth to a second son in the United States. At one point she complains to the city employees who were showing them apartments that were available to the family. "Mom was upset because the apartments...didn't meet her standards," Padilla writes, acknowledging a sense of entitlement that many Americans find infuriating. In a review for the *Washington Post*, Latina journalist Marcela Valdes wrote that she was "intensely ambivalent" about the book.

But Liz Robbins was enthralled, as she made clear not only in her review in the *Times* but also in an interview with Padilla that was aired on C-SPAN. She had no questions about the contemptuous insults Padilla leveled at those who oppose illegal immigration. He denounces them as "haters." He gloats that because of the rising numbers of people like him, "We are in the ascendant. America is ours." He concludes the book with a taunt: "Demography is a bitch. Holla at me if you want me to break it down for you." She didn't question his intemperance or arrogance, no doubt because she found nothing questionable about it. A graduate of Cornell, she gushed with admiration for Padilla, who had earned honors at Princeton. Robbins is married to the editor of the Spanish-language news service of the Associated Press in New York. She has far more in common with Padilla than with those who find his story outrageous rather than inspiring.

THE MORE THINGS CHANGE, THE MORE THEY STAY THE SAME

The *Times* did expand its news coverage of Middle America and the working class in the era of Trump. At the editorial board there was a major change in 2017 when Lawrence Downes accepted a buyout the paper had offered as a cost-cutting measure. Downes reportedly had clashed with new editorial page editor James Bennet over an issue that had nothing to do with immigration. But any hope that the vacancy would be filled by someone whose temperament was less like Downes's and more like Jack Rosenthal's was dashed by the announcement that veteran Washington journalist Michelle Cottle had been hired as the lead editorial writer on issues involving national politics.

Cottle, who would work from the *Times* bureau in Washington, was well traveled in Washington journalism circles. She had worked at the *Atlantic, National Journal,* the *New Republic, Washington Monthly, Newsweek,* and the *Daily Beast.* The editors who jointly announced her hiring praised her for writing with "passion, nuance and wit since the Clinton administration."

I cringed at the thought of Cottle weighing in on the politics of immigration. In 2013 I had a good view of Cottle in action as she provided the most flagrant, un-nuanced example of contempt for working-class Americans I have ever seen in print.

The offensive piece was Cottle's story for *The Daily Beast* about a march and rally at which a group called the Black American Leadership Alliance—which was allied with the restrictionist Federation for American Immigration Reform—had teamed up with members of the Tea Party for a march down Pennsylvania Avenue. Their purpose was to mark the 50th anniversary of Martin Luther King's March on Washington for Jobs and Freedom. Together they opposed an immigration reform bill that had just been passed by the Senate and was referred to the House, the so-called Gang of Eight bill. Opposing the bill's promise of legalization, a.k.a. amnesty, the groups demanded that lawmakers "recognize the devastating effects illegal immigration and amnesty have on low-skilled workers, particularly those in minority communities."

I was also there that sweltering summer day, watching the march and the rally at a park near the Capitol. I will describe the scene fully in Chapter Six, which is the story of the divide between black workers concerned about jobs and black politicians concerned about showing solidarity with Latinos in the Democratic coalition. For now, suffice it to say that Cottle's story skipped past the concerns of the blacks in order to heap contempt on the whites. She wrote with a gleefully condescending malice. In her rendering, the protesters were a pitiful assemblage who hadn't really marched at all. Instead they had "drifted" down Pennsylvania Avenue. And of course, they weren't just ordinary white people; they were "lily white" as they wilted under the heat of the brutal sun and Cottle's withering prose. Cottle oozed venomous contempt and snarky ridicule for the sweating proletariat. She lived a life well insulated from their working-class vexations. She and her husband owned a seven-bedroom, eight-bathroom home. It was in Chevy Chase, Maryland, just outside the District of Columbia, but well within the Beltway bubble.

When Cottle was hired at the *Times,* no one took note of her rant at the restrictionist gathering five years earlier. But a few months later, a volcanic eruption followed the announcement that the *Times* had hired a young Harvard Law School graduate named Sarah Jeong to write editorials on technology and the Internet. Jeong's expertise and talent were beyond question, but her incendiary Twitter account was not. It was soon revealed that between 2013 and 2015, Jeong, a Korean-American, had repeatedly lashed out at online tormenters. Her targets weren't just those who were trolling her, but white men in general. "White men are bullshit," said one Jeong tweet. Throwing more fuel onto the fire, she wrote: "White people have stopped breeding. You'll all go extinct soon. That was my plan all along."

After Jeong joined the *Times,* her Twitter storms were revived and led to furious demands that she be fired. The *Times* defended her, explaining that "her journalism and the fact that she is a young Asian woman have made her a subject of frequent online harassment" and that she had responded "by imitating the rhetoric of her harassers." But a year later, amidst continuing controversy, Jeong left the editorial board and became a "contract contributor" to the opinion pages.

The Cottle and Jeong hires took place several months after Arthur Gregg Sulzberger was named publisher at the *Times.* At 37 he succeeded his father, who at 66 stayed on as chairman of the New York Times Company. I was concerned that the generational change would mean a further ratcheting up of the paper's loose-borders liberalism. So I was encouraged in early 2020 when the op-ed page published an essay in which I made the liberal case for restricting immigration.[41] As I read the 970 readers' comments that accompanied the story online, I was happy to see many endorsements from liberal readers. Here are some excerpts from the comments, which provide evidence that many readers of the *Times* dissent from its Upper West Side sensibility:

- From Los Angeles: "It amazes me how so many of my progressive friends can't draw connections between the real effects of immigration and the 2016 election. They want to believe opposition is all bigotry and propaganda, while at the same time they blue-sky every single instance of migration. I'd suggest they might want to engage with restrictionists on a more tolerant basis. If we can't have a civil discussion, then only uncivil people will talk about it."
- From Washington, D.C.: "if the Democrats want to have a winning candidate for the presidential race, they would be well advised to take a moderate position on immigration...I reject Donald Trump on almost every level, including how he's treated people at the southern border, but he [has] tapped into a very real security/anxiety among the US electorate. and this is primarily why he was/has been effective with a lot of moderates. Some of it's racism, some of it's a sense of fairness, some of it's cultural unease, some of it's economics, or a mix of these. No matter, it will matter."
- From Idaho: "Why is any business allowed to hire anyone without verifying that they have a valid Social Security Number? Why must those earning the minimum wage have to compete with un-documented Immigrants who are willing to work for lower wages and longer than 40 hours a week without overtime ? Why must the hard working Poor of America have to have their wages remain stagnant, see their jobs disappear so that the wealthy can hire live in Maids, Gardeners, Nannies whom they treat as Economic Slaves."
- From North Carolina: "I am a social democrat and I completely agree with this piece. When people are financially insecure as they are due to massive and yawning inequality, immigration only adds to their distress. We must not be cruel but we must also restrict the flow of migrants effectively and reassure the people they aren't at risk of losing wages."

- From Pennsylvania: "I (a naturalized citizen from India) am watching in astonishment, as some of my fellow Indian immigrants complete 20 years in standing in line, waiting for their green card, while the democratic candidates refuse to distinguish between legal and illegal immigrants."

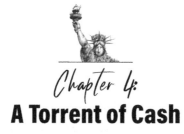

Chapter 4:

A Torrent of Cash

Charitable Foundations Bankroll the Immigrant-Rights Movement

> **The fields of psychology, sociology and anthropology have long attracted liberals, but they became more exclusive after the 1960s, according to Dr. Haidt. "The fight for civil rights and against racism became the sacred cause unifying the left throughout American society, and within the academy," he said, arguing that this shared morality both "binds and blinds."**
>
> *–Article on social psychologist, Jonathan Haidt,* New York Times, *2011*[1]

Backstory: The most valuable real estate in American journalism is the front page of the Sunday *New York Times.* It is a showcase for in-depth reporting, especially long-form investigations into major issues. In April 2011, a story that occupied the top of the front page and then jumped to an entire inside page, presented an investigative profile of John Tanton, the Michigan ophthalmologist and conservationist whose concerns about overpopulation led him first to activism with groups like the Sierra Club, Planned Parenthood, and Zero Population Growth, and then to decades dedicated to organizing the modern movement to restrict immigration.

Tanton, who died in 2019 at the age of 85, is a central figure in the history of immigration restrictionism. His role was so wide-reaching and controversial that he is the focal point of Chapter Five. But I mention the *Times* story here to use it as a bridge from Chapter

Three's examination of the newspaper's role in the immigration debate to this chapter's investigation of the activism of a network of liberal foundations, which are concentrated in Manhattan and share the cosmopolitan ethos of the *Times*.

In both instances, we see powerful institutions whose biases trace our country's divisions along lines of ideology, class, and geography. Both have proclaimed that it is a moral responsibility to welcome illegal immigrants. But while that position certainly merits vigorous discussion in the search for reform, both have weaponized their moral concerns. They have launched them with accusatory fury at those who disagree. They stirred the populist resentment and alienation that led to the election of Donald Trump.

The 2011 story about John Tanton was provocatively headlined "The Anti-Immigration Crusader." The gist, the "nutgraph" in journalistic terms, was that Tanton had undergone an "evolution from apostle of centrist restraint to ally of angry populists and a man who increasingly saw immigration through a racial lens." The story was written by Jason DeParle, an accomplished reporter who in 2019 would publish a book about immigration in which he acknowledged that, "Over the years, I've intermittently engaged with restrictionist leaders, liked some of them and sympathized with some of their concerns." He added the salient observation that the restrictionist "movement runs the gamut from toxic provocateurs like [pundit and author] Ann Coulter...to folksy Roy Beck, the founder of NumbersUSA, whose slogan is 'no to immigrant bashing' but yes to 'economic fairness' for American workers."[2]

I respect DeParle as a reporter. Having spoken with him a few times, I like him as a person. Unlike most at the *Times* who report or editorialize about immigration, he manages his biases fairly, keeping his mind and his notebook open for opposing views. When we spoke as he was in the reporting stage of his story on Tanton, I asked that he consider the central role that the Carnegie Corporation of New York played in bankrolling a multimillion-dollar campaign to smear restrictionists. But while DeParle's piece would note in passing that immigrant-rights activists had produced a video that coupled pictures of Tanton with "images of Klan members and Nazis," he wrote nothing about Carnegie's underwriting of the campaign. He had advised me of this ahead of time, attributing it to an editor's decision. "I used the Carnegie stuff, but it got cut," he said in an email. "Maybe I can come back to it."

My response was based on years of frustration with immigration coverage in *The Times*. In a blog post I wrote that I could expect to see the *Times* report on Carnegie's funding of immigration activists about the time I see Porky Pig flying down Pennsylvania Avenue.

Nine years later, I've still made no sighting of porcine aviators over Washington. That is why this chapter begins with a look at Carnegie's bankrolling of intolerant, hostile activism. Long before Donald Trump descended a Trump Tower escalator to assail Mexican immigrants as he announced his presidential candidacy, Carnegie and other foundations were spending millions on campaigns to insult, defame and defenestrate restrictionists.

CARNEGIE'S CAMPAIGN

In 2008, the Carnegie Corporation of New York, the charitable foundation established by Pittsburgh steel titan Andrew Carnegie, awarded a grant of $200,000 to Capitol News Connection, a nonprofit, Washington-based news service whose programs were heard on public radio stations around the country. The foundation's grants database reported that the money would "enable CNC to deepen and enhance" its reporting on the immigration debate "particularly during an election year and during the opening of a new administration and Congress."[3]

In 2010, as the grant's two-year funding period was coming to an end, Capitol News Connection reported on a study by the Immigration Policy Center, which advocates for expansive immigration policies. It reported the center had found that immigrants and the children of long-established immigrants had doubled their presence in the electorate between 1996 and 2008.[4]

I heard the story on Washington's public radio station WAMU. The story piqued my interest because of its unmistakable political message. I wasn't aware of the Carnegie grant at the time. But with a little work on Google and news databases, I learned that Carnegie money was at work on every level of the story:

- Carnegie funded voter registration drives in many parts of the country.
- Carnegie funded the Immigration Policy Center, which was the research arm of the American Immigration Council, an activist group that says its mission is to "strengthen America by honoring our immigrant history and *shaping how America thinks about and acts toward immigrants and immigration*."[5] (Emphasis added).
- Carnegie funded Capital News Connection, whose story concluded with a blunt warning about the might of the rapidly growing immigrant vote: "Candidates, especially those in close elections, would do well to take heed," the reporter warned.[6] It wasn't the blatant intimidation of a street thug selling "protection" by saying it would be a shame if anything bad happened to a shop. But it rhymed.

With these efforts to boost the immigrant vote and then publicize its success through public radio, Carnegie achieved a sort of vertical integration of the news. Ironically, CNC, whose story did not disclose Carnegie's multi-level involvement, had proclaimed a commitment to investigate the influence of money in Washington.[7]

Carnegie's funding of CNC was part of an aggressive, multimillion-dollar effort to influence news coverage of immigration issues. At times the foundation's descriptions of its grants have explicitly acknowledged the intention not to report the news but to "shape" it in order to influence public opinion.

With its overtly partisan immigration activism, Carnegie has veered away from the vision of its founder, Pittsburgh steel titan

Andrew Carnegie. Naming his foundation the Carnegie Corporation of New York, he commissioned it to promote "the advancement and diffusion of knowledge and understanding," and he called for it to work for "real and permanent good."

Since its creation in 1911, the Carnegie Corporation has funded many remarkable initiatives. Best known is its funding of community libraries, which Andrew Carnegie regarded as cradles of democracy. It has funded research across a broad spectrum of policy issues and scholarly endeavors, including efforts to curtail nuclear proliferation, establish Head Start, create public television, and improve the education of teachers.

Carnegie's current president is Vartan Gregorian, an Iranian-born Armenian-American, who assumed leadership of the foundation in 1997, after serving as president of Brown University. Mindful of Andrew Carnegie's founding mandate, Gregorian wrote: "The Corporation is committed to the idea of investing in a wide range of *both competing and complementary scholars and institutions* [emphasis added] as one way we can increase and help to create knowledge." He aspired to "augment the sources of knowledge that may be drawn upon to inform American leaders and citizens about the issues on the nation's agenda, and thus enrich discussion and debate about them."

Gregorian's vision was consistent not only with Andrew Carnegie's wishes but also with the foundation's obligation, as a tax-exempt charity, to operate in a nonpartisan fashion for the public interest. But it has embraced the highly partisan ideological forces that a 1995 *New Republic* article found widespread at charitable foundations. "The preponderance of foundation grants to advocacy groups.... suggests that foundations are less devoted to the reasoned pursuit of the public good than to the multiculturalist dogmas propounded by their staff," it reported.[8]

GERALDINE MANNION, CARNEGIE'S IMMIGRATION ACTIVIST

The driving force behind Carnegie's immigration activism has been Geraldine Mannion, the longtime director of the foundation's Strengthening U.S. Democracy program. Mannion, whose family immigrated to the U.S. from Ireland when she was a child, is a prominent figure in the tight-knit community of charitable foundations. She is co-founder of the Four Freedoms Fund, which has provided tens of millions of dollars to support immigrant-rights groups. FFF has received more than $50 million in Carnegie grants. Much of that money has been earmarked "to push back against proposed anti-immigrant policies"[9]—a category that in Mannion's lexicon includes any effort either to stop illegal immigration or limit legal immigration.

Carnegie's militancy intensified after the 2007 collapse of efforts to pass a comprehensive immigration reform bill. A $6.5 million Carnegie grant financed the startup of an advocacy group called America's Voice, giving it a mandate "to more directly challenge those who oppose immigration reform."[10] That nine-word strategy statement would reverberate loudly across the immigration debate, anticipating an effort to convince journalists to shun not only the Federation for American Immigration Reform, but also the Center for Immigration Studies and NumbersUSA. As we will see in Chapter Six, America's Voice teamed up with the National Council of La Raza, the Center for American Progress, and the Center for New Community to carry out the campaign to "Stop the Hate."

One of the most forceful critics of that campaign was Tom Barry, a staunchly liberal advocate of comprehensive immigration reform. Calling the campaign "unprincipled," Barry challenged "the foundations that have supported this smear campaign to disassociate themselves from such character-assassination tactics." He disliked the tactic of telling the press to shun the restrictionist groups. "One wonders just whom the media is supposed to talk to about the restrictionist cause if reporters are to reject these three influential institutes as illegitimate," he wrote.

Tom Barry was a strong but lonely voice on the left, where Carnegie and Geraldine Mannion were part of what social psychologist Jonathan Haidt calls "a tribal moral community," bound together so intensely by a sacred principle that they were blind to opposing views. Mannion was clearly delighted with America's Voice's leading role in the attack. Under her direction, Carnegie gave America's Voice another $2 million in 2010. The grant award praised the group for providing "faster and edgier communications" and "innovative strategies [that] have helped to influence media coverage of the issue in new ways."[11]

As demonstrated by Carnegie's funding of Capitol News Connection and the related voter-registration effort, the foundation has not only spent heavily to encourage immigrants to naturalize, register, and vote. It has also bankrolled thinly veiled admonitions about the electoral risks of opposing comprehensive immigration reform. In 2012, Frank Sharry of America's Voice warned that Republicans' resistance to reform put them on a path to political suicide with the fastest-growing group of new voters in the nation."

Through its financing of efforts to get out the vote and support expansive immigration reform, Carnegie inevitably became entwined with Democratic politics. As we've seen, its grants were crucial to the activism of America's Voice. They were also essential to the mission of the Center for Community Change, which sought to harness the power of the ballot box to create "a whole different national agenda."

The strategizing was guided by two Democratic power centers: The New Democratic Network, which sought to harness changing demographics to consolidate a "permanent Democratic majority"; and the Center for American Progress, which the *New Republic* in 2016 would describe as so "stuffed to the gills" with Democratic operatives" that it was essentially "Hillary Clinton's government-in-waiting."

SPENDING BIG TO THWART ENFORCEMENT

The Carnegie Corporation invested heavily in advocacy for comprehensive immigration reform. But its grant-making demonstrated that, like many activists whose central goal was legalization for unauthorized immigrants, Carnegie wanted to thwart worksite enforcement. In other words, it wanted to defeat a critical element of comprehensive immigration reform.

For example, a $1 million grant to the Center for Community Change—which Carnegie earmarked "to help immigrants advocate for their needs"[12]—financed opposition to E-Verify, a computer-based system intended to stop the employment of unauthorized workers. Carnegie joined forces with those who wanted E-Verify to be voluntary, a concept that makes no more sense than voluntary income taxes. Carnegie had aligned itself with those who complain that the immigration system is broken but systematically undermine an essential component of the proposal to reform it.

Carnegie also funded a campaign by the Mexican American Legal Defense and Education Fund (MALDEF) to mount legal challenges against states and municipalities that had passed ordinances to target illegal immigration. Some local governments, for example, had forbidden landlords to rent property to persons they knew to be unauthorized. Carnegie helped to ensure that such efforts would lead to costly legal battles. Several high-profile legal challenges led to court rulings that the local governments had exceeded their authority. The bitter irony for the cities was that their efforts to enforce the law in the absence of federal enforcement were found to be an illegal intrusion into the federal government's sphere of responsibility.

Carnegie's defense of unauthorized immigrants included funding not just for the liberal left but also for the libertarian right. The foundation awarded a $25,000 grant to the open-border, free-trade Cato Institute to promote the book, *Let Them in: The Case for Open Borders*, which was written by Jason Riley, a member of the *Wall Street Journal* editorial board. An additional grant of $150,000 was earmarked to help Cato to "bring its unique libertarian perspective to bear on the public debate" by opposing proposals for a national system of worker identification.[13] That effort featured warnings that an identification system would be a slippery slope toward totalitarianism. It united Cato with the strange bedfellows of the ACLU.

OTHER MAJOR FOUNDATIONS JOIN THE FIGHT FOR MORE IMMIGRATION

In the overwhelmingly liberal world of charitable foundations, Carnegie is hardly alone in its immigration advocacy. The effort to thwart immigration restriction has included George Soros's Open Society Foundation, the Tides Foundation, Atlantic Philanthropies, and at least a dozen smaller foundations. My estimate, based primarily on examination of the foundations' online grants' databases, is that between 2001 and 2020 foundations invested more than $400 million to support expansionist policies.

Just between 2008 and 2015, the Ford Foundation distributed $109 million in dozens of grants earmarked for "protecting immigrant and migrant rights." Although illegal immigrants by definition did not have a right to be in the United States, Ford claimed to be protecting a *human right* to come to the United States. Ford said its human-rights initiative on immigration "works to secure equal rights and opportunities for all"—that is, without regard to legal status—and to "integrate them into a broader social justice."[14]

The irony here, of course, is that U.S. immigration law establishes limits in an effort to ensure order, fairness, and pragmatic functionality. But in the world of liberal foundations, the imperatives of equality and inclusiveness are the ultimate authority. No principle of restriction is to be tolerated because restriction is seen as a form of oppression directed against people of color.

THE FORD FOUNDATION

The Ford Foundation's long history of funding social activism includes underwriting the 1960s' launch of the Southwest Council of La Raza, the Mexican-American organization that changed its name to National Council of La Raza as it sought broader visibility and influence. In 2017, NCLR changed its name to UnidosUS in response to criticism that "La Raza" (The Race) was anachronistic and divisive and not welcoming for those from other Latin American countries, whose numbers have boomed since the 1980s.

In recent years, Ford has spent heavily on legal defense of illegal immigration. Its grantees include the National Immigration Law Center, the Immigrant Legal Resource Center, the National Immigration Project of the National Lawyers Guild, the National Immigrant Justice Center, the American Immigration Council, and, of course, the American Civil Liberties Union.

Ford Foundation president Darren Walker said the foundation's "most important obligation is to stand with courageous and creative visionaries on the front lines of social change."[15] It funds the vision of Deepak Bhargava, an immigrant from India who is the executive director of the Center for Community Change.

According to the *Chronicle of Philanthropy*, Bhargava believed that Congress would not pass a controversial measure like comprehensive immigration reform "unless throngs of people are in the street."[16] Ford gave millions to organizations across the country to fill the streets with demonstrations, much of which was coordinated by the CCC's Fair Immigration Reform Movement. As we have seen, the marches in several cities in 2006 provoked a backlash from people who dissented from the vision of a country that welcomed everyone who wanted to come. *Arizona Republic* columnist Ed Montini wrote that the demonstrations "shocked and frightened" many people. "Regular people were outraged, and they told elected officials as much," Montini wrote.[17]

But the CCC's ability to move its people helped it gain influence in high places. In late 2008, the chairwoman of its board, Cecilia Muñoz, the top lobbyist for the National Council of La Raza, was named director of intergovernmental affairs for the incoming administration of President-elect Barack Obama. In that job she would be Obama's principal adviser on immigration policy.

GEORGE SOROS AND THE OPEN SOCIETY FOUNDATIONS

George Soros, with the billions he acquired in high-risk investing as the head of a hedge fund, provides a particularly vivid example of great wealth at work in the immigration debate.

Soros has described himself as a stateless statesman. In a 1995 profile, journalist Connie Bruck said he had "the instincts of the outsider; he was distrustful of government, disdainful of the establishment, allergic to institutions generally." She cited his "tendency to beatify one side and demonize the other." She described him as "an extremely undemonstrative person, who appears cold, detached, and insular."[18] Soros, then, is not one to be impressed with the classically conservative social bonds of loyalty, tradition, and mutual obligation. In other words, George Soros is no Edmund Burke, for whom warm localized attachments were "the first principle... of public affections."

In his advocacy of open immigration, Soros is a post-national man, averse to sentiments of national identity and cohesion, and confident in the energizing power of open borders and unrestricted immigration. Such sentiments have motivated Soros funding for the Center for American Progress. To us skeptics, who believe that immigration should be contained within reasonable limits, Soros's certitude brings to mind Burke's critique of revolutionaries who "are so taken up with their theories about the rights of man that they have totally forgotten his nature."

One Soros grantee is the National Day Laborer Organizing Network (NDLON), which resists efforts by cities and towns to restrict hiring sites they believe have become public nuisances. NDLON sued Redondo Beach, Calif., which had adopted an ordinance that prohibited standing on a street or highway and soliciting work from anyone in a motor vehicle.

In 2011 the U.S. Court of Appeals for the Ninth Circuit ruled that the ordinance was so broadly written that it violated the constitutional guarantee of free speech. In an angry dissent that illustrated one fault line in the immigration debate, one member of the court wrote that the ordinance was a reasonable attempt to control the problem caused by men who "litter, vandalize, urinate, block the sidewalk, harass females and damage property."[19] But NDLON pressed its case, denouncing a similar ordinance in Fairfax, Virginia, which it said was "nothing more than an ugly and xenophobic attempt to get rid of the Latinos on the sidewalk looking for work."[20]

Soros's Open Society Foundations are active on multiple fronts opposing enforcement of immigration law. Some grants advanced other rights. For example, a 2011 grant to the Immigrant Defense Project provided $400,000 "to protect the legal, constitutional, and human rights of immigrants with criminal arrests and convictions." Another grant used euphemistic framing to designate $200,000 "to protect the legal rights of immigrants facing deportation as a result of interactions with the criminal justice system."

The Immigrant Defense Project takes a hard line against enforcement. Its director in New York declared that the U.S. deportation system is so unjust that "we cannot justify sending anyone into detention and deportation, a system that only compounds and exacerbates the unfairness that many immigrant and low-income communities have historically faced through the criminal (in)justice system."[21]

ATLANTIC PHILANTHROPIES

Atlantic Philanthropies was founded by billionaire Charles Feeney, who built his fortune with a chain of duty-free shops. It was a major funder of the Center for Community Change. Before the 2014 elections, Atlantic Philanthropies issued a grant "to ensure policy-makers at the state and federal levels are attuned to Latino voting power and its immigration policy objectives."[22] The foundation gave $9 million to America's Voice, including a $1 million grant in 2014 with an explicitly political purpose. The money was designated for "a national media narrative that affirms the relationship between the growing Latino electorate and the demand for immigration reform."[23] In other words, it was intended to remind politicians of the growing power of the Latino vote. It was an effort to make expansive immigration policies a self-fulfilling ultimatum. And because it was a not-so-subtle celebration of growing Latino politico clout, it was bound to stir anxiety among those whose power was being diminished.

Some Americans have been provoked to anger as they survey the shifting demographic, political, and economic landscape. Others have surrendered to a despairing sense of displacement. Small towns concentrated in the Midwest have suffered the double-whammy inflicted by decisions of politicians and corporate chiefs to allow the in-sourcing of low-wage immigrant labor and the out-sourcing of industrial jobs that once supported a blue-collar middle class. Many agreed with Donald Trump's assessment that they had been invaded by immigrants and betrayed by American elites. Many were defiantly proud in claiming to be one of the Trump-supporting "deplorables" decried by Hillary Clinton in an infamous display of condescension and contempt shortly before the 2016 election.

New Yorker film critic Pauline Kael famously said that those who voted for Richard Nixon were "beyond my ken"—occupants of a different political and moral universe. Program officers at many foundations are similarly alienated from those who favor immigration restrictions. They are, however, thoroughly supportive of immigrants and immigration activists. For example, consider Cecilia Muñoz, the daughter of Bolivian immigrants who in her role as director of the White House Domestic Policy Council became President Obama's top adviser on immigration policy. In 2000, when Muñoz was the lead lobbyist for the National Council of La Raza, she received a MacArthur Foundation "genius" grant.

THE INSULAR WORLD OF MANHATTAN

Heavily concentrated in Manhattan, liberal foundations occupy an insular world of tremendous wealth, privilege and sophistication. But they show little understanding of those beyond the Hudson who have struggled in an era of mass immigration and globalization.

Andrew Carnegie's father was a Scottish handloom weaver who lost his job after the 1840s introduction of the steam-powered loom. The young Carnegie wrote that his father's displacement "was disastrous to our family." It would seem reasonable, therefore, to expect that the Carnegie Corporation would be sympathetic to the concerns of American workers confronting displacement by both immigration and globalization. But Carnegie and the other foundations have chosen not to acknowledge any moral ambiguity. I searched in vain through their grants' databases, reports, and public pronouncements for some recognition that mass immigration has created both winners and losers. Instead, I found repeated, almost ritualistic, invocations of the blessings of unrestricted immigration. I also found grant after grant that was used to finance media and public relations campaigns to demonize those who oppose such views.

In their partisan zeal, these foundations have strayed from their responsibility to work for the broad public good rather than for a narrow, particular ideology. Consider this excerpt from *The Carnegie Reporter,* the foundation's own publication. In 2008, when Carnegie's funding of Capital News Connection was part of a surge in aggressively politicized grant-making, it proclaimed:

> *At this moment of national conversation, the Corporation expects to be on the front lines of this important national debate about the evolving relationship between immigration and our democratic American society. Our grantees are asking the questions, conducting the research, and working with men and women who want an immigration system that is worthy of Emma Lazarus's fabled words at the base of the Statue of Liberty.*

This is a warm sentiment. But it is simplistic and disingenuous. It obscures the fact that Carnegie grantees are not asking questions about immigration's place in our society because they begin with the answers, which include the condemnation of those who don't share their expansionist goals. Rather than informing and enlarging the debate, they are seeking to stifle it.

The open-borders sensibility that is so manifest at the foundations is a badge of membership among woke liberals, especially in their cultural capital, Manhattan. It is seen in the Democratic activists who pressured candidates for the party's 2020 presidential nomination to endorse decriminalization of unauthorized immigration and free medical care for the 11 million people now living illegally in the United States. It represents a radical departure from the centrist views that prevailed among Democrats for decades. That pragmatic sensibility was essential to their ability to work in a bipartisan spirit to enact IRCA.

Consider the work of the Senate Judiciary Committee during the debate that led up to IRCA's enactment. The committee advised that "the ability of the American people to welcome aliens into their day-to-day life experiences has limits." It expressed polite skepticism about the *relevance of* Emma Lazarus's poem, "The New Colossus," to policy making a full century after it was written. Observing that the poem is "cited in nearly all discussions of U.S. immigration policy," it dissented from the poem's implicit call for open borders. The committee reached a conclusion that remains valid today:

> *In an earlier time, the nation could welcome millions of newcomers, many of whom brought few skills, but did bring a willingness to work hard....Immigration can still greatly benefit America, but only if it is limited to an appropriate number and selected within that number on the basis of immediate family reunification and skills which truly serve the interest of a highly developed nation.*

PAUL KRUGMAN'S BRAVE, PRAGMATIC COLUMN.

In 2006, economist Paul Krugman, a Nobel Prize winner dissented from what he saw as the errant romanticism of the expansionists.

A staunch liberal, he began one column in the *New York Times* with observations that amounted to a pre-emptory self-defense against the inevitable claims of racist intent. Krugman said Emma Lazarus's poem "still puts a lump in my throat." He professed gratitude that "the door was open when my grandparents fled Russia."[24] These familial chords, Krugman said, made him "instinctively, emotionally pro-immigration." Then he introduced the big "but" that was the theme of his column:

> *But a review of serious, nonpartisan research reveals some uncomfortable facts about the economics of modern immigration, and immigration from Mexico in particular. If people like me are going to respond effectively to anti-immigrant demagogues, we have to acknowledge those facts.... while immigration may have raised overall income slightly, many of the worst-off native-born Americans are hurt by immigration—especially immigration from Mexico. Because Mexican immigrants have much less education than the average U.S. worker, they increase the supply of less-skilled labor, driving down the wages of the worst-paid Americans ... modern America is a welfare state, even if our social safety net has more holes in it than it should—and low-skill immigrants threaten to unravel that safety net.*

For a liberal of Krugman's stature, this was a pronouncement as brave as it was pragmatic. Rooted in the labor-market circumstances of his time, it was a dissent from the sentimentality of the Emma Lazarus poem, which was written in 1883, when the U.S. population had just reached the 50-million mark. Krugman concluded, "Realistically, we'll need to reduce the influx of low-skill immigrants."

THE ROOTS OF POPULIST UNREST

A vigorous immigration debate makes room for those who want to probe the moral ambiguity and the dilemmas inherent in the tension between competing values. On the one hand, it is admirable to want to maintain the American tradition of welcoming immigrants as a source of vitality, creativity, and renewal. But it is also admirable to want to regulate—in other words, to restrict—immigration in order to preserve our ability to cohere as a nation and cooperate in the challenging project of democratic governance. Those of us who identify as restrictionists have a range of views as to how much immigration we should have and what we should do about those who violate our laws. But fundamentally, most of us believe that if immigration is unrestricted, if it is shaped by the romance of Emma Lazarus's poem or the let-it-rip libertarianism of free markets and open borders, it will inevitably provoke a populist backlash, especially in an era when globalization, automation, and free trade have already had brutal consequences for millions of working-class families. Among those who feel an embittered sense of abandonment and betrayal, a movement toward populism is perhaps inevitable.

In his book *The Populist Explosion*, journalist John Judis made an assessment that applies here. "In both Europe and the US, populist movements have been most successful at times when people see the prevailing political norms—which are preserved and defended by the existing establishment—as being at odds with their own hopes, fears, and concerns. The populists express these neglected concerns and frame them in a politics that pits the people against an intransigent elite." Judis's book was published in October of 2016, one month before Donald Trump was elected president of the United States.

AFTERWORD

In August 2019, the *New York Times* published an expose about the woman whose fortune had become the principal source of funding for John Tanton and the restrictionist movement. It was an impressive piece of reporting. It was based on months of research that took the reporters across the country for dozens of interviews and a deep dive into archives, court files, and government records. It certainly cost the *Times* tens of thousands of dollars, a price tag that few newspapers can now afford. While most papers have seen their business model destroyed by the Internet, the *Times* has prospered by selling digital subscriptions to readers around the world.

Reporters Nicholas Kulish and Mike McIntire traced the personal life and the political activism of Cordelia Scaife May, an heiress of the Pittsburgh-based Mellon family, which amassed a fortune in banking and major holdings in such corporations as Gulf Oil and Alcoa. She died in 2005 at the age of 76.

May emerged from a troubled childhood with a passion for protecting natural habitats and a fascination with birds. An admirer of Margaret Sanger, the founder of Planned Parenthood, she had a measured concern for overpopulation that evolved into a fretful fixation on immigration. She believed that immigration to the U.S. should be balanced with emigration from the U.S. because overpopulation was "the root cause of unemployment, inflation, urban sprawl, highway (and skyway) congestion, shortages of all sorts (not the least of which is energy), vanishing farmland, environmental deterioration and civil unrest."

The *Times* story documented how, like John Tanton, May sometimes allowed her beliefs to be tainted as immigration surged in the 1970s and 1980s. "When we hear of immigrants, we instinctively think of Mexicans because they are the most numerous and given the greatest press coverage," she wrote in a letter to a cousin. "In truth, we are being invaded on all fronts." She cited the influx of Filipinos, residents of the Caribbean islands and South America, "Orientals and Indians" coming across the Canadian border, and Cuban refugees who "breed like hamsters."

The *Times* story makes a convincing case that May's affinity for John Tanton's concerns resulted in her emergence as the central, indispensable funder for the restrictionist movement. *Times* graphic artists created a Venn diagram that showed the tens of millions she distributed not only to the three major restrictionist groups (FAIR, NumbersUSA, and the Center for Immigration Studies) but to several others that Tanton was involved involved with. Those secondary organizations included Californians for Population Stabilization and the Immigration Reform Law Institute.

This is solid reporting, documenting spending that surprised me in its breadth. But the reporters betray the shallowness of their understanding of the debate with their tendentious framing of the fact that May's Colcom Foundation supports "groups that spent decades agitating for policies now pursued by President Trump: militarizing the border, capping legal immigration, and prioritizing skills over family ties for entry." Far from the fixations of small minded agitators, these policies have been endorsed not only by the U.S. Commission on Immigration Reform headed by Barbara Jordan, but also a variety of public opinion polls. While many Americans do not want the "militarizing" of the border—a loaded and imprecise term—they do overwhelmingly favor strong measures at the border to stop illegal immigration.

The *Times*' most egregious unfairness was the story's guilt-by-association reference to the 2019 massacre of shoppers at an El Paso Walmart. The story reported: "Though their methods radically diverged, Mrs. May and the killer in the recent mass shooting in El Paso applied the same language, both warning of an immigrant 'invasion,' an idea also promoted by Mr. Trump." Underscoring the moral of their story, the reporters concluded: "In many ways, the Trump presidency is the culmination of Mrs. May's vision for strictly limiting immigration."

Here the ideological reach of the reporters' tendentious conclusion exceeds the grasp of their solidly assembled facts. It is an example of the epic failure of the *Times* in recent years to understand that the rise of Donald Trump represents the culmination of the vision of those who have encouraged and supported illegal immigration and obstructed efforts to curtail it ever since the days of the Truman administration. As we saw in Chapter One, back then a presidential commission was so struck by the intensity of the illegal influx that it described it as "a virtual invasion." Today, at the *New York Times*, "invasion" is a shibboleth that betrays one as small minded and anti-immigrant. For many Americans, the word expresses a stunned recognition of their government's ability to control the border.

I share the vision of John Rohe, the Tanton biographer and director of philanthropy for the Colcom Foundation, which May established in 1998 to support not only the restrictionist movement but a host of philanthropic causes. "We should have a pro-immigrant, nonracial immigration policy," Rohe told the *Times*. "It should not be based on race. It's only based on the numbers."

Finally, I want to acknowledge that because Colcom is a major funder of the Center for Immigration Studies, where I am a senior research fellow, I might not have been able to write this book without its support.

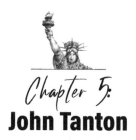

Chapter 5:
John Tanton

Nativist Puppeteer or Environmentalist Johnny Appleseed?

> **Opponents and supporters alike have long agreed that Dr. Tanton had an outsize influence on national policy for an eye doctor living nearly 800 miles from Washington in a resort town on Lake Michigan......[He was] also deeply concerned about the impact of the rapidly growing human population on the planet......Dr. Tanton's ideas prefigured many of the debates about white identity politics that have taken hold on the right wing.**
>
> —New York Times, *July 18, 2019*[1]

During a visit to Phoenix in 2010, I stopped by the *Arizona Republic* newsroom to talk with former colleagues at the paper, which had been my professional home from 1986 until 2002. One of them mentioned that a reader had recently complained about a story that quoted Steve Camarota, director of research at the Center for Immigration Studies, where I began working a year earlier. Camarota has a doctorate in public policy analysis from the University of Virginia. His work has been cited by the Supreme Court and the National Academy of Science. It wasn't the quote itself that had upset the reader. Camarota had made a straightforward observation about the reasons for the decline of Arizona's unauthorized immigrant population to an estimated 460,000 in 2009 from 560,000 a year earlier. He noted that the state "has had a very bad job market and it has had a very robust enforcement scene." Earlier that year, Arizona Gov. Jane Brewer had signed controversial legislation that, while aimed at stopping illegal immigration, was known nationally as the "show-me-your-papers-law" because it had empowered police to determine the legal status of people encountered in the normal course of their work.

The reader's complaint was that the story had identified CIS as a "think tank in Washington, D.C. that favors reductions in immigration." He said the *Republic* should have described CIS as part of "the John Tanton network," which he thought should be identified a group of white nationalists and racists directed by Tanton, who founded FAIR in 1979 and later was instrumental in the establishment of the Center for Immigration Studies and NumbersUSA.

The reader was a volunteer with an organization called Nativism Watch. It was a new weapon in the campaign to exclude restrictionists from the national debate. I called it *reductio ad Tanton*. Its strategy was twofold: to claim that the three major restrictionist organizations were puppets dancing under strings manipulated by Tanton, and to demonize Tanton as a sinister mastermind like Emmanuel Goldstein in George Orwell's *1984*. Goldstein was the leader of the Brotherhood, the underground movement that sought to topple the totalitarian state dominated by Big Brother. He was the target of the Two Minutes Hate, which was a rite of exorcism to purge his corrupting influence. His image was projected onto a screen in a public square filled with loyalist automatons who scream in obligatory fury. "He was the primal traitor, the earliest defiler of the party's unity," Orwell wrote. "All subsequent crimes against the Party, all treacheries, acts of sabotage, heresies, deviations, sprang directly out of his teaching."[2]

Nativism Watch sprang from the work of Heidi Beirich and Mark Potok's Intelligence Project at the Southern Poverty Law Center. Beirich and Potok claimed to be advocates of truth and tolerance but instead orchestrated a campaign of distortion and character assassination against restrictionists. In a lurid 2002 report, they branded Tanton as the sinister "Puppeteer." Six years later, as we will see in the next chapter, they helped launch a "We Can Stop the

Hate" campaign that juxtaposed photos of Tanton with images of Klansmen and Nazis. A desire to counter such tactics was a major motivation for me to come to work at CIS.

AN INVITATION TO COFFEE IS TURNED DOWN

After learning about the criticism of the *Republic* article, I sent an email to the complaining reader, a Phoenix immigration activist named Chris Fleischman. I introduced myself and invited him to meet for coffee or a drink. My tone was cordial. "I would like to know more about your concerns," I wrote. "And I would like to share with you some of my own."

Fleischman promptly sent me a polite but frosty reply. "I must decline your offer because I do not wish to associate myself with someone who is connected with CIS," he wrote. "The organization has troubling ties to white nationalism, and I do not have time to give to anyone in that position. If you leave your position with the John Tanton Network, I would be happy to talk with you and treat you to a beverage." That was my last communication with Chris Fleischman. But it was just the beginning of my effort to learn about him and Nativism Watch, which enlisted activists in other parts of the country in an effort to shape the news.

I learned that Fleischman was no callow youth, no campus militant. He was a middle-aged engineer who had worked in the aerospace industry. He was deeply, sincerely engaged in advocacy for the undocumented. His Facebook page had a photo of him holding a sign that, in an apparent reference to illegal immigration, posed the question: "Who are YOU to judge?" Another photo showed a poster that read, "I pledge to break ICE's hold on my community and country." A third, posted in protest of an Arizona law that targeted illegal immigrants, showed him with a poster that merged the sunburst at the center of the state flag with a swastika. Like Beirich and Potok, he claimed to see Nazis always lurking in the background.

THE UNITED CHURCH OF CHRIST

Nativism Watch was a project of the Chicago-based Center for New Community (CNC). CNC is led by the Rev. David Ostendorf of the United Church of Christ. In church circles, Ostendorf is known for the fiery certainty in his moral convictions. He has said the church's work on behalf of immigrants should be righteously militant, going beyond "resolutionary Christianity" to "revolutionary Christianity."[3] In a statement that helps explain the rationale for Nativism Watch, Ostendorf declared, "When we unite for justice and expose the architects of contemporary organized racism, we create a space for people to take control of their own narratives." And so, in the world of Chris Fleischman, it was righteous and true to expose and muzzle groups like the Center for Immigration Studies in order to empower illegal immigrants and those who defended them.

The United Church of Christ is known for its aggressively righteous activism. During the 2008 presidential campaign, the UCC's Rev. Jeremiah Wright achieved national notoriety as the pastor to Sen. Barack Obama. A video of one of Wright's sermons exploded onto the political scene, showing Wright's denunciations of the U.S. government for abuse of American Indians, Japanese-Americans, and African-Americans. "God damn America!" Wright thundered repeatedly. Obama distanced himself from the remarks and eventually disavowed Wright.

The Center for New Community's immigration activism has been supported by a series of grants from the liberal foundations we encountered in Chapter Four. The Carnegie Corporation provided $200,000. The Ford Foundation gave CNC $500,000 to "reframe the debate on immigration." Three years later, Ford gave another $300,000 for CNC to "provide research and analysis combating anti-immigrant extremism." Meanwhile, George Soros' Open Society Foundations provided $300,000 for "general support."

The man who supervised Nativism Watch was the CNC's national field director, Eric K. Ward. Ward is a professional activist. He has had many jobs on the social justice front. Before joining CNC, he was a field organizer for an organization named the Northwest Coalition Against Malicious Harassment. After leaving CNC, he worked at the Ford Foundation and then Atlantic Philanthropies, helping to select grantees. For a short time, he was a fellow with the Southern Poverty Law Center. Then he became executive director of the Western States Center, whose declared mission is to "strengthen inclusive democracy so that all people can live, love, and work free from fear."[4]

I had first learned about Ward a year earlier, when he appeared on NPR's "Tell Me More" program along with Cornell professor Vernon Briggs, a labor economist and a member of the Center for Immigration Studies board of directors. Ward took offense at Briggs's observation that illegal immigration has negative effects on the job prospects of African Americans. That was a longstanding concern of many black leaders, including two who sit on the CIS board. But to Ward it was a smoke screen behind which lurked the snarling face of racism. He angrily claimed that Briggs's comment was part of CIS strategy to "use the plight of African Americans as a ploy to hoodwink the American public."

Briggs rebutted the criticism with characteristic civility. Noting the alarm that Barbara Jordan had expressed about illegal immigration, he said, "Barbara Jordan was no racist." Then he named other African-American leaders who had voiced similar concerns: A. Philip Randolph, W.E.B. Du Bois, Booker T. Washington, and Frederick Douglass. Ward was as undeterred by historical fact as he was uninterested in Briggs's record as an advocate for the African-American working class. That advocacy was made explicit in the book Briggs wrote when he was an assistant professor at the University of Texas at Austin. There he collaborated with Professor Ray Marshall (who would become secretary of labor in the Carter administration) in writing a 1967 book titled *The Negro and Apprenticeship*. They made the case for programs to train young African-Americans at a time when they had virtually no presence in most of the nation's highly skilled craft unions. They decried "the almost universal failure of recruiting drives, the lack of programs to prepare Negro youth for entry into the skilled trades, and the lackadaisical attempts to gather and distribute information about specific apprenticeship programs." A review in the scholarly journal *Industrial and Labor Relations Review*, praised the book as "vital reading for anyone affecting such policies and activities." For decades Briggs had been an advocate for American workers. In the 1960s, while teaching at the University of Texas, he had helped Cesar Chavez organizing farmworkers in the Rio Grande Valley who were losing their jobs to strike breakers brought in from Mexico. For Eric Ward, however, Vernon Briggs was fair game.

JOHN TANTON: BRIGHT LIGHT AND DARK SHADOW

Like Vernon Briggs, John Tanton is more complex and respectable than the diabolical caricature fabricated by activist lefties for whom character assassination is just another weapon to be deployed in their heroic struggle. While I met him only once, I felt compelled to study his background when I came to CIS, knowing that he was a controversial figure. I came to see him as a man of bright light and deep shadow, someone whose track record offered much to admire and much to lament.

There is much to admire in Tanton's lifelong environmentalist concerns. His sensibility was marked by an acute perception of the threat that population growth and sprawl could pose to the natural world. In the midst of one preservationist battle he said, "We have a responsibility to preserve these particular acres, so there will be something left for those who come after us." This core conviction led him eventually to activism against unchecked immigration. Indeed, when he founded FAIR in 1979, he launched the modern restrictionist movement. But in the ensuing years, as mounting immigration from Mexico made him fearful that the U.S. would face a divide like that threatening to divide French-speaking Quebec from the rest of Canada, Tanton saw immigration as also a cultural and linguistic threat. Always an inveterate organizer, eager to build networks and alliances, he developed a no-enemies-to-the-right blind spot that prevented him from seeing the toxicity of some of his friends. This drew him toward an intense ethnocentrism that at times crossed the line and entered the perilous territory of white nationalism.

One of Tanton's friends, former Colorado Gov. Richard Lamm, regarded him as "a remarkable man, very deep and complex." But Tanton was also exasperating. He had a tin ear for the sensitivities and moral ambiguities of immigration policy, and he showed scant empathy for the anguished predicaments of many migrants. And so, this man from rural Michigan, who did more than anyone else to establish the modern movement to restrict immigration, also did more than anyone else to undermine that movement. While I met Tanton only once, speaking to him briefly when I was still a reporter, my research made me think of him as the restrictionists' proverbial eccentric uncle, capable by turns of eliciting admiration and exasperation. His fundamental concerns were admirable and sometimes even prescient. But his mistakes made it easy for unscrupulous enemies like Heidi Beirich and Eric Ward to find us all guilty by association with some very bad actors on the far right. The story of how it all happened is worth telling.

A SMALL-TOWN DOCTOR IN A BIG NATIONAL DEBATE

John Tanton was born in Detroit in 1934 to parents who yearned to escape the city for a life on the land. When he was 10, they moved to the farm near Saginaw, where his mother had been raised. That was the beginning of his immersion in the natural world and his love of landscapes never touched by the developer's hand. "Gathering the hay, monitoring the cloud formations, and learning the growth cycles caused John to resonate with the pulsations of the land," wrote John Rohe, a conservationist, and Tanton biographer who supported Tanton's ventures through his work as director of philanthropy at the Colcom Foundation.

Tanton graduated from Michigan State University in 1956 with a degree in chemistry. He went on to earn his M.D. and a master's degree in ophthalmology from the University of Michigan. In the 1960s, when he was ready to launch his medical practice, he and his wife, Mary Lou, settled in the northern Michigan town of Petoskey. He soon became an activist and an organizer of environmental causes. Tanton founded the regional Audubon Society and helped start the local chapter of the Sierra Club. He and his wife joined the Nature Conservancy and the League of Conservation Voters. He was appointed to the state's Wilderness and Natural Areas Advisory Board. In 1965 he cofounded Michigan Planned Parenthood.

The range and intensity of Tanton's interests were remarkable. Reporter Jonathan Tilove of the Newhouse News Service found Tanton to be "a relentless figure of perpetual self-improvement and civic engagement."[5] He wrote of Tanton's joy at learning about the chemical structure of chocolate, the complexities of microeconomics, beekeeping, gardening, hikes in the woods, and discussions of great books. Tanton made his home in the small town of Petoskey, a salon in the woodlands by Little Traverse Bay. He loved ideas. He relished discussing them, debating them, in a wide-open, free-wheeling style fueled by his ceaseless, compulsive curiosity. It was a characteristic that endeared him to friends. But his inability to moderate his intensity would get him into trouble.

PAUL EHRLICH AND THE POPULATION BOMB

The pivot point in Tanton's evolution from provincial polymath to activist on the national stage was the 1968 publication of *The Population Bomb,* a runaway bestseller by Stanford biologist Paul Ehrlich. Written with the fervor of an Old Testament jeremiad, the book was a provocative updating of the Malthusian warning that unrelenting population growth would overwhelm mankind's capacity to produce food. Drawing apocalyptic scenarios of mass starvation and societal collapse, Ehrlich warned, "We must rapidly bring the world population under control, reducing the growth rate to zero or making it negative."[6] Critics who called Ehrlich's doomsday scenarios preposterous claimed vindication when breakthroughs in agricultural science miraculously boosted crop yields. His defenders cautioned that his warnings, while premature, remained prescient.

Ehrlich's clarion call jolted Tanton, arousing his already acute ecological instincts. It infused him with a new sense of urgency, a passion to avert the existential threat of multiplying human numbers. Long accustomed to acting locally in Michigan, he acquired a more prominent profile when he became national president of Zero Population Growth. Ehrlich had cofounded ZPG to harness the public alarm his book had stirred and to urge Americans to limit the size of their families. His movement received a powerful, popular culture boost when late-night television host Johnny Carson was so struck by Ehrlich's message—delivered with an affable bluntness—that he made the doomsday professor a frequent guest on his show. From 1971 to 1975, Tanton was chairman of the National Population Committee of the Sierra Club. But one Tanton critic, exemplifying the tendency to exaggerate his influence, falsely wrote in the *Los Angeles Times* that he was the club's executive director.[7] That came in 1997, during the club's titanic struggles over immigration policy, which we'll explore in Chapter Nine.

In 1979, frustrated that he could not persuade his ZPG colleagues to make reduced immigration a central goal, Tanton founded FAIR, the Federation for American Immigration Reform. Mimicking Ehrlich's effort to jolt the public into action, FAIR placed a full-page ad in the *Chicago Tribune* and other newspapers that combined a simple declarative sentence about immigration history with a provocative and pessimistic question about its future: "Our Grandparents Came to America To Escape Poverty and Despair. Will Our Children Want to Leave for The Same Reasons?"[8] Later, in an effort to encourage local and state governments to take action against illegal immigration, FAIR created the Immigration Reform Law Institute.

Tanton would have been more effective if he had maintained his focus on concerns about human numbers and environmental stewardship, which resonated powerfully with the public. But he became increasingly worried about the cultural ramifications of a particular kind of immigrant, the Mexicans, who represented by far the largest cohort of newcomers. Indeed, between 1970 and 2008, the Mexican-born population of the U.S. grew from 700,000 to some 12 million. In the 1980s, emigration from Central American countries torn by civil war, economic misery, and natural disaster also soared. Never before had immigration been so dominated by the speakers of one language. In 1983, as many observers worried that a Quebec-style separatist movement could form in the U.S., Tanton founded a group called U.S. English to oppose bilingualism, which he said was fine for an individual but bad for a country. Joining Tanton as co-founder was S.I. Hayakawa, a former Republican U.S. senator from California who had declared on the Senate floor, "When people speak one language they become as one; they become a society."[9]

In the 1980s, the immigration debate unfolded against a background of mounting cultural tensions. Multiculturalism emerged as a powerful movement for diversity and against what was called the oppression of the white patriarchy. Ethnic and racial identity groups became more assertive in their conviction that assimilation was a form of cultural hegemony. Then came an episode that embarrassed Tanton and alienated many who had shared his fundamental concerns.

TANTON'S TROUBLING AND TROUBLESOME MEMO

In 1988, just before Arizona voters approved a ballot proposition that U.S. English had advanced to make English the state's official language, the *Arizona Republic* published a memo that Tanton had written two years earlier, as Congress held heated debates over the Immigration Reform and Control Act that it would pass late in the year. Tanton's memo made vivid his unease about Mexican immigration.

Here are the excerpts that received the most attention:

ON THE POLITICAL IMPLICATIONS OF DEMOGRAPHIC CHANGE: *"As whites see their power and control over their*

> *lives declining, will they simply go quietly into the night? Or will there be an explosion?"*

> **ON CULTURAL INFLUENCES:** *"Will Latin-American migrants bring with them the tradition of the mordida (bribery), the lack of involvement in public affairs, etc.?... Will blacks be able to improve (or even maintain) their position in the face of the Latin onslaught?"*

> **ON THE LATINO BIRTHRATE:** *"Perhaps this is the first instance in which those with their pants up are going to get caught by those with their pants down."*

Tanton later said he had been provocative in order to stimulate discussion within a small circle of colleagues and that he intended the memo to remain confidential. That was foolish on both counts. The *Republic's* headline concisely stated how the memo had provoked outrage and made Tanton the story; it read, "'English' Advocate Assailed, Proposition Foes Call Memo Racist."[10]

Publication of Tanton's provocative ruminations brought a storm of condemnation. Tanton was condemned as racist, anti-Hispanic, anti-immigrant, and anti-Catholic. Opponents of U.S. English labeled it "the Nazi memo." Former Tanton allies renounced him, including Linda Chavez, a prominent member of the U.S. English advisory board who had joined because she believed that English fluency was essential to Hispanics' successful integration in American life. She denounced the memo as "repugnant" and "anti-Hispanic" as she announced her resignation.[11] Journalist Walter Cronkite, one of the most admired men in the United States, also left the board.

Tanton's memo was an embarrassment, not just to him but also to those who had worked with him. It betrayed both his cultural tone-deafness and his political naïveté. As the criticism of his memo mounted, he himself resigned, lamenting that the discussion of U.S. English had "come to center more around me in the last week or 10 days."[12] Tanton resigned in embarrassment and as an embarrassment to the restrictionist movement, which found it difficult to get a fair hearing amid the din of anti-Tanton outrage.

In fairness, it is important to note that Tanton, however awkwardly and intemperately, was expressing concerns that should be part of any rigorous discussion of immigration. He raised issues that had long been discussed by writers who were known for their sympathy for Latino immigrants but who were undeterred by the strictures of political correctness.

For example, in 2001, Earl Shorris, a noted humanitarian, author, and student of Latino history and culture, warned that although the Latino middle class would grow with immigration, many migrants "will transport the woes of the old country to the United States. The real tragedy, however, is that failure produces failure and the multiplier effect of dropouts marrying dropouts and producing children who will drop out promises a 21st-century Latino underclass of enormous size."[13]

In 2002, Sam Quinones, the acclaimed *Los Angeles Times* reporter who chronicles the lives of Mexican immigrants with respect and empathy, found good reason to criticize some aspects of Mexican culture. "Little about Mexican politics and economics is worth transplanting," Quinones wrote. "Political and economic traditions in Mexico keep poor people poor and reward the rich. Mexican immigrant assimilation is necessary to keep these nasty traditions at bay and for the United States to continue being the kind of place Mexicans wanted to emigrate to in the first place."[14]

In 2007, writer Ashley Pettus, who would go on to establish a foundation to help marginalized people in the Third World, had this observation about immigration in *Harvard* magazine: "Will the current tide of poor, low-skilled Hispanic labor migrants (legal or not) gradually blend into the American mainstream like their European predecessors? Or will they remain a growing but segregated population, marginalized by race, class, language, and culture?"[15]

Tanton's fretful comments on Latino immigration lacked the empathetic grace notes with which writers like Sam Quinones write about immigrants. So he was pilloried for his blunt indiscretions. He would acknowledge the gratuitous negativity of his infamous memo. He particularly lamented the pants-down crack as "a throw-away line I should have thrown away."[16] How ironic it is that a man who was so acute in his perception of the disorder and instability that can result from uncontrolled immigration was himself a threat to the movement that advocated immigration limits.

Tanton had revealed the shadowy side of his ideology. It loomed even larger with the disclosure that FAIR had received $1.2 million from the Pioneer Fund, which was known for funding research into theories of genetically based inferiority or superiority. Tanton protested that FAIR had used the money only for general operations and that many university-based scholars had also received money from the fund. But reputational damage had been done. Immigrant-rights advocates, their guns loaded with ammunition from the Southern Poverty Law Center, spread the misinformation that Tanton dominated the restrictionist movement long after he had faded into the background. I have seen no Tanton influence during my decade at the Center for Immigration Studies. He has attended none of our meetings, nor has he even visited our office. If CIS embraced his nativist, arguably white nationalist views, I would not have come to work at CIS. After taking the job, I told my wife that I would have to resign if CIS worked with racists at the fringe of restrictionism. I have never had to face that circumstance. Moreover, CIS has supported both my objective, journalistic research and my relatively liberal position in support of another IRCA-style amnesty, as long as this time the enforcement side of the deal is credible. That would require immigrant-rights advocates to acknowledge the need for limits and commit themselves to enforcing those limits.

HEIDI BEIRICH'S BACTERIA HYSTERIA

I have sometimes thought of putting together a collection of Heidi Beirich's absurd attacks on Tanton. If I did, the centerpiece would be the red alert she issued after reading a 1997 profile of Tanton in the *Detroit Free Press*. Here is the passage that summoned the outrage of the always-primed-for-outrage Beirich:

> *In his characteristically blunt manner, Tanton explained his obsession with immigration, likening the flood of humanity to America's shores over the past 400 years to a plate of bacteria in a medical lab. "You put a bug in there and it starts growing and gets bigger and bigger and bigger. And it grows until it finally fills the whole plate," Tanton said. "It uses up the medium. And then maybe it crashes and dies."*[17]

Tanton's analogy was a provocative means to sound the alarm about relentless demographic expansion since the days of Columbus. It was a discussion of a process, known as exponential doubling, that had long been described by the late University of Colorado physics professor Albert Bartlett to dramatize the environmental dangers posed by the rapid growth of the U.S. population. It was a lecture-hall hyperbole, an exaggeration for effect. For Heidi Beirich, it was an outrage, grotesque and intolerable. She saw it as a bigoted rant, a racist affront that that demanded repudiation. Beirich declared in anguish that Tanton "*has compared immigrants to bacteria!*"[18] The phrase became a slogan and a battle cry in the fight for unchecked immigration. Google Tanton's name together with "compared immigrants to bacteria" and you'll see what vacuous indignation Heidi and her friends at the National Council of La Raza, and America's Voice have wrought.

TANTON'S DUBIOUS FRIENDS

The description of Tanton as the Dr. Evil of immigration policy is a grotesque distortion. But Tanton has no one to blame but himself for the criticism he has drawn for his dalliances with some extremist figures on the nativist right. Consider Tanton's work on behalf of Sam Francis, who in 1995 was sacked from his job as a columnist at the *Washington Times*. Francis lost that position after a series of offenses. They included a speech in which he said whites "must reassert our identity and our solidarity, and we must do so in explicitly racial terms through the articulation of a racial consciousness as whites."[19] He also mocked Southern Baptists who declared that slavery was a sin.

Undeterred by Francis' blatant white nationalism, Tanton suggested FAIR hire Francis to be an editor. Fortunately, FAIR had the good sense to reject that idea. But the episode illustrated that Tanton, who did so much to establish the framework for reasonable and responsible restrictionism, was a carpenter with a perverse attraction to termites.

Having failed to inflict Francis on FAIR, Tanton had his way in 1998 when he selected an editor for his quarterly journal, the *Social Contract Press*, whose mission is to examine "trends, events, and ideas that have an impact on America's delicate social fabric." His choice was a man named Wayne Lutton, who, like Sam Francis, was a talented writer with a doctorate and a preoccupation with what he saw as the impending doom of the white race because of a flood of immigration. In 2001, Lutton joined the editorial board of the newspaper published by the Council of White Citizens. That notorious group was an offshoot of the White Citizens Council, which long resisted desegregation in the South. To put it mildly, this is not a connection that can be useful to anyone who wants to play a constructive role in the national immigration dialogue.

When I wrote a report criticizing Tanton's blunders and excesses, his allies at the white nationalist blog VDARE.com—(named for Virginia Dare, the first English child born in North America)—accused me and the Center for Immigration Studies of "undermining the patriotic struggle."[20] This perverse notion of patriotism is a big problem at the fringes of contemporary restrictionism. It has been the material for more broad-brush smears of those of us whose efforts to restrict immigration have nothing to do with repugnant notions of white identity and everything to do with our conviction that for immigration to be successful it must be limited.

FAIR'S FIRST EXECUTIVE DIRECTOR GETS IT RIGHT

One of the best decisions Tanton ever made was his choice of Roger Conner to be FAIR's first executive director. Conner had the humanitarian qualities, political sophistication, and broad-based appeal that Tanton lacked. As a young graduate of the University of Michigan Law School, Conner had helped win passage of the 'state's first environmental protection law. He also persuaded the state's Supreme Court to issue a permanent injunction against oil drilling in the Pigeon River Country Wilderness. The son of a short-order cook, Conner was a lifelong liberal who understood the struggles of the working class. As he told an audience at Washington's Howard University in 1983, "if the immigrants coming in were competing for jobs with architects, lawyers and engineers, the immigration problem would have been solved a long time ago."[21]

Nearly three decades later, when he was teaching at Vanderbilt Law School, Conner regretted that he had not restrained Tanton's indiscretions. He said Tanton's commitment to FAIR's mission and the depth of his decency and generosity had been "so profound that the people around him disregarded things that we should have called him on."[22]

Tanton failed to understand the dangers of his big-tent philosophy that welcomed even avowed white nationalists. "You have to avoid even the appearance of bigotry," Conner told me. A moment later he added, "The risk of a big-tent philosophy was, and is, that if you don't explicitly exclude the fringe groups from your tent, you can ruin it for the majority of Americans—those of us who are just as opposed to intolerance or racism as we are to excessive immigration."

In contrast to the SPLC's depiction of Tanton as "the puppeteer," Conner describes him as the immigration restriction movement's Johnny Appleseed, a man who sowed organizational seeds and moved on to the next idea. "He would talk to anybody, from rich people to small donors, from labor groups to environmentalists, from liberals to conservatives, and he tried to talk their language about why immigration reduction should fit into their particular agenda," Conner said. "Like a Johnny Appleseed of public policy, his aim was to get people to plant trees and join the debate."

STEPHEN COLBERT AND THE IDEOLOGY OF LATE-NIGHT COMEDY

Four decades after Johnny Carson's concern about overpopulation promoted the movement called Zero Population Growth, Comedy Central's Stephen Colbert cited the work of the SPLC to mock John Tanton and the Center for Immigration Studies. His late-night show in April of 2012 was painful for me because I had long enjoyed the zany genius of his portrayal of a right-wing television news anchorman.

I was a fan of Colbert's despite the excesses of his open-borders liberalism. I admired his empathy for the undocumented. I laughed when his character proclaimed there could be only one response to illegal immigration: "Wall, moat filled with flames, fire-proof alligators." I loved the silliness of his faux endorsement of restrictionism with his proclamation that the U.S. is "an unwavering beacon of limitless freedom, which people the world over see and say, 'I want to live there. I want to be an American.' That's why we must erect a 40-foot-high wall."

But Colbert lost me on the night in April of 2012 when he resorted to the cheapest of all the rhetorical assaults. He cited a CIS report on the connection between immigration and population growth to highlight the CIS connection to John Tanton and to insinuate that CIS was an ally of the Ku Klux Klan.

The report was solid work. It written by Steven Camarota, the CIS director of research, and Leon Kolankiewicz, an environmental scientist who had been a Peace Corps volunteer in Honduras and married a Honduran woman with whom he had two sons. They made the case that "future levels of immigration will have a significant impact on efforts to reduce global CO2 emissions."[23] They explained that once immigrants adopt American patterns of consumption their carbon footprint becomes much larger than it was in their native countries. Their conclusion was scientifically undisputable. But to Stephen Colbert it was fair game for ridicule because—at least for the purposes of The Colbert Report—it emitted the acrid odor of a burning cross.

With his trademark wink-wink, double entendre, Colbert issued a proclamation: "Lefty environmentalists, you can trust this study because it came from the Center for Immigration Studies, which was founded by John Tanton, who, according to the Southern Poverty Law Center, has for decades been at the heart of the white nationalist scene and has met with leading white supremacists. Now, I'm sure he's just pressuring the Klan to make their cross burnings carbon neutral."

It was vintage Colbert. It was a manic, gleeful assault that turned a complex situation upside down. His shtick delighted the studio audience by flashing the screen with a rhetorical coup de grace, mocking the CIS concern about carbon as "Ku Klux Konservation."

As I took it all in at home, I felt sick to my stomach. I was used to the tiresome attacks of the SPLC, the CNC, and their allies. But this was character assassination played for laughs, and it was a mockery of concern about immigration's undeniable connection to population growth and environmental damage.

The bitter taste of that moment has lingered in my memory. I never again looked at Colbert with the same admiration for his comedic gifts. Now I saw him as guilty of a corrosive cheap shot. That's why 1 reacted reflexively two years later when the receptionist in our office called out that someone from The Colbert Report was on the phone and wanted to talk to Mark Krikorian, our executive director. I jumped up and sprinted to Mark's office as he was about to pick up the phone. "You know this isn't about a real conversation, right?" I said. "You know this is all about mockery and asking how it feels to be pals with the KKK."

In 2017, Caitlin Flanagan—without specifically referring to the Colbert hit piece—made the case that such raucous displays of liberal bias had become so commonplace on late-night television that they antagonized conservatives across the country. Writing in the *Atlantic,* she argued that late-night comedy hosts had piled on so much ridicule that they seemed to be on the same team as the journalists who despised Donald Trump as a hack whose appeal was limited to the ignorant and resentful. Flanagan opined that after the election "one had to wonder whether some part of [Trump's] ground game had been conducted night after night after night on television." She said that when Republicans see the incessant barrage of mockery from such hosts as Colbert, Samantha Bee, Jimmy Kimmel and Seth Meyers, "they don't just see a handful of comics mocking them.... they see exactly what Donald Trump has taught them: that the entire media landscape loathes them, their values, their family, and their religion."

Flanagan's story was headlined "How Late-Night Comedy Fueled the Rise of Trump."[24]

Chapter 6:
The "Intelligence Project" of the Southern Poverty Law Center

McCarthyism as a Business Model

> **The people who will give big money through the mail are either on the far right or the far left. They're true believers. You can't fire them up with a middle-of-the-road cause or candidate. You've got to have someone who can arouse people."**
> —*SPLC founder Morris Dees*[1]

> **The Southern Poverty Law Center demonizes respectable political opponents as "hate groups"—and keeps its coffers bulging.**
> —City Journal, *2017*[2]

In early 2008, a year before the Center for Immigration Studies offered me the chance to pursue the investigative and explanatory reporting that the Internet-induced newspaper recession had made increasingly unaffordable, the National Council of La Raza announced a campaign to "Stop the Hate" in the national immigration debate. The centerpiece of the campaign was the Southern Poverty Law Center's designation of the Federation for American Immigration Reform as a "hate group." It was a bold move, placing FAIR on a black list occupied by such groups as the Ku Klux Klan and the American Nazi Party. It injected into the debate the tactics of McCarthyism, the use of dramatic, unsubstantiated charges to vilify FAIR so that it would be shunned by the media and denied participation in the national discussion.

As someone who believes that rigorous and civil discussion is vital to our democracy, I had been concerned about the sudden intensification of hostilities. I wanted to know how it had come about. That meant looking into the work of the Montgomery, Ala.-based SPLC.

My knowledge of the SPLC was sketchy at the time. I knew it had done important work in the 1970s and 1980s against the Ku Klux Klan, winning lawsuits that drove several groups of white-hooded fanatics into bankruptcy. Its lawyers also won a court order requiring Alabama State Troopers to hire blacks and in a separate case forced the Montgomery YMCA to integrate. I admired these accomplishments. But I was uneasy about the contradiction between the attack on FAIR and the SPLC's claim to be a force for tolerance and understanding in our pluralistic society.

The first stop on my trail of research into the SPLC was a 2000 story in *Harper's* written by Ken Silverstein, an old friend of mine and one of the best investigative reporters in the country.[3] Silverstein reported that the SPLC had taken a cynical turn.

"Today, the SPLC spends most of its time—and money—on a relentless fund-raising campaign, peddling memberships in the church of tolerance with all the zeal of a circuit rider passing the collection plate." Turning his attention to SPLC founder Morris Dees, a hero to many, Silverstein quoted a former Dees associate who compared him to a disgraced pair of hustling television evangelists, calling him "the Jim and Tammy Faye Bakker of the civil rights movement." Citing SPLC reports to the IRS on its $44 million income from contributions and investments in 2000, Silverstein said the center had become: "one of the most profitable charities in the country." Even more surprising than this account of the SPLC's finances was Silverstein's conclusion that the center had become a racket engaged in the systematic bilking of its supporters. Wrote Silverstein:

> *The Ku Klux Klan, the SPLC's most lucrative nemesis, has shrunk from 4 million members in the 1920s to an estimated 2,000 today. But news of the declining Klan does not make for inclining donations to Morris Dees and Co., which is why the SPLC honors nearly every nationally covered "hate crime" with direct-mail alarums full of nightmarish invocations of "armed Klan paramilitary forces" and "violent neo-Nazi extremists."*

Silverstein's story, published in a prominent national magazine, was the most detailed in a string of exposes going back to the early 1990s. For me, it foreshadowed the cynicism that I discovered when I investigated "We Can Stop the Hate" campaign, which received its most potent weaponry from Heidi Beirich and Mark Potok of the SPLC's Intelligence Project.

FAILED REFORM SETS THE STAGE

The backstory for the "We Can Stop the Hate" campaign was as the 2007 defeat of the reform legislation sponsored by a bipartisan pair of Senate heavyweights, Massachusetts Democrat Edward Kennedy and Arizona Republican John McCain. The bill had several key components. First, like the 1986 immigration reform, it coupled legalization (a.k.a. amnesty) with a plan to stop future illegal immigration at the worksite. It also included a program for "temporary workers" that was aimed at winning the support of employers. And it included a point system along the lines of the one used in Canada to select immigrants.

The McCain-Kennedy bill was defeated because it had opponents across the political spectrum. Influential labor unions opposed the temporary worker program as a corporate ploy to drive down wages. Restrictionists on the pro-labor left and the social-conservative right complained that amnesty would reward illegality, punish those who worked within the system, and repeat the worksite failure of the 1986 act. Immigration activists said the point system was elitist and discriminated against the unskilled poor. An analysis in Real Clear Politics concluded that the bill was "profoundly out of step with public opinion," as indicated by a Rasmussen poll showing that by a margin of more than two-to-one Americans said it was a higher priority to gain control of the nation's borders than to provide legal status to illegal immigrants and that 75 percent said it was very important to "improve border enforcement and end illegal immigration."

The most intense criticism came from talk radio. Rush Limbaugh led the assault. He warned that millions of legalized immigrants, along with the relatives who would eventually come to join them, would add so many liberal voters that conservatives would be swamped. Limbaugh dubbed the bill *The Comprehensive Destroy the Republican Party Act.* Sen. Trent Lott, a Republican from Mississippi who endorsed the bill, complained. "Talk radio is running the country." That prompted the accusation from Limbaugh that some Republicans had made common cause with Democrats against the will of the people. "This amnesty bill...is a battle between Washington and the people, and they know it," Limbaugh said. "So, you got a Republican talking about talk radio the way liberals talk about talk radio." It was an early taste of populist disillusionment with the Republican establishment. Lott wouldn't have to face it much longer. He was about to become a lobbyist, co-founding a firm that would become "one of the top 20 lobbying shops" in Washington, according to the Center for Responsive Politics.[4]

What killed the immigration reform bill was not a straight up-or-down vote on its merits. Rather, the Senate voted 54–46 not to cut off debate and move to a vote on the bill. While Republicans provided most of the resistance, they were joined by nearly a third of the Democrats, the fading remnant of liberals who believed restriction was necessary to protect American workers. This group was joined by Vermont Independent Sen. Bernie Sanders, who thundered against the guest worker plan as a scheme to depress wages and boost corporate profits. Said Sanders, "At a time when millions of Americans are working longer hours for low wages and have seen real cuts in their wages and benefits, this legislation would, over a period of years, bring millions of low-wage workers from other countries into the United States."[5]

THE NCLR-SPLC ALLIANCE

Cecilia Muñoz, the National Council of La Raza's chief immigration lobbyist, was crestfallen at the collapse of the reform bill. She pointed to "a wave of hate" from talk radio and called for a strategy to resist it. *Miami Herald* columnist Andres Oppenheimer urged La Raza to launch "an all-out campaign to expose anti-Latino bigots in the media, entertainment, and politics."[6] NCLR executive director Janet Murguia agreed. "We do need to rethink our strategy," she said. "There is no question about it." The three influential Latinos made no mention of the Federation for American Immigration Reform. But FAIR would soon become the principal target of the NCLR's new strategy, at the suggestion of the the SPLC's Potok and Beirich.

In July of 2007, less than a month after the reform bill fizzled in the Senate, the SPLC launched the Hatewatch Blog, which according to Beirich would "share tantalizing tidbits and serious commentary about the world of hate." Hatewatch would operate in the tradition of the SPLC's Klanwatch, which had long monitored the activities of the notorious Ku Klux Klan. Potok and Beirich wanted to turn their guns on the Federation for American Immigration Reform.

Potok, the son of a Holocaust survivor, had specialized in covering extremist groups as a reporter for *USA Today* before moving to the SPLC in 1997. He was employed there for 20 years, becoming editor of The Intelligence Project. In a blunt acknowledgement of the strategy of designating hate groups he said, "Our purpose is to destroy them or to politically nullify them."[7]

In the fraught political environment around immigration, the job of self-appointment hate-group monitor was fraught with risk and moral hazards. Zealous activists seeking attention and financial support could designate opposing views as hate speech and extend the insult by naming those who expressed them as hate groups. That was a risk to which both Potok and Beirich were inclined by ideology and temperament.

Beirich, a graduate of Berkeley, completed doctoral work at Purdue, where she studied white nationalism and wrote her dissertation about Spain's attempt to purge its judicial system of the fascist legacy of Francisco Franco. She is a postmodern militant, a cultural Marxist committed to the proposition that immigration restriction is a system of oppression, a social construct designed to oppress minorities. She saw the problem as inherent in American political and social structures. Expressing a conviction that she shared with many immigration activists, she told ABC news, "I think sometimes Americans forget that this country was founded on white supremacy."

I drew on a variety of sources, both human and documentary, to assemble the story of Beirich's and Potok's work targeting FAIR. In October of 2007, as immigration activist groups assessed the fallout from the failure of the Senate reform bill, they traveled to Washington for a meeting at the offices of the Center for American Progress, a liberal think tank closely aligned with the Democratic Party. CAP fellow Henry Fernandez was assembling a task force that included the National Council of La Raza, the Mexican American Legal Defense and Education Fund, and the National Immigration Forum.

The group's official name was "The Anti-Hate Table." Among themselves they shortened it to "The Hate Table." Their job, as their funders at the Open Society Institute would explain, was to be "focused on anti-immigrant hate rhetoric and violence."[8] Additional funding came from the New York-based Hagedorn Foundation, which said it would be used to "undermine the effectiveness of and push back against the organizations injecting hate into public, anti-immigrant discourse."[9]

The "Anti-Hate Table," with its heroic posture of righteous resistance to bigotry, had a magnetic appeal for the program officers at liberal foundations. But how should it proceed? What would be its strategy? Talk radio was too powerful to take on. The big hitters—Limbaugh, Savage, Hannity, Glenn Beck—were capable of instantaneous and overwhelming response on hundreds of radio stations around the country. Potok and Beirich proposed a strategy to target the Federation for American Immigration Reform. By labeling FAIR as a hate group and then mounting a campaign to spread the word, they said, they could badly damage FAIR. "We'll take them out," they promised, according to someone with direct knowledge of the discussion. They were received like heroes.

One of the group's first challenges was a plausibility problem. Since they had long criticized FAIR without applying the incendiary "hate group" label, they needed something new to justify tagging FAIR with their version of the Scarlet Letter. So Potok cooked up a cover story. He said that after learning that FAIR officials had met with a right-wing group from Belgium, he "decided to take another look at FAIR." And then, behold: "When our work was done, it was obvious that FAIR qualified as a hate group."

This was a laughable ruse. The single FAIR official at the meeting in question was Jack Martin, a communications officer who met with the Belgians when they were in Washington It was the sort of low-level meeting Martin had routinely held during his career in the State Department. "I've met with visitors from dozens of foreign countries who are traveling here," Martin told me. "The fact that I met with them does not mean I agree with their politics. I've met with officials from Communist China, and that doesn't mean I'm a communist."

Nor is Martin, who was stationed in Mexico, a nativist. He and his wife adopted a Mexican child, not a common move for nativists or haters. But Martin's Belgian connection was good enough for the SPLC's hate police. In December 2007, the Hatewatch blog announced that the SPLC had decided that FAIR was a hate group. The news was topped with the grandiose headline: "FAIR: Crossing the Rubicon of Hate." Potok was at least candid in acknowledging the motivation for the designation, "What we are hoping very much to accomplish is to marginalize FAIR," he announced. "We don't think they should be a part of the mainstream media."

In the following months, through the dark magic of guilt by association, the SPLC set out to spread the reputational stain to the Center for Immigration Studies, NumbersUSA, and other restrictionists. The malice of the attack surprised even some immigrant-rights activists. One of them was Tom Barry, director of the TransBorder Project at the Center for International Policy. Barry was a widely respected liberal journalist. He would be a finalist for a 2010 National Magazine Award for his investigation of the burgeoning system of private prisons in which federal authorities detained illegal immigrants. Barry opposed restrictionists but believed they should be heard under the norms of democratic civility. He wrote that by slapping the hate-group label on FAIR, the SPLC had "provided highly explosive ammunition for the character assassination campaign."

Said Barry, who opposed the policies of restrictionist groups but was alarmed at the blatant attempt to muzzle them, "Trying to stick a label of 'extremist' on institutes that have massive memberships, good relations with the media, and good standing on the Hill is a measure of how desperate and isolated the pro-immigration forces that have embraced this strategy really are."

THE ASSAULT BEGINS

Armed with the just-in-time decree from Alabama, the National Council of La Raza made it the centerpiece of a national "We Can Stop the Hate" campaign. On CNN, NCLR executive director Janet Murguia presented the smear as a smoking gun. The SPLC had made it official, she said, "FAIR is a known, documented hate group!"[10]

As the campaign unfolded over a period of months, it placed full-page ads in *Politico* and *Roll Call*, newspapers directed at Washington's political class.[11] "The Federation for American Immigration Reform (FAIR) Is Designated a HATE GROUP by the Southern Poverty Law

Center," said one ad, using bright red boldface to highlight "FAIR" and "HATE GROUP." It added, "Extremist groups, like FAIR, shouldn't write immigration policy." It urged supporters to take the message to the House and Senate: "Tell Congress, Don't Meet with FAIR." The website of America's Voice, one of the Anti-Hate Table partners, took note of other residents of the netherworld to which FAIR had been banished. "Other SPLC hate groups include: The Ku Klux Klan, the American Nazi Party, and the Aryan Nations."

Beirch and Potok presented themselves as independent watchdogs, trustworthy arbiters of hate and intolerance. They even called themselves journalists. But the website of the "We Can Stop the Hate" campaign revealed that they were part of the team. It listed the SPLC as one of the campaign's "allies," a group that also included the highly partisan Media Matters for America, the Anti-Defamation League, and the Leadership Conference for Civil Rights, and, of course, the Center for American Progress, which is essentially an arm of the Democratic Party.[12]

Despite that acknowledgment in the small-print of the website, Potok and Beirich had their way with the credulous reporters on the immigration beat. In style and substance the SPLC duo were Jacobins, ruthless and radical, convinced of the righteousness of their brand of hate. But they had claimed the mantle of civil rights crusaders, and reporters went along with the ruse. They wrote many stories about the SPLC's designation of FAIR. Not one examined Potok's justification for the designation. Not one identified the SPLC as an ally of the campaign to attack FAIR. The *Washington Post* described the center as "an independent group based in Montgomery, Ala., that monitors racist organizations." Here is a representative sample of other descriptions of the SPLC[13]:

- "a civil rights organization" —*The Des Moines Register*[14]
- "a civil rights group based in Montgomery, Ala., with a history of monitoring racist organizations" —*Cox News Service.*[15]

- "a group that tracks hate crimes nationwide." —*Arizona Daily Star*[16]
- "a Montgomery, Ala.,-based civil rights group that monitors extremist activity" —*Nashville Tennessean*[17]
- "a watchdog group" —AP story in *San Jose Mercury News, Chicago Tribune, Richmond Times, Lexington Herald Leader, and Grand Rapids Press*[18]

Most of the reporting added no context beyond a denial by FAIR, which found itself in the awkward position of the man who is asked if he has stopped beating his wife. The stories simply reported that FAIR denied the allegations. A notable exception was the work of David Crary, a national writer for the Associated Press. Crary noted that the SPLC had critics who "contend that the periodic reports on hate groups exaggerate the threat to public safety and inflate the total by including entities that are little more than websites or online chat rooms."[19] He also noted that FAIR's position is that immigration policy should reflect "no favoritism toward or discrimination against any person on the basis of race, color, or creed."

THE MARKETING GENIUS OF MORRIS DEES

The credulous reporting on the SPLC, characteristic of reporters on the immigration and civil rights beats, had long been essential to the success of the SPLC's charismatic flimflam man, Morris Dees. So the story of Morris Dees is worth a serious look.

Dees was born in rural Alabama in 1936. From the time he was a boy he dreamed of accumulating great wealth. In the 1960s, as a student at the University of Alabama, he built a small fortune by obtaining the birthdates of fellow students and writing letters to their parents, offering to deliver a freshly baked cake for the big day. "I learned to write sales copy, to design an offer, and to mail at the most opportune time," Dees would recall.[20] Dees and his business partner used direct-mail marketing to pitch everything from cookbooks to tractor cushions. They eventually sold their company for $6 million.

Dees founded the SPLC in 1971 and began doing admirable work the cause of civil rights. Dees built a national reputation with the innovative tactic of claiming that KKK groups should be held financially responsible for the violent acts of their members. For work such as this, Dees won numerous awards and honorary university degrees. He had tremendous success as a fundraiser for George McGovern, the Democratic candidate for president in 1972. The magic of his fundraising letters lay in the sense of intimacy and urgency that they stirred. Dees' prose reflected his Baptist roots. "Like the evangelist who came to our summer revivals, I asked in McGovern's name for the reader to 'join hands with me now.... I believe this is a time to heal,'" he wrote.[21] It was a call to join a sacred cause. To the astonishment of the Democratic Party, it brought a windfall to McGovern, who was so grateful that he gave Dees the mailing list of his nearly 700,000 donors. They soon began receiving appeals to support the SPLC.

Dees understood that in politics, money is attracted to passion and partisanship. He liked candidates he could paint in bold ideological colors. For that reason, he was initially reluctant to take the job of chief fundraiser for Jimmy Carter's 1976 presidential campaign. He worried that Carter was too moderate to attract donors. "Jimmy's a political animal—he backs down on the issues," Dees said. "You can't raise money through the mail for just any candidate. You've got to have a candidate who's way out on the extremes—a Reagan, a Wallace, a McGovern, a Goldwater. The people who will give big money through the mail are either on the far right or the far left. They're true believers. You can't fire them up with a middle-of-the-road cause or candidate. You've got to have someone who can arouse people."[22]

That insight into human nature has been central to the communications strategy of the SPLC. Three decades later, Beirich and Potok would take it to the Anti-Hate Table. What is perhaps most remarkable is that it worked for so long, despite the accumulating evidence of its hypocrisy and excess.

THE SPLC'S HOMETOWN PAPER TAKES A HARD LOOK

Until the early 1990s, the SPLC and the swashbuckling Dees basked in the admiration of reporters at his hometown paper, the *Montgomery Advertiser*. Journalists there had formed friendships with liked-minded idealists on the SPLC staff. "There aren't a lot of young liberals in Montgomery, as you might imagine, and those are the people we associated with," said Jim Tharpe, the paper's managing editor. He said *Advertiser* reporters had been "essentially boosters for the SPLC; we parroted their press releases." But then, according to Tharpe, disillusioned former SPLC staffers told reporters, "You guys really ought to look at this place, something's just not right there."[23]

In 1994, the *Advertiser* published an investigative series titled "Rising Fortunes: Morris Dees and the Southern Poverty Law Center."[24] Reporter Dan Morse found that the real-life Dees was less admirable than the figure portrayed by actor Corbin Bensen in the film "Line of Fire." Hollywood, Morse wrote, had portrayed Dees as "a fearless crusader who uses the courtroom to do what the FBI and no one else can—stop hate groups." But former friends and associates of Dees told a different story. "Some who have worked with Dees call him phony, the 'television evangelist' of civil rights who misleads donors into thinking the center desperately needs their money," Morse wrote. "Others acknowledge his long list of accomplishments but call him vindictive and two-faced, a man obsessed with grooming his image." One of the most damning assessments came from Millard Fuller, Dees's former business partner, who had gone on to found Habitat for Humanity. "He leaves a trail of bodies behind him, of broken relationships," Fuller said. "It's just how he treats people."[25]

An *Advertiser* editorial that accompanied the investigative series asserted that while the KKK "deserves the scorn of all reasonable people," Dees was continuing to publicize his work against it "not because the Klan is a major threat, but because it plays well with liberal donors."[26] Speaking on the theme of opportunism posing as idealism, Gloria Browne, a black woman and a former lawyer at the SPLC, told the newspaper, "The market is still wide open for the product, which is black pain and white guilt."[27]

The series was impressive investigative journalism. It was named as a finalist for a Pulitzer Prize. Then Dees called on George McGovern and other political friends to write letters to the Pulitzer board on his behalf and against the *Advertiser*. Bill Kovach, one of the country's most esteemed journalists and former curator of the Nieman journalism foundation at Harvard, said he believed that the letter-writing campaign was unprecedented in the history of the Pulitzers. The *Advertiser* did not win the award.

At a conference hosted by Harvard's Nieman Foundation for Journalism, Jim Tharpe, the *Advertiser*'s managing editor when the series was published, said the series got scant notice beyond its circulation area. "The story really didn't get out of Montgomery, and that's a real problem. The center's donors are not in Montgomery; the center's donors are in the Northeast and on the West Coast. So the story pretty much was contained in Montgomery where it got a shrug-of-the-shoulders reaction. We really didn't get much reaction at all, I'm sad to say."

THE PROGRESSIVE MAGAZINE DESCRIBES THE DEES FORMULA

One of the red flags that had drawn the *Advertiser's* attention was the 1988 article in *The Progressive* magazine titled "How Morris Dees Got Rich Fighting the Klan."[28] It reported on Dees's fundraising success with wealthy Jewish donors on the East and West Coasts. Of course, many Jews, mindful of Torah admonitions to pursue justice and of centuries of persecution, are eager to support noble-sounding causes. In his mailings to zip codes that had many Jewish residents, Dees signed his pleas with his middle name—Seligman—which he had received in honor of a family friend, but which was intended to suggest (non-existent) Jewish heritage. Attorney Tom Turnipseed, a former Dees associate, told Cox News Service, "Morris loves to raise money. Some of his gimmicks are just so transparent, but they're good."[29] Turnipseed described a Dees fundraising letter whose return envelope carried "about six different stamps." The purpose of the ruse was to present the appearance of an organization struggling to keep going. As Turnipseed noted: "It was like they had to cobble them all together to come up with 35 cents."[30]

In an interview, Ray Jenkins, a journalist who worked many years at the *Advertiser* and later became an editor at the *Baltimore Sun*, told me his assessment of the SPLC under Dees. "They've done some good work," he said. "It's just that Dees' ego is so smarmy that it gets all over you and you can't abide him." Jenkins said he has an indelible memory of Dees parking his Rolls Royce at a spot reserved for him at the SPLC. It was such ostentation that prompted the comparison of Dees with notoriously extravagant television evangelists.[31]

While critics saw Dees as a cynic and hustler who posed as the real-life Atticus Finch, admirers paid little attention to his flaws. "How do you say something bad about a guy who sticks up for Jews and blacks?" asked Jesuit priest Raymond Schroth in an article for the *National Catholic Reporter*.[32] Schroth's answer—"With trepidation"—did not dissuade him from a negative assessment of the Dees modus operandi. "If the problem is nuanced, complicated...he provides a prism, based partly on fear, through which we can view the issue," Schroth wrote. "The Internet is out of control; hate groups are poisoning the World Wide Web. His Southern Poverty Law Center, with your help, will save you."

In 2001, writing in *The Nation*, JoAnn Wypijewski observed: "No one has been more assiduous in inflating the profile of [hate] groups than the millionaire huckster Morris Dees." Ripping the SPLC as "puffed-up crusaders," Wypijewski condensed the Dees strategy to this: "Hate sells; poor people don't."[33]

CASHING IN ON THE RISE OF TRUMP

Despite the periodic exposes, the SPLC continued to rake in millions from liberals in the thrall of Morris Dees. Every year it raised millions of dollars with direct-mail appeals signed by Dees. In its 2007 report to the IRS as a tax-exempt, charitable organization, it showed contributions and grants totaling $32,398,000. By 2015 it had boosted that figure to $52 million. Its endowment grew from $34 million in 1990 to $319 million in 2017. Dees's total compensation as chief trial counsel was $406,000 in 2015. In its cult-like deification of Dees, the SPLC's public relations apparatus hailed Dees as a figure of uncommon dedication and saintly altruism, a fearless protector standing like a rock against the hateful hordes. The Winter 2008 issue of the *SPLC Report* was an eight-page tabloid. It included seven photographs of Morris Dees. It is the sort of idolatry that is hard to find outside North Korea. On December 15, 2009, donors received an email that began: "Spirits are unusually high today at the Southern Poverty Law Center—we're celebrating Morris's birthday....Please take a moment to honor him by sending a personalized birthday message along with a special tax-deductible gift to support his work."

Such cynicism notwithstanding, the SPLC continued to attract idealistic young activists who did admirable work, for example, their representation of immigrants whose illegal status has made them vulnerable to exploitation by employers. SPLC attorneys also deserve recognition for their work on behalf of persons seeking relief from deportation. But the acclaim for such efforts provided cover for the "hate group" hysteria of Beirich and Potok at The Intelligence Project. They received a pass from many reporters, who lack either the time or the inclination to look beneath the gleaming surface. But in recent years the organization's allure came under suspicion as hate-group strategy became increasingly flagrant and partisan. "They're hate activists," warned a 2013 essay in *Foreign Policy*. "There's nothing wrong with that—advocating against hate is a noble idea. But as activists, their research needs to be weighed more carefully by media outlets that cover their pronouncements."[34]

TARGETING THE CENTER FOR IMMIGRATION STUDIES

One of the most glaring journalistic failures to scrutinize the SPLC unfolded in early 2017, when Heidi Beirich announced that Hatewatch had designated the Center for Immigration Studies as a hate group. The breakdown was most evident in the work of two accomplished reporters, Joel Rose of NPR and Nicholas Kulish of the *New York Times*. Both reported the reputational assault on CIS as if it were the well-considered judgment of a responsible arbiter. Neither subjected it even to a rudimentary credibility check.

The slanted coverage was doubly painful for me. First, as a member of the CIS staff, I had skin in the game. Second, as a former reporter, I disliked the suspension of basic rules of journalistic fairness. But I understood that most of us reporters lean left. So I conducted a thought experiment, pondering how journalists would respond if a conservative group launched a campaign to disgrace a prominent rival on the left. If the attack were truly damaging, I concluded, reporters would demand evidence to support the charges. If the charges proved to be bogus, reporters would expose the sham. Then, depending on the importance of the issue, editorial writers might register outrage, and investigative reporters might check for patterns of similar distortions in the past.

I thought of a pertinent admonition from one of the heroes of modern journalism, the late Murray Marder of the *Washington Post*. In the 1950s Marder broke away from the pack of reporters who spread the hysterical red-baiting accusations of Sen. Joseph McCarthy. "The press can't simply report flatfooted a smearing accusation against someone's loyalty," said Marder. "The press should ask the accuser, 'What do you mean? What justification do you have?' That's real work, and it's called journalism."[35]

There was no such skepticism in the work of Joel Rose, despite NPR's commitment, spelled out in the *NPR Ethics Handbook*, to "rigorously challenge...the claims that we encounter" and to "take special care with news that might cause grief or damage reputations." Nor at the *New York Times*, whose mission is to present "all the news that's fit to print."

The Rose story, clocking in at precisely three and one-half minutes, might have worked as the introduction to a longer, rigorous report. But it was Rose's only crack at the controversy. Far from taking "special care," it was superficial and irresponsible.

As Rose introduced the SPLC's hate-group accusation, Beirich said of CIS, "Their ideas are rooted in racism." On the issue of the timing of the attack, Rose observed, "Heidi Beirich says that's because CIS puts out a weekly newsletter that links to articles the law center considers racist and anti-Semitic." Then Mark Krikorian defended CIS, saying its mission was "to make immigration skepticism intellectually respectable." And a spokesman for the open-borders Cato Institute said of Krikorian, "He's not an angry guy. He's fun to talk to."[36] Fair enough.

But Rose did nothing to examine the accuracy of Beirich's claims. This gaping hole in his story was a flagrant violation of NPR's commitment to rigorous reporting, which its Ethics Handbook makes explicit under the heading "These are the standards of our journalism."

In the *Times*, Nicholas Kulish, picked up Beirich's insinuation that CIS is anti-Semitic. He reported that the SPLC claimed the center had "circulated" articles by Holocaust deniers. He failed to note that Beirich did *not* claim to have found denialism or anti-Semitism in any report, analysis, congressional testimony, or other statement written or spoken by anyone at CIS. The means of circulation was a triviality, a weekly listserv that compiled links to dozens of articles from across the ideological spectrum.

Beirich's accusation was akin to a corrupt prosecutor indicting someone for complicity in a crime he had nothing to do with. Contrary to Kulish's reporting, Beirich had cited a single Holocaust denier. But his denial did not appear in the article that was included in the listserv. Compounding the deception, Beirich omitted the fact that the listserv that allegedly "promoted" hateful views included articles that *celebrated* immigration. One was titled "How Immigration Has Changed the World—for the Better." Another was written by economist Giovanni Peri, one of the most prominent academic advocates of expansive immigration. Yet another item was a *New York Times* editorial that condemned Donald Trump's claim that Mexican-American judge Gonzalo Curiel was biased against him because of his immigration policies. The editorial warned that the danger of Trump's allegations "is that they embolden Mr. Trump's many followers to feel, and act, the same way."

The same could be said about the SPLC's reckless accusations of hatred.

Beirich's most laughable bit of hate-mongering concerned CIS fellow John Miano, a former computer programmer who became a lawyer because he wanted to represent American workers improperly displaced by recipients of H-1B visas. An admirer of Ann Coulter, the aggressively conservative critic of U.S. immigration policy, Miano took advantage of an opportunity to meet her by attending a party hosted by Peter Brimelow, a former *Forbes* reporter and publisher of the white nationalist website VDARE. That was enough for the SPLC's kangaroo court to find him guilty of hating immigrants.

One Beirich complaint, about CIS's commissioning of work from a Harvard Ph.D. Jason Richwine, is not so easy to dismiss. During the 2013 debate over proposed comprehensive immigration reform, Richwine became a controversial figure for his 2009 Harvard dissertation, which examined IQ differences among races and suggested that because such differences could be predictive of socioeconomic success or failure they should be considered in the selection of immigrants. While the dissertation was good enough to pass muster at Harvard, and while Richwine has been unfairly attacked as a racist, I thought that the decision to affiliate with him was a gift to those who sought to discredit CIS. I still feel that way.

THE PRESS FINALLY TURNS A SKEPTICAL EYE ON THE SPLC

Despite the poor reporting by Blitzer and Rose, this time Beirich's stunt was a flop, at least in contrast with the big success she and Potok had with their 2007 attack on FAIR. This time the SPLC came in for some tough-minded reporting on a string of Beirich stunts, including the attack on CIS.

Here are three examples:

- *Politico*: "Is tough immigration control really a form of hate, or just part of the political conversation? Does rejecting a religion make you an extremist? At a time when the line between 'hate group' and mainstream politics is getting thinner and the need for productive civil discourse is growing more serious, fanning liberal fears, while a great opportunity for the SPLC, might be a problem for the nation."[37]
- *Real Clear Politics*: "Scaring the beejesus out of people requires new bogeymen, and lots of them. In recent years, you can find yourself on the SPLC's "hate map" if you haven't gotten fully aboard on gay marriage—or the Democratic Party's immigration views. In other words, the Dees' group classifies individuals and organizations as purveyors of 'hate' for holding the same view on marriage espoused by Barack Obama and Hillary Clinton until mid-2012."[38]
- *The Weekly Standard*: "Reporters should be ashamed of treating it [the SPLC] as an arbiter of respectability."

Prager University, the conservative, online media non-profit, produced a video that neatly turned the tables on Beirich and Dees. It labeled the SPLC "The 'Anti-Hate' Group That is a Hate Group."

I was relieved to see the powerful reporting and commentary, which included an incisive comment from Cornell professor William Jacobson: "For groups that do not threaten violence, the use of SPLC's 'hate group' or 'extremist' designation poses a danger of being exploited as an excuse to silence speech and to skew political debate. It taints not only the group or person, but others who associate with them. It has a very chilling impact on political debate...It seems that CIS has been placed on the hate-group list because SPLC disagrees with CIS's positions on immigration."

A year later, SPLC credibility continued to crumble, with word that it had agreed to pay $3.375 million to settle claims that it had maliciously defamed the Quilliam Foundation as "anti-Muslim extremists." Required by the settlement to acknowledge the shoddiness of its work, the SPLC said that upon further review, it realized that the foundation had made "valuable and important contributions to public discourse."

Anyone who gives fair consideration to the work of CIS—reports, analyses, investigative pieces, commentaries, and blog posts—can see that it makes valuable and important contributions to the immigration debate. It is a debate that our country needs. It should be conducted in a spirit of civility and decency that the SPLC has sought to destroy. Donald Trump's ugly xenophobia has made him their perfect foil. In the year after Trump was elected, the SPLC raised $132 million, swelling its endowment to $477 million. George and Amal Clooney donated $1 million in response to the violence in Charlottesville, Va., by white nationalists. "We are proud to support the Southern Poverty Law Center in its efforts to prevent violent extremism in the United States," the Clooneys said. I doubt they knew much about the SPLC's work beyond the fact—widely reported in the press—that it monitors hate groups. They were likely unaware of the SPLC's role in poisoning the immigration debate and aggravating the polarization of our country. The remarkable irony of the SPLC is that it is itself a hate group that amassed great wealth by posing as posing as defender of tolerance while screaming "Hater!" and "Racist" at those who called for immigration limits.

DAY OF RECKONING FOR DEES

In 2019 the myth was finally exploded by SPLC staff who accused Dees of sexual harassment and racist abuse that, they said, had been covered up for years. Dees was abruptly fired amidst a spate of revelations about his self-aggrandizement and hate-mongering. *The New Yorker* published an essay titled "The Reckoning of Morris Dees and the Southern Poverty Law Center." Its author was a former employee who came to believe that the center's motto should be: "The SPLC—making hate pay."

In the wake of Dees's firing and other resignations, and the spate of articles about his multiple abuses, the *New Yorker* article about the reckoning for him and the SPLC included an assessment from Yale law professor Stephen Bright, who had long cast a skeptical eye on the man and his organization. Said Bright, "These chickens took a very long flight before they came home to roost." So long that the SPLC wreaked terrible damage on the national immigration debate. Its efforts to muzzle responsible organizations that argued for reasonable limits on immigration helped to foment the backlash that led to the election of Donald Trump.

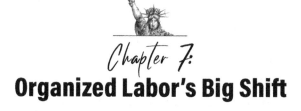

Chapter 7:

Organized Labor's Big Shift

Those who want to sharply curb illegal immigration include conservatives, liberals and most unions. Their just cause is badly damaged because their ranks also include disgusting racists. On the other side is...an equally odd combination of groups that usually fight one another: liberals, militant Latinos, conservatives, a few unions and, of course, employers who love the cheap labor of illegal immigrants.... Let's stop tempting illegal immigration and use counterfeit-proof work authorization cards to make the landmark 1986 immigration reform law succeed.

—*Harry Bernstein,* Los Angeles Times *labor columnist, 1992*[1]

Samuel Gompers, the founder of the American Federation of Labor, had no patience for advocates of open borders. "Those who favor unrestricted immigration care nothing for the people. They are simply desirous of flooding the country with unskilled as well as skilled labor of other lands for the purpose of breaking down American standards," Gompers said.[2] He made that populist declaration in 1918, but it could have come from nearly any American labor leader until the final years of the 20th century.

In the aftermath of World War I, the United States was shaken by religious intolerance—aimed primarily at Catholics and Jews—and fear that Bolsheviks and anarchists would destabilize the country by recruiting from the influx of European immigration. But business interests pushed for expansionist policies. According to historian John Higham, they wanted "a revival of heavy immigration, expecting it would beat down an inflated wage-scale and curb the increased power of the unions."[3] In 1922, the Imperial Wizard pro tempore of the resurgent Ku Klux Klan proclaimed a mission to build national solidarity by guarding "the interest of those whose forefathers established the nation."[4]

In 1924 Congress passed the Reed-Johnson Act, also known as the National Origins Act, to reduce the influx of Southern European Catholics and Eastern European Jews. The blatantly discriminatory restriction, followed by the Great Depression and World War II, drastically curbed the immigrant influx for decades. It also tightened the labor market, helping to set the stage for a robust labor movement and the rise of the blue-collar middle class. Some historians, with a nod to the national motto, believe that by diminishing the cultural tumult of *pluribus* it aided the consolidation of a cohesive *unum* that was further enhanced by the country's economic primacy following World War II.

During the presidency of Lyndon B. Johnson, labor's sway over Democrats was a major factor in the decision by Congress to terminate the bracero program, which since 1942 had brought millions of low-wage farm workers to the U.S. under an agreement with Mexico. The labor movement also took an aggressive stand against illegal immigration. At a congressional hearing in 1981, AFL-CIO secretary-treasurer Thomas Donahue called for employer sanctions legislation to stop the hiring of unauthorized immigrants. Said Donahue, "Federal law must provide effective penalties for employers who hire illegal aliens.... The quickest and the best way to stop illegal immigration is to stop giving jobs to illegal immigrants."[5]

As we saw in Chapter One, the early iterations of the Immigration Reform and Control Act were known as Simpson-Mazzoli, taking the names of the principal Senate and House sponsors. The legislation divided two key elements of the Democratic coalition: Hispanics who said the law would discriminate against them, and labor unions who said the lack of employer sanctions had harmed its members for years. In 1984, a presidential election year, a front-page story in the *New York Times* reported on the controversy under the headline, "Bill on Aliens a Divisive Issue for Democrats." The story said Walter Mondale, the frontrunner for the Democratic nomination, had expressed support for legislation sponsored by Rep. Ed Roybal to mandate stronger enforcement of labor laws in order to discourage employers from hiring unauthorized workers, who were vulnerable to exploitation. Meanwhile, the Reagan administration was showing diminished support for Simpson-Mazzoli while Reagan and the Republican Party were "ardently wooing Hispanic voters in the belief that many share Mr. Reagan's conservative views on national defense and social issues."[6]

IRCA was an effort to forge a compromise that would cut off the jobs magnet while providing amnesty to unauthorized immigrants who had been in the country for at least five years. But as we have seen, illegal immigration not only continued after IRCA, it gathered momentum and grew rapidly. As the 20th century neared its end, the influx was part of a combination of powerful forces, including globalization and automation, that meant trouble for organized labor. By 1990, only 14 percent of the workforce was unionized, down from 35 percent in 1955, the year the American Federation of Labor merged with the Congress of Industrial Organizations, establishing the AFL-CIO.

The labor movement faced an existential struggle that was complicated by an internal dispute over employer sanctions and immigration policy generally. The strains came into view in 1990 as another group of strange bedfellow allies—including Utah Republican Sen. Orrin Hatch, Massachusetts Democratic Sen. Edward Kennedy, and the National Council of La Raza—called for repeal of IRCA's employer sanctions.

We'll take a close look at this controversy in the next chapter. But for now, I'll just note that Harry Bernstein, a feisty advocate of the working class who in 1990 wrote a column on labor issues for the *Los Angeles Times*, noted the division within organized labor.

"While a couple of unions trying to organize illegals have joined the campaign against punishing employers who hire them, the 14 million-member AFL-CIO warns that ending sanctions would be 'an open invitation to unscrupulous employers' to step up the hiring of undocumented workers."[7] With characteristic bluntness, Bernstein wrote that "one of the dumbest things Congress could do would be to tell employers that it's OK to hire those underpaid, easily abused illegals to compete with workers here."

THE SERVICE EMPLOYEES INTERNATIONAL UNION

One of the unions organizing unauthorized workers was the Service Employees International Union. SEIU President John Sweeney, the son of immigrants from Ireland, worked energetically to expand membership. A pivotal moment was his 1995 election as president of the AFL-CIO. From that position he pushed aggressively against the efforts of Sen. Alan Simpson and Rep. Lamar Smith to mandate rigorous improvement of the worker identification system. That Republican duo, as we have seen, was thwarted by the left-right coalition that opposed immigration restriction.

In 1997, the AFL-CIO published *Not Your Father's Union Movement: Inside the AFL-CIO*. It reported that the labor giant was "devoting more resources than labor has ever done in the past to organize immigrant workers."[8] Many of them were working illegally, having used counterfeit documents to game the system.

The labor movement faced the irony that illegal immigration, which it had long decried as a danger, was replenishing its ranks. *Not Your Father's Union Movement* did not directly acknowledge that awkward reality. Instead, it said a campaign to organize hotel workers in Los Angeles was aimed at helping "workers whose authorization expires but who then correct their immigration status."[9] The delicate phrasing was a means of avoiding recognition of what union organizers well understood: that many of the workers had never had authorization in the first place. Union organizers plowed ahead, and by 2000, Latino immigrants were 60 percent of the janitors in Los

Angeles, up from 10 percent in 1970, according to a UCLA sociologist who studied the industry.[10]

Successful union organizing was another consequence of the failure of worksite enforcement. The AFL-CIO felt compelled to adapt to the reality of a feckless enforcement system, that, as it noted, "leaves unpunished unscrupulous employers who exploit undocumented workers.[11]

A PIVOT POINT AT A HOLIDAY INN EXPRESS

And so, unions became more assertive in their recruitment of and advocacy for the unauthorized. A pivotal moment was the 1999 firing of eight workers at a Holiday Inn Express in Minneapolis after they tried to join Local 17 of the Hotel Employees and Restaurant Employees International Union. The hotel owners, claiming to be surprised to learn that they had hired illegal immigrants, called in the INS, whose agents arrested the union-organizing troublemakers. But the union defiantly rallied around the workers, putting up the $18,000 it took to get them out of jail. It also mobilized protests on their behalf.

Lawyers for the hotel workers invoked employment and labor law on their behalf. They complained to the Equal Employment Opportunity Commission and the National Labor Relations Board that the hotel had discriminated against the workers by paying them less and making them work harder than non-immigrant workers. They also claimed that the firings were illegal retaliation for workers' attempt to organize. The NLRB and the EEOC agreed, filing a lawsuit against the hotel owners. The suit produced a $72,000 settlement for the workers, seven of whom were allowed to stay in the country to continue their legal battle.

The Minneapolis story, which highlighted both the brazenness of some employers and the power of organized resistance, jolted the AFL-CIO into action. In a dramatic move, the AFL-CIO's executive council passed a resolution calling for an end to employer sanctions and a sweeping amnesty. That historic shift was the lead story on the front page of the *Washington Post*, where the headline blared, "Unions Reverse on Illegal Aliens."[12]

"I think we've really come full circle," said John Wilhelm, president of the Hotel Employees and Restaurant Employees Union. "The labor movement is on the side of immigration in this country." The *Post* reported that 75 percent of HERE's members were immigrants. The reversal was not well received by the *New York Times* editorial board, which had not yet embraced the ideology of inclusiveness for all migrants, regardless of legality. In retrospect, the *Times* editorial criticizing labor's retreat can itself be seen as the paper's final insistence on the need for immigration limits and firm enforcement. In that sense, the editorial was itself historic. It warned:

> *Amnesty would undermine the integrity of the country's immigration laws and would depress the wages of its lowest-paid native-born workers.... The primary problem with amnesties is that they beget more illegal immigration. ... Amnesties signal foreign workers that American citizenship can be had by sneaking across the border, or staying beyond the term of one's visa, and hiding out until Congress passes the next amnesty. The 1980's amnesty also attracted a large flow of illegal relatives of those workers who became newly legal. All that is unfair to those who play by the immigration rules and wait years to gain legal admission.*
>
> *It is also unfair to unskilled workers already in the United States. Between about 1980 and 1995, the gap between the wages of high school dropouts and all other workers widened substantially. Prof. George Borjas of Harvard estimates that almost half of this trend can be traced to immigration of unskilled workers. Illegal immigration of unskilled workers induced by another amnesty would make matters worse. The better course of action is to honor America's proud tradition by continuing to welcome legal immigrants and find ways to punish employers who refuse to obey the law.*[13]

The editorial identified the risks that had long made labor resist large-scale immigration. But the likelihood of wage suppression was just one half of the dilemma that organized labor faced at the end of the millennium. The other half was that continued efforts to thwart illegal immigration would antagonize many dues-paying members and alienate potential recruits. The events at the Minneapolis Holiday Inn Express clarified the stakes.

Nevertheless, the AFL-CIO's resolution did not signal a complete reversal of opposition to illegal immigration. While calling for amnesty, it also advocated stepped up efforts to stop illegal immigration at the border. Moreover, the AFL-CIO continued to oppose the guest-worker programs that employers wanted as part of any new immigration reform package. That position was a major reason for the decision by several unions, led by the Service Employees International Union, to split off from the AFL-CIO in 2005. The SEIU endorsed a guest-worker program as part of an alliance with business organizations that included business support for a sweeping amnesty.

The hunger of employers for imported workers posed a tricky problem for labor's liberal advocates. Barney Frank, the outspoken Democratic representative from Massachusetts, acknowledged that an expansion of the immigrant workforce would be "bad for blue-collars." But he found a rationale for going along. Immigrants' votes, he noted, would help put Democrats in control of Congress, which could then pass legislation to strengthen unions. And then, he said, "you would offset the negative effect on the income of the workers."[14] Frank's rationalization represented another milestone in the Democrats' long slide away from opposition to illegal immigration.

COMPREHENSIVE REFORM REPEATS THE FORMULA FROM 1986

The core of the comprehensive immigration reform bill taken up by the Senate in 2007 was basically a reprise of the old compromise of the Immigration Reform and Control Act of 1986. It combined amnesty (which advocates now preferred to call "earned legalization" because they want to avoid association with the failure of IRCA) with plans to fortify the worker verification process and to build up the Border Patrol. Those provisions were not a problem for most of the labor movement. But the AFL-CIO fought the bill because it was convinced that another section, which would have allowed the annual importation of hundreds of thousands of temporary workers, would help employers hold wages down. "If approved, it would have only perpetuated the problems it intended to solve," said AFL-CIO President John Sweeney.[15]

Six years later, the Gang of Eight reform bill that won Senate passage got a tremendous boost from a compromise on temporary workers. It eased labor's fears by putting a cap on the guest workers who could be admitted to the country. But the bill withered in the House of Representatives as Republican Speaker of the House John Boehner, fearing a debate would cause a rupture within his caucus, refused to bring it up. Reform advocates, confident that the bill had enough support to pass the House, furiously condemned the Republicans as obstructionists. Many members of the Republican establishment also disapproved of the legislative blockade. They feared that the hardline on immigration would alienate Latino workers who, in large part because of decades of immigration, had grown into an electoral force, especially in such crucial swing states as Florida and Colorado.

Meanwhile, the AFL-CIO grew stronger in its immigration advocacy. In 2016, as polls showed that whites without a college education formed the core of Donald Trump's support, the labor powerhouse produced a video in which its president, Richard Trumka, a former coal miner from Pennsylvania, urged workers to reject Trump. "A campaign fueled by contempt and exclusion is bad for working families and undermines the values that make America great," he said.[16] But Trumka faced a rupture within his own ranks. As Donald Trump's victory made strikingly clear, millions of working-class Americans supported him because he vowed to protect

American workers from illegal immigrants and unfair trade agreements. Exclusion was just what they were looking for.

HOW ENFORCEMENT OPPONENTS ADVANCED IN THE 1990S

One week after the AFL-CIO's dramatic move to oppose employer sanctions and favor amnesty in February 2000, the National Immigration Forum (NIF) sponsored a panel discussion on the state of the immigration policy debate. The participants, all allies in the battle for legislation to grant legal status to illegal immigrants, noted with satisfaction the changes in the political panorama since the early 1990s.[17] Four observations provide a metric of how far those who opposed enforcement had advanced in the 1990s.[18]

- Frank Sharry of the National Immigration Forum marveled at the change since 1995. "Just five years ago, Governor Pete Wilson was preparing to be a contender for the presidency on the heels of Proposition 187," said Sharry. "Congress and the administration were preparing to enact the toughest crackdown on immigrants in 70 years. And immigrants were viewed as easy targets, blamed for everything from recession, to wage stagnation, to deficits." Now, Sharry said, the economy was booming and [Federal Reserve Chairman] "Alan Greenspan repeatedly warns that without increased immigration, wages, prices, inflation, and interest rates will go up, threatening the economic expansion we are enjoying as a nation."
- Cecilia Muñoz of the National Council of LaRaza cited "record numbers of naturalizations" among Latino voters as a sign of growing political influence. She said that in that year's presidential campaign, "the candidates have responded to these changes in the electorate by paying their respect to Latino voters and to immigrant voters." Muñoz, long influential in Democratic circles, would become President Obama's top adviser on immigration policy.

- Muzaffar Chishti of the Union of Needletrades, Industrial and Textile Employees (UNITE) hailed the AFL-CIO's decision to stop resisting illegal immigrants and recruit them instead. He said the move signaled a recognition of new realities, including the fact that in some areas of the country "about one-half to three-fourths of new entrants into the low-wage labor market are immigrants."
- John Gay, a lobbyist for the American Hotel and Lobbying Association, said, "The greatest problem we face is that we cannot find the number we need of essential workers, as we call them, the lesser skilled and unskilled workers." Gay was co-chair of an organization formed by the Chamber of Commerce and low-wage employers—in such fields as hotels, restaurants, nursing homes, and home building – who were pushing for immigration reform. It was called the Essential Worker Immigration Coalition (EWIC). The name was an exercise in irony. It showed workers more respect than their paychecks offered. Gay's duties on Capitol Hill included lobbying against legislation to raise the federal minimum wage. At the state legislature level, his organization also sought to block legislation for mandatory sick leave.

Low wages, of course, are a function of loose labor markets. As the U.S. jobless rate dipped to 4 percent in 2000, EWIC sent a letter to members of Congress pleading for help. "The global workforce market should be more readily available to businesses in order to meet workforce needs,"[19] it said. Alex Aleinikoff, former general counsel of the INS, wrote in amazement that "labor, business, and political elites are praising as 'essential workers' the immigrants they used to call 'illegal aliens.'"[20]

WARNINGS OF A BACKLASH AND ANOTHER VIEW OF THE WORKSITE FAIT ACCOMPLI

Contrarian liberals and social conservatives pushed back against the expansionist campaign. An article in *Foreign Affairs* in the fall of 2000 made a case for resisting employers' efforts to loosen labor markets by providing visas to foreign workers. It reported that the intense immigration of the 1990s was "creating special burdens and tensions" in states from California and Arizona to New Jersey. The article, written by the foreign affairs columnist for the *San Diego Union Tribune*, concluded with a warning: "If Congress and the next president do not come up with reasonable solutions... the field will be clear for the unreasonable solutions advanced by politicians such as Pete Wilson and Pat Buchanan and discriminatory initiatives like Proposition 187."[21] Buchanan, who had made opposition to illegal immigration the centerpiece of two 1990s runs for the Republican presidential nomination, was the Reform Party's candidate in the 2000 race. He decried an "immigration invasion that will alter the ethnic character and Western culture of America forever, risking a breakup of the nation."[22]

Louis Uchitelle, who wrote about economics for the *New York Times,* took another measure of INS' enforcement work. "The agency now concentrates on picking up aliens who have committed a crime," he reported in 2001. "The rest are in effect allowed to help American employers fill jobs." Commenting on that situation, Robert Bach, the INS official who designed the strategy, showed how far enforcement had fallen as he observed: "It's just the market at work, drawing people to jobs, and the INS has chosen to concentrate its actions on aliens who are a danger to the community."[23] We will see more of Bach in Part Three as we examine the immigration policies and politics of the Clinton administration.

Uchitelle reported that the INS retreat from worksite enforcement helped explain why the economy had registered smaller pay increases than economists had expected in the tight labor market produced by the booming economy. He observed that while Alan

Greenspan was worried that a tight labor market would push wages up and thus fuel inflation, the INS decision to let the job market work "may be inducing more workers to immigrate" in search of a job. "That would dilute the labor shortage—and the wage pressure that worries Mr. Greenspan," he wrote. "In fact, it may already be doing so."

Greenspan, the country's most famous libertarian, was a former disciple of Ayn Rand, a passionate free-market enthusiast. His libertarian enthusiasm for the wage-suppressing effects of low-skilled immigration made him an ally of the immigration expansionists who have come to dominate liberal political circles. Meanwhile, Harry Bernstein, a powerful voice of the liberal case for immigration restriction in the interests of American workers, was nearing the end of his career.

DISSENT FROM THE LAST OF THE GREAT LABOR REPORTERS

During his three decades at the *Los Angeles Times*, Harry Bernstein was first a labor reporter and then became a labor columnist, a position that allowed him to state his opinions openly and forcefully. As a reporter from 1962 to the 1990s, he chronicled the struggles of working Americans and the decline of labor unions. In 1986 he warned that as workers lost political power, "the economic gap between the prosperous and middle America continues to widen ... [and] could bring a danger of social and political unrest."[24] He criticized efforts by the Reagan-era National Labor Relations Board to frustrate union-organizing efforts. When Bernstein died in 2006, at the age of 83, Judge Stephen Reinhardt, a former labor lawyer, hailed him as "the last of the great labor writers." Added Reinhardt, who was then a judge on the U.S. Ninth Circuit Court of Appeals, "In the days when labor relations were a major part of life in this country, he made it a fascinating subject for the entire community."[25]

Bernstein was outspoken in his insistence that illegal immigration was destabilizing and should not be tolerated. He rejected the claim that illegal immigrants took jobs that Americans won't do.

"The truth is that employers hungering for really cheap labor hunt out the foreign workers," he wrote in 1992.[26] Three years later he insisted, "The truth is that citizens and other legal residents of this country do the very same jobs done by illegal immigrants in a few states like California. And there are very few real labor shortages."[27]

Bernstein had endorsed IRCA. But he was upset by its failure at the worksite. "Congress wisely granted amnesty to nearly 3 million illegal immigrants, and, as part of a compromise, included in the new law a weapon aimed rather inaccurately at the massive economic and social problems that the illegal immigrants pose for this country," he wrote.[28] The law had failed, Bernstein asserted, "because employer penalties were almost entirely unenforced." Nevertheless, he favored another amnesty, saying that those who wanted to expel millions of illegal immigrants were proposing "an ugly and impossible task." He insisted that a new law could succeed only if Congress and the White House resolved to "stringently enforce much tougher laws containing severe penalties against employers who hire illegal immigrants."[29]

Bernstein, then, was a liberal restrictionist. "Those who want to sharply curb immigration include conservatives, liberals and most unions," he observed. "Their just cause is badly damaged because their ranks also include disgusting racists."[30]

In 1992, Bernstein lamented the decline of the labor beat in American journalism, writing that as union membership dropped, "editors of the newspapers made the decision that unions were not as important as they once were, and that pushed the unions down further." In a tone that seemed almost wistful, he added, "If the public had a thorough understanding of unions, there would be more support for them." In 1994, Vermont Congressman Bernie Sanders was chagrined that while the program lineup at PBS had three business shows, "there is not one regularly scheduled program on PBS ... reflecting the interests of working people and organized labor."[31] Sanders charged that the absence of such reporting was widespread in American media, reflecting the concentration of media ownership in the hands of corporations hostile to workers. There was another dynamic at work, however. By the 1990s, newspaper reporters and editors were turning their attention elsewhere. The labor relations beat had been eclipsed by coverage of race relations, gender issues, and the struggle for diversity and equality. Moreover, by the 1990s far fewer reporters and editors came from the working-class backgrounds that had long been commonplace in newsrooms.

MICKEY KAUS ON LIBERALS' "CONTEMPT FOR THE DEMOGRAPHICALLY INFERIOR"

This absence of journalistic interest in the working class was a symptom of the decline of civic solidarity lamented by Mickey Kaus in his 1987 book, *The End of Equality*. Kaus, an editor of *The New Republic*, reported on the estrangement between workers and affluent professionals, some of whom harbored a "smug contempt for the demographically inferior."[32] Kaus sees labor's opposition to immigration restriction as part of the problem. "We need a government that works, an economy that's hot, and people have to make enough money to live a life of dignity," he argued in 2010 as he made a quixotic run for the U.S. Senate. "That's what the unions and the Latino lobby are getting in the way of."[33]

As we have seen throughout this book, there is a broad, strange-bedfellows, left-right coalition that has thwarted efforts to establish reasonable immigration limits. The left has moved steadily away from the principles of restraint that liberals used to assert, in the interests of workers and the common good of our country. Barbara Jordan, as the head of the Clinton-era Commission on Immigration Reform, insisted that "it is both a right and a responsibility of a democratic society to manage immigration so that it serves the national interest." Jordan was a civil rights icon and a nationally revered voice of moral authority, and no one on the expansionist side of the debate dared to launch an ad hominem attack on her. Yet, as Boston College immigration scholar Peter Skerry has noted, liberals have "come to treat opposition to illegal immigration and constraints on illegal immigration as unacceptable, even racist."[34]

Such moral posturing and self-satisfaction are commonplace in elite circles of American life. Those who dismissed or disdained advocates of immigration limits stoked the resentment of millions of Americans who rose up against the political establishment. They elected a man who identified with their grievances and claimed to share their outrage. They wanted to overturn a system that had turned against them. They voted for Donald Trump out of frustration and anger at the failures of their government to defend their interests. Despite the Immigration Reform and Control Act of 1986, the federal government only pretended to be determined to stop illegal immigration.

Chapter 8:

The Divide Between Black Workers and Black Politicians

> **It stands to reason that if new immigrants are predominantly poorly skilled and educated, they will compete most directly with native-born Americans who are poorly skilled and educated. This competition will reduce the wages for such labor, making the plight of poorly educated and skilled Americans more difficult....it will become evident that immigration not only contributes to growing inequality in general, but makes life more difficult for black workers in particular** —*Nathan Glazer, 2000*[1]

In 2013, as the U.S. Senate was about to debate a comprehensive immigration reform bill, journalist Roland Martin interviewed Rep. Maxine Waters, a Democrat from south-central Los Angeles who supported the bill. Martin, an African American like Waters, spoke of the frustration of black workers who had been displaced by unauthorized immigrants. He said that whenever he talked of immigration on his radio show, "Nine out of ten callers, African Americans, they were not feeling immigration reform, So there's a very interesting disconnect, if you will, from black political leaders, black civil rights leaders, and regular, ordinary people who are saying, 'Look, those are a lot of jobs that we used to have.'"[2]

Waters, who represented a Los Angeles-area district whose Hispanic population had grown steadily, downplayed the divide. A member of Congress since 1991 and a former chair of the Congressional Black Caucus, she assured Martin that blacks would eventually come around to her side. "You know, these issues are issues that are evolving," she said. "And as you know, we had a lot of African-Americans who had difficulty coming along with gay issues, for example ....This is a country of immigrants. These immigrants are going to have a path to citizenship. And it will all work out. It has to."

The divide between the black political class and the black working class is one of the least examined subplots in the national immigration story. It has received little attention in the national press. It is one of those issues—like the connection between immigration-led population growth and environmental concerns, which will be the subject of the next chapter—whose political and cultural cross currents are particularly uncomfortable for liberals.

It is also a touchy issue for black politicians and civil rights leaders who work with Latinos to build the Democratic coalition and advance a host of liberal causes.

Many prominent blacks see the immigrant-rights movement as part of the larger civil rights struggle. They talk of blacks and Hispanics as natural allies in the struggle for equality. They are suspicious of conservatives whose concerns for immigration's effects on blacks strike them as strangely inconsistent with their resistance to affirmative action and other social initiatives. Journalist Leonard Pitts, Jr. has called out Republicans for what he sees as cynical attempts to arouse resentment against certain groups. Wrote Pitts, "It's the feminists' fault,' they said. Or the Hispanics, the Muslims, or the gays.'"

DISMAY AT THE SILENCE OF CIVIL RIGHTS LEADERS

On the other hand, prominent blacks who dismiss the street-level competition between blacks and Hispanic immigrants face dissent from blacks who don't support the immigrant-rights movement.

As Earl Ofari Hutchinson wrote in *The Latino Challenge to Black America*, many blacks have "declared the movement a threat to their interests and rejected the position of the civil rights leaders who backed immigration reform." Hutchinson quoted black conservative Deneen Moore's refutation of the notion of moral parity, "The civil rights movement was a fight for justice and equality," Moore said. "Illegal immigrants are fighting the rule of law."[3]

Joe Hicks, the former executive director of the Southern Christian Leadership Conference's Los Angeles chapter, has stood on both sides of the divide. At a rally against California Proposition 187 (the 1994 attempt to cut off education and public services to illegal immigrants), Hicks declared, "We've got to send a message to the rest of the nation that California will not stand on a platform of bigotry, racism and scapegoating."[4] But in 2014 Hicks had a different perspective. He expressed dismay that civil rights leaders were "strangely silent on the economic threat illegal immigration poses to millions of low-skilled black workers."[5] Donald Trump must have had this in mind when he told a 2016 campaign rally in Des Moines, "Every time an African-American citizen, or any citizen, loses their job to an illegal immigrant, the rights of that American citizen have been violated."[6]

VAN JONES SEES AN OPPORTUNITY FOR TRUMP

In early 2016, CNN anchor Van Jones said the immigration debate presented an opportunity to then-presidential-candidate Donald Trump to appeal to African Americans. "People assume African Americans won't listen to Trump," Jones said, calling for attention to be paid to the fact many blacks "have been uncomfortable with Mexican immigration and Latino immigration for a long time."[7]

Trump received only 8 percent of the black vote, while Hilary Clinton received 88 percent. But his aggressive opposition to illegal immigration was such a dramatic contrast to Clinton's soft-on enforcement policies that it may help explain the low black turnout. As the political website FiveThirtyEight observed regarding the Democrats' strategy: "Painting Trump as a bigot did not motivate more African-Americans to vote."[8]

A REBUKE FOR LIBERALS IN EBONY MAGAZINE

This great divide on immigration has been apparent since at least 1979, when an article in *Ebony* lamented the "public silence of contemporary Black leaders" about the loss of jobs to undocumented Hispanic workers.[9] The article was a rebuke of "liberals [who] find themselves unable to consider cogently the devastating effects of illegal aliens upon Blacks when two minority groups are in conflict."

In recent years one such scenario unfolded in Tar Heel, N.C., home of the world's largest pork-processing plant. Operated by Smithfield Foods, it slaughters 32,000 pigs a day, running them through disassembly lines where they are sliced into various cuts.[10] The transformation of the plant to a majority-Hispanic workforce was part of North Carolina's startling demographic change during the 1990s, when the Hispanic population grew by 394 percent, from 76,726 to 378,963. By 2008 that figure had reached 601,000, half of whom were unauthorized immigrants. That meant North Carolina had the country's eighth-largest illegal immigrant population.[11]

Many Latino newcomers found work at Smithfield plant. "They were good people, hard workers," said Wade Baker, an African American who worked at the plant from 1994 to 2002. Baker said there was widespread belief among Smithfield workers that the company's hiring decisions were part of its anti-union strategy. "They started hiring Mexicans to help beat the union," he said. "They would fire blacks for penny-ante things because they knew there were lots of Mexicans ready to come to work. And they knew they could control the Mexicans and make them afraid to vote for the union."

"FOR AFRICAN AMERICAN WORKERS, IT GOES WAY BACK"

One of the most outspoken critics of such displacement of black workers is Frank Morris, former executive director of the Congressional Black Caucus Foundation, former dean of graduate studies at Morgan State University in Baltimore, and a member of the board of the Center for Immigration Studies. "Less skilled, less educated American workers are those most hurt by immigration," said Morris. He noted that the category includes many whites. "These are the ones that no one really speaks for. No one really identifies for these folks. And for African American workers, it goes way back."[12]

Morris points to the anguish expressed in 1853 by Frederick Douglass, the great abolitionist. Wrote Douglass: "Every hour sees the black man elbowed out of employment by some newly arrived emigrant, whose hunger and whose color are thought to give him a better title to the place....It is evident, painfully evident to every reflecting mind that the means of living, for colored men, are becoming more and more precarious and limited. Employments and callings, formerly monopolized by us, are so no longer."

In 1895, W.E.B. DuBois pleaded with leaders of American industry to hire blacks rather than recruiting workers in Europe. Three decades later black leaders supported federal legislation that—by excluding Southern European Catholics and Eastern European Jews— drastically reduced the immigrant influx for four decades. *The Messenger*, a New York-based African American magazine, said the legislation "gives the Negro worker a strategic position. It gives him power to exact a higher wage.....and to compel organized labor to let down the bars of discrimination against him."[13]

"A SUBSTANTIAL REDISTRIBUTION OF WEALTH"

In the last decades of the 20th century, it was immigration from Mexico that most affected black Americans. The General Accounting Office reported in 1988 that employers had used unauthorized immigrants to displace several thousand unionized black and Hispanic janitors in Los Angeles. Those American workers had won labor contracts that paid up to $12 an hour. But that wage was high enough to make them vulnerable to displacement by non-union janitorial companies that hired newcomers who were eager to work for far less.[14] The GAO also reported on a similar situation in Southern California agriculture, where labor contractors used illegal immigrants to drive down wages and benefits. Harvard economist George Borjas has written that across the U.S. economy, immigration has caused "a substantial redistribution of wealth away from workers who compete with immigrants and toward employers."[15] He estimates that "these wealth transfers may be in the tens of billions of dollars per year."[16]

Between 1960 and 1995, California's immigrant population grew six-fold, from 1.3 million to eight million. During the same period, the immigrant share of the state's population jumped from 8.2 to 24.1 percent. While nearly 2 million were illegal immigrants, even legal immigration was large enough to affect labor markets. In 1998, researchers at the Rand Corporation estimated that the income of African American men without a high school diploma would have been 10 to 16 percent higher had there been no immigration.[17]

AN ENCOUNTER WITH SENATOR OBAMA

In 2006, I had a brief opportunity to ask then-Senator Barack Obama about immigration's effect on young blacks. I was in a group of reporters standing just off the Senate floor as he walked by on his way to the chamber. I asked how he would respond to those who say illegal immigration has displaced young black men from the workplace. Obama kept moving as he said, "Well, there are a lot of other issues facing young black men." That was it. The future president kept moving.

Obama was certainly correct. William Julius Wilson has written that many blacks are "embedded in ghetto neighborhoods, social networks, and households that are not conducive to employment."[18] Crime and antagonistic behavior are also problems, especially in the black underclass of many inner cities. Many employers say Latino workers are more reliable and cooperative than blacks. The tragic result is that job opportunities are denied to large numbers of responsible young black men who are eager for an opportunity to work.

The Pew Research Center, reporting in 2006 on its survey of blacks' views on immigration, observed, "For blacks, the growing presence of immigrant workers adds to the formidable obstacles they face in finding a job." Pew said the problem was particularly acute in Chicago, where, "Fully 41 percent of African Americans say they or a family member have lost a job, or not gotten a job, because an employer hired an illegal immigrant." That was nearly double the rate reported by blacks nationally, and nearly triple the rate for Chicago-area whites.[19]

Terry Anderson, an African American mechanic and anti-illegal immigration activist in Los Angeles, told a 1999 congressional hearing that the problem was not confined to unskilled black workers. "I am talking brick layers," he said. "I am talking concrete. I am talking roofers. I am talking framers. I am talking body and fender men who were taking $20 an hour in the 1970s. Now they can't get a job in South Central unless they are willing to make seven or eight dollars an hour. This is ridiculous."[20]

Meanwhile, immigration activists and their liberal supporters tend to be so attuned to the legal, political, and economic struggles of unauthorized immigrants that they give little attention to the debate among blacks. Black politicians are typified by the members of the Black Congressional Caucus, whose desire for good relations with their Hispanic colleagues has muted labor-market concerns. Terry Anderson told the congressional hearing of his frustration with black elected officials. "We have gone to them. We have begged them, 'please help us,' and a deaf ear is turned. It has been my experience, my personal experience, that when black elected officials talk, they speak in terms of minorities and people of color. When the advocates of the illegal alien speaks, he speaks about Latinos. We are always left out of the equation. We are never included in the equation. We have laws on the books to address these problems, but we are not—nobody has the resolve to step forward and use these laws."

BLACK TEENAGERS BECOME DISCOURAGED

In California and several other states, anxiety about immigration's labor-market effects was part of the background against which Congress in 1978 created the Select Commission on Immigration and Refugee Policy. (See Chapter One.) At a hearing in Los Angeles, the commission heard from Reuben Vaughn Greene III, who said, "Black teenagers are at a special disadvantage, since many of the jobs they qualify for are taken by illegal aliens. ... Most unfortunate is the fact that they become discouraged, not only with their condition but with society in general. Sooner or later, this spells trouble for us all."[21]

The select commission's executive director, Lawrence Fuchs, was an immigration scholar whose liberal bona fides included past membership on the board of MALDEF. But as Fuchs took note of the displacement of young blacks from the workplace, he was struck that black leaders were "increasingly reluctant to do anything that would conflict with the leadership of Mexican-American national organizations."[22] Fuchs identified the political and cultural dynamic at work in that reluctance. He observed that in the debate that preceded passage of IRCA, "Mexican-American leaders repeatedly said that employer sanctions were their civil rights issue, and black leaders accepted that view in order to strengthen the nascent coalition." And so, the entire black caucus followed the lead of their Mexican-American colleagues in opposing employer sanctions and worksite enforcement.

THE REV. JESSE JACKSON AND THE BATTLE OF 1984

Congressman Ed Roybal, the most influential Latino opponent of employer sanctions, found an important ally in the Rev. Jesse Jackson, the renowned civil rights leader. In 1984, when Roybal introduced an amnesty bill that excluded employer sanctions, Jackson was seeking the Democratic nomination to run against Ronald Reagan in that year's presidential election. Jackson, whose candidacy drew on his "Rainbow Coalition" of ethnic and religious groups, condemned the Simpson-Mazzoli legislation as racist.

Jackson was particularly active in courting Latino support in California before that state's Democratic primary election. He dramatized his outrage at employer sanctions proposals by leading a protest march in downtown Los Angeles. "There is a virtual hysteria against the undocumented," he declared. "This hysteria is fueled by a combination of myth, stereotype, meanness and political expediency." Jackson then proceeded to go to his own extreme, likening advocates of employer sanctions to the people responsible for two infamous episodes in U.S. history: the 1942 executive order that led to the internment of many Japanese-Americans, and the agreement between northern and southern states that once allowed blacks to be counted as three-fifths of a person for the purpose of determining a state's representation in the House of Representatives.

Roybal's uncompromising position and Jackson's pandering to Latino voters prompted a *Washington Post* editorial that criticized both men for their "ugly misrepresentations" about employer sanctions:

> *Rep. Edward Roybal (D-Calif.) has warned that a section of the bill to punish employers who hire illegal aliens would result in legal aliens having to wear dog tags around their necks. Jesse Jackson has said repeatedly that Simpson-Mazzoli would force aliens to carry passbooks similar to those carried by blacks in South Africa. The fact is that Simpson-Mazzoli specifically repudiates a national identification card as a means of establishing employee eligibility for lawful resident aliens and citizens.... The identification would be used only when applying for a new job, and by everyone eligible to work—not just aliens.*[23]

In the ensuing vote, Roybal and Jackson prevailed with House Democrats, who voted 138–125 against the bill. But Republicans voted 91–73 for the bill, allowing it to pass with a five-vote margin. That vote took place shortly before the Democratic National Convention in San Francisco, where immigration loomed as a source of intra-party turbulence. Jackson added to the drama by leading a march to the Mexican border, claiming the moral authority of Jesus, Gandhi, and Martin Luther King. Said Jackson, "Just as Jesus marched to Jerusalem, and Gandhi marched to the sea, and Martin Luther King marched to Washington, we must march to the border and cross lines of race, language, and culture."[24]

Lawrence Fuchs took a dim view of Jackson's posturing, which he saw as self-serving and destructive. "Jackson's hyperbolic opposition...removed any possibility that national black leaders would support employer sanctions," Fuchs wrote.[25] Driven by his need to court the Latino vote, Jackson did not acknowledge that in the absence of worksite enforcement of employer sanctions, blacks would continue to suffer discrimination from employers who preferred to hire illegal immigrants.

Although Jackson pulled many Democrats away from Simpson-Mazzoli, some liberals continued to endorse it. A *New York Times* editorial said the legislation could "prevent the growth of a larger underclass and ... protect us from the terrible divisiveness that would result from large-scale illegal immigration in the future."[26]

MONDALE'S DILEMMA

Jesse Jackson's hard line made life especially difficult for Walter Mondale, President Carter's vice president and the frontrunner for the 1984 Democratic presidential nomination. As far back as 1970, Mondale had expressed alarm that "we have a massive poverty population coming into the country virtually every day from Mexico."[27] But as he sought the presidency in 1984, Mondale faced the contradictory task of wooing Mexican-American support without antagonizing labor-movement allies who urged support for Simpson-Mazzoli.

On the horns of that dilemma, Mondale equivocated.[28] That provoked Mexican-American delegates at the convention, who threatened to embarrass him by boycotting the first ballot. They relented only after Mondale and his running mate, Representative Geraldine Ferraro, met with Latino delegates, denounced Simpson-Mazzoli and promised to help defeat it. Ferraro left no doubt about her allegiance to the cause of killing the bill. "The bill is wrong because it is discriminatory," she said. "The bill is wrong because it targets in on individuals just because they are who they are. The bill is wrong because it looks to deprive individuals of their ability to get jobs. The bill is wrong, wrong, wrong!"[29] Those words and that position gave the Democratic Party a forceful, historic shove in the direction of loose borders and lax enforcement.

The *New York Times*, which had vigorously endorsed Simpson-Mazzoli, gloomily assessed the post-convention scene. It predicted "bleak days for immigration reform" because of what it called "pandering to Hispanic leaders" by the contenders for the Democratic presidential nomination. Lamenting the demise of the Simpson-Mazzoli bill in that session of Congress, the newspaper made a pointed observation about the forces aligned against that reform effort: "The bill had plenty of enemies, including growers and the Chamber of Commerce. But none inflicted wounds more grievous than Hispanic leaders and lobbyists."[30]

THE AFTERMATH

The employer sanctions regime eventually established by IRCA was too flimsy to be effective. But the left-right coalition wanted to eliminate it entirely. In 1990, they welcomed a GAO report that, on the basis of a nationwide survey, found that 19 percent of the nation's 4.6 million employers had effectively acknowledged some form of discrimination. Generally, that meant either that employers had avoided hiring applicants whose appearance or accent seemed foreign or that they had demanded verification of work eligibility only from persons they suspected were foreign.

As we saw in Chapter Two, the response of Democratic Sen. Edward Kennedy and Republican Sen. Orrin Hatch was to introduce legislation to repeal employer sanctions. The old battle lines formed again. IRCA opponents claimed that the GAO had made their case. IRCA supporters pointed to the GAO's finding that "much of the reported discrimination appears to come from employers who are confused about how to comply with IRCA's verification requirements." Rather than risk being penalized, wary employers turned away some workers. The GAO recommended that the government improve employer education, reduce the number of documents that workers could present, and make the documents harder to counterfeit.[31]

Against this turbulent background, a group of prominent blacks, including Coretta Scott King, the widow of Martin Luther King, Jr., came forward with an appeal to keep employer sanctions in place. Repeal, they said, would enable continued "discrimination against brown U.S. and documented workers, in favor of cheap labor-- the undocumented workers."[32] Nevertheless, the convention of the National Association for the Advancement of Colored People called on Congress to abolish sanctions. Its vote reversed the NAACP's long-standing support for worksite enforcement, which, as immigration scholar Michael Fix noted, had "great political and symbolic value for the law's proponents."[33]

The employer sanctions dispute revealed the fault lines dividing liberals on illegal immigration. NAACP executive director Benjamin Hooks believed the GAO report left his organization little choice but to vote against employer sanctions. That position, however, prompted Harry Bernstein, the outspoken liberal labor columnist at the *Los Angeles Times*, to criticize both the GAO and the NAACP.

Bernstein noted that within the GAO, the report had come under attack. He added his own criticisms and complained that NAACP leaders were using the report "as the excuse for joining militant Latinos and others in a campaign to be nicer to companies that use illegal aliens as a source of cheap, exploitable labor." Bernstein went on to note that the GAO had not recommended terminating employer sanctions but instead had called for simplifying the I-9 process, which was the centerpiece of worker identification.

Those observations did nothing to soften the resistance of Ed Roybal or his allies, including Raul Yzaguirre of the National Council of La Raza. Yzaguirre repeatedly called opposition to employer sanctions "the transcendent civil rights issue of our time."[34] In his effort to keep black legislators on his side, that proved to be an effective tactic.

THE SEPARATE PEACE OF MAXINE WATERS

By the end of the 1990s, Hispanics had replaced blacks as the nation's largest minority group. The Hispanic population grew 58 percent in the 1990s, reaching 35.3 million. Meanwhile, the black population grew by 16 percent to 34.7 million. It was against this background that Mervyn M. Dymally, a prominent black member of the California Assembly, made this poignant observation: "Latinos have always been our natural allies, except for one setback, and that's the differences over immigration.[35]

No California politician has understood the need for Latino support better than Maxine Waters, whose south-central Los Angeles district's influx of Latinos has coincided with an out-migration of blacks. Her coalition-building strategy has featured energetic advocacy for comprehensive immigration reform and equally strong criticism of its opponents. Waters brought both passions to a 2011 House hearing that was titled "Making Immigration Work for American Minorities."

At the hearing, Republicans cited research from Harvard economist George Borjas, who concluded that immigrant labor had reduced the wages of Americans in low-skill jobs by 7.4 percent.[36] Democrats countered by quoting Yale's Gerald Jaynes, a professor of economics and African American Studies who insisted that the negative impacts of immigrant workers on blacks were "mostly absent, and modest at worst for only a small segment of lowest-skilled workers."

Professor Carol Swain of Vanderbilt, a conservative black scholar of immigration, was a witness for the Republicans. Swain testified that she was "dismayed by... the fact that the black leadership, whether we are talking about the NAACP or the Congressional Black Caucus, has done a very poor job of representing the interests of black Americans as well as legal Hispanics in their districts." Testifying at the invitation of the Democrats, Wade Henderson of the Leadership Conference on Civil Rights defended the Congressional Black Caucus and disputed the claim that immigrants were a cause of black unemployment. Henderson said the difficulty blacks have in finding work was linked to "many other challenges disadvantaged populations have faced in the United States."

Waters decried what she saw as a cynical Republican effort to split the black-Latino coalition and undermine its legislative agenda. "As a member of Congress representing both Latinos and African Americans, I am very disappointed with the majority's effort to pit minorities against one another in a blatant attempt to derail comprehensive immigration reform," she said. "The Congressional Black Caucus and the Congressional Hispanic Caucus have been at the forefront in championing progressive policies that take into account the challenges that American minorities confront. One need only review the Republicans' voting records to understand their political priorities, and it does not include a deep concern for the working class or American minorities."

Although Waters's district is heavily Latino, many of her constituents are illegal immigrants not eligible to vote. She has easily won reelection in her overwhelmingly Democratic district in part because she has benefited from what the *New York Times* called a long-established modus vivendi in which "black and Latino politicians ... have collaborated behind the scenes to carve out safe elective enclaves for members of the City Council, the State Legislature and Congress."[37] Waters's immigration advocacy has certainly made good political sense. It has protected her left flank from a potential primary challenge. It has not shielded her from the skepticism of journalists like Roland Martin and the criticism of prominent blacks who seek to protect black workers.

THE CONDESCENSION OF AN ELITE WHITE REPORTER

Frank Morris is particularly aggrieved by attempts by Waters and others to portray the fight for illegal immigrants as a continuation of the great civil rights struggle led Martin Luther King, Jr. Morris stated his case at a 2013 event in Washington to mark the 50th anniversary of King's historic March on Washington for Jobs and Freedom. It was there that King delivered his "I Have a Dream" speech, lamenting that the black man "finds himself in exile in his own land."

Morris spoke at the end of a march to the Capitol that was led by a group called the Black American Leadership Alliance and supported by members of the Tea Party. Their purpose was to invoke the memory of Dr. King's concern for jobs as they called on Congress to reject legalization for illegal immigrants. Morris was indignant that immigration activists had sought to claim King's mantle. Noting that the civil rights movement had fought the systematic denial of basic rights guaranteed by the Constitution, he expressed outrage at the attempt to make that struggle "equivalent to non-citizens going into another country, demanding rights they do not have, and demanding that laws that were supposed to protect American citizens not be enforced."[38]

Morris's speech was the thematic heart of the march, which concluded with a rally on a sweltering afternoon. It had assembled blacks and whites in a demonstration of goodwill, solidarity, and citizenship that Martin Luther King would have found moving. There were many poignant moments, as when young black men held up for the cameras a sign that identified the marchers as "American Citizens—Black &White—Against Illegal Immigration." Tea Party members carried signs that read "American Jobs for American Workers."

It was this demonstration of black-white solidarity that was the subject of the 2013 *Daily Beast* column by Michelle Cottle that I mentioned in Chapter Three.[39] It was a museum-quality specimen of the elite liberals' capacity for withering contempt. It was an exhibition of the can-you-believe-these-rubes denigration that was stoking a backlash in populist corners of American culture like "South Park," the animated sitcom. One episode gave voice to a character who laid into Rosie O'Donnell for her Cottle-like attitude. "People like you teach tolerance and open-mindedness all the time," he seethed. "But when it comes to Middle America, you think we're all evil and stupid country yokels who need your political enlightenment."

Writing in the *Wall Street Journal*, former presidential speech writer Peggy Noonan satirically observed that Capitol Hill advocates of expansive immigration were convinced of their moral superiority. "They are inclusive and you're not, you cur, you gun-totin' truck-driver's-hat-wearin' yahoo. It's all so complex, and you'd understand this if you weren't sort of dumb."[40] Noonan's satire, written in 2007, was aimed at the kind of arrogance that in 2016 propelled Hillary Clinton to scorn Trump supporters as "a basket of deplorables." She believed they were irrelevant—until the votes came in.

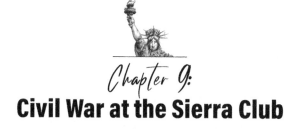

Chapter 9:
Civil War at the Sierra Club

> **"To explore, enjoy, and protect the planet. To practice and promote the responsible use of the Earth's ecosystems and resources; to educate and enlist humanity to protect and restore the quality of the natural and human environment; and to use all lawful means to carry out those objectives."** —*Sierra Club mission statement*

> **"The raging monster upon the land is population growth. In its presence, sustainability is but a fragile theoretical concept."** —*Edward O. Wilson*[1]

In the spring of 1970, rising national awareness of degradation of the nation's water, air, and open lands led to the convocation of the first Earth Day, an effort to mobilize the public that launched the modern environmental movement. CBS television anchorman Walter Cronkite reported that 20 million Americans had participated in what he called "a day dedicated to enlisting all the citizens of a bountiful country in a common cause of saving life from the deadly byproducts of that bounty." Americans gathered on college campuses and urban parks to learn what they could do to counter pollution and ease the degradation of entire ecosystems. The *New York Times* noted that one concern was the growth of the U.S. population, which three years earlier had passed the 200 million mark. Balloons stamped with the family-planning advice to "Stop at Two" floated above the crowds, it reported.[2] A *Times* editorial greeted the sense of common purpose against an existential threat: "Unless all can live and work together for a better environment, all may suffocate together," it warned. Cronkite anchored a special report titled "Earth Day: A Question of Survival."

The nation's political leaders responded to the swelling sense of urgency. President Nixon signed an executive order creating the Environmental Protection Agency. Congress enacted legislation to establish a national environmental policy, placing "the profound influences of population growth" first on its list of concerns.[3] The blue-ribbon Commission on Population Growth and the American Future concluded that "the gradual stabilization of our population would contribute significantly to the nation's ability to solve its problems."[4]

For years the Sierra Club was at the forefront of advocacy for efforts to limit the growth of the U.S. population in order to avoid environmental degradation. In 1968, the club published *The Population Bomb,* the best-selling environmental jeremiad that warned of catastrophe if the world's population continued its rapid growth. At a 1980 congressional hearing, club representative Judith Kunofsky testified: "It is obvious that the number of immigrants the United States accepts affects our population size and growth rate. It is perhaps less well known the extent to which immigration policy, even more than the number of children per family, is the determinant of the future number of Americans."[5] In 1989, the Sierra Club board took the position that immigration "should be no greater than that which will permit achievement of population stabilization in the United States."[6]

Then the club began a period of long, traumatic division. It began with two issues concerning the club's makeup and identity. Club leaders sought to diversify membership beyond their overwhelmingly white, middle-class core. Meanwhile, Latino activists, asserting their groups' rapidly growing numbers, admonished the club that if it wanted to recruit from their ranks, it needed to support the twin causes of social justice and environmental justice. They formed alliances[7] with other people of color and demanded that the club support their calls for more immigration.

It is no exaggeration to say that the fights within the Sierra Club became a civil war. Sierrans who had traditionally been united by a broad environmental consensus, split bitterly over immigration policy. What one side valued as essential environmental stewardship the other scorned as a form of oppression by an entrenched white elite. Inevitably, the battles were fiercest in California, home of the club's headquarters and the greatest concentration of its members.

DEFINING THE CLUB'S IDENTITY

John Muir, one of the most important advocates of wilderness preservation in American history, founded the Sierra Club in 1892. At that time California's population was 1.2 million. A century later, when the club's immigration struggle began, California was home to nearly 30 million people. One catalyst for the club's immigration struggle was the first People of Color Environmental Leadership Summit, which took place in 1991. The club's executive director, Michael Fischer, was in attendance, along with the director of the National Resources Defense Council. At one point in the proceedings the two men were summoned to the stage to face questioning about their policies and intentions. What ensued was a three-hour harangue that Fischer later described as "incoming rounds of [accusations that they were] racist, insensitive, thoughtless obstacles to progress."[8] Two decades after Tom Wolfe wrote that black radicals had introduced other minority activists to the art of intimidating or "mau-mauing" second-level bureaucrats he called "flak catchers," the summit laid it on the heads of two major environmental organizations. It staged a drama that might've been called "Mau-Mauing the Tree Huggers."

Shortly after the summit, a chastened Fischer demonstrated his remorse and declared his commitment to the activists' cause. He said the club needed "a friendly takeover" by people of color. The alternative, he said, was that the club would "remain a middle-class group of backpackers, overwhelmingly white in membership, program and agenda – and thus condemned to losing influence in an increasingly multicultural country."[9] Fischer essentially pleaded guilty to the charge that the club was beset by the elitist snobbery of members whose principal concern was to protect the wilderness. He wanted to show solidarity with those who demanded that attention be paid to the harm that chemical plants, power generating stations, and waste dumps inflicted on communities of the poor and people of color.

Fischer's conversion met resistance. Some members of the Club protested that he was pushing the club toward social justice activism and away from its core mission of conservation. In 1992, the *Los Angeles Times* reported that he was resigning. "Not only are there long weeks away from my family, but the job is an exhausting one," Fischer explained. That same year, the U.S. Census Bureau provided a metric for the intensity of the immigration debate. It announced a striking revision of its previous projections that the U.S. population would level off at about 300 million by the middle of the 21st century. The bureau's new finding was that the country's population growth, driven primarily by immigration, was on course to reach 400 million by 2050 and then to keep growing.[10]

To replace Fischer, the Sierra Club board selected Carl Pope, who had been working as the club's associate executive director. Pope's background included outspoken advocacy for immigration limits. He had been a lobbyist for Zero Population Growth in the early 1970s, when the U.S. was issuing about 400,000 green cards per year, the *New York Times* reported that Pope "says we can't hope to absorb all those who want to come in." He even challenged the poetic mythology of immigration. "Immigration is a sentimental symbol whose day is long past," he said. "We could take in 100,000 immigrants and still serve that symbol."[11] In other words, Pope believed that the ethos of "Give me your tired, your poor" was an anachronism that needed to give way to new priorities in a new era. After taking the top post at the Sierra Club, he reaffirmed those convictions. He said that although all nations should curb population growth, "The United States and other developed nations have a special responsibility because of our disproportionate consumption of world resources. Our goal in the United States should be achieving domestic population stabilization."[12]

Pope took that position in a 1992 letter to the editor of the *New York Times*. Nevertheless, the following year, the Sierra Club board took a position that, while not directly addressing immigration or population, was an effort to find common ground with immigrant rights activists who claimed immigration was a basic human right. In a statement that signaled solidarity with the activists, the board declared that "to achieve our mission of environmental protection and a sustainable future for the planet, we must attain social justice and human rights at home and around the globe."[13]

In 1994 National Public Radio reporter Isabel Alegria provided a revealing look at the ideological cross currents buffeting the environmental movement as it sought to resolve the conflict between traditional environmental concerns and the cause of inclusiveness and diversity. At this time, Pope still wanted to hold the line on immigration. He told Alegria that it made no sense to urge Americans to limit the size of their families without also taking a position on policies that regulate the annual flow of immigrants. Alegria, drawing a line under that concern, concluded, "So Pope says the Sierra Club is now debating a population policy that includes a call for immigration reform."

Then Alegria introduced Cathi Tactaquin, the U.S.-born daughter of a farmworker who had immigrated from the Philippines. She was a founder of the National Network for Immigration and Refugee Rights. Alegria observed that Tactaquin was "alarmed by growing ties between anti-immigrant groups and environmentalists."[14] She saw immigration as a human right. She wrote that respect for the right to immigrate was essential "if groups like the Sierra Club want to broaden their appeal to the diverse communities that make up the human element of the environment."[15]

The rise of environmental justice activism and the ongoing mobilization of Latinos, many of whom in 1994 were battling California's anti-illegal immigration Proposition 187, intensified feelings on all sides. Activists claimed that if the Sierra Club supported reduced immigration, it would be making common cause with California Governor Pete Wilson and the Republican Party. The Sierra Club board decided to stay out of the debate. It voted to "take no position on immigration levels or on policies governing immigration into the United States."[16] But that was far from the end of the controversy.

"NOT FEWER PEOPLE, BUT BETTER LIVES FOR PEOPLE"

The year 1997 was a pivotal time in the debate over population, environmentalism, and immigration. The National Academy of Sciences published its conclusion that immigration would play "the dominant role" in the growth of the U.S. population. The study projected that between 1995 and 2050, the population would jump from 263 million to 387 million. Those numbers represented both immigrants and their offspring. Of the 124 million additional people in 2050, "80 million will be the direct or indirect consequence of immigration." The study intensified the debate within the Sierra Club, where the cohort that had long favored reduced immigration clashed with a much newer cohort of environmental justice advocates. Tactaquin was named to the club's National Population Committee. There she was joined by immigration activist Santos Gomez, who was named to the committee immediately after joining the club. Gomez spoke out forcefully against those who favored immigration limits. "If you use that language, you're fighting a losing battle," he warned. "The first objective is not fewer people on the plant, but better lives for people."[17] Gomez, of course, was referring to the middle-class standard of living that was a core part of the American dream that drew many immigrants to the U.S.

In addition to their participation in the Sierra Club, Tactaquin and Gomez were leaders of a San Francisco environmental justice organization called the Political Ecology Group. PEG was a militant group whose declared purpose was to build "alliances to confront environmental destruction, racism, sexism, homophobia and corporate power."[18] Employing some of the most confrontational rhetoric in the immigration debate, it said environmentalists who sought to reduce immigration were attempting to "foment a hateful anti-immigrant atmosphere."[19] That was a warning that restrictionist concerns had political and social consequences. Ratcheting up the intensity of the rhetoric, PEG, with Tactaquin in the lead, condemned such concerns as "the greening of hate." It is a catchy phrase, still used to intimidate people who see themselves as advocates for the greening of immigration policy.

Dave Foreman, a fiery member of the Sierra Club board and an advocate of radical conservation measures, responded with equal intensity. He ripped PEG as "race-baiting hooligans of the left" who had made it impossible to have an "honorable, decent, and fair" discussion. He warned that "white middle-class guilt" could paralyze the Sierra Club.[20] But *San Francisco Examiner* columnist William Wong found good reason for the club to feel guilty. "Why should an illustrious environmental organization join immigrant-bashing ideologues like Pat Buchanan!" he wrote. Calling attention to wasteful American consumption patterns, he proposed an alternative set of priorities for the club: "Go after monster sport-utility vehicles... Go after monster single-family homes...Go after monster food packaging."[21]

SIERRANS FOR U.S. POPULATION STABILIZATION

The club's new position on immigration antagonized Sierrans who said it was a de facto "policy to have no policy." A central figure in this group was UCLA professor Ben Zuckerman, a renowned astronomer. He was also a passionate outdoorsman, conservationist, and population activist who was known to eschew air travel in order to minimize his carbon footprint. Stating his population case in the *Los Angeles Times,* he wrote: "Because the average American consumes so much, we 270 million Americans have as much environmental impact as the more than 4 billion people who live in all the developing countries of the world."[22]

In an effort to force the Sierra Club to reengage in the politics of immigration, Zuckerman and allies founded Sierrans for U.S. Population Stabilization (SUSPS). Leveraging the club's unusually open system of participatory democracy, they launched a petition drive that succeeded in bringing the issue up for a vote by the club's entire membership of some 550,000, about a third of whom lived in California. As it appeared on the ballot of the club's 1998 election, their proposal would have directed the club to advocate for "an end to U.S. population growth at the earliest possible time" through reduction of immigration and births.

SUSPS won endorsements from such national figures as Earth Day founder Gaylord Nelson, former Secretary of the Interior Stewart Udall, and famed Harvard biologist E.O. Wilson. Wilson's books included *The Diversity of Life*, which describes the extinction of entire species during the 20th century as the result of human activities. "The raging monster upon the land is population growth," he wrote. "In its presence, sustainability is but a fragile theoretical concept."[23]

The club's board launched an aggressive communications strategy to defeat SUSPS by drawing attention on some unsavory characters who supported SUSPS. At the top of their list was David Duke, the notorious white nationalist and former Grand Wizard of the Ku Klux Klan. Carl Pope declared that if the club pushed for immigration limits, "we would be perceived as assisting people whose motivations are racist."[24]

Such tactics infuriated Gaylord Nelson. "People have been silenced because they are scared to death of being charged with being a racist," he said. "But racism has nothing to do with it. It's a question of numbers."[25] Pope countered that the SUSPS effort was "seen by people in immigrant communities as saying: You are a form of pollution."[26] Indeed, immigration activists made immigration policy a litmus test of the club's commitment to diversity. Carlos

Quirarte of the club's Los Angeles chapter warned that if SUSPS won, he would quit. "I am a Chicano and blood is thicker than water," he said.[27]

As the club prepared for the vote in early 1998, the board put its finger on the scale of electoral fairness. Despite club rules that entitled SUSPS to a straight up or down vote, the board offered an alternative proposal to "address the root causes of migration by encouraging sustainability, economic security, health and nutrition, human rights and environmentally responsible consumption."

The 14 percent of Sierrans who voted sided heavily with the board, whose alternative proposal received 46,935 votes while the SUSPS proposal received 31,345 votes. It was a thumping rebuke, but Ben Zuckerman refused to be discouraged. Charging that the board had unfairly manipulated the process, he said the SUSPS effort was "a respectable initial showing by grassroots members up against virtually the entire club bureaucracy."[28] He vowed that SUSPS would be back. Meanwhile, Cathi Tactaquin pressed her case. "There's a need for a broader human rights movement for people with or without documents," she said. She added that enforcement of immigration laws had propagated "a climate of fear, repression, and discrimination against immigrants and people of color."[29]

DAVID BROWER RESIGNS

The Sierra Club's position on immigration angered David Brower, the legendary Sierran who during his tenure as executive director from 1952 to 1969 transformed the club from an easy-going group of a few thousand back-country hikers to a 70,000-member powerhouse in the thick of environmental politics. Once the best rock-climber of his generation, he became the most influential environmental activist in the United States. Brower was known for eloquence, charm and a fiercely stubborn refusal to compromise. He was an inspiration to friends who joined in campaigns like his successful 1960s effort to thwart the plans of the Bureau of Reclamation to construct dams at the edges of the Grand Canyon. Brower could be an exasperation to foes, including those on the club's board who in 1969 forced him out as executive director because of his combativeness and what they saw as his unwise spending priorities. Brower took his inexhaustible activism elsewhere, founding Friends of the Earth and the Earth Island Institute, and advising the League of Conservation voters.

In the 1980s and 1990s, Brower claimed vindication, His stature as an environmentalist legend propelled his election to the board, where he pressed his conviction that "you don't have a conservation policy unless you have a population policy." Shortly before his death in 2000, at the age of 88, Brower resigned from the board. "The world is burning and all I hear from them is the music of violins," Brower said, objecting to inaction on such issues as immigration, overpopulation, wilderness preservation, and mass transit. "The planet is being trashed, but the board has no real sense of urgency." Clearly exasperated, he warned, "Overpopulation is perhaps the biggest problem facing us and immigration is part of that problem. It has to be addressed."[30]

THE ISSUE RETURNS: THE CLUB ELECTION OF 2004

Ben Zuckerman's determination to press on was encouraged by his easy victory in his 2002 run for a seat on the Sierra Club board. He saw the victory as a measure of support for his challenge to the club's hierarchy and his conviction that overpopulation was the root cause of environmental crises. As a profile in the *Los Angeles Times* put it, Zuckerman believed that the club's leadership had been stricken by fear: "Fear of being called racist. Fear of losing minority-group members and fear of forfeiting financial support from big business and foundations."[31]

Zuckerman's sense of urgency drew support from *Los Angeles Times* columnist James Ricci, who cited a club official's contention that immigration to the U.S. would slow when conditions in the sending countries did not compel them to leave. Taking Zuckerman's side in the debate, Ricci opined that the club had capitulated to the notion that immigration would continue until "conditions here become equally bad, the swollen masses just as poor, the environment just as degraded."

Zuckerman's insurgency gained momentum in 2003 when two allies were also elected to the board. They were Paul Watson, who had been named by *Time* as one of the environmental heroes of the 20th century and who was known for forceful tactics to disrupt seal and whale hunting, and Doug La Follette, the Wisconsin secretary of state, one of the organizers of the first Earth Day, and author of *The Survival Handbook: A Strategy for Saving Planet Earth.*

With its eye on the five board seats that would be up in the 2004 election, SUSPS began recruiting more like-minded candidates. The three who signed on were:

- Richard Lamm, former Democratic governor of Colorado, who had first won election in 1974 with a vow to limit the state's growth. Lamm criticized U.S. immigration policies for propelling growth. A member of the board of the Federation for American Immigration Reform, he acknowledged that he was running because he wanted to engage the Sierra Club in the effort to limit immigration. "I have been monomaniacal in some ways about how America is ducking this issue," he said. "I have a grandchild in utero. If that child is long-lived, she might see a billion Americans."[32]
- Frank Morris, former head of the Congressional Black Caucus Foundation, who had long decried the effects of low-wage immigrant labor on black workers. Morris was also a member of the boards of FAIR and the Center for Immigration Studies
- David Pimentel, a Cornell entomologist who had written academic articles with such titles as "How Many Americans Can the Earth Support?" and "Will Limits of the Earth's Resources Control Human Numbers?"

Once again, Carl Pope would lead the institutional counter attack. Once again, accusations of guilt-by-association were the principal tactic. Felicity Barringer of the *New York Times* reported, "Pope and Larry Fahn, the board president, contend that members of the internal faction supporting those candidates have ties to racist groups or Web sites – a claim first made by a staff member at the Southern Poverty Law Center."[33]

Of course, the "internal faction" was SUSPS, whose leaders included Ben Zuckerman. Zuckerman's casual connection to John Tanton, a former member of the club's National Population Committee, attracted the outrage of the Southern Poverty Law Center's Mark Potok, who described the men as close allies. Zuckerman called the claim nonsense, saying that while he and Tanton shared the concern about immigration and population, they had met exactly once. In contrast to Tanton's provincial background and friendships with white nationalists, Zuckerman was a native New Yorker with a long commitment to social justice. His first involvement in political activism came when he was a teenager and he rode a bus to Washington to join a march for civil rights.

The variety and complexity of restrictionists' concerns are quickly obliterated when the SPLC mud-slinging begins. Indignant that Zuckerman had once described Tanton as "courageous" and "a great environmentalist," Potok said, "We are concerned that a club director ... would defend Tanton, whose ties to bigots and bigoted groups have been well documented."

Potok rang the alarm about a racist cabal at the gates. "Without a doubt, the Sierra Club is the subject of a hostile takeover attempt by forces allied with Tanton and a variety of right-wing extremists," Potok declared.[34] His boss, SPLC founder Morris Dees, soon joined the fray. Warning that SUSPS represented "the greening of hate," Dees put his name on the ballot and proceeded to portray the election as a Manichaean struggle. "A hostile takeover of the Club by radical anti-immigrant activists is in the making," he warned. "Please save the Sierra Club from takeover by the radical right."[35]

Zuckerman by this time had his fill of the SPLC's accusations of extremism and racism. He condemned the Potok letter as "unadulterated garbage." He listed five errors in a single Potok paragraph, beginning with the false claim that Tanton was the force behind the club's 1998 referendum. "He had nothing to do with it," said Zuckerman, exasperated at the recklessness of the SPLC.[36]

Once again, the board put its hand on the scale of electoral balance. It ordered that ballot materials sent to members include an "Urgent Election Notice," a warning that "outside groups ... are urging their supporters to join the Club as a means to influence club policy in line with their non-environmental agendas."[37] The board also directed that an article attacking SUSPS be distributed to club chapters around the country. Chapters in at least eight states—California, Utah, Texas, Louisiana, Kansas, Ohio, West Virginia, and Massachusetts, published it in their newsletters under the same headline: "Outside Interests Push to Hijack Sierra Club."

The article was a hit piece that set a new low for cynicism and mendacity in a dispute that had plenty of both. It made the absurd allegation that "Zuckerman has compared immigration to cancer."[38] Since the writer didn't say what the alleged comparison actually was, a reasonable reader might have speculated that he had condemned immigration as a deadly disease attacking the body politic. But the allegation was itself a hijacking of a reference Zuckerman had made to famed Western writer Edward Abbey, the author of such classic works as *Desert Solitaire* and *The Monkey Wrench Gang*, who has been hailed as "the Thoreau of the West" and "a voice crying from the wilderness for the wilderness." Zuckerman, in presenting his argument for limiting immigration in order to limit sprawl and damage to the environment, quoted Abbey's trenchant observation that "Growth for the sake of growth is the ideology of the cancer cell." The article, by making a hash out of the fact that neither Ed Abbey nor Ben Zuckerman had compared immigration to cancer, was a stunt based on the flagrant misrepresentation of a quotation.

Carl Pope also stirred the pot of innuendo. The *New York Times* quoted him as saying that although he didn't believe Lamm, Morris, and Pimentel were actually racists, they were "in bed with racists."[39] In *U.S. News and World Report,* conservative columnist John Leo, wrote: "Good grief. Next we'll be hearing that FDR was a commie because Stalin fought on his side during World War II."[40]

Richard Lamm, a longtime civil rights activist who had been a vice president of the NAACP chapter at the University of California, responded with a mix of astonishment and dismay. "I hurt," he told the *New York Times.* "Because nobody has ever, ever brought a stain on my reputation like this small clique of people in the Sierra Club. Not in my worst campaign."[41]

In the spring of 2004, as the election results came in from a record high 22 percent of club members, SUSPS was routed. In a field of 17 candidates, from which five would be elected, the SUSPS candidates placed 11th, 12th and 15th. Acknowledging the effectiveness of the scorched-earth campaign, David Pimentel conceded, "The Old Guard did a really effective job on us." The SUSPS response was more pointed, complaining that club leaders had conducted "an unprecedented campaign of disinformation, fear mongering and hostility."[42]

SUSPS persisted in its conviction that the Sierra Club would one day have to acknowledge the environmental consequences of unrestrained immigration. Jim Montevallo of *E Magazine* penned a concise formulation of that conviction: "There's a minefield in the American environmental movement, and its name is population. Because negotiating that minefield is so dangerous, many environmental groups and leaders have stopped trying to cross it. But to ignore population as a central issue while talking freely about sprawl, air and water pollution, loss of biodiversity, agricultural land and animal habitat, global warming, and many other crucial environmental issues is to deny reality."[43]

CARL POPE AND THE ANONYMOUS $100 MILLION DONOR

In the months before the 2004 vote, SUSPS had made a desperate, last-ditch effort to force Carl Pope to answer a question about the club's immigration politics. Richard Lamm and Frank Morris demanded to know why Carl Pope had not disclosed the identity of donors who had contributed a whopping $102 million to the club. As the *Los Angeles Times* reported, the two men "questioned whether any of the anonymous donors had been behind what they called the 'smear campaign'" against SUSPS. Said Morris: "We've been attacked as racists and nationalists and haven't been able to understand the severity of the attacks. This could be it."[44]

Carl Pope, bound by a promise of confidentiality, shrugged off the suspicion. "These anonymous donors want to remain anonymous," he said.[45] That put the issue on ice until six months after SUSPS lost the election, when the story roared back to life as the *Los Angeles Times* identified the principal donor as David Gelbaum, a publicity-shy mathematical genius who had amassed a fortune as the head of a hedge fund. Although Gelbaum maintained he had not played a role in the election, he acknowledged that Pope had been aware of his position on immigration. Said Gelbaum, "I did tell Carl Pope in 1994 or 1995 that if they ever came out anti-immigration, they would never get a dollar from me."[46]

Pope acknowledged receiving Gelbaum's warning but said the board had already decided not to engage on the issue. Richard Lamm wasn't buying it. The club had been "caught red-handed ... they sold out one of the most important environmental issues of our time."[47] A decade later, Lamm's resentment of Pope was still palpable. "I've had all kinds of people disagree with all kinds of my positions," he said, recalling attacks he received for advocating abortion rights and for opposing a campaign to bring the Olympics to Colorado when he was governor. "I'm not a fragile person. But there is a level of debate that goes beyond decency, where you attack someone's character more than his ideas. It was Carl Pope that was the energy, the power behind those attacks. I'll never forget it. I guess I still resent it."[48]

THE GELBAUM-ZUCKERMAN DICHOTOMY

David Gelbaum is an important figure in the Sierra Club civil war for reasons beyond the still-unresolved controversy over the effect of his immigration ultimatum. He presents a fascinating contrast with Ben Zuckerman.

Zuckerman and Gelbaum approached immigration from contrasting moral perspectives and sensibilities. Zuckerman was attuned to what he saw as the negative consequences—environmental, social, and political—of overpopulation. He had become as committed to preserving the majesty of open spaces as he was to probing the mysteries of the celestial vastness.

Gelbaum was married to a Mexican-American woman. He spoke poignantly about the moral direction he received from his immigrant grandfather, Abraham, who had been a watchmaker in Ukraine before fleeing persecution of Jews early in the 20th century. In an interview with the *Los Angeles Times*, Gelbaum talked of a conversation with his grandfather. "I asked, 'Abe, what do you think about all of these Mexicans coming here?' Abe didn't speak English that well. He said, 'I came here. How can I tell them not to come?'" That led Gelbaum to his bottom line: "I cannot support an organization that is anti-immigration. It would dishonor the memory of my grandparents."[49]

Zuckerman and Gelbaum are emblematic figures. Both are committed conservationists and humanitarians. Both are acutely attuned to the imperatives of their moral sensibilities. Zuckerman is driven by his conviction that failure to take urgent, pragmatic action to reduce environmental damage would be a form of generational malpractice. Gelbaum acts out of a sense of family obligation and moral conviction.

In 2018, as the Trump administration encountered widespread criticism for separating children from their parents after they were detained by the Border Patrol, Sierra Club Executive Director Michael Brune issued a statement of resistance. Its righteous outrage at

Trump's draconian tactics also provided a measure of how the club's immigration politics had changed since 1990.

"Trump's administration threatens immigrants, workers, women's health, LGBTQ rights, clean air, clean water, climate safeguards, and so much more. It's more important than ever to show that our diverse movement is united for justice. The Sierra Club is in total solidarity with immigrants, communities of color, Muslims, women, and all those who may be threatened under the Trump administration. The struggles to protect our communities and our environment cannot be separated. We are proud to take this opportunity to resist xenophobia and speak up for what's right."

Part 3
THE UNRAVELING

A Cautionary Tale of Failed Immigration Reform

The Immigration Reform and Control Act of 1986 has never come close to the goal that President Ronald Reagan identified when he signed it into law. Reagan said the legislation was intended to "establish a reasonable, fair, orderly, and secure system of immigration."[1] In a more precise formulation, a Department of Justice report in 1996 said the goal was "to reduce the magnet of jobs that draws illegal immigrants to this country and preserve those jobs for U.S. citizens and aliens authorized to work in the U.S."[2]

In Parts One and Two of this book, we examined many of the causes of the failed reform: structural flaws written into the legislation, the political clout of business interests, the policy reversals by important members of the Democratic coalition, and the conviction of many liberals that enforcement of immigration limits was a violation of the principles of inclusiveness and diversity that had become their core value. In Part Three we will see the unraveling of enforcement as it played out in the administrations from Reagan through Obama. Along the way we will examine the ambivalence of public opinion that, while strongly favoring limits on immigration, often recoiled from the harsh consequences of enforcing those limits.

As enforcement failed, the U.S. population of illegal immigrants grew from about 3.5 million in 1990 to its peak of 12.2 million in 2007. During that 17-year span, the unauthorized population grew at an annual average of more than 500,000 persons, most of them drawn by the job magnet that IRCA was intended to deactivate. The influx validated a warning issued the bipartisan Select Commission on Immigration and Refugee Policy long before IRCA was enacted. In its 1981 report to Congress, the commission recommended a sweeping legalization but cautioned that unless legalization was combined with "strong, new efforts to curtail illegal migration" it "could serve as an inducement for further illegal immigration."[3]

Although IRCA required employers to verify that new hires were authorized, it provided no reliable process to verify the authenticity of documents that new hires presented for the Employment Eligibility Verification form, commonly known as Form I-9. Lawmakers, in an effort to accommodate workers from a wide variety of backgrounds and social classes, allowed them to present documents issued by a plethora of state, tribal, and federal agencies. Moreover, employers were required to accept a document that "reasonably appears on its face to be genuine." The result, for many employers, was confusion and frustration.

In a more general sense, the I-9 process created a moral hazard, a system of incentives that enables illegal immigrants to pretend to be legal while employers pretend to believe them. The I-9 process became an administrative Potemkin village, an elaborate façade of legality. In 2006 David Martin, former general counsel of the Immigration and Naturalization Service, wrote that fraud had reduced the I-9 process to "an empty ceremony."[4]

The weakness of verification, the paucity of INS investigative resources, and tactical mistakes in levying fines on early violators, soon put IRCA's worksite enforcement component on a course to collapse. What followed was three decades of slow, steady enervation. The exceptions were episodic exercises of political expedience when the administrations of Presidents Bill Clinton, George W. Bush and Barack Obama conducted crackdowns in an effort to win public support for "comprehensive immigration reform" legislation that would once again combine legalization with promises of enforcement. The crackdowns, the thought, would ease suspicions that Washington would once again walk away from enforcement once another legalization program was in place. That skepticism, still widespread, was the inevitable result of the collapse of IRCA's promise to demagnetize the worksite for illegal immigrants.

In the decades after IRCA's enactment, INS leaders were forced to bow to pressure from Congress, including some elected officials whose early support for IRCA withered under pressure from employers. The INS mandated restrictions on the worksite raids that special agents conducted across the country to arrest illegal immigrants. Agents had sometimes raided businesses with such excessive force that they provoked public outrage. One result was that budgets in INS district offices around the country were "reprogrammed" away from worksite enforcement to less controversial work. Disgruntled special agents cited instances when colleagues had been detailed away from investigative work and assigned, for example, to work as an usher at a naturalization ceremony, or staff a public information desk,[5] or adjudicate petitions for naturalization.[6]

The most striking policy feature of the 34 years since IRCA became law has been the failure of successive administrations and congresses to reform IRCA's critical birth defect, its weak defective I-9 worker verification process. That deficiency remains, despite the efforts of many critics both within and outside the government. The most consistent critic has been the watchdog Government Accountability Office, whose many admonitions to Congress made it function like a Greek chorus in the protracted drama of IRCA's failure. The chapters that follow here will show how the familiar forces on the left and right that ensured IRCA's initial defects worked against efforts to repair them. Their efforts caused the unraveling at the worksite, thereby fomenting the populist backlash that took shape first in California, then in Arizona, and then across the country. One early manifestation of public frustration was the emergence of populist firebrand Pat Buchanan, whose 1990s runs for the presidency foreshadowed the emergence of Donald Trump.

Chapter 10:

The Reagan-Bush Years:

Small Government ideology meets big government reform

> **The act I am signing today is the product of one of the longest and most difficult legislative undertakings of recent memory. It has truly been a bipartisan effort, with this administration and the allies of immigration reform in the Congress, of both parties, working together to accomplish these critically important reforms. Future generations of Americans will be thankful for our efforts to humanely regain control of our borders and thereby preserve the value of one of the most sacred possessions of our people: American citizenship.** *—President Reagan at signing ceremony for the Immigration Reform and Control Act of 1986*

In October of 1987, Alan Nelson, the commissioner of the Immigration and Naturalization Service, called a press conference at INS headquarters in Washington. Flanked by senior staff on one side and statistical charts on the other, with an American flag behind him, Nelson stood at a podium and projected the confidence of an Army general in charge of a military campaign.

Nelson's purpose was to report on his agency's progress in implementing the Immigration Reform and Control Act, which had been passed nearly a year earlier. He pointed to a chart showing that the 1,124,931 arrests that the Border Patrol had recorded in the just-completed fiscal year represented a 30 percent drop from the year before. That, Nelson declared, demonstrated "that the immigration bill is beginning to work, that knowledge is out there, not only among American employers but potential illegal entrants."[1]

Turning to the agency's program to educate employers about their responsibilities under IRCA, Nelson said it was on track to complete a million informational visits by the following June. His personnel had also sent out seven million booklets that explained employers' obligation under the law to fill out a new document—dubbed Form I-9—to verify that new employees were authorized to work in the United States.

"The law is beginning to work...to discourage illegal immigration by turning off the magnet of jobs," Nelson said. He reported that employers were responding well to the INS effort to encourage their voluntary compliance. But he added the cautionary note that the six-month educational period provided by the law was over, so employers who failed to comply after receiving an initial warning from the INS were now subject to fines.

John Schroeder, the assistant commissioner for employer-labor relations, came to the podium to amplify Nelson's call for cooperation from employers, whose hiring practices IRCA was bringing under federal scrutiny for the first time. Schroeder had spent most of the previous year spreading the word around the country. In Dallas, for example, he spoke at an Hispanic Chamber of Commerce seminar titled "The New Immigration Reform Law and What Business Must Know and Do."

At the press conference, Schroeder praised the "good corporate citizenship" he had observed in visits with corporations like McDonald's, with its half-million employees, and Hyatt Hotels, with its workforce of 85,000. He said such relationships were "real good building blocks as far as the ability to show that it's not a difficult task to comply" with IRCA.

A BUSINESS-FRIENDLY CULTURE FOR IRCA ENFORCEMENT

In an interview in 2016, Schroeder recalled the business-friendly culture Nelson wanted to establish in the administration of IRCA.

"His yardstick was not how many fines did we issue this month," Schroeder said. "It was how many people did we educate this month."[2]

Indeed, a few weeks before Nelson's press conference, the owner of Blackie's House of Beef, a popular restaurant in the nation's capital, had marveled at the change from days when INS agents chased his busboys and left him with a depleted crew. "Now they come to visit you and have you work with them," he told *The Washington Post.*[3]

Nelson's emphasis on the nice-cop strategy reflected the business-friendly politics of the Reagan administration. But at that 1987 press conference he also displayed the tough-cop credentials he had received from IRCA. Nelson announced that a Quality Inn in nearby Arlington, Va., just across the Potomac from Washington, had become the first business to be fined under IRCA's employer sanctions provisions. He said the fine was necessary because the motel's managers had ignored an INS warning that they had hired unauthorized workers from Mexico, Guatemala, El Salvador, and Bolivia, "They just absolutely weren't complying in any respect," Nelson said. "And so we issued the fine."

Nelson's display of toughness on the east coast was replicated by the INS district office in Los Angeles, home to the country's largest concentration of illegal immigrants. Employers began to adjust their business practices as word spread that the federal government was serious about enforcing the new law. Ten days after Nelson's press conference, the *Los Angeles Times* reported that hotel operators in Orange County were raising wages in anticipation of a tighter labor market. "Let's be realistic," said one business executive. "It just makes sense there will be greater competition for a smaller pool of employees."[4]

And so, when IRCA hit the one-year mark, it seemed to be working according to plan. The indications were that it was demagnetizing the American workplace. By tightening the labor market, it promised to make the law of supply and demand work on behalf of

American workers rather than the employers who had relished the loose labor markets provided by illegal immigration.

THE WORKSITE GETS WISE TO THE MYTH OF ENFORCEMENT

But it didn't take long for the myth of IRCA might to be knocked down. Seven months after Nelson's press conference, the *Los Angeles Times* examined hiring practices at hotels, car washes, janitorial services, landscaping companies, and construction firms. It concluded that IRCA's employer sanctions "simply aren't working." Most employers said they could not tell whether the documents workers submitted for the I-9 process—birth certificates, Social Security Cards, green cards, and a host of others—were legitimate, the paper reported. "Many acknowledge that they knowingly accept questionable documents, while others are ignoring the law's requirements altogether."[5]

By 1989, the number of Border Patrol arrests dropped below one million for the first time in seven years. Skeptics suggested that was more an indication of the success of IRCA's amnesty than of its provisions for worksite enforcement. Those who had received amnesty no longer had to avoid the Border Patrol, they noted.

Meanwhile, immigration researchers at the University of California at San Diego reported that amnesty recipients were drawing unauthorized friends and relatives to join them by providing financing for the trip and assistance in finding work.[6] In 1990, the number of apprehensions jumped 23 percent to 1.2 million.[7] "The trend is not in the right direction," INS spokesman Duke Austin acknowledged.[8]

Also in 1990, two prominent immigration researchers warned that employers' initial belief that the federal government was serious about enforcing IRCA was "dissolving into complacency as employers experience the low probability of an actual INS visit."[9] Those researchers, future INS Commissioner Doris Meissner and her future director of planning Robert Bach, would play pivotal roles in a controversial INS move to focus enforcement resources only on the most egregious violations of IRCA. With that decision, the INS effectively acceded to the illegality that became entrenched in U.S. worksites during the 1990s. We will examine the work of Meissner and Bach in the next section of this paper.

In its failure to agree on a credible worker verification process, Congress, as we have seen, had dropped IRCA into the lap of the INS with a crippling birth defect. That flaw was then compounded by the nice-cop culture that Congress and the Reagan administration had demanded. As some INS agents would ruefully put it, they were expected to act like Officer Happy.

This was bound to be a dicey proposition for INS special agents. Trained as criminal investigators, they had always had the job of arresting illegal immigrants and removing them from the country. But now, instead of just conducting searches or quick-strike worksite raids to arrest illegal immigrants, they were required to master the unfamiliar techniques of employer-labor relations. The potential for problems stirred anxiety at INS headquarters and at the Justice Department, which oversaw the agency.

"Suddenly you had a law enforcement workforce who were going to be interfacing with American citizens and businesses," said Anne Veysey, who was an analyst in the INS enforcement division. Veysey said there was alarm at the risk inherent in a situation involving agents accustomed to rounding up illegal aliens—as they were commonly known—who were not likely to complain. Under IRCA, those same agents were now investigating the hiring practices of American businesses whose executives often had friends in high places. "They were greatly fearful of that concept," Veysey said.[10]

And then there was the matter of self-interest at a government bureaucracy that, because of IRCA, would grow budget and size. The INS did not want to establish a regulatory and enforcement regime so tough and punitive that it could antagonize business leaders and possibly lead to the repeal of employer sanctions. As one INS attorney put it, "If sanctions is sunset, we lose jobs and money."[11]

That anxiety took shape in an INS directive designed to regulate the regulators. Before agents could audit an employer's I-9 forms, they would have to notify employers three days in advance. "What that meant was that [during those three days] duplicate records were being created," Veysey said. The constraint aroused agents' suspicion that important people wanted to stifle worksite enforcement. "There was a constant battle with people who wouldn't allow us to actually take an enforcement posture," said Veysey.

THE INS INVESTIGATIONS DIVISION

IRCA created an enormous new set of responsibilities for the agents who worked under Jack Shaw, a former FBI agent who was the INS assistant commissioner for investigations. Their ranks, depleted by underfunding from Congress, had shrunk to about 900 nationwide when IRCA was passed. While Congress had authorized a near doubling of that force, the protracted congressional appropriations process led to hiring delays, which were followed by months of training before rookie agents were put to work.

The manpower shortage added to the difficulty of a task that some already thought was logistically impossible as well as politically unpopular. Even if the agents somehow reached Nelson's initial goal of visits to a million businesses, that would mean six million businesses went unattended in the vastness of the U.S. economy.

One of IRCA's principal congressional sponsors, Rep. Charles Schumer (D-N.Y.), ridiculed the employer-labor relations initiative. Schumer mocked it as "this idiotic education program" and called for more robust enforcement. "No one expects you're going to have an INS agent in every factory all the time," he said. "But if employers know they're going to be enforced rather stiffly, they're going to obey the law."[12]

The most severe impediment to the work of INS investigators was the proliferation of the counterfeit documents trade. Counterfeiters had long been active on a relatively small scale. But after IRCA required employers to demand documentary proof of work authorization, the industry boomed. For less than $200, street-level salesmen could provide a suite of phony documents—Social Security Cards, birth certificates, driver's licenses, visas—that made the holder appear to be authorized to live and work in the United States. Under the law, unless investigators found I-9 files whose documents were obviously fraudulent, employers could assert that they had acted in good faith and were therefore in compliance with the law.

A JAMMED ENFORCEMENT AGENDA, AT THE WORKSITE AND BEYOND

Even if INS special agents had received no new duties under IRCA, they would have had their hands full. In addition to pursuing illegal immigrants, they were expected to track hardened criminals and remove them from the country. They also had the jobs of investigating smuggling rings, money laundering schemes, and a category of crimes known as benefits fraud that involved efforts to obtain work authorization, green cards, naturalization and other benefits. One common scheme involved bogus marriages between a citizen and a foreigner whose only true love interest was a green card.

Meanwhile, the growth of the INS investigations division was meager in comparison. The number of special agents did grow from 1,004 in 1987 to 1,625 at the end of the George H.W. Bush administration in 1993. But given the size and complexity of their responsibilities, they were badly understaffed. "We were given an impossible task," Jack Shaw said in 2017. "We did the best we could, but we couldn't really do anything more than present an illusion of enforcement. The resources just weren't there."[13]

Failure under the circumstances Shaw faced was probably inevitable. Shortly after IRCA was passed, the investigative workload grew dramatically because of a category of fraud triggered by a deal that Rep. Schumer cut to get the bill passed. To placate the powerful California growers, Schumer agreed to a provision for "special agricultural workers" who would be eligible for amnesty if they had worked 90 days in the fields. One of Schumer's negotiating partners in this SAW deal was California Senator Pete Wilson.

The SAW program demonstrated the congressional inclination to turn immigration policy into a piñata stuffed with visas for the benefit of influential constituencies. It triggered an avalanche of bogus applications for amnesty. Many of the applicants had never held a hoe in their lives, but they showed up at INS amnesty processing centers with proof of eligibility provided by the phony document industry. Labor contractors also got into the action. Some charged $1,000 for affidavits falsely attesting to the 90 days of work for former "employees."

The result, reported the *New York Times,* was "one of the most extensive immigration frauds ever perpetrated against the United States Government."[14] The SAW program had been expected to accommodate about 350,000 migrants.[15] But more than 1.3 million applied and 1.1 million were approved.[16] Fraud was rampant, Shaw recalled in 2017. But because of political and institutional pressures as well as a shortage of INS agents, only a small fraction of those responsible for the fraud were prosecuted. Shaw summarized the instructions he received from his superiors this way: "You can't stop the process. You can't weed out who's legit and who's not legit. Get them through the system." He said the workforce demands of growers in California and Washington prevailed.[17]

THE BORDER PATROL AND EMPLOYER SANCTIONS

In an effort to distribute the worksite enforcement workload, the INS assigned Border Patrol agents to the employer education program. Many agents enjoyed the work. They found it to be an interesting change of pace from their usual duty of tracking illegal immigrants. "It meant you were in plain clothes and you weren't sweating in the desert," recalled retired agent Fernando Lucero, who worked in west Texas.[18]

Another retired Border Patrol agent, Mike Moon, said he had enthusiastically welcomed IRCA's attempt to shut off the job magnet. "I worked on the premise that if we started getting employers' attention, the word would get out," said Moon. "I thought that hiring people legally would become similar to paying your income tax."[19]

A similar optimism energized special agents of the INS Investigations Division. "There was a palpable excitement," recalled Dan Cadman, also retired. "Naive as it sounds in retrospect, we felt on the cusp of great things."[20]

That can-do spirit soon began to fade. While some of the factors that undermined efforts to stop illegal immigration were written into IRCA, others were the result of administrative decisions. INS attorneys, seeking to avoid lengthy legal battles, routinely negotiated with businesses found to have violated IRCA. But instead of backing up agents' efforts to impose heavy fines, as the law provided, the attorneys frequently agreed to accept sharply reduced amounts that left investigators shaking their heads in demoralized disbelief.

INS agents suffered the morale-draining effects of seeing their investigative work result in fines so low that employers could shrug them off as a minor business expense. Bill Yates, a career INS official, recalled that "issuing fines that the attorneys mitigated down to nothing was not inspiring work."[21]

Mike Moon talked of one such case involving an El Paso Walmart that was charged with knowingly hiring five unauthorized Mexican workers to assemble bicycles. Moon called it a flagrant violation. "They were warned once and they did it again," said Moon, recalling that while the fine was originally assessed at $10,000, Walmart ended up paying about $3,000. "For a corporation as big as Walmart a fine like that is considered just more overhead, just part of the cost of doing business," Moon said. He added that the case was "a real morale killer" for agents in the field.

Morale had long been a problem at the INS. The agency's dysfunction had been laid bare in 1981 by a Pulitzer Prize-winning investigative series in the *New York Times*. The stories portrayed the agency as "a bureaucratic stepchild beset by political interference and official indifference, an agency mired in mountains of unsorted paper and hampered by lost and misplaced files, and with a record of selective enforcement, brutality and other wrongdoing."[22]

Alan Nelson, a former San Francisco attorney who had become commissioner in Reagan's second year as president, would resign under pressure in 1989, early in the term of President George H.W. Bush. He stepped down after an audit ordered by Attorney General Richard Thornburgh turned up evidence of continuing dysfunction. President Bush replaced him with Gene McNary, the Republican county executive of St. Louis County, Missouri, where he had directed Bush's presidential campaign. McNary, like Nelson before him, came to the job with no background in immigration policy.

FRUSTRATED AGENTS LOOK AWAY FROM THE WORKSITE

Many special agents, disillusioned by what they saw as the politicization of worksite enforcement, gravitated toward investigative work that would not be stifled by the bureaucracy. Others became disillusioned with worksite enforcement because they found little satisfaction in arresting busboys or dishwashers.

During the 1980s, as immigration surged across the U.S., law enforcement officials attempted to adapt to the growing involvement of non-citizens in drug trafficking, human smuggling, and related violent crimes that required sustained investigative work. Yates was assigned to the multi-agency Organized Crime Drug Enforcement Task Force, which sought INS expertise in prosecuting criminals for violation of immigration laws. This was a variation on the strategy that decades earlier had enabled federal agents to bust gangster Al Capone for tax evasion.

There were other opportunities for INS agents to take on hardened criminals. The Anti-Drug Abuse Act of 1988 expanded the INS role in the arrest and deportation of serious offenders. In the early 1990s, Attorney General William Barr ordered the INS to assign agents to anti-gang enforcement efforts. Some agents would eventually take assignments with the Joint Terrorism Task Force, a nationwide partnership of law enforcement agencies.

Robert McGraw was one of the agents assigned to investigate drug-trafficking by foreigners. In a 2017 interview, McGraw recalled that he encountered Jamaicans whose fathers had cut sugar cane in Florida but who themselves became members of violent trafficking gangs.

McGraw said he found such work more worthwhile and interesting than worksite enforcement, especially given the constraints imposed on employer sanctions work. "Cops are pretty practical people," McGraw said in an email. "Why go through the motions on worksite enforcement when we can enforce the law in such a manner that is truly important to the nation we cherish and swore to defend?"[23]

The IRCA mandate that employers accept documents that "reasonably appear to be genuine" resulted in legal battles over that standard's meaning for I-9 audits. In one instance an appeals court overturned the administrative law judge's ruling that a Sizzler restaurant in Phoenix had knowingly hired an unauthorized Mexican immigrant named Armando Rodriguez. The INS attorneys argued that Sizzler employee Ricardo Soto should have been alerted to the fraud by the misspelling of Rodriguez's name on the Social Security card he presented. They also said the fraud would have been apparent if Soto had compared the card with the sample Social Security card in the employer's handbook the restaurant had received from the INS.

The court disagreed. "We can find nothing in the statute that requires such a comparison," it wrote. "Moreover, even if Soto had compared the card with the example, he still may not have been able to discern that the card was not genuine. The handbook contains but one example of a Social Security card, when numerous versions exist."[24]

That ruling highlighted another problem that made the I-9 process a source of torment and confusion for employers. The handbook presented them with 29 different documents that workers could present—including Social Security cards, immigration documents, birth certificates, school records—some of which were produced in multiple formats. The General Accounting Office (whose name was changed in 2004 to the Government Accountability Office) would practically plead with the INS to trim the list of acceptable documents. But bureaucratic inertia stalled that effort, which was further complicated by the INS's effort to make the I-9 process user-friendly for persons—such as Native Americans on reservations—who might not have ready access to official documents. In 1999 the GAO reported that the agency "has made little progress toward its goal of reducing the number of documents that employers can accept to determine employment eligibility."[25]

THE PAPER CURTAIN

In 1991, the Urban Institute Press published *The Paper Curtain*, a book that compiled research on the worksite enforcement effort. Its title told the tale of the weakness of the employer sanctions effort. In a de facto rebuke of the INS, researchers cautioned that in order for enforcement to succeed it "must systematically reinforce the perception that the government attaches high priority to enforcing the law." They followed that general criticism with the specific admonition that "violations must be pursued aggressively—and lead to substantial fines and prosecutions."[26]

Researcher Michael Fix found problems that derived from the administrative decentralization that was entrenched in INS culture. The 34 district directors across the country had a remarkable amount of decision-making autonomy, Fix learned. The result, he said, was a nationwide patchwork of enforcement priorities. For example, in New York, Miami, and San Antonio, efforts to report drug dealers "dominated the enforcement agenda, and in Houston sanctions enforcement was almost entirely eclipsed by a local preoccupation with prosecuting fraud" by those who submitted bogus documents in an effort to prove they were eligible under IRCA's provisions for amnesty.[27]

The researchers found wide discrepancies in the fines levied against employers. Some districts preferred complex investigations that produced heavy fines for a few employers. Others focused on identifying paperwork violations associated with the I-9 forms that led to minor fines for many employers. "The INS does not need complete uniformity in the amount of the fines it levies, but there shouldn't be that sharp a variation," said Fix. "People have to be treated similarly place to place."[28]

The discrepancies highlighted another organizational problem at the INS, the free hand that district directors around the country were given to run their operations. As a result, wrote former INS general counsel Raymond Momboisse in 1989, the agency "functions as if it were composed of numerous totally independent units....and there has been no national uniformity in the enforcement of the law or implementation of policy."[29] Momboisse said the agency had become "totally decentralized and totally disorganized. There is a void of confidence, a feeling of drift, a loss of direction and motivation."[30]

In an effort to rationalize the work of the Investigations Division, the INS in 1991 issued a directive for a standardized use of investigative agents' time, with 30 percent to be used to investigate criminal aliens, 30 percent on fraud, and 30 percent on worksite enforcement.[31] Commissioner Gene McNary took employer education off the agents' to-do list.

The agents often worked in teams that focused on a particular enforcement area. The problem was that there were too many scams and too few agents. Supervisors in each area of enforcement—criminal aliens, smuggling, marriage fraud, and employer sanctions—competed for reinforcements. Meanwhile, Gregory Bednarz, a career INS agent who eventually became acting assistant commissioner for investigations, suffered through a yearly budgetary process in which requests for more enforcement resources—especially more agents—were routinely hacked to pieces as they ran the gauntlet of review at the INS, the Department of Justice, Office of Management and

Budget, and congressional appropriators. "Very few of our requests for enhancements survived," said Bednarz in 2017.[32]

By 1990, the dysfunction at INS was only part of the explanation for the increasingly apparent failure of IRCA enforcement. The fundamental problem remained the same: the failure of Congress four years earlier to equip IRCA with a credible system of worker identification. Congress had bowed to the demands of the powerful left-right coalition that was led by business and ethnic groups but also included church groups, immigration lawyers, business libertarians, and civil libertarians who warned that proposals for secure identifiers would foster a big-government assault against privacy rights. They also feared that IRCA would induce many employers to avoid hiring anyone who looked or sounded foreign.

In 1990 those same activist groups came together to demand that Congress repeal sanctions. Their warnings of discrimination had just received powerful confirmation in a report from the General Accounting Office, which found that IRCA had indeed caused "a widespread pattern" of discrimination.[33] That finding prompted a hearing before the Senate Judiciary Committee, where Massachusetts Democrat Edward Kennedy joined with Utah Republican Orrin Hatch in calling for a repeal of sanctions.

At that hearing, Mario Moreno of MALDEF provided a poignant call for repeal as he asked for consideration of "the indignity, the pain, and the grim reality faced by minorities and foreign born workers" who were not being hired because of employer sanctions. He told the story of a Mexican-American job seeker who had been born in the United States but was turned away by an employer who demanded that he produce a document from the INS—which as a born citizen he never needed or received. "How much discrimination shall be tolerated by a nation committed to equal justice under the law?" Moreno asked. "We believe that the answer is none."[34]

That hearing featured tense exchanges between Kennedy's allies—from MALDEF, the National Council of La Raza, the Conference of Catholic Bishops, and the American Bar Association—and the Senate's leading advocate of employer sanctions, Wyoming Republican Alan Simpson.

In a gesture that combined civility, irony, and exasperation, Simpson addressed these sometimes bitter antagonists as "the groups" or, ironically, as "old friends." In 1986 Simpson had reluctantly accepted severely compromised provisions for identification in order to win passage of a bill that would–at least and at last–outlaw the hiring of illegal immigrants. In 1990 Simpson ridiculed the notion that sanctions would be abolished. "We all know damn well it isn't going to be repealed," he said. "Go check with your friendly AFL-CIO and find out." In a reference to the president of the AFL-CIO, he said, "Thank heaven for Lane Kirkland."[35]

As the failure of enforcement became increasingly evident during the 1990s, the AFL-CIO would eventually reverse that position. As we have seen, it would give up the fight against illegal immigrant workers and adopt a survival strategy based on recruiting them and pressuring Congress to grant them legal status.

The move to repeal sanctions fizzled in 1990, despite the efforts of the National Council of La Raza, whose president, Raul Yzaguirre, called it "the transcendent civil rights issue of our time."[36] Yzaguirre's organization was overtaking MALDEF as the most influential advocate of illegal immigrants. Cecilia Muñoz, the NCLR's senior immigration policy analyst, wrote a paper that called on Congress not only to repeal sanctions but also to "reject proposals to develop any type of identity card" to improve the worker verification process.[37] The first page of her report described the NCLR as an organization whose mission was to "improve life opportunities for the more than 20 million Americans of Hispanic descent."

A STRUGGLE OVER WORKER VERIFICATION

In late 1990, as Congress debated legislation to expand legal immigration, a dispute erupted between Hispanic representatives allied with the NCLR and Sen. Simpson, who had long claimed to be pursuing immigration policy in the broad national interest.

The dispute concerned Simpson's attempt to insert a provision for a pilot project to develop a secure driver's license that would include a biometric component, perhaps a fingerprint, and the driver's Social Security number. His hope was to develop a form of identification that would eventually be used to stop illegal immigration at the worksite.

Simpson's effort was blocked by a group of Hispanic members of Congress who were led by Rep. Ed Roybal of California. During floor debate, Roybal associated Simpson's effort with a particularly sinister form of racism. "It is ironic that South Africa has just abandoned its notorious pass-card identification program that has been an essential element of its hated apartheid system," he said. Such overwrought language, reflective of emotions that were rooted in the discrimination Roybal had experienced as a young man in East Los Angeles, was common in the debate over proposals for more secure worker identification. For civil libertarians and free-market conservatives, calls for more efficient identification stirred anxieties of Big Brother totalitarianism.

THE PROBLEM OF CRIMINAL ALIENS

That 1990 Senate hearing on employer sanctions foreshadowed a problem that would spread across the country in the 1990s. During that decade, as the nation's illegal immigrant population surged, the INS increasingly focused its enforcement attention on those whose violations of law went beyond immigration infractions. Because they were seen as an immediate threat to public safety, they became a prime concern of congressional appropriators who controlled the INS budget.

At the hearing Sen. Paul Simon asked Gene McNary about the case of Jose Ramon Orantes Pleitez, an illegal immigrant who had been arrested in New York, then released pending a deportation hearing, for which he failed to appear. Orantes Pleitez fled to Illinois, where he was detained by police for trespassing at an Air Force base. Police brought his illegal status to the attention of the INS, which declined to take him into custody because he had not been convicted of a crime. He then stole a pickup truck that he crashed into two pedestrians, killing them both.[38]

"He's an illegal alien, and at the present time that is not a priority situation for our law enforcement people," said McNary. Jack Shaw joined in with a statement about INS priorities in the face of an overwhelming workload. "Our focus today is on criminal aliens," said Shaw, adding that the INS was receiving about 100,000 calls annually from law enforcement agencies across the country who had detained illegal immigrants. But unless they had been convicted of a crime, they were not a priority for Shaw's agents. Over the next 15 years, Congress would repeatedly appropriate funds to provide the INS with more detention space to hold criminal aliens whose proliferation, in large measure, was the result of the failure of worksite enforcement.

Chapter 11:
The Clinton Years:
First Term Vigilance, Second Term Negligence

> **When it comes to enforcing our nation's immigration laws, we mean business. We are determined to restore the rule of law to our Nation's immigration system.**
>
> —*President Bill Clinton, February 1996*

> **We never really did in any serious way the enforcement that was to accompany the legalization of the people who were here illegally.**
>
> —*Doris Meissner, Clinton's Commissioner of the Immigration and Naturalization Service, 2007*

Bill Clinton became aware of the political dangers of chaotic immigration long before he became president. In 1980, when Clinton was governor of Arkansas, he lost reelection to a challenger whose TV ads portrayed him as weak in his response to rioting Cuban refugees at Fort Chaffee, Ark., where they were being held for screening. The turbulence intensified anxiety among those who thought the U.S. was under siege and the government was complicit in the foreign intrusion. Years later, the *Washington Post* reported on that episode under the headline "The forgotten story of how refugees almost ended Bill Clinton's career."[1]

In 1993, during Clinton's first months in the White House, a series of incidents seized the nation's attention and aggravated its immigration angst:

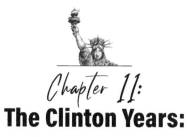

- Zoe Baird, Clinton's choice to be attorney general, withdrew her name from consideration, conceding to the fury that followed revelations that she had hired two illegal immigrants from Peru as a nanny and chauffeur, and then failed to pay Social Security taxes.
- A Pakistani who had applied for asylum in the U.S. killed two CIA employees in a shooting rampage outside the agency's headquarters in suburban Washington. CBS reporter Leslie Stahl reported on 60 Minutes about rampant abuse of the asylum system by foreigners who appeared at Kennedy Airport with phony documents. They were admitted into the country and received permits to work until their asylum hearings, for which few appeared. "It's so easy to defeat the system," an INS official told the *New York Times*. Another official added, "The aliens have taken control. The third world has packed its bags and it's moving."[2]
- A Kuwaiti who had entered the U.S. with fraudulent documents and asked for asylum blew up a yellow Ryder rental van filled with explosives in the garage below the North Tower of the World Trade Center.
- The Golden Venture, a dilapidated cargo ship smuggling several hundred Chinese ran aground off New York. Ten people drowned or died of hypothermia in their attempt to reach shore. The story of that tragic odyssey alerted Americans to the brutal world of the "snakeheads," smugglers who were funneling tens of thousands of Chinese into the U.S. at a per capita cost of $30,000 or more.

The drumbeat of stories warned of disorder, danger, and lawlessness in an immigration system that was under-regulated and overwhelmed. Public concerns intensified when the nightly television news showed thousands of Haitian and Cuban "boat people" approaching the Florida coast, their faces etched in hunger and desperation.

The Clinton years, 1993 to 2001, were a decisive time in the story of illegal immigration. At first, INS enforcement expanded in response to public outcry and Clinton's determination to avoid another Fort Chaffee-style political debacle. Then it imploded under an array of economic, political, demographic, and social pressures. This allowed an immense and protracted burst of illegal immigration from Mexico. Word spread that U.S. employers' interest in Mexican labor was strong, worksite enforcement was weak, and it was easy to get lost in the interior of the United States.

Late in the decade, as the U.S. economy boomed and the unemployment rate dropped to four percent, Richard Stana of the GAO sized up the state of worksite enforcement at a congressional hearing. Stana said most illegal immigrants "are well aware that the enforcement mechanism is modest and that they stand a good chance, once across the border, to find employment."[3] The *Washington Post* reported that flimsy enforcement combined with the easy availability of fraudulent documents to create a "pull factor that encourages people to risk crossing the border illegally...or to use various other means to gain entry."[4] IRCA enforcement went bust long before the economy's dot-com bubble collapsed at the end of the decade. Far from shrinking illegal immigration, IRCA had encouraged it. Instead of deactivating the jobs magnet, IRCA had supercharged it.

In 1994 President Clinton recognized the political danger in the populist backlash against illegal immigration. Nowhere was the climate more tense than in California, where Republican Governor Pete Wilson was blaming Washington for the chaotic influx that played out in plain view every night just south of San Diego. Initially far behind in the polls, Wilson rode Proposition 187, the anti-illegal immigration ballot measure that was passed with 59 percent of the vote, to an easy reelection victory.

Clinton, wary of both the backlash and a potential challenge from Wilson in the presidential election of 1996, ordered Attorney General Janet Reno to California. There she directed a buildup of the

Border Patrol, which launched Operation Gatekeeper in an attempt to impose order on the borderlands chaos. Border fencing, cameras, and lighting were part of the effort as Reno vowed that the Clinton administration would deliver "a secure border that is fully defensible against illegal immigrants."[5] She then added a steely-eyed pledge: "We will not rest until the flow of illegal aliens has abated." Such never-retreat declarations from officials in the Clinton administration became a regular feature of 1990s immigration reporting.

To understand the Clinton administration's failure to fulfill that pledge, it is useful to look at an assessment that respected demographer Jeffrey Passel would make seven years after Clinton left office. Writing for the Pew Hispanic Center, Passel observed, "The spread of immigration flows to new areas (largely driven by new settlement patterns of unauthorized Mexican immigrants) has transformed the political issue of immigration from a largely local concern (in six states) in the early 1980s to a national issue now."[6]

But in 1994, Clinton was focused on short-term political danger. Operation Gatekeeper calmed the chaotic corridor that stretched north from Tijuana, thereby easing Clinton's political problem. However, it didn't close the gate. It merely shifted it to remote stretches of the border. Smugglers, so wily and tough that Mexican slang named them "coyotes," adjusted their routes and raised their prices.

INS criminal investigators were surprised by the intensity of the counterfeit-documents trade that served illegal immigrants once they reached their destination. "There's so much money associated with it that every time we arrest and prosecute a ring, there's always somebody to step in behind them," said John Brechtel, who supervised INS investigations in Los Angeles.[7] When agents in Los Angeles busted a counterfeiting ring, they seized 115,000 blank documents—including green cards and Social Security cards—with an estimated street value of $5 million.[8]

Despite such arrests, the phony-document trade was so lucrative that other groups rushed in to meet the demand from illegal immigrants. Labor economist and immigration expert Philip Martin reported that despite Operation Gatekeeper many illegal border-crossers made it past the Border Patrol on their first attempt. In the understated tone of someone drawing attention to an obvious problem that has long been overlooked, Martin said "Many believe that the INS should devote more resources to interior enforcement to prevent unauthorized workers from obtaining U.S. jobs."[9]

BARBARA JORDAN AND THE U.S. COMMISSION ON IMMIGRATION REFORM

As Janet Reno was pouring federal resources into the border, the U.S. Commission on Immigration Reform, under the leadership of civil rights icon and former Democratic congresswoman Barbara Jordan, presented a proposal to repair the hole that counterfeit documents had punched into worksite enforcement. The commission called for pilot programs to test systems for a computerized registry of information supplied by the INS and the Social Security Administration. Employers would be able to access the registry by telephone to learn if Social Security numbers presented by new hires were valid and had been issued to someone authorized to work. While the commission acknowledged that there could be challenges to such a system, its 1994 report to Congress asserted that the pilot programs would provide "an opportunity to determine the most cost-effective, fraud-resistant, and non-discriminatory method available." That report, titled "U.S. Immigration Policy: Restoring Credibility,"[10] became the basis for legislation sponsored by Republicans Alan Simpson in the Senate and Lamar Smith in the House.

The commission's report and the legislation it inspired drew fierce opposition from the left-right coalition that had long resisted immigration enforcement. Lucas Guttentag of the ACLU warned that the proposals to reform worker verification were "merely a launching pad for a national computer registry and a de facto ID card system that will make human guinea pigs of millions of people in the states where the system is supposed to be tested," The National

Rifle Association joined in, sounding an alarm about government intrusion into personal privacy. Cecilia Muñoz of the National Council of La Raza, fearing that employers would only check the status of minorities, denounced Jordan's proposal as "worse than Big Brotherism" for Latinos.[11] Republican insider, free-market advocate, and Microsoft lobbyist Grover Norquist orchestrated a protest that likened the proposal to Nazi dehumanization of Jews. "We had guys walking around with tattoos on their arms," he said. Stephen Moore of the libertarian Cato Institute added another note of Manichean struggle. He said Jordan had made "an evil proposal.....the camel's nose under the tent for a national ID card."[12]

Conflicting political considerations put the Clinton White House on a zigzag course. While Clinton was attuned to growing public anxiety about illegal immigration, he had political allies and donors who wanted expansive immigration policies and compassion for illegal immigrants. Meanwhile, economic and demographic forces were intruding from south of the border. In Mexico an economic crisis in 1995 wiped out a million jobs,[13] even as the Mexican working-age population was exploding in a baby boom that between 1970 and 2000 would swell the population from 53 million to 100 million. The result was an exodus to the United States, much of it illegal and much of it to Arizona, where schools, hospitals, and social service agencies experienced tremendous new demands for their services

In his 1995 State of the Union address, Clinton talked tough about illegal immigration. "All Americans, not only in the states most heavily affected but in every place in this country, are rightly disturbed by the large numbers of illegal aliens entering our country," he said. "The jobs they hold might otherwise be held by citizens or legal immigrants. The public services they use impose burdens on our taxpayers." Clinton pledged "to better identify illegal aliens in the workplace as recommended by the commission headed by former Congresswoman Barbara Jordan."

Clinton introduced a theme repeatedly raised by Jordan. "We are a nation of immigrants, but we are also a nation of laws," he said. "It is wrong and ultimately self-defeating for a nation of immigrants to permit the kind of abuse of our immigration laws we have seen in recent years, and we must do more to stop it." Jordan issued a blunt warning that failure to manage immigration would provoke an anti-immigration backlash. "Unless this country does a better job in curbing illegal immigration, we risk irreparably undermining our commitment to legal immigration," she said.[14] The possibility of a populist backlash against unchecked immigration was given ominous form by Sen. Dianne Feinstein, D-Calif. "Ladies and gentlemen, let me say to you what I honest-to-God believe the truth. If we cannot effect sound, just and moderate controls, the people of America will rise to stop all immigration."[15]

Clinton's initial endorsement of Jordan's recommendations aligned him with a formidable and beloved national figure whose stature he had acknowledged in 1994 when he awarded her the Presidential Medal of Freedom. Jordan was "the most outspoken moral voice of the American political system," Clinton said. He also said Jordan had "captured the nation's attention and awakened its conscience in defense of the Constitution, the American dream, and the community we share as American citizens." Elaine Jones, director of the NAACP Legal Defense Fund, added this: "Barbara understood that the law was the fabric of society."[16]

RHETORIC MEETS REALITY, AND LOSES

Clinton's soaring rhetoric clashed with the brutal reality of the American workplace, where many business leaders were delighted with the availability of low-wage unauthorized workers. The attractiveness of unauthorized workers to unscrupulous employers was famously described by Ray Marshall, President Carter's liberal secretary of labor, who observed that they worked "hard and scared."

During the 1990s many states that had experienced little immigration for decades—including Georgia, North Carolina, and

Iowa—saw rapid growth in their immigrant populations. While estimates at the time put the annual growth of the unauthorized population at about 250,000, demographers would later double that estimate as they got a clearer picture of the dimensions of the influx. The Pew Research Center would report that between 1990 and 2000 the nation's illegal immigrant population grew from 3.5 million to 8.6 million. So the average annual increase exceeded 500,000.[17]

California continued to attract the largest numbers of newcomers, both legal and illegal. But even there the INS Investigations Division, which had the job of enforcing employer sanctions, remained a 98-pound weakling. In 1995 the *Los Angeles Times* took the measure of the mismatch, reporting that in Southern California "only 30 to 35 INS agents monitor almost half a million employers in a vast area stretching from San Clemente to San Luis Obispo, and east to the Nevada and Arizona borders." "Sanctions have not been supported with resources," said Jack Shaw, who directed the INS investigations division. "If we're not visible, no one takes the law seriously."[18]

CONGRESSMAN BONILLA GETS LUBY'S OFF THE HOOK

Lee Bargerhuff, the Patrol Agent in Charge of the Border Patrol's San Antonio station, received a lesson in the politics of enforcement in 1995 when a secretary interrupted his briefing of special agents who were about to conduct a worksite raid at a Luby's cafeteria. U.S. Rep. Henry Bonilla, who represented the city, was on the phone. A year earlier Bonilla, a Republican, had called for a crackdown on illegal immigration. But this time he had a different message. Somehow he had found out about the impending raid. He wanted Bargerhuff to go easy on Luby's, whose corporate headquarters were in San Antonio. Constituent service trumped worksite enforcement.

"The congressman told me Luby's was an important corporate citizen, and he said that surely we could work something out," Bargerhuff recalled in 2017.[19] Bargerhoff replied to the congressman that if Luby's had been willing to address INS concerns about its hiring practices, there would be no need for a raid. "As politely as I could, I told him my orders didn't come from him and that he wasn't in my chain of command," Bargerhuff recalled. He said he then resumed the briefing, only to be interrupted again, this time by a blunt message from the headquarters of the Laredo sector. "They told me the operation was scrubbed," he said.

At the INS office in Atlanta, district director Tom Fischer received a stream of calls in 1995 from people who were alarmed at the crowding of schools and neighborhoods resulting from the big migrant influx. "They were asking me, 'What the hell are you guys doing and why don't you do something about this?'" Fischer later recalled.[20]

Meanwhile, an INS colleague in Arkansas, where the poultry industry was matching the health-conscious public's growing appetite for poultry with its own appetite for immigrant labor, wrote a memorandum that assessed the situation there. "The large number of illegal aliens and our inability to deal with them has brought criticism and the notion that we have become an inept agency unable to enforce our immigration laws in the interior of the United States," the internal memo said. It called for action "to change this negative perception, enhance our image and regain the confidence of our citizens."[21]

Those concerns generated an enforcement campaign that took its name from an admonition Fischer had received from his wife's aunt. "She asked me, "Why aren't you protecting American workers" Fischer said. Condensing those last three words to their initials, he introduced Operation SouthPAW, a new attempt to deliver on IRCA's old promise.

SouthPAW mobilized dozens of INS agents to pursue tips that came primarily from authorized workers and the public. They conducted raids at construction sites, carpet factories, hotels, poultry plants, and other worksites in Georgia, Alabama, Arkansas, Tennessee, and the Carolinas. They arrested 4,044 unauthorized workers, about 90 percent of whom were from Mexico. The rest were from 40 other countries in Latin America, Asia, Eastern Europe, Africa, and the Middle East. In a pamphlet titled "Worksite Enforcement: Reducing the Job Magnet," the INS boasted that because of their removal $55.7 million in wages were made available to legal American workers."[22] Adding a new twist to the old tactic of worksite raids Fischer worked with employment agencies to fill suddenly vacant jobs with authorized workers. He touted the results in regular statements to the press. "We're going to ensure that the American worker is protected," Fischer said as he supervised a 1996 raid at a carpet factory in Dalton, Ga.[23]

SouthPAW triggered alarms at the National Immigration Forum, a Washington-based advocacy group that tied together the left-right coalition for expansive immigration. "It smacks of a kind of police approach," said Frank Sharry, the forum's executive director, who wanted the INS to back off. *USA Today* observed that "immigration advocates, many of whom have supported Clinton, are growing increasingly bitter, convinced he's been influenced by public resentment of illegal immigrants."[24]While that argument would gain political power as both legal and illegal immigration continued to grow, Tom Fischer received so much support that top-level INS officials who wanted to rein in the raids kept quiet. "They really couldn't shut us down because the public reaction was so good," said Fischer.[25] For Clinton, who was as attuned to public unrest over illegal immigration as he was fixated on his campaign for re-election, it was a bad time to accede to the wishes of Frank Sharry and his allies.

THE 1996 BATTLE IN CONGRESS

The 1994 mid-term elections put Republicans in control of the House and Senate for the first time in 40 years, enabling two Republicans, Sen. Alan Simpson and Rep. Lamar Smith of Texas, to become chairmen of the immigration subcommittees in their respective chambers. Because the national mood had grown stern about illegal immigration, they were confident of winning enactment of the

Jordan commission's proposals for stopping illegal immigration and redesigning legal immigration.

Testifying at a Senate hearing before the election, Jordan issued a call to action "It is both a right and a responsibility of a democratic society to manage immigration so that it serves the national interest," she said. Later she declared that the commission found that there was "no national interest in continuing to import lesser-skilled and unskilled workers to compete in the most vulnerable parts of our labor force. Many American workers do not have adequate job prospects. We should make their task easier to find employment, not harder."[26]

Simpson and Smith had hoped to win mandates for a robust and mandatory system to verify workers' legal status. They failed. Their effort to boost worksite enforcement was cut down to a pilot project in a few states where employer participation would be voluntary. The two lawmakers also adopted the Jordan commission's recommendations to redesign legal immigration policy to prioritize the speedy reduction of nuclear families while curtailing the "chain immigration" system. That system allowed a single immigrant gradually to bring an extended family to the U.S, including siblings, cousins, parents, and grandparents.

The reform proposals for legal immigration also drew intense resistance. President Clinton backed off his endorsement of Jordan's proposal, bowing to opposition that included organizations of Asian-Americans who wanted to protect the chain immigration. Karen Narasaki of the National Asian Pacific-American Legal Consortium denounced the commission's recommendations as "an attack on the Asian community."[27] Silicon Valley entrepreneurs joined in to protect their access to skilled foreign workers. The effort to reform legal immigration policy was routed by its well-organized and influential opponents.

A SPLIT BETWEEN DEMOCRATS

While most members of the Democratic coalition opposed Simpson and Smith, some held to the traditional Democratic concern for working-class Americans. That concern had launched the long debate that culminated in the 1986 passage of IRCA. But as illegal immigration became entrenched and Hispanic political power grew, many Democrats abandoned the old liberal efforts to stop illegal immigration. Latino activists had become an important part of the Democratic coalition.

A 1996 debate on the floor of the House of Representatives included a vivid exchange between two of the most liberal Democrats put the party's divide in sharp relief. John Conyers of Michigan invoked the civil libertarian argument about the dangers of government regulation. "This is the famous camel's nose under the tent amendment," Conyers warned indignantly. "This is the one where it starts off real nice. Not to worry, folks. It is okay. Trust us....We will do it just like we did the Japanese internment program when we said we are going to find out who the Japanese are that need to be rounded up."[28] Like many other Democrats, Conyers was a crusader for social justice who came to see efforts to stop illegal immigration as a social injustice.

The response from Barney Frank of Massachusetts blended incredulity with sarcasm about the internment camp analogy. "We are not talking about camels, noses and tents," Frank said. "We are talking about whether or not we have a rational approach to enforcing the laws against illegal immigration. I have to say that, of all the things in my life that puzzle me, why so many of my liberal friends have such an aversion to this simple measure is the greatest....To turn this into some act of oppression makes no sense whatsoever."[29]

Alan Simpson was accustomed to accusations of big-government oppression from the left-right coalition that had fought immigration enforcement for decades. In 1996 he was also infuriated by what he saw as cynical machinations at the Immigration and Naturalization Service. At issue was a blatantly misleading INS press release that suggested there was no need for such legislative action because immigration was slowing on its own, due to a reduced demand for green cards. Questioning Meissner at a Senate oversight hearing where she was the only witness, Sens. Simpson and Feinstein accused the INS of politically motivated deception to derail the proposal to reduce legal immigration.

"What [the press release] created was a real distortion in what we were trying to do and made it falsely look like we were reducing the numbers, when in fact the numbers were increasing dramatically," said Feinstein. "I think it created, for me at last, a major credibility problem....because this was hotly contested" in the Judiciary Committee. Sen. Simpson, declaring his respect for Meissner, said he did not blame her for the press release. But he cautioned her that she had been "ill-served" by others at the INS, people who "have simply political interests at heart, and that does not serve the country's interest well."[30] He did not name names.

NO LOBBY FOR AMERICAN WORKERS

The Jordan commission's work represented a high-water mark of efforts to stop illegal immigration and to reduce legal immigration. When she died in early 1996, at the age of 59, those efforts lost their most powerful voice, the voice least likely to be silenced by claims of guilt by association with bigots or Big Brother. Simpson and Smith lost a powerful ally at a crucial point in the legislative calendar. In a tribute to Jordan, Simpson said, "If she had been here, we would have gotten a lot further."[31]

In 1997, Robert Reich, who had been labor secretary during President Clinton's first term, lamented the absence of a Washington lobby that could challenge the tenacious and well-funded coalition that hacked away at the efforts to enact measures for effective worker verification. "There's no National Association of Working Poor," said Reich. "There's no special-interest lobbying group working on behalf of very poor people trying desperately to find and keep jobs."[32]

Susan Martin, who had worked at Barbara Jordan's side, was part of a team of Georgetown University researchers who in 2007 issued a blunt assessment of protracted congressional failure to enforce immigration law within the U.S. They reported: "Despite acknowledgment of IRCA's ineffectiveness in stemming illegal immigration by analysts from a multiplicity of political perspectives, disciplines, and institutions cross-cutting the academic, government, labor, and advocacy communities, there has been little political will for worksite enforcement since its passage in 1986. In its place, Congress has primarily channeled resources towards securing the southern border."[33]

THE JOHN HUANG CONNECTION

An investigative report by the *Boston Globe* detailed a campaign by Asian-Americans to persuade President Clinton to reverse his early endorsement of Jordan's proposal to end chain migration. The *Globe* reported that the reversal "brought the White House in line with the top priority" of Asian-Americans who had contributed heavily to his campaign.[34]

The *Globe* conducted a follow-the-money investigation of the advocacy of John Huang, an immigrant from Taiwan who in 1992 had raised $250,000 for Clinton's first presidential campaign.[35] Four years later, he was credited with raising about $3 million for Clinton's re-election. By then he was a vice chairman of the Democratic National Committee, The *Globe* reported that Huang "waged an intensive effort to influence Clinton's migration policy."

In a remarkable coincidence, Huang had earlier been appointed to a policymaking position at the Commerce Department for which he was "totally unqualified" according to the congressional testimony of a former undersecretary for international trade.[36] Huang worked under Charles Meissner, the Assistant Secretary of Commerce in charge of international economic policy and husband of INS commissioner Doris Meissner. Charles Meissner died in the 1996 plane crash in Croatia that took the lives of Commerce

Secretary Ron Brown and others. In 1999 Huang pleaded guilty to a felony conspiracy charge for violating campaign finance law. His story is an example of the links between campaign fundraising and public policy in Washington

TOUGH TALK ON DEPORTATIONS

Just before the 1996 election, the White House held a press briefing to boast about record numbers of deportations of illegal immigrants. "I am proud once again to announce that the Clinton administration's determination to remove criminal aliens and other deportable aliens from the United States has produced record results," Meissner announced.[37]

She said 67,094 illegal immigrants—criminal and non-criminal—had been deported in the 1995 fiscal year. In a dutiful tribute to Clinton that echoed statements from the White House and the Justice Department, Meissner contrasted his performance to that of his predecessors. "For too many years, under-enforcement of our nation's immigration laws undermined their credibility," she said. "But this administration's unprecedented expansion of and support for strong but fair enforcement of immigration laws...is restoring that credibility."

In another bow to Clinton's leadership, Meissner declared that the INS "means business when it comes to enforcing immigration laws in the workplace." That echoed language Clinton had used the day after Pat Buchanan's surprising second-place finish in the Iowa caucuses, when he issued an executive order barring companies that had knowingly hired unauthorized workers from receiving government contracts. "American jobs belong to America's legal workers," Clinton said. "This executive order will make clear that when it comes to enforcing our nation's immigration laws, we mean business. We are determined to restore the rule of law to our Nation's immigration system."[38]

Clinton's restoration project faced a panorama of brazen worksite illegality. A day earlier, INS agents had arrested 20 Mexicans and

Hondurans at the construction site for a $200 million federal office building directly across from the INS offices in Atlanta. Four days before that, agents arrested 22 Mexicans working at Camp Lejeune, a Marine Corps base in North Carolina, where they were employed by companies that had received federal contracts worth $37 million.

Despite the stern rhetoric from the president and the INS commissioner, the illegal immigrant population continued to surge as the business of evading IRCA continued its boom. In 1997, when Meissner and Reno called in the press to trumpet that year's deportations of 112,000 illegal immigrants that year, reporters pointed to reports that the nation's illegal immigrant population was increasing dramatically.

USA Today reported that Meissner "could not predict when the stepped-up enforcement efforts would substantially reduce the overall number of illegal immigrants."[39] Said Meissner, "I would not want to speculate on that. I think the important point is that all the trend lines are in the right direction." Janet Reno, using another phrase that became a Clinton administration favorite, declared that the record deportation figures showed the effectiveness of the administration's strategy to establish "a seamless web of enforcement from the border to the workplace." Despite Reno's best intentions, the "seamless web" was a myth that was mocked by the reality of both the border and the worksite.

THE BACKLASH BUILDS, BUT FARMERS CALL THEIR FRIENDS

As illegal immigration gathered strength, so did the backlash against it. In 1996 Patrick Buchanan ran for the Republican presidential nomination on a populist platform that foreshadowed the Donald Trump campaign 20 years later. In contrast to Trump, he brought a grace note to his campaign, praising Mexicans as "a good people," but he bluntly declared that illegal immigrants had "no right to break our laws and come into our country and go on welfare and, some of them, commit crimes." Buchanan wanted to unwind trade agreements and vowed to "stop this massive illegal immigration cold."[40]

In many parts of the U.S. elected officials aligned themselves with public anger, declaring their own frustration with illegal immigration and their determination to stop it. But on the rare occasions when INS agents cracked down on industries that were backbones of local economies, members of Congress switched to ad hoc displays of righteous indignation against the heavy hand of the immigration police. And so it was in 1998, when Bart Szafnicki of the INS office in Atlanta led an operation to arrest dozens of unauthorized Mexican workers who were harvesting Georgia's $80 million Vidalia onion crop.

The farmers of Vidalia had given up on obtaining workers through the H-2A temporary worker program. They complained that the program was too complex and cumbersome. When Szafnicki's men showed up in their fields, the farmers demanded that their elected representatives protect them from financial catastrophe. Congressional offices erupted in responsive outrage. "What the INS has done with gestapo tactics has been to eliminate the labor supply," said the chief of staff for Republican U.S. Rep. Saxby Chambliss.[41]

Another Georgia Republican, U.S. Rep. Jack Kingston, was outraged despite his previous alarm at the "explosion of illegal immigrants" and his insistence that, "We have no need to apologize for cracking down on those who flout our laws by entering illegally."[42] Kingston joined U.S. Sen. Paul Coverdell and other members of Georgia's congressional delegation in condemning "the apparent lack of regard for farmers in this situation and the intimidation tactics being employed by federal officials." Szafnicki called out a pointed question as Coverdell passed by at a public event. "Can you tell me which laws you passed that you want me to enforce?" he asked.[43]

Pulled between constituents who were usually not organized to press their concerns about illegal immigration and employer groups that were often well organized behind Washington lobbyists, many members of Congress adopted separate strategies for border and interior enforcement. They heaped appropriations on the Border

Patrol to demonstrate their determination to defend the rule of law. But on the home front, they protected constituent employers who expected them to intervene with the INS.

David Martin, the INS general counsel from 1995 to 1998, would describe the trend a decade later. Martin observed that "significant interest group pressure quietly helps push Congress toward underfunding these enforcement endeavors, and there has been no equivalently organized constituency pushing back."[44] Efforts to improve the worker verification process "generate determined resistance among a highly influential interest group," Martin wrote. He went on to describe the inclination of Congress to walk the path of least resistance: "Border measures, in contrast, step on almost no influential toes. Border crackdowns are therefore used to demonstrate enforcement seriousness, alienating few and placating many. But focusing only on the border is an ineffective way to master our enforcement problems. The key fulcrum for effectiveness is the workplace."

In a 2017 interview, Martin elaborated on his observation of the behind-the-scenes process by which financial support was drained from worksite enforcement. "We knew that groups like the Chamber of Commerce were well organized and very savvy and had good communications channels with the appropriators," Martin said. "That's where it would show up. It also showed up in internal deliberations, as the president's budget was being put together—what would be funded and what wouldn't—plus the departmental and DOJ decisions as to what they would prioritize."[45]

A prime example of enforcement schizophrenia on Capitol Hill is the 1996 immigration bill, which carried the cumbersome name: "The Illegal Immigration Reform and Immigrant Responsibility Act of 1996." The legislation mandated the hiring of thousands of new Border Patrol agents to keep the undocumented out of the country, but it also frustrated efforts to keep them out of the workplace. Moreover, the bill produced something akin to a legislative card trick. While legislators authorized 300 additional INS worksite investigators each year for three years, Republicans in control of the appropriations committees blocked funding for those positions. That prompted Sen. Ted Kennedy to complain that "when it comes to enforcing the immigration laws in the workplace, one has to wonder whether our Republican friends are really serious."[46]

Kennedy's complaint prompted Arizona Republican Jon Kyl to aim an accusatory finger at the White House. Sen. Kyl didn't want Republican fingerprints to be alone on the card trick. He said the Clinton administration had failed to assert its influence on behalf of efforts to boost worksite enforcement. "If there is any blame for not having adequate appropriations, I do not think you can just lay it at the doorstep of Congress," he said. "It is the responsibility of both the administration and the Congress to ensure that in laying out these new challenges and responsibilities we have got to fund it as well as authorize it adequately."[47]

MORALE FALLS, RAIDS DIMINISH

While Meissner and the White House declared their commitment to the rule of law, INS agents in the field remained frustrated at the paucity of resources that Congress provided to deal with a problem that was expanding dramatically across the country. Belying repeated assurances of the Clinton administration's vigilance and determination, the GAO reported that worksite enforcement accounted for less than four percent of INS enforcement work in the 1996 fiscal year. Moreover, most arrests produced meager results because, as the Department of Justice's inspector general reported, "INS does not have adequate resources to house and deport most of the illegal aliens it encounters in the worksite."[48]

Morale dwindled. Agents in the field believed INS headquarters was turning its back on worksite enforcement. Tom Fischer, directing the Atlanta office, recalled that at meetings with his peers from other parts of the country, "Everybody would moan and groan" about the lack of support. "That assessment was echoed by Bart Szafnicki, who as assistant district director for investigations in Atlanta had worked under Fischer. "It always felt like you had to battle to do your job," Szafnicki said in a 2016 interview. "You were thwarted one way or another. A lot of it was subtle. They would be trying to focus your energies in another direction." He said it was clear that many people at high levels looked askance at those who believed that INS raids were an essential tactic in the effort to deter illegal immigration. "Sometimes it was like they thought you were Don Quixote tilting at windmills."

In the summer of 1996, a worksite raid in Alan Simpson's home state of Wyoming provided a case study of the excess and clumsiness that eroded public support for roundups of illegal immigrant workers. According to a *Denver Post* account about the raid in the tourist town of Jackson Hole, some suspects were "nabbed on the street merely because their skin was brown", while others were loaded into a horse trailer stinking from manure.[49] Although the worst abuses were apparently committed by local police who had assisted in the raid, the resulting uproar tainted the INS, which initiated the operation. Said INS official Joe Greene, "We flubbed it.... We're not going to do business like that anymore."

As if to demonstrate the futility of the raid, some of the deported workers returned to Jackson a week or two later. One news story told of grim conditions that made Americans shun work there. "American workers won't take those jobs because they don't pay a living wage," said one resident. "Mexicans are willing to live 10 people to a two-bedroom apartment." Another said Mexicans "work lots of overtime for straight pay, and they won't go complaining about it to the labor board."[50]

Syndicated columnist Lars-Erik Nelson used the Jackson Hole episode to criticize IRCA's fatal structural flaw. "The law rewards ignorance," he wrote. "There is virtually no penalty for hiring illegal aliens. All you need is a blank look, a shrug of the shoulders and an innocent, hurt voice when it is suggested your ragged $2-per-hour dishwashers, speaking in unknown tongues, might not be legal residents."[51]

RISING ANGER FROM A RESTIVE PUBLIC

Public frustration was commonplace in communities that experienced an intense illegal influx. Sen. Chuck Grassley, R-Iowa, reported on constituent complaints about the seeming inability of the INS to respond to calls for help. Grassley told of a police chief who "had released a truckload of illegals because the INS would not or could not pick them up." INS commissioner Doris Meissner responded that the demand for INS special agents exceeded the agency's supply. "We are moving as quickly as we can, given the staffing that we have," she said. "And as soon as we have more, Iowa is on the list."

Three years later Congress would provide funding for the INS to station "quick response teams" in Iowa and nine other states where illegal immigration boomed in the 1990s: Arkansas, Colorado, Georgia, Iowa, Kentucky, Missouri, Nebraska, North Carolina, and South Carolina. That effort prompted a warning from labor union organizer Muzaffar Chishti that such cooperation "will do irreparable harm to law enforcement and public safety" because "if local police are known to have a cooperative relationship with the INS, members of immigrant communities are not likely to report crimes or assist officers investigating crimes."[52] And so the tensions grew, steadily compounding in variety and complexity as the illegal influx continued. Enforcement advocates wanted tough measures. Defenders of illegal immigrants warned of the costs of alienating the newcomers. The INS, chronically beleaguered, underfunded, and hounded by critics on all sides, struggled to find its way in a fraught social and political environment.

Sen. Kyl of Arizona, the state that received much of the illegal traffic deflected from California by Operation Gatekeeper, told Meissner that he had received "considerable correspondence" seeking information about the Border Patrol's buildup there.[53] The Border Patrol added 400 agents between 1996 and 1998, growing to 1,200 in that border state. Meanwhile, the investigative team responsible for monitoring tens of thousands of employers in the vast northern 2/3 of the state was only allowed to grow from six agents to seven.

As a result, the agent in charge of investigations, Tony Esposito, said he had to ignore 75 percent of even the most detailed and promising tips brought to his office. "I don't have anybody to assign them to," he said. The headline on the *Arizona Republic* story that reported Esposito's predicament neatly encapsulated the problem: "Illegals on Job Being Ignored: Border Patrol Buildup No Help at Work Sites."[54]

And so, as interior enforcement failed, the rising tide overwhelmed the flimsy barriers set against it.

A BUNGLED RAID ACCELERATES RETREAT FROM THE WORKSITE

Throughout the second half of the 1990s, worksite enforcement was beset by problems old and new. Senator Simpson complained that the INS routinely settled employer sanctions fines for 42 cents on the dollar, thereby undermining the effort to incentivize compliance with the laws.[55] The GAO pointed to problems at the Department of Labor, which had agreed to work with the INS to identify employers who knowingly hired unauthorized workers. The GAO reported that Labor had "generally limited" its cooperation with the INS because it feared that "unauthorized workers fearing possible removal from INS could be discouraged from complaining about labor standards violations."[56] Those labor violations were the DOL's principal responsibility and primary concern.

If a researcher had produced a graph to measure the INS's sagging commitment to worksite enforcement, it would have been the mirror image of a graph tracking the increase in the size of the illegal immigrant population. In 1998 the INS Miami office, for example, investigated only 126 employers, compared to 711 in 1988 when the agency believed it had political support and a mission to shut off the job magnet.[57]

One of those 1998 investigations in Miami culminated in a raid that became infamous for its excesses. It unfolded at a Miami flower wholesaler, First Paragon Floral, where the INS had been alerted to the presence of unauthorized workers. Agents arrested 23 people—from Nicaragua, Honduras, Columbia, Peru, and Chile. Most were unauthorized. But as agents forcefully hustled workers into vans, coworkers screamed—truthfully—that some were authorized. Fights broke out and a larger melee ensued. Agents "commanded workers to sit on a wet floor, then held them in a cooler where flowers are stored at 34 degrees," reported the *Miami Herald*.[58] One woman complained an agent had grabbed her by the hair, knocked her to the ground, and kicked her in the back. Rep. Lincoln Diaz-Balart, a Republican from Miami, was furious at the INS. "They mistreated people," he said. "They pushed and hit."[59] He was joined by Miami-Dade County Mayor Alex Penelas, who said, "These people were treated like a herd of cows."[60]

The raid at First Paragon Floral was an enormous embarrassment for the INS. Meissner apologized, and INS headquarters ordered that future raids be directed only at "major violators," which it defined as employers "who intentionally and repeatedly engage in illegal hiring; are involved in other criminal activity, including smuggling and fraud," and those who "hire unauthorized workers and subject them to abusive work conditions."[61] This was a major redirection of resources away from the broad American workplace and toward the narrow band of egregious offenders.

That retreat signaled another trend at the INS. The new constraints on INS worksite enforcement would be fully articulated in an interior enforcement strategy document drafted at the direction of Robert Bach, the INS executive assistant commissioner for policy and planning.

Bach, a sociologist of strong liberal leanings, came to the INS from the State University of New York-Binghamton, where he had been director of the Institute for Research on Multiculturalism and International Labor. In a 1978 research paper titled "Mexican Immigration and the American State," Bach took a deterministic view of U.S. immigration policy, writing that "the American state permitted and indeed had to permit illegal immigration to meet its various commitments to different sectors of capital and labor."[62]

One of Bach's research partners was Doris Meissner. In 1990, while Bach was still at Binghamton and Meissner directed the Immigration Policy Project at the Carnegie Endowment for International Peace, they co-authored an analysis of worksite enforcement that took a less ideological and more pragmatic approach than Bach's earlier paper. They wrote that past experience had demonstrated that employer sanctions could be effective, but only if policy-makers committed to "a sustained effort over a period of years and a willingness to adjust law and practice to reflect experience." Echoing a concern that had been repeatedly stated by Barbara Jordan, they wrote, "A generous evolving immigration policy cannot sustain public support in the absence of effective deterrents to illegal immigration."[63]

After Meissner became commissioner, she brought Bach to INS headquarters to help her chart the agency's course. Together they would adjust INS strategy to reflect what they saw as the realities emerging from the growing economic, social, and political imperatives that emerged from the turbulence of the mass illegal immigration of the mid- and late-1990s.

JACK SHAW'S ATTACK ON MEISSNER AND BACH

At the end of 1998 Jack Shaw retired from the INS and went public with his frustration with Meissner and Bach at a congressional hearing. It was a strong, if modulated denunciation of their leadership, particularly regarding enforcement of IRCA and other aspects of immigration law. But the hearing was almost entirely ignored by the Washington press. Perhaps reporters were turned off by the hearing's drab title: "Designations of Temporary Protected Status and Fraud in Prior Amnesty Programs."[64]

In his oral testimony to the House Subcommittee on Immigration and Claims, Shaw summarized years of frustrated attempts to interest Meissner in his ideas regarding interior enforcement. He poured out his frustration at what he felt was the marginalization of the investigations division, which he had directed from 1984 to 1995. "I would hope that the Congress...shares my expectation, and yes, my sense of frustration in waiting for INS senior management to propose, seek funding for, and enthusiastically endorse and implement a cohesive, fully integrated interior enforcement strategy," he said. He concluded with a cry of the heart, calling for INS senior management to recognize "the professional competence, fidelity and dedication of the long-overlooked coterie of special agents of the INS."

The power of Shaw's attack on Meissner and Bach was blunted because he confined his strongest criticism to the written statement he submitted for the record. Even there Shaw's critique was elliptical as he assessed the influence of the coalition of immigration advocates that Alan Simpson icily referred to as "the groups."

Said Shaw: "Immigration advocacy groups exert a strong interest in areas of INS policy formulation... and they are not prone to endorse strong enforcement actions away from the land borders to deny aliens immigration benefits." Referring to Bach only by his title, Shaw said that at a strategy planning meeting, "[T]he executive associate commissioner for policy and plans noted that there are operational sensitivities to take into account and no strong public consensus for INS enforcement activities in the interior of the United States." Clearly referring to Meissner and Bach, he said, "INS top management remains reticent and lukewarm" about enforcement.

Shaw also blamed Congress for slighting interior enforcement while lavishing money on the Border Patrol. He drove this point home by inserting in the record an excerpt from an article in the Raleigh *News and Observer*:

> *A raid last March at El Mandado, a Hispanic grocery and cafe in North Raleigh, came after the INS received phone calls about a story in The News & Observer that profiled a store employee and documented his illegal border crossing. Last year, when INS agents charged two Mexicans in Sanford with smuggling deaf countrymen into the United States to*

> *sell trinkets, the raid sprang from efforts in New York and elsewhere to break up a larger ring.*
>
> *In reality, the INS still strikes little fear in illegal immigrants here.*
>
> *After leaving his home in Mexico in 1996, Rogelio, 42, now a landscaper in Durham, was caught three times in a single month after crossing the Texas border with a smuggler. Yet when he made it to North Carolina on the fourth try, he was in the clear.*
>
> *"En Carolina del Norte, no hay problemas con La Migra," said Rogelio, who asked that his name be changed for publication. Translation: In North Carolina, immigration authorities pose no problems.*
>
> *Instead of focusing on states like North Carolina, the INS tends to keep its binoculars focused on the Mexican border.*
>
> *As Congress boosted the Washington-based agency's budget 163 percent in six years, the enforcement priority has been clear. Each year through 2002, the INS is to deploy an additional 1,000 Border Patrol agents, for a total of 12,000.*
>
> *Yet almost half the illegal-entry problem has nothing to do with border enforcement. The INS' own statistics show that four of every 10 undocumented immigrants enter the country legally—usually on short-term tourist or work visas—and then stay.*[65]

Despite the vivid newspaper account, Shaw's presentation was so subdued and understated that it had little effect. It had the impact of the proverbial tree that falls in the depths of a forest where there is no one to hear it. As a call for public outrage and mobilization on behalf of worksite enforcement, it was a dud. But in his public expression of frustration with INS leadership, Shaw gave voice to the disaffection from Doris Meissner that ran deep among the corps of INS investigators whose duty was to enforce the nation's immigration laws. Meissner had many admirers in and out of the INS, but there were few special agents among them. She declined to be interviewed for this report.

DORIS MEISSNER AND THE SPECIAL AGENTS

INS investigators, also known as special agents, were immersed in a conservative culture of commitment to the rule of law. They were attuned to the risks and dangers of loose borders, illegal immigration, the plethora of scams used to cheat the system, and the rising threat from international terrorist organizations.

INS Commissioner Doris Meissner, by contrast, was a liberal immigration scholar and Washington technocrat, appreciative of the diversity and dynamism that immigrants bring to the country and alert to the shifting currents of immigration politics. While Meissner understood that law enforcement was essential to the integrity and viability of the immigration system, she was most interested in fulfilling the INS responsibility to attend to those who sought naturalization and other services. Indeed, after taking the reins at the agency, Meissner declared that her goal was to put the "N" back in INS.

"Doris seemed to be uncomfortable with the enforcement side of the house," said Anne Veysey, an analyst in the investigations division during the Clinton administration.[66] "She was much more comfortable with giving than with enforcing." Several agents described Meissner in identical terms, saying that while she was "a nice person," she was "not an enforcement person. Two former supervisory agents, recalling Meissner's visits to investigations offices in Virginia and Phoenix, said she was clearly physically uncomfortable in the agents' presence.

The two cultures clashed in ways both subtle and overt. Veysey recalled documents she had sent to Meissner that came back with the phrase "illegal aliens" scratched out. "We were told that Doris didn't like that," she said. That term had long been used in legal documents, news reports, and research papers to identify those who had violated immigration law, and Meissner herself had used the term in the 1990 research paper she co-authored with Robert Bach. But as time passed, it was increasingly seen as offensive, especially by advocacy groups whose influence grew throughout the 1990s. They preferred the more dignified "undocumented immigrants," a term that conservatives often rejected with the observation that the "undocumented" frequently had multiple sets of fraudulent documents. Meissner was not sympathetic with such reasoning. "She wanted a kinder, gentler immigration service," Veysey said. And so, the divide within the INS sometimes presented a microcosm of the broader national debate, which could break down on issues of semantics well before any discussion of policy.

Gregory Bednarz, the acting assistant commissioner for investigations from 1995 to 2002, still vividly recalls a moment that he says encapsulated Meissner's aversion to enforcement. It came after Meissner and other top-level INS staff attended a 1995 briefing by a CIA analyst who came to INS headquarters. Meissner attended at the suggestion of the INS intelligence division. In an email to Meissner, Bednarz had described it as a "Threat Assessment of Islamic Fundamentalist Groups and Impact upon INS." Bednarz recalled that after the briefing, Meissner dismissed it as "a waste of time."[67] Such moments explain the wry quip that circulated among high-level agents who were detailed temporarily from field offices to INS headquarters. They joked that the experience allowed them to understand what it had been like to live in occupied France during World War II.

Some of the former agents contacted for this book expressed admiration for Doris Meissner. "She was probably the most knowledgeable commissioner we had with respect to the scope of her understanding of immigration, with that hole when it came to immigration enforcement operations," said William Yates. One former enforcement agency executive said the joking references to occupied France began before Meissner's tenure and reflected a long-established cultural divide at the INS. Former INS general counsel David Martin said the cultural divide between INS law enforcers and a service-oriented commissioner who had to navigate tricky political currents of Capitol Hill was no surprise.

Indeed, the weak enforcement regime at the Clinton-era INS may be seen as typifying the style of a president who, according to veteran critic of the Washington establishment Kevin Phillips, "abandoned his populist outsider postures to compromise with established lobbies, power brokers, and congressional leaders."[68]

Under Clinton, the growth of illegal immigration ran a parallel course with the rise of poverty. "Since 1990, about 90 percent of the increase in people living below the government's poverty lines has come among Hispanics," columnist Robert Samuelson would write in 2006. "That has to be mainly immigrants and their U.S.-born children." Citing the difficulties unchecked immigration causes for previous immigrants, Samuelson wrote, "There's a paradox. To make immigration succeed, we need to curb some immigration."[69]

UPROAR OVER A NEW ENFORCEMENT STRATEGY

Four days after the hearing where Shaw went public with his frustrations, newspapers published stories about the new INS enforcement strategy that had been written under Bach's direction. Deportation of criminal aliens would be the Number One priority. In descending order of priority, investigators would also pursue smuggling rings that brought illegal immigrants to the U.S., fraudulent efforts to receive immigration benefits such as green cards or other visas, and employers who not only knowingly hired unauthorized workers but also compounded the offense by abusing them

The Scripps Howard News Service reported that critics described the plan as "a first step toward amnesty" for illegal immigrants.[70] One of the critics was Jack Shaw. "It is amnesty in another name," said Shaw. "INS is ducking the bullet on the responsibility of providing resources to the field offices to detain and remove" people who were illegally in the country.

More criticism came from an INS official quoted in the story. "This says if you can get in get a job and stay out of trouble your chances of being deported are zero," the official said. "You have to wonder about the message it is sending to people thinking about coming here as illegal immigrants." The strategy seemed to contradict an observation Meissner and Bach made in their 1990 analysis of enforcement when they wrote, "Compliance can only be assured over the long run if the enforcement is credible."[71]

The *Washington Post* observed that the new strategy "affords a measure of relief to the estimated 5.5 million illegal immigrants living in the United States and the thousands of businesses that employ them." But reporter William Branigin added that the strategy was "generating intense criticism within the INS and among advocates of a tougher stand on illegal immigration. They say the new policy undermines the INS's commitment to removing illegal aliens, essentially ignoring them as long as they do not commit a crime that brings them to the agency's attention.[72]

Branigin, respected for the depth of his reporting and the breadth of his sources, added this trenchant analysis: "The change... reflects the political reality that has doomed previous crackdowns on illegal employment. According to INS insiders, neither the Democrats nor the Republicans have demonstrated the political will to seriously reduce the illegal work force, in large part because key constituencies oppose such efforts. On the Democratic side, interior enforcement directed against undocumented workers tends to alienate lawyers, ethnic lobbies, civil rights groups and, increasingly, unions trying to organize the newcomers. For the Republicans, work-site raids often pose problems because they arouse bitter complaints from business and agricultural interests."

Lamar Smith, furious at the INS's new direction, called another hearing to condemn it. "What's the new strategy?" he asked in his opening statement. "It is a bright flashing sign that says to potential illegal aliens: 'Come to the United States. Once you make it, you are home free.'"[73] Bach responded that worksite raids provided too little bang for too many bucks. He noted that in the 1998 fiscal year, the INS had arrested 13,897 illegal immigrants at worksites across the county, or about 45.6 apprehensions per INS investigator work-year. "At that rate, it would take an enormous increase in investigative resources to begin to have an impact on the number of illegal resident workers in the United States," he said.[74] Bach believed that the illegal immigrant population had grown so large that raids were an anachronism, a prohibitively expensive remnant from an earlier time.

Sitting with Bach at the hearing was Mark Reed, the director of the INS's Dallas-based Central Region. As his Exhibit A in support of the new strategy, Reed told the story of one of the largest enforcement operations in INS history, the 1992 raid at a meat processing plant in Grand Island, Nebraska. "We took about 200 agents, helicopters, K9 groups," Reed said. "We arrested over 300 people at the plant. It got national coverage. And nothing happened. When we went back again this year, that same plant had that many, if not more, unauthorized workers." Seven years on, Reed said, "That is just not a strategy that we have enough [agents] to do."

OPERATION VANGUARD

At the time of that hearing, the new INS strategy was taking dramatic shape in an operation that Reed was directing at worksites across Nebraska. Called Operation Vanguard, it was an effort to shut off the illegal-immigrant employment magnet at every meat-packing plant in the Cornhusker state, which was home to more than 100 of them. The methodology was remarkably simple. After I-9 audits identified about 4,000 apparently unauthorized workers, INS agents scheduled them for interviews to discuss their status. Three thousand of them failed to show up and lost their jobs. The remainder, able to correct errors in their personnel files or INS records, kept working.

The *Wall Street Journal* opened a window on meatpacking in Nebraska with a story about the hiring practices of industry giant IBP.[75] According to the *Journal*, the company hired recruiters who placed radio advertisements that offered wages of $8 an hour, bus transportation to the U.S., and health insurance to persons authorized to work in the United States. The fraudulent document industry solved the problem of work authorization for many workers. Some came with counterfeit papers, while others bought or borrowed genuine documents that had been issued to someone else.

Complicating the enforcement challenge for the INS was the recidivism rate among deportees, which was so high it threatened to make a mockery of time and expense involved in deportations. Many deportees, especially those who had been returned to Mexico, simply made a turn through the border's revolving door and came right back. "It is simply a cat and mouse game to believe that just by apprehending someone and removing them to their country of origin, that you have finished your job," said Bach. "They are coming back." He cited a 1997 study that found that 75 percent of those deported from the Los Angeles County jail system returned to the United States within six years and got into another round of trouble with the criminal justice system.

The counter-argument, making the case for a deportation strategy, also was well represented at the hearing. Former INS agent Thomas Hammond predicted that Operation Vanguard would be futile because the workers it scared out of one job would simply move down the road and find another. The deterrent effect of possible deportation would be lost and word would go out that the coast was clear, he said. "When smuggled illegal aliens are allowed to remain, they announce their success to their friends, relatives, and countrymen; and the result is more smuggled aliens," he said.[76] Adding to the criticism, Robert Hill, an immigration attorney who had served on the Jordan Commission, noted that the commission had endorsed deportation as essential to credible deterrence. Expressing alarm at the new INS strategy, Hill said that in recent months he had observed "the deterioration of a system that appears to be collapsing under its own weight."[77]

Vanguard would collapse under the political and financial weight of the Nebraska meatpacking industry. But to put that development in a larger frame, it is useful to understand how Vanguard came into being. Eric Schlosser provided a taut description of its socio-economic background in his best-selling expose *Fast Food Nation: The Dark Side of the All-American Meal*:

Wrote Schlosser:

> *The industrialization of cattle-raising and meatpacking over the past two decades has completely altered how beef is produced. Responding to the demands of the fast food and supermarket chains, the meatpacking giants have cut costs by cutting wages. They have turned one of the nation's best-paying manufacturing jobs into one of the lowest-paying, created a migrant industrial workforce of poor immigrants, tolerated high injury rates, and spawned rural ghettos in the American heartland. Crime, poverty, drug abuse, and homelessness have lately taken root in towns where you'd least expect to find them. The effects of this new meatpacking regime have become as inescapable as the odors that drift from its feedlots, rendering plants, and pools of slaughterhouse waste.*[78]

THE BACKSTORY OF OPERATION VANGUARD

In a 2017 interview Mark Reed told the story of the political roots of Vanguard.[79] The story began with an urgent request to the INS from the Nebraska and Iowa delegations in the House of Representatives. They asked Doris Meissner for a meeting to complain about the explosion of illegal immigration in their states. Reed accompanied Meissner to the meeting, where they endured a heated recitation of complaints from towns across the two states.

"They were upset," Reed said, "They said our inability to control the border was adversely affecting their states. It was the old complaint. The schools were being overrun. The health care was being overrun. The judicial system was being overrun. Basically their lifestyle was being overrun because we were unable to stop the flow of people across the border. They were very agitated. If there had been food at that meeting, I think they would have thrown it at us." Reed responded by laying out what became the Operation Vanguard strategy. The congressional offices responded enthusiastically and asked Reed to give them regular updates.

The cheering for Reed's efforts did not last long. Although Vanguard was an operational success, it proved to be a political failure, a repeat in the Northern Plains of the political firestorm that had swept across the onion fields of southern Georgia. The Nebraska meat industry, pointing to the operation's cascading effects for the state's cattle and hog producers, hired former Nebraska Senator Ben Nelson, a Democrat, to lobby on its behalf. Nelson said it had been "ill-advised for Operation Vanguard to start out in a state with such low unemployment and an already big problem with a shortage of labor."[80] Sen. Chuck Hagel, a Republican, also lined up with the meat industry. And a task force appointed by Gov. Mike Johanns called for an amnesty for unauthorized workers in the state.[81]

It was an intense political backlash on behalf of a dominant industry whose excesses had provoked a populist backlash. Meissner got the word to Reed. "She told me we would have to rethink Vanguard," Reed said in 2017. "I knew then that it was dead."

And so instead of taking Vanguard on the road, the INS put it on ice. And instead of demonstrating the commitment of the federal government to respond to grassroots public concerns by enforcing IRCA, Vanguard demonstrated the futility of a crackdown on a powerful industry when that industry has become accustomed to access to unauthorized workers. The INS response brought to mind the observation of Grover Norquist that in Washington, "intensity trumps preference." In other words, diffuse public opinion is no match for a powerful lobby.

In the absence of systematic and sustained enforcement, illegal immigrants continued to make the dangerous border crossing, heading for Nebraska and many other parts of the country. One metric of the influx came from the desert mountains of the Border

Patrol's Tucson Sector, where arrests reached 616,000 in 2000, up from 139,000 in 1994.[82]

In late 2000 as the Clinton presidency neared its end, Doris Meissner resigned as commissioner of the Immigration and Naturalization Service. She later helped establish the Migration Policy Institute, a respected research organization whose work tends to support an expansive immigration policy. She is an advocate of the comprehensive immigration reform legislation that would provide sweeping legalization for illegal immigrants, boost legal immigration, and provide employers with ready access to low-wage workers from abroad.

DORIS MEISSNER AND A C-SPAN CALLER FROM NORTH DAKOTA

In 2007, as the Senate neared a vote on comprehensive reform legislation, Meissner said it would provide a more effective enforcement regime than was possible under IRCA. Then she made what amounted to a repudiation of her claim at a 1996 Senate hearing that under President Clinton "the INS is showing that it means business when it comes to enforcing immigration laws in the workplace." Seven years after leaving government service, Meissner acknowledged, "We never really did in any serious way the enforcement that was to accompany the legalization of the people who were here illegally."[83]

Six years later, when comprehensive reform proposals returned in slightly different form in the so-called Gang of Eight bill, Meissner appeared on C-SPAN to support the proposal for a sweeping legalization coupled with fines and other requirements. "We are talking about accountability—on the part of the people who violated the law by being here illegally as well as by the society overall for having allowed this for so many years," she said.[84]

Then a caller—Phil from Minot, North Dakota—identified himself as the owner of a construction business and made an anguished and angry case that it was the government that should be called to account.[85]

Said Phil: "You have people in this country trying to run their businesses legally. They pay their taxes. They pay their workers compensation. They pay their insurance. And you have other businesses hiring illegal immigrants. They hire them. They know they can't cover them with insurance. They pay them less money and they don't cover them with workers comp. They don't cover them with liability insurance. So they can bid the job way cheaper than anybody running their business legally. If you're running your business legally, you're not hiring illegal immigrants. So I don't hire illegal immigrants.... So I have to bid my job to cover my expenses in this country. So I am going out of business because you guys are allowing people to hire illegal immigrants....And they're really damaging this country. I don't understand how people cannot see this. I mean they are putting me out of business because I won't work illegal immigrants."

Meissner responded: "You know, you are describing very vividly what our dilemma as a country and as a society is. It is why immigration reform is so urgent. This is an unacceptable situation. It's an unacceptable situation for exactly the reasons you described. It creates a completely uneven field in labor markets, particularly in sectors like the construction sector. So we have to get ahold of it. But politically, it has not been possible for the Congress to come to an agreement. The only institution in our society that can resolve this is the Congress, by putting a new system of laws into place."

As Meissner well understood, business interests like those that resisted IRCA in the 1980s and that fought worksite enforcement in the 1990s are a mighty obstacle to such an effort. In 1981, when Meissner was the acting commissioner of the INS and Congress was beginning the debate that ultimately led to passage of IRCA, she testified at a Senate hearing that although an employer sanctions law was needed to stem illegal immigration, "implementation of the law is not designed to be and will not be anti-employer."[86]

Testifying at the same hearing Cornell University labor economist Vernon Briggs said one benefit of employer sanctions legislation was that it "sets the moral tone....that it is an illegal act for an employer to hire an illegal alien." Briggs then added the admonition that "there is not much sense in going through with the employer sanctions if you are not going to have some kind of credible identification system linked with it."[87]

In 1986 Congress managed to pass a law, but after efforts to establish a credible identification system had been thwarted. Credibility was sacrificed in the name of compromise and for the benefit of intensely organized special interests.

A LABOR MOVEMENT MILESTONE IN MINNEAPOLIS

Another major chapter in the erosion of worksite enforcement began to unfold in the fall of 1999, when workers at a Minneapolis Holiday Inn Express supported a union organizing effort. (See Chapter Seven.) Hotel management, claiming to have just become aware of their illegal status, fired them and called the INS.

After the workers were arrested, the gambit backfired. The union organized protests. The Equal Employment Opportunity Commission and the National Labor Relations Board sued the employers for retaliatory firing and won a financial settlement for the workers, who were allowed to stay in the country.[88] The story received national attention and became a major factor in the decision of the AFL-CIO's executive council in 2000 to call for an end to employer sanctions and for a blanket amnesty for illegal immigrants. That historic move was the lead story on the front page of the *Washington Post,* whose headline announced, "Unions Reverse On Illegal Aliens."[89]

Former INS general counsel Alex Aleinikoff noted with apparent surprise a comment that Robert Bach had made about the state of worksite enforcement. Bach told the *New York Times* that unauthorized workers ran little risk of arrest "unless the employer turns a worker in, and employers usually do that only to break a union or prevent a strike or that kind of stuff."[90] In a piece for the *American Prospect* the following year, Aleinikoff retorted, "That, of course, is precisely the AFL-CIO's complaint. Employer sanctions have not kept undocumented immigrants out of the workplace, and unscrupulous employers rarely face penalties. Instead, the law has provided employers with a justification for firing workers engaged in union activity."[91]

WARNINGS OF A BACKLASH AND ANOTHER VIEW OF THE WORKSITE FAIT ACCOMPLI

A 2000 article in *Foreign Affairs* magazine made a case for resisting employers' efforts to loosen labor markets by providing visas to foreign workers. It reported that the intense immigration of the 1990s was "creating special burdens and tensions" in states from California and Arizona to New Jersey. It quoted Georgetown University immigration expert Susan Martin, who had been the executive director of the Jordan Commission. In its reports to Congress, the commission predicted that when the economy sagged, the country could expect a backlash "that could be greater than it was in California." The article concluded with a warning: "If Congress and the next president do not come up with reasonable solutions along the lines proposed by the Jordan Commission, the field will be clear for the unreasonable solutions advanced by politicians such as Pete Wilson and Pat Buchanan."[92]

The following year, *New York Times* reporter Louis Uchitelle took his own measure of INS' enforcement work. "The agency now concentrates on picking up aliens who have committed a crime," he reported. "The rest are in effect allowed to help American employers fill jobs." His story included this anodyne observation by Robert Bach on the jobs panorama opened up by INS inattention at the workplace. "It's just the market at work, drawing people to jobs, and the INS has chosen to concentrate its actions on aliens who are a danger to the community."

Uchitelle reported that leniency at the INS helped explain why the economy had registered smaller pay increases than economists had expected in the tight labor market of the time. The wage-suppressing effect drew the approval of Alan Greenspan of the Fed because it helped keep a lid on inflation. Greenspan, perhaps the country's most famous libertarian, smiled approvingly at the economic effects of mass immigration.

Liberal economist Jared Bernstein would note a less benign consequence. Bernstein said illegal immigration contributed to what he called an economic "crunch" suffered by American workers. Unlike Greenspan and Robert Bach, Bernstein didn't think it was a good idea to sit back and let employers have access to workers from around the world for whom an American minimum wage represented a major upgrade. Taking the classic liberal stance in defense of American workers, Bernstein wrote what amounted to a lament of the policies of the federal government:

> *I hate to go to the Big Brother place. But we need to get between employers addicted to an endless flow of cheap labor and unauthorized immigrants for whom a substandard job here is a step up. We have the technology to implement a reliable system that tells employers whether they're hiring an illegal worker. What we have lacked thus far is the political guts to mete out serious punishment to those employers who ignore the law.*[93]

Chapter 12:

The George W. Bush Years:

The Search for Reform Meets the Credibility Gap

> **You've got to understand why they're here. They're motivated out of the deep love of their children and their wife. They're working just as hard as any other mom or dad do, for the same reason: They have an obligation and a responsibility. These people need to be treated with respect.**
>
> *—President George W. Bush, 2004*

> **A comprehensive reform bill must hold employers to account for the workers they hire. It is against the law to hire someone who is in the country illegally. Those are the laws of the United States of America, and they must be upheld.**
>
> *—President George W. Bush, 2006*

When Texas Governor George W. Bush ran for president in 2000, he often talked respectfully of those who entered the U.S. illegally in search of work. "Family values do not stop at the Rio Grande," he said "If you're a mother or dad and you can't find work close to home, and you're worth your salt, you're coming."[1] Bush's genial rhetoric was an expression of the "compassionate conservatism" that was the theme of his campaign. It was also a sharp departure from the alarm in his party just four years earlier. The 1996 Republican platform declared that "illegal immigration has reached crisis proportions."[2]

After Bush became president, his choice to be Commissioner of the INS was James Ziglar, a former banker and a libertarian in the business-friendly, and open-borders tradition of the *Wall Street Journal*. Ziglar was a frequent contributor to the Republican Party and a boyhood friend of Sen. Trent Lott, R-Miss. His background, including a stint as Sergeant at Arms of the Senate, provoked skepticism about his qualifications to run the INS. An editorial in the *San Diego Union-Tribune* scoffed, "He is, to put it politely, a purely political appointee."[3]

Ziglar became Commissioner of the Immigration and Naturalization Service just five weeks before September 11, 2001. The horrors of that day jolted the agency away from his plan to improve services for those who had qualified for green cards. It was the enforcement mission that took on new urgency, especially the job of tracking those who sought to inflict more damage. His libertarian sensibility was out of tune with the times. Barely a year after coming to the INS, Ziglar resigned.

The staff report of the 9/11 Commission criticized the INS for failure to understand the national-security implications of its work. "Prior to September 11 immigration inspectors were focused on facilitating the entry of travelers to the United States," the report observed. "Special agents were focused on criminal aliens and alien smuggling, and those handling immigration benefits were inundated with millions of applications. Thus, on the eve of the 9/11 attacks, the INS found itself in a state of disarray."[4]

The staff report also highlighted the cultural and ideological breech at the INS that became pronounced during the tenure of Doris Meissner. As we have seen, Meissner's chilly relationship with the INS investigations division was exemplified by her dismissal of a 1995 CIA briefing on terrorism as "a waste of time." The staff of the 9/11 commission provided another indication that Meissner regarded terrorism as irrelevant. It reported that in a 2003 interview, Meissner did not recall the briefing and "told us she never heard of Usama Bin Ladin until August 2001, nearly 10 months after she left the INS."[5]

MEXICO DEAL GOES DOWN, BORDER PATROL BUILDS UP

Another casualty of the 9/11 attacks was President Bush's immigration-policy initiative with Mexican President Vicente Fox. The two leaders, both elected in 2000, quickly developed what news reports touted as a "dos amigos" relationship. It was aimed at opening the border to a freer flow of Mexican labor and providing legal status to Mexicans living and working illegally in the U.S. After the 9/11 attacks, those ideas were put on hold.

Meanwhile, the flow of illegal immigration remained intense despite the Border Patrol buildup ordered by Congress. In 2002 the Public Policy Institute of California reported that it found "no statistically significant relationship between the build-up and the probability of migration. Economic opportunities in the United States and Mexico have a stronger effect on migration than does the number of agents at the border."[6]

A central premise of the Immigration Reform and Control Act was that worksite enforcement would shut off the job magnet that attracted illegal immigration. But instead of correcting the defects that energized the magnet with fraud, Congress bankrolled a multi-billion-dollar border-industrial complex, with contractors competing to provide surveillance cameras mounted on towers, mobile surveillance units, ground sensors, unmanned aircraft to supplement a regular air force of helicopters and planes, border fencing illuminated by stadium lights, and fleets of new four-wheel-drive trucks. From a force of 3,200 when IRCA was passed, the Border Patrol grew to nearly 10,000 agents in 2001, on its way to 19,000 by the end of the Bush presidency.

THE CREATION OF ICE

Following passage of the Homeland Security Act of 2002, the law enforcement responsibilities of the INS and the Customs Service were merged under the Department of Homeland Security. Then those responsibilities were divided between two new agencies, Customs and Border Protection and the Bureau of Immigration and

Customs Enforcement, which is now known as Immigration and Customs Enforcement, or ICE. Within ICE the Homeland Security Investigations division handles not only legacy INS duties such as worksite enforcement and pursuit of smuggling and benefits fraud but also the legacy Customs responsibilities in such areas as drug trafficking, cybercrime, money laundering, intellectual property theft, and enforcement of export laws.

The ICE merger was not a happy union. Agents from "legacy INS" regarded it as a hostile takeover in which Customs imposed its will, showing little regard for those who had sought to enforce immigration laws. "The organization is stagnated in a convolution of identities and cultures brought over from INS and Customs," ICE official Philip Wrona acknowledged in his thesis for the Naval Postgraduate School.[7] He wrote that many legacy INS agents, feeling disdained and dominated by legacy Customs, sought work elsewhere. He noted their complaints "that they are continually demeaned when they hear legacy Customs agents refusing to perform INS enforcement work because it is not real criminal enforcement work." Wrona quoted a legacy INS employee at ICE as saying, "We hear from the legacy Customs... [that] 'we'll be a lot better off when we get rid of this immigration shit.'"

The Government Accountability Office, which had long pointed with urgent concern to the structural flaws of INS worksite enforcement, maintained its vigilance after the Department of Homeland Security took charge of ICE. It reported that worksite enforcement in the post 9/11 era was constrained by "limited resources and competing priorities for those resources."

Priority number one was national security. Indeed, ICE issued a memo requiring field offices to request approval from headquarters before investigating any worksite not related to "critical infrastructure," such as airports and nuclear power plants.[8] While that rule was later relaxed, the GAO reported, "Eight of the 12 offices we interviewed told us that worksite enforcement was not an office priority unless the worksite enforcement case related to critical infrastructure protection." According to the GAO, in 1999, the INS had devoted about nine percent of its agents' work-years to worksite enforcement, but in 2003, the worksite received only four percent of agents' work years.[9]

THE EXPANDING DIMENSIONS OF CRIME

Against this background of listless enforcement, the illegal immigrant population continued to surge, thereby expanding the dimensions of the enforcement challenge in what became a self-propelled downward spiral of illegality. In a report titled "Numerous Daunting Enforcement Issues Facing ICE," the GAO reported that:

> *The number of individuals smuggled into the United States has increased dramatically, and alien smuggling has become more sophisticated, complex, organized, and flexible. Thousands of aliens annually illegally seek immigration benefits, such as work authorization and change of status, and some of these aliens use these benefits to enable them to conduct criminal activities. Hundreds of thousands of aliens unauthorized to work in the United States have used fraudulent documents to circumvent the process designed to prevent employers from hiring them. In many instances, employers are complicit in this activity.*[10]

That report was one of several candid official acknowledgements of the alarming dimensions of the challenge to law enforcement. The Justice Department, for example, describing the nexus between immigration and the proliferation of drug trafficking, reported that in the Washington-Baltimore area, "the dramatic increase in the Hispanic population has enabled Colombian, Dominican and, increasingly, Mexican, Guatemalan, and Salvadoran criminal groups and gangs with ties to drug source and transit countries to operate more easily."[11]

Another reason that ICE agents were spending such little time at the worksite was that they were occupied with more direct threats to public welfare. They conducted Operation Cross Check to deport violent offenders and members of transnational gangs. Operation SOAR (Sex Offender Alien Removal) targeted those who had been convicted of sex offenses. In 2004 the *Baltimore Sun* reported that Operation Predator had led to the arrest of "more than two dozen illegal immigrants and green-card holders who have criminal sex-offense records."[12]

ALONG THE ARIZONA BORDER

In George W. Bush's first term, the Border Patrol detailed hundreds of agents—at tremendous expense for motel lodging alone—to the Arizona border, which included the most active smuggling corridors. By 2004 the patrol's Tucson sector had 2,200 agents, up from 287 a decade earlier. But even a force that size could not control the sector's 261 miles of border.

In 2005, I spoke with a 28-year-old Mexican man outside Phoenix who was surprised at how easy it had been to come across near Nogales. He said he had been part of a small group that was led by a smuggler who charged $1,100 for a two-hour hike through the desert to a rendezvous with a car that took him to Phoenix. "Next time I'll do it myself," he said as he stood on a street, hoping to be picked up by a contractor for a day's work.

To be sure, the risk of arrest at the border was rising. In 2005 the Border Patrol arrested 1,600 illegal crossers every night. But agents acknowledged that for every one they arrested, two to four others got away. Some smuggling organizations, handling hundreds of people per week, adopted the strategy of deliberately sending a group of 15 or 20 toward Border Patrol agents. They knew that for the next several hours while the agents were processing and transporting their clients, the way would be clear for other groups to make it through to rendezvous points with a smuggler's vehicle. They also knew the migrants who had been used to distract the Border Patrol would soon be released into Mexico, where they could rest before crossing again in a day or two.

A single chart in a report from the Congressional Research Service is the statistical equivalent of a smoking gun in the case against the Bush administration's commitment to enforcement. It showed that in contrast to 1999, when federal agents initiated 443 fines against employers for hiring unauthorized workers, they issued 16 in 2003. Criminal cases dropped from 109 in 1999 to four in 2003. During the same four-year period fines collected from offending employers declined from $3.6 million to $212,000.[13]

Such hard facts about soft enforcement presented a problem of political staging for the Bush White House, which was energetically promoting immigration reform legislation sponsored in the Senate by Republican John McCain and Democrat Edward Kennedy. Much like IRCA in 1986, their legislation would promise to match legalization for illegal immigrants with worksite enforcement to prevent future waves of illegal immigration.

But the Bush administration's record of ineffectual enforcement at the worksite created a credibility gap as vast as the Mexican border. The legislation's provisions for the annual importation of hundreds of thousands of guest workers for up to six years received a skeptical evaluation from researchers concerned about its labor-market effects. Jared Bernstein of the Economic Policy Institute said the program "basically takes all the low-wage labor employers say they need and wraps it up with a big ribbon."[14] Lindsay Lowell of Georgetown University called the six-year limit a "shell game" that would divert attention from the fact that workers and their families would inevitably form attachments that would inevitably create pressures for legislation to allow them to stay permanently in the United States.[15]

AN ENFORCEMENT OFFENSIVE

In the spring of 2006, ICE launched a campaign to demonstrate its newly found enforcement bona fides. During the 12 months from

April 2006 to March 2007, agents conducted a dozen major worksite operations. They went big and bold at the outset, with the largest single worksite enforcement action ever taken—coordinated raids at 40 locations of IFCO Systems, a pallet manufacturing company. It resulted in the arrest of seven current and former managers as well as 1,187 unauthorized workers. More than half the company's workforce had used Social Security numbers that were either fake or belonged to someone else. IFCO eventually agreed to pay $20.7 million in civil forfeitures and penalties for the massive fraud.[16]

Later that year ICE agents arrested nearly 1,300 workers at Swift meat-processing plants in Iowa, Minnesota, Nebraska, Colorado, Utah, and Texas. Those raids highlighted the industry's reliance on unauthorized workers to sustain a business model that had begun years earlier and steadily brutalized the worksite. The model began with the relocation of plants from big cities to rural areas and the replacement of skilled butchers with less-skilled workers who would make the same repetitive cuts thousands of times a day on the dangerous and rapidly moving "disassembly line." Severe wage reductions were another key ingredient. Government data showed that in 2006, wages in the industry were 45 percent lower than they had been in 1980, adjusted for inflation.[17]

In between those two major enforcement actions, President Bush took up the task of assuring the public that his administration was ready to build on IRCA's promise and redeem its failings. "A comprehensive reform bill must hold employers to account for the workers they hire," Bush told the U.S. Chamber of Commerce in a speech at its headquarters, which is located directly across Lafayette Park from the White House. "It is against the law to hire someone who is in the country illegally. Those are the laws of the United States of America, and they must be upheld."[18]

The *Washington Post* cast doubt on the president's commitment, raising the suggestion of political expedience as it cited data from Government Accountability Office. The *Post* reported that despite the administration's vow to crack down at the worksite, it had "virtually abandoned such employer sanctions before it began pushing to overhaul U.S. immigration law."[19]

In an attempt to show that he understood public frustration in Arizona—then ground zero of illegal immigration—Bush sent 6,000 National Guard troops to the border. He called for more detention facilities to hold those arrested by the Border Patrol while they were processed for deportation. And he declared that worksite enforcement must be so tough that it would "leave employers with no excuse for violating" the law.

A CALL TO GET SERIOUS BEYOND THE BORDER

Silvestre Reyes, who became El Paso's Democratic congressman after retiring from the Border Patrol, was not impressed with the rhetoric or the headline-grabbing call-up of the National Guard. Reyes believed that what was needed was a sustained crackdown on rogue employers. He had been chief of the Border Patrol in McAllen, Texas, when IRCA was passed in 1986, and his agents had been part of the earliest employer sanctions work. As word filtered through Mexico that the United States was getting serious, Reyes said, apprehensions in his area dropped by as much as 80 percent.

Reyes had earned his borderlands credibility. His success as the architect of the 1994 Operation Hold the Line, a show of Border Patrol force that imposed order on the chaotic line between El Paso and Juarez, had launched his political career. After Bush's speech, Reyes insisted that a determined commitment to worksite enforcement would enable it to work again. "It would have been much more effective had he announced he was directing the secretary of Homeland Security to identify 1,000 agents that would fan out throughout the country and start doing employer sanctions," he said.[20]

THE NEW BEDFORD RAID

The risks inherent in aggressive worksite enforcement were highlighted by a 2007 ICE raid on a manufacturing plant in New Bedford,

Mass., that produced accessories such as ammunition belts, rucksacks, and other gear for the U.S. military and other customers.

Federal agents arrested 361 of the company's workers, mostly from Guatemala, Honduras, and El Salvador. Prosecutors then charged the owners with conspiring to hire illegal immigrants, helping them obtain fraudulent documents, and failing to train them to handle dangerous chemicals and machinery. News accounts told of other abuses, including shabby working conditions and fines for taking bathroom breaks of more than two minutes. There was even an alleged scheme to deny workers overtime pay by issuing separate checks to indicate that they had worked for two companies.[21] Such was life when illegal workers were afraid to complain about illegal employers.

Critics condemned the New Bedford raid as excessive and cruel, especially for children who were left on their own after their parents were arrested. An ICE spokesman insisted that the agency's efforts to avoid such a situation had been frustrated when parents didn't truthfully answer agents' questions. There were misunderstandings all around, perhaps inevitable under the turbulent circumstances of a raid that was intended to remove unauthorized workers from their jobs and from the country.

Sen. Kennedy said worksite raids in general "unfairly penalize vulnerable workers."[22] Other critics were less measured. In an op-ed column for the *Boston Globe*, two officials of the American Civil Liberties Union likened ICE tactics to a campaign of ethnic cleansing. "The United States went to war to stop Slobodan Milosevic's attempt to 'ethnically cleanse' Kosovo in 1999," they wrote. "We should ask ourselves how, just eight years later, we came to be carrying out a policy that involves such similar tactics—lightning raids, mass arrests, packed detention centers, and mass deportations."[23]

DHS Secretary Michael Chertoff acknowledged the raid's connection to the push for the immigration reform bill. "I believe the credibility of [DHS] as a partner in immigration reform is enhanced by our determination to enforce our immigration laws firmly as well as fairly," he said.[24] Chertoff's statement may have been an accurate reflection of his intentions. But it flew in the face of two decades of federal failure that undermined both the integrity of the law and public confidence that the federal government was serious about enforcing immigration law at the worksite.

"THE AMERICAN PEOPLE FEEL LIKE THEY WERE SCAMMED"

In the summer of 2007 the comprehensive reform bill failed in the Senate, collapsing under the weight of a populist uprising that signaled widespread public frustration with illegal immigration. One of the most pointed acknowledgements of that frustration had come earlier, in a 2006 Senate hearing that was titled "Immigration Enforcement at the Worksite: Learning from the Mistakes of 1986."[25] There Texas Republican John Cornyn described IRCA's legacy of governmental failure and public disillusionment.

"The American people feel like they were scammed the last time we were on this subject 20 years ago," said Cornyn. He went on to sum up concerns that had accumulated for two decades. "I feel very strongly that, unless we are serious about making the system work and we actually appropriate the money, hire the people, train the people, actually put them in place, create the databases, create the secure identification card to make this work, we will find ourselves here once again, with not 12 million people illegally in the United States but maybe 24 million or more," he said.

A few weeks earlier, Doris Meissner made a similar assessment of the requirements of credible enforcement if comprehensive reform were passed. "There will need to be not only massive infusions of resources," she said on C-SPAN. "There will need to be a great deal more management acumen, a great deal more administrative skill and commitment devoted to implementing these reforms. These reforms involve enormous workload challenges."[26]

THE GROWERS' SENSE OF ENTITLEMENT

The failure of enforcement is an expression of political expedience. It allows Congress to satisfy both the public clamor for border security and the demands of organized business interests for access to a large supply of cheap labor. In 2016 Stewart Baker, who was the DHS Assistant Secretary for Policy under George W. Bush, described his meeting with growers who asserted with smug satisfaction that the federal government's policies had protected their access to unauthorized workers. Said Baker, "They introduced themselves along the lines of 'We hire illegal workers illegally; that's what we do, and the system allows it, and we depend on it.'"[27]

The growers' sense of entitlement and the political might they muster have long been powerful shapers of immigration enforcement policies. For decades, the labor demands of agriculture in the West and South were the tail wagging the dog in this area of governance. In 1951, 35 years before IRCA was passed, the *New York Times* reported the complaint by three INS officers "that a powerful 'pressure group' of farmers annually was forcing suspension of law enforcement against illegal Mexican immigrants in order to get cheap labor."[28] In the 31 years since IRCA was passed, a reliance on illegal-immigrant labor has become characteristic of other sectors of the economy. That entrenchment, along with the growing importance of ethnic political organizations, explains why Congress has shown little interest in providing the resources necessary for credible worksite enforcement. Instead, the nation's lawmakers have sought to placate and pacify the public with ritualistic calls to secure the border and enormous expenditures on the Border Patrol.

In 1985, when Robert Bach was a college professor, he described a leftist theoretical perspective on such an enforcement regime in a capitalist society. Identifying the native U.S. working class as members of the dominant social group, he wrote: "Employing migrants from culturally and racially distinct origins is identified here as a common strategy used by the employer class against organizations of domestic workers. Hence, the benefits brought about by a subordinate minority in the labor market accrue not to all members of the dominant group, but only to members of the employer class. Such benefits are extracted precisely against the interests of the domestic proletariat, which is pitted against the new sources of labor."[29]

Richard Stana of the GAO offered a more pragmatic assessment of the problem. For years Stana, whose organization serves as a watchdog for Congress, attempted to prod Congress to get serious about worksite enforcement. As he put it with characteristic understatement at a congressional hearing, "Achieving an appropriate balance between border and interior enforcement resources could help create a credible framework for deterring those considering illegal entry and overstay."[30]

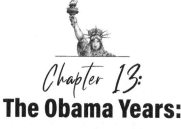

Chapter 13:

The Obama Years:

A "More Thoughtful Approach" Meets a More Powerful Backlash

> **Today, our immigration system is broken—and everybody knows it. Families who enter our country the right way and play by the rules watch others flout the rules. Business owners who offer their workers good wages and benefits see the competition exploit undocumented immigrants by paying them far less. All of us take offense to anyone who reaps the rewards of living in America without taking on the responsibilities of living in America. And undocumented immigrants who desperately want to embrace those responsibilities see little option but to remain in the shadows, or risk their families being torn apart.**
>
> —*President Barack Obama, November 12, 2014*

In 2006, when Senator Barack Obama was contemplating a run for the White House, he published *The Audacity of Hope: Thoughts on Reclaiming the American Dream*. Obama wrote of "the classic immigrant story" he saw still unfolding as a "story of ambition and adaptation, hard work and education, assimilation and upward mobility."[1]

Yet Obama also sounded a cautionary note. He said mass migration from Latin America had roiled labor markets and stoked understandable resentment in broad swaths of the American public. Noting the tensions that had arisen between blacks and Latinos in his hometown of Chicago, he wrote:

> *There's no denying that many blacks share the same anxieties as many whites about the wave of illegal immigration flooding our Southern border—a sense that what's happening now is fundamentally different from what has gone on before...If this huge influx of mostly low-skill workers provides some benefits to the economy as a whole... it also threatens to depress further the wages of blue-collar Americans and put strains on an already overburdened safety net.*[2]

During his 2008 campaign for the presidency, Obama's pursuit of the Latino vote included a speech to the National Council of La Raza's annual convention. There, as he pledged to make immigration reform "a top priority in my first year as president," he criticized the Bush administration's frequent use of worksite raids. He highlighted in vivid detail the excesses that had marred some of the operations launched by ICE special agents. Something is amiss, Obama said, "when communities are terrorized by ICE immigration raids, when nursing mothers are torn from their babies, when children come home from school to find their parents missing, when people are detained without access to legal counsel."[3]

Another Obama objection to Bush's policies was that they often resulted in the deportation of illegal workers while leaving illegal employers untouched. And so, shortly after he became president, Obama came under pressure from immigration advocates who were furious that ICE agents in Bellingham, Wash., had raided a plant that rebuilt car engines. They arrested 25 illegal immigrants from Mexico, Guatemala, and El Salvador and processed them for deportation. "What are Latino and immigrant voters to think?" complained the executive director of the National Immigration Forum. "They turn out in massive numbers and vote for change and yet 'Change We Can Believe In' turns out to be business as usual."[4]

Homeland Security Secretary Janet Napolitano stepped in to placate the critics. She publicly rebuked ICE for the raid. Soon the workers were not only released, they were also granted work permits so that they could help prosecutors make the case against their former employers.

Two months after the Bellingham raid, ICE rolled out an enforcement strategy that targeted rogue employers. Much like the policy of the late-Clinton-era INS, it prioritized the prosecution of the worst illegal employers—those who not only made hiring unauthorized workers part of their business plan but also mistreated the workers or schemed with smugglers to bring them in.

This was the centerpiece of what Obama called "a more thoughtful approach than just raids of a handful of workers." *Nation's Restaurant News*, a trade publication, got the word out. "ICE agents are encouraged to prosecute employers after finding evidence of mistreatment of workers, trafficking, smuggling, harboring, visa fraud, document fraud, and other violations," it reported.[5] By administrative decree: the de facto threshold for enforcement had been raised well above the de jure standard established in 1986.

TAKING ACCOUNT OF THE OBAMA WORKSITE STRATEGY

The most important tool of the new strategy was an old IRCA enforcement stand-by that had become so prominent in Operation Vanguard: audits of the I-9 form that employers were required to have on file for each new worker. Janet Napolitano said the audits, sometimes called "silent raids" by immigration advocates, were aimed at illegal immigration's demand side. Soon she was boasting that ICE in the Obama era was racking up far more audits and imposing more fines than it had during the Bush administration.

Indeed, the 2,196 worksite audits ICE carried out in 2010 quadrupled the Bush administration's 2008 tally. And in 2013, the most active year of the Obama era, ICE boosted the number to 3,127.[6] Still, the numbers on the worksite enforcement scoreboards of both administrations represent a tiny fraction of one percent of the nation's employers. They also provide a metric of the decline of enforcement over the years since IRCA. In 1990, for example, the INS not only conducted 5,118 audits. It also carried out 9,588 investigations based on leads about suspected violations.[7] The GAO then tracked a steady decline in the number of lead driven investigations, which dropped to 5,767 in 1993.

ICE director John Morton said the agency was imposing "smart, tough employer sanctions to even the playing field for employers who play by the rules."[8] But enforcement in the Obama era affected no more than a tiny portion of the vast field of the American workplace, which employed more than seven million unauthorized workers. Worksite enforcement lacked the methodical consistency and the visibility needed to make it an effective deterrent. It was comparable to a highway patrol policy to issue speeding tickets only to the most egregiously defiant drivers—those who not only exceeded the speed limit but also careened recklessly down the highway.

A STRUGGLE OVER DEPORTATIONS

The Obama strategy renewed an old debate with Lamar Smith. The Republican congressman from Texas argued that robust deportation was essential to a deterrence strategy to demonstrate that illegal immigration would not be tolerated. Smith also believed that a failure to remove unauthorized workers was a betrayal of American workers. "Seven million people are working in the United States illegally," Smith said. "These jobs should go to legal workers, and securing these jobs for Americans and legal immigrant workers should be a priority of the federal government."[9]

The decision to target illegal employers rather than the workers they hired was consistent with Obama's hopes to sign legislation that would grant legal status to millions of illegal immigrants. In the meantime, however, the administration had the duty to enforce the laws that were still on the books. This presented a dilemma that Morton wrestled with in public. "We've got to have some sort of balanced reform that gets us back to very meaningful enforcement, where the rules do matter and there's integrity in the system," Morton said. "And at the same time we have a very firm but fair means for people who have been here a very long time to gain some sort of path to citizenship."[10]

No enforcement issue was more delicate for John Morton and the White House than deportation. Congressional appropriations bills had given the executive branch a legislative mandate to carry out 400,000 deportations annually. All illegal immigrants were, by definition, subject to deportation unless they received special consideration from the courts or Congress. This was an awkward circumstance for a president whose advocacy of sweeping legalization had helped him win 70 percent of the Hispanic vote in 2008. His response was a two-fold strategy.

First, Obama invoked prosecutorial discretion to target high-priority offenders, including violent criminals, persons who re-entered the country after being deported and recently arrived illegal immigrants. This would have the effect of shielding those who had established themselves in the U.S. and stayed away from additional legal trouble. Such persons are sometimes described has having established "equities" in U.S. society.

Second, the administration cooked the books of deportation accounting. Many of those counted as deportees had been arrested near the border and speedily returned to Mexico. Historically, such offenders had been classified as "returns" as opposed to "removals," which are reported as deportations. Obama himself acknowledged that in the official tallies of deportations "the statistics are a little deceptive" because his administration had prioritized illegal immigrants who had committed felonies, not just the misdemeanor offense of illegal entry. "Our enforcement priority is not to chase down young people who are following all the other laws," he said.[11] The *Los Angeles Times*, after an examination of deportation data, reported that "expulsions of people who are settled and working in the United States have fallen steadily since [Obama's] first year in office, and are down more than 40% since 2009."[12]

CECILIA MUÑOZ: FROM LA RAZA TO THE WHITE HOUSE

President Obama's top adviser on immigration policy was Cecilia Muñoz, the longtime vice-president and top lobbyist at the National Council of La Raza. Early in his first term Obama named Muñoz as the White House liaison with local and state governments. Newspaper profiles called Muñoz, whose parents were immigrants from Bolivia, a "fierce" and even "ferocious" advocate of illegal immigrants.[13]

Muñoz had a long record of opposing enforcement. Shortly after IRCA was passed in 1986, she called for repeal of employer sanctions. In the mid-1990s, she blasted the Jordan Commission's call for a computerized registry of authorized workers, calling it "worse than Big Brotherism" for Latinos.[14] Later she was active in the effort to block implementation of E-Verify, the computer-based system of worker verification. In 2000 the MacArthur Foundation awarded her a "genius" grant in recognition of her immigration advocacy. She also served on the boards of two foundations that donated millions of dollars to advocates for unauthorized immigrants, the Open Society Institute and the Atlantic Philanthropies.

One of Muñoz's jobs at the White House was to defend Obama against the criticism of Latino activists who expected him to use his bully pulpit to press immediately for sweeping immigration reform. Meanwhile, enforcement advocates complained that the priority system was granting a de facto free pass to illegal immigrants who eluded the Border Patrol and used fraudulent documents to cheat the worksite verification system. They ridiculed the analogy that Cecilia Muñoz used to defend Morton's prosecutorial discretion. "If you were running the police department of any urban area in this country, you would spend more resources going after serious criminals than after jaywalkers," said Muñoz. "DHS is doing the immigration equivalent of the same thing." Fox News reported that story under the headline: "White House Compares Illegal Immigration to Jaywalking."[15]

MARIA HINOJOSA COMES CALLING

When journalist Maria Hinojosa called on the White House as she worked on a 2011 *Frontline* documentary about the deportation controversy, Cecilia Muñoz got the job of defending the administration. In an intense encounter with Hinojosa, who often straddled the line between reporting and advocacy, Muñoz said the administration was obligated to carry out the deportation policies mandated by Congress.

"As long as Congress gives us the money to deport 400,000 people a year, that's what the administration is going to do," Muñoz said. "That's our obligation under the law. We will be strategic about how we do it.... But Congress passed a law, and Congress appropriates funds to implement that law, and the executive branch's job is to enforce it. How we do it matters a lot, but the president can't say to the Congress, 'I'm not going to bother to enforce this particular law because these are really compelling people.' That's not how democracy works."[16]

The interview was an excruciating task for Muñoz. The *Frontline* documentary told stories of heartbreak for the children who stayed in the U.S. after their parents had been deported. The *Washington Post* reported that Muñoz had been "targeted as a traitor by fellow Latinos in a highly personal, ethnic-based campaign against the president's deportation policies."[17] Hinojosa's brother, UCLA professor Raul Hinojosa, ratcheted up the pressure on the White House. He said activists believed that Obama was "prepared to sacrifice Latino families in a constant effort to placate the right" in pursuit of "an immigration reform negotiation that is not taking place."[18]

In early 2012, as President Obama neared the end of his first term, he appointed Muñoz to the top White House job concerned with immigration. She became director of the Domestic Policy Council, which oversaw policy development for immigration and other issues such as education and health care. *Government Executive*, whose readership is primarily high-level employees of the federal government, reported that Muñoz's appointment was a "signal to Hispanic voters that Obama has not given up on immigration reform, despite the lack of progress in his first term."[19]

Latino politicians and activists pressured Obama to assert executive authority to protect illegal immigrants from immigration enforcement. Obama, a former lecturer on constitutional law, demurred. "Now, I know some people want me to bypass Congress and change the laws on my own," he said. And believe me, right now dealing with Congress.... the idea of doing things on my own is very tempting. I promise you. Not just on immigration reform. But that's not how our system works."[20]

In the summer of 2012, four months before a presidential election in which Obama was counting on Latino support, he changed course. He announced a program to suspend temporarily the threat of deportation and to grant work permits to the "Dreamers," the most sympathetic group of illegal immigrants, who had come to the U.S. before age 16. His executive order established a program called Deferred Action for Childhood Arrivals, or DACA. He said congressional inaction had forced his hand.

Conservative critics charged Obama with taking a hammer to constitutionally established separation of powers. Charles Krauthammer denounced the move as a "brazen end run" around constitutional constraints and "the perfect pander" to Hispanic voters that would also have the effect of creating "a huge incentive for yet more illegal immigration."[21] He contrasted the president's action with his earlier resistance to demands that he act on his own. A year earlier Obama had said, "With respect to the notion that I can just suspend deportations through executive order, that's just not the case, because there are laws on the books that Congress has passed."

In the November election, Latinos gave 71 percent of their votes to Obama and just 27 percent to Republican Mitt Romney, who had favored constraints on illegal immigrants that would induce them to "self-deport." The Obama victory led Republican Party leaders to make an assessment of the nation's immigration-driven demographic transformation. In their somber "autopsy" report, they concluded: "we must embrace and champion comprehensive immigration reform. If we do not, our Party's appeal will continue to shrink to its core constituencies only."[22] That report would reverberate across the Republican landscape, particularly in the emergence of a New York tycoon and reality TV star named Donald Trump.

THE GANG OF EIGHT

In 2013, the bipartisan Gang of Eight senators—four Democrats and four Republicans—won Senate passage of a comprehensive reform bill. The measure was adopted by a wide margin despite warnings that it was once again fatally flawed by inadequate measures for worker verification. Then all eyes turned to the House, where Speaker John Boehner, fearing a fracture of his unruly caucus, refused to bring the bill up for a vote.

The following year, 2014, saw a steady escalation of tensions on both sides of the immigration divide. In March, Janet Murguia of NCLR used the Obama administration's inflated deportation statistics to ratchet up the pressure on him to circumvent the Capitol Hill logjam. In a speech at the NCLR's annual awards dinner, Murguia blasted Obama as "the deporter-in-chief," and demanded that he "stop tearing families apart."[23] Her dramatic break with the president made headlines across the country as she called on Obama to use his executive authority to protect more unauthorized immigrants. Obama, who wanted his presidency to be remembered as a parting of the waters for illegal immigrants, directed his legal advisers to draft a plan to do just that. The White House aimed for a rollout before the November mid-term elections.

Meanwhile, tensions also rose within the GOP. Gang of Eight member John McCain warned that failure to endorse the Senate-passed reform would be "catastrophic" for the GOP. "I have a tendency to agree with the head of the U.S. Chamber of Commerce, who said it doesn't matter who runs in 2016 if we don't do immigration reform," McCain said.[24] Then came the fateful month of June. In Virginia's Seventh Congressional District, a little-known economics professor named David Brat, who made opposition to the comprehensive reform bill a centerpiece of his campaign, won a stunning Republican primary victory over House Majority leader Eric Cantor, who had tried to advance the reform. That seismic result sent shivers across the political landscape, including Democratic moderates who asked Obama to hold off any new executive action until after the November mid-term.

Another shock originated in the Rio Grande Valley of Texas, where tens of thousands of asylum-seeking Central Americans children were pouring across the border and looking for the Border Patrol to take them in. Intensive news coverage of the dramatic scene heightened the immigration anxiety that had been a major factor in Cantor's defeat. News accounts described Cantor as a casualty of immigration reform. His downfall was a crushing blow to those who had clung to the lingering hope that the reform would become law.

In late November, after the mid-term elections, Obama issued an executive order that delighted advocates of unauthorized immigrants. He established a program that would be known as DAPA—Deferred Action for Parents of Americans and Lawful Permanent Residents. It was intended to shield several million more people from enforcement of federal immigration law. Obama pitched it as a measure to target deportations at "felons, not families." DAPA, however, was halted by a federal judge in a 2015 decision that was upheld a year later by a deadlocked Supreme Court.

A TALE OF TWO SENATORS: SCHUMER AND PORTMAN

Barely noticed within the immigration Sturm und Drang at the White House, a drama unfolded in the Senate Chamber in 2013 that in the long run may be more important to the effort to repair the nation's broken immigration system. It was a struggle over proposals in the Gang of Eight bill to replace the much-maligned I-9 worker verification process, which remained in place despite decades of reports about its inadequacies and pleas for Congress to replace it with a system less vulnerable to fraud.

The drama was a battle of wills between two emblematic figures in the immigration debate, a Democrat and a Republican, whose approaches were shaped by their contrasting personalities, sensibilities, and conceptions of the challenge of reforming immigration law, especially at the worksite.

The Democrat was Chuck Schumer, a liberal from New York. He is a man of perpetual motion, who relishes being in the thick of the action and at the center of attention. He is driven by a will to cut deals, stroke egos, forge alliances, and build consensus to get bills passed. "I love to legislate," Schumer said in 1998, during his first campaign for the Senate. He described that art this way: "Taking an idea—often not original with me—shaping it, molding it, building a coalition of people who might not completely agree with it."[25]

Schumer is a compulsive deal-maker. His urge to reconcile opposite sides of an issue seems to be an extension of his knack for brokering romances within his staff. The *New York Times*, describing Schumer's inclination to "cajole, nag, and outright pester his staff... toward connubial bliss," called him "the Yenta of the Senate."[26]

Schumer was a key broker of the Immigration Reform and Control Act of 1986. The *Houston Chronicle* reported then that he "was so determined to forge enough compromises to pass the bill that some lobbyists dubbed him 'The Monty Hall of Immigration,'" in a reference to the host of the frenetic television game show "Let's Make a Deal."[27] Schumer cut the deal to placate California agribusiness by offering amnesty not just to illegal immigrants who had been in the country for five years but also to farm workers who had picked crops for a mere 90 days. That Special Agricultural Worker amnesty, as we have seen, would be swamped by fraud.

The other participant in the drama was Rob Portman, an establishment Republican from Ohio. He operates in a lower key. He is as understated as Schumer is brash, as polished as Schumer is rumpled. He has the physical confidence of an outdoorsman who has kayaked the length of the Rio Grande and who once worked on a Texas cattle ranch. Despite those interests, the Capitol Hill newspaper *Roll Call* pointed to Portman's "Midwestern wonk character" as "part of his appeal." It described him as "most comfortable rattling off statistics about the deficit."[28] His credentials as former head of the Office of Management and Budget and chief U.S. trade representative are part of a packed resume that made him a finalist to be Mitt Romney's vice presidential running mate.

Portman immersed himself in immigration policy in the late 1970s as a staffer on the Select Commission on Immigration and Refugee Policy, whose work we examined in Chapter One. Chaired by the Rev. Theodore Hesburgh, president of Notre Dame, SCIRP comprised 16 members—four from the Senate, four from the House, four cabinet members, and four members of the public. Its final report, issued in 1981, laid the policy foundations on which IRCA was passed five years later.

If Schumer can be seen as the id of immigration policymaking—eager and insistent—Portman is the superego, assessing risks and warning of consequences. If Schumer is its broker, Portman is its quality-control engineer. If what Schumer fears most is failure to produce a bill, Portman warns about the futility of passing a defective bill that is bound to fail. Schumer was the irrepressible driving force within the bipartisan Gang of Eight, a group whose efforts Portman viewed with a mixture of admiration and skepticism.

Portman supported the Gang of Eight bill's provisions to address the concerns of important groups, especially the advocates of illegal immigrants who would be put on a path to citizenship and the employers who would be given access to hundreds of thousands of additional immigrant workers. But he believed that the bill, far from solving the problem of worker verification, would compound it, extending past failures far into the future. Rather than showing Congress's ability to solve problems, he believed, it would demonstrate its capacity to perpetuate them. He was convinced that the promised reform would prove to be another damaging policy failure.

Portman was haunted by IRCA's failure. He saw it as corrosive not only of immigration control but also of public trust in government. "The 1986 bill casts a long shadow on this place," Portman said in his June 26 exchange with Schumer, "and we've got to be sure we don't repeat those mistakes."[29]

During the long debate that preceded its passage, as the Senate moved toward its vote on the Gang of Eight bill in late June, Portman joined Montana Democrat Jon Tester in offering an amendment that aimed to strengthen E-Verify, the Internet-based program that allows employers to check whether a new hire is authorized to work. They believed that the version of E-Verify included in the Senate bill was vulnerable to fraud. Their warning echoed a concern voiced by the *New York Times* back in 1980, when the House of Representatives was in the early stages of a debate that led to IRCA: "Without effective verification, there can be no effective enforcement of the borders," said a *Times* editorial. "Without effective enforcement, there can be no immigration reform worthy of the name. The choice for the House is clear: legislate or pretend."[30]

Portman believed that the Senate bill was a form of pretending. He thought worker verification had been compromised to placate powerful political and economic interests, just as it had been in 1986. "Look, it is, frankly, not a very popular part of the legislation, and over the years it hasn't been," Portman said. "In 1986 it wasn't. That is why it was never implemented, because there is sort of an unholy alliance among employers, among those representing labor union members, among those representing certain constituent groups who feel there might be some discrimination or other issues."

Portman insisted that the Senate take a firm stand: "We believe—and I am passionate about this, as you can tell—that if we don't fix the workplace, we cannot have an immigration system that works," he said.

As detailed in his amendment, Portman wanted to expedite the rollout of E-Verify, putting it on a more rapid timetable for large employers than called for in the Senate bill. To improve the accuracy of E-Verify and reduce identity fraud, he wanted to strengthen the photo-matching process known as Photo Tool, which would enable employers to match a photo ID provided by the employee with a digital photo stored in an E-Verify database. Portman wanted to double the federal grant money to states that make their driver's license photos available to E-Verify. He proposed to address privacy concerns by prohibiting the use of those shared photos for anything other than E-Verify.

Portman and Tester wanted Senate Majority Leader Harry Reid (D-Nev.) to allow a brief floor discussion of their amendment and a separate vote. Portman explained his frustration with Reid's refusal. "To not have a separate debate and a separate vote on this amendment, on this issue," he said, "does not give us the possibility of sending this over to the House with a strong message and maximizing the chance the House of Representatives will see that strong bipartisan vote on this important issue of workplace enforcement.... It is that simple."

Schumer, ironically, said he supported the upgraded E-Verify of the Portman-Tester amendment. But he was trying to guide the bill past a quarrel between Reid and Chuck Grassley over how many amendments would be brought to the floor before the final vote. For Schumer, the Portman amendment had become a nuisance, an obstacle in the way of an historic bill that would bring legalization for millions and provide employers access to hundreds of thousands of additional foreign workers every year. With his eyes on that big prize, Schumer was irritated by Portman's fixation on technical detail.

Schumer used multiple tactics on the Senate floor, soothing Portman and then cajoling him. Harry Reid mocked Portman's refusal to have the amendment subsumed into the several hundred pages of an amendment that Schumer had just brokered with Sens. Bob Corker (R-Tenn.) and John Hoeven (R-N.D.).

That amendment sought to win Republican votes by doubling the Border Patrol and spending an astonishing $42 billion on border security. Such extravagance made sense only as a ploy to win a few Republican votes. It had little chance of surviving the legislative gauntlet. But Reid, irritated at Portman's stubbornness, accused the Ohioan of theatrics, complaining, "He wants a big show out here to have a separate vote."

Portman conceded Reid's point. Normally un-theatrical, Portman believed that the debate was necessary. Given the long history of failed enforcement, he believed the debate would help build a record of firm congressional intent. He believed it would allow Congress to make a statement of atonement for the sins of IRCA. It would be a statement that this time Congress was serious, that it would not accept a failure like the one that had followed IRCA, that it would insist on developing, funding, implementing, and enforcing a system that would deliver what Congress promised.

Schumer was the expansively reformist liberal. He was determined to take bold action, confident in his good intentions, and eager to pass a bill. Portman was the cautiously reformist conservative. He was wary of promises that would exceed the grasp of legislation and thereby aggravate the problem it sought to control.

The contrasting priorities of these two lawmakers will almost certainly re-emerge in any future congressional discussion of immigration reform. The challenge for those who seek reform will be to enact legislation that incorporates necessary compromises and trade-offs without crippling enforcement within the interior of the United States.

EPILOGUE:

Donald Trump: Hardline at the Border, Retreat from E-Verify

> **In the fall of 2018, an unprecedentedly large caravan of would-be border crossers—peaking at 7,000 people—headed toward the United States from Central America. Trump demagogically seized on the caravan as a voting issue before the November midterm elections....Demagogues don't rise by talking about irrelevant issues. Demagogues rise by talking about issues that matter to people, and that more conventional leaders appear unwilling or unable to address: unemployment in the 1930s, crime in the 1960s, mass immigration now.**
>
> *—David Frum, speechwriter for President George W. Bush and conservative critic of President Donald Trump*[1]

One of the principal reasons for Donald Trump's stunning victory in 2016 was his ability to harness the latent electoral might of Americans whose alienation from civic life had been stoked by resentment toward politicians and elites who had opened the U.S. to unchecked immigration and free trade. Trump's populist nationalism galvanized this cohort and made it the core of his base. Washington's failure to manage immigration was his central theme. He vowed that when he was president, "Americans will finally wake up in a country where the laws of the United States are enforced."[2] He pledged to repulse the "invasion" and defend American communities with an aggressive "deportation force." His vision of an "impenetrable, physical, tall, powerful, beautiful southern border wall,"[3] sent a thrilling jolt through the raucous thousands who jammed his rallies. "Build that wall!" they chanted in the staccato cadence of football fans urging the home team to "Hold that line!"

Trump's dark vision of illegal immigrants as a criminal horde contrasted vividly with Hillary Clinton's "Stronger Together" country of inclusiveness. Clinton's website's immigration page showed her immersed in a sea of Spanish-language signs. She seemed to have a winning strategy in a country transformed by demography. Then came her shocking defeat in an election shaped by Trump's success in framing her as a symbol of corrupt and arrogant elites who had betrayed the country and insulated themselves from the shocks induced by their indifference.

Trump's immigration politics were opportunistic and malleable. Back in 2012, after Mitt Romney's bid to unseat President Barack Obama had failed, he said Republicans needed to adjust to new demographic realities. He ridiculed Romney's policy of "self-deportation," which was based on the proposition that if illegal immigrants were denied access to such necessities as jobs and drivers licenses, many would return on their own to their home countries, thereby sparing both themselves and the government the trauma of forced removal. Trump ridiculed the idea as "crazy," and "maniacal," a deal-killer with immigrant communities. "He lost all of the Latino vote," Trump said. "He lost the Asian vote. He lost everybody who is inspired to come into this country."[4]

And so, just four years before he was elected on promises of militant exclusion of illegal immigrants, Trump was lining up with the growing ranks of Republicans who called for accommodation. The spirit of inclusiveness became GOP doctrine in 2013 when the Republican National Committee, releasing a report on its "autopsy" of the 2012 election, said that unless the party embraced comprehensive immigration reform, it "will continue to shrink to its core constituencies only."[5]

Sometime between Romney's defeat and the publication of the autopsy, Trump recalculated his position and junked the GOP's electoral GPS. He concluded it was foolish to alienate the potentially huge block of voters who believed uncontrolled immigration was part of their problem. He registered his dissent with a Tweet that asked, "Does @RNC have a death wish?"[6] He didn't elaborate. But there wasn't much interest anyway. As *Politico* would observe, "Pundits laughed it off as the buffoonish ramble of a fringe New York billionaire."[7] Washington's political class dismissed Trump as a reality TV showboat and perpetual self-promotion machine.

Donald Trump would have the last laugh. His ambition was fueled by the mockery he faced at the 2011 White House Correspondents' Association dinner. There, as a glowering Trump watched from a table, President Obama ridiculed his attempt to propagate the "birther" conspiracy theory, which held that Obama was not a legitimate president because he had not been born in the U.S. Obama, who had just provided certified copies of his birth certificate to prove he was born in Hawaii, sarcastically observed that Trump "could finally get back to focusing on the issues that matter, like did we fake the moon landing [and] what really happened at Roswell." At the same dinner, comedian Seth Meyers feigned surprise at the news that Trump might run for president as a Republican "because I just assumed he was running as a joke."[8] Trump's hunger for vindication drove him. He wasn't likely to win the presidency, he knew, but a national political campaign would give him a platform and build his brand.

Trump's interest in the political possibilities of immigration anxiety grew when he began working with political consultant Sam Nunberg. "When I started putting him on conservative talk radio in 2013—Mark Levin's show and guys like that—they kept asking him about immigration," Nunberg would recall. "That opened his eyes."[9] Immigration shot to the top of Trump's issues list. By the time he spoke at the 2013 Conservative Political Action Conference (CPAC) he was convinced that a populist campaign on immigration would energize members of the working class who leaned Republican but had been unable to relate to the patrician Romney. Showcasing his warning that illegal immigration was an existential threat to the

GOP, he predicted that "the 11 million illegals, if given the right to vote...will be voting Democratic." Echoing his "death wish" Tweet, he said Republicans who called for amnesty were "on a suicide mission."[10]

STEVE BANNON AND BREITBART

No Trump adviser was more important than Steve Bannon. The Richmond, Va.-born son of a telephone lineman, Bannon was a rumpled former Navy officer, investment banker, filmmaker, and pugnacious provocateur. In 2012 he became executive editor of the right-wing news website Breitbart.com after the death of founder Andrew Breitbart, who a year earlier had touted Trump's political potential. Trump would be a credible presidential candidate, he said, because "Celebrity is everything in this country."[11]

Bannon was a political brawler who was disgusted at the Wall Street recklessness and self-dealing that in 2008 had brought the economy to the verge of collapse. He was appalled by what he saw as the decadent axis that connected the bankers of Wall Street to the lobbyists of Washington's K Street. He professed a commitment to working people who were struggling in the new economy that the elites had rigged to enrich themselves. He believed that Washington was so detached from the rest of the U.S. that it was like a foreign country. So, he named the Capitol Hill townhouse where Breitbart put its Washington office "the Breitbart embassy." He saw politics as cultural and economic warfare to be waged with a relentless will to power. After Breitbart editor-at-large Ben Shapiro resigned, he said Bannon had turned Breitbart into "Trump's personal Pravda."[12] Bannon himself described the website as "the platform for the alt-right," a term for the loose conglomeration of far-right conservatives, white nationalists, and militant immigration restrictionists.

Bannon deployed the Breitbart site as heavy artillery in a twilight struggle. His reporters often obliterated the border between straight reporting and overt partisanship. He made Breitbart the pulsating nerve center of a movement whose voice was amplified by the Drudge Report, social media, and conservative radio figures like Levin, Rush Limbaugh, Sean Hannity, and Laura Ingraham. One of their first battlegrounds was the 2014 Republican primary election in Bannon's old hometown of Richmond.

To the slack-jawed bewilderment of the political world, Eric Cantor, the Majority Leader of the House of Representatives who had piled up a $5 million campaign war chest, was toppled by a little-known college professor named David Brat, who had raised less than $231,000. Relentless coverage from Breitbart made up the difference, with admiring stories of Brat's opposition to comprehensive immigration reform. "I'm against amnesty of any sort, granting citizenship to those who've broken the law," Brat said.[13] His supporters labeled Cantor—who opposed a blanket amnesty but was willing to consider it for adults who had arrived illegally as children—as soft on illegal immigrants. That made him vulnerable to attack, and Breitbart led the charge.

Brat won with a margin of 12 points. It was an historic thumping that validated the strategy Trump was pursuing. A post-election Breitbart story was headlined: "DONALD TRUMP: CANTOR'S DEFEAT SHOWS 'EVERYBODY' IN CONGESS IS VULNERABLE IF THEY SUPPORT AMNESTY."[14] The story quoted Trump scolding the Republican establishment for not responding to the immigration concerns of ordinary Americans. Looking ahead to 2016, he provided a sketch of a candidate who could reclaim the presidency for the GOP. It was a self-portrait. "It needs to be somebody who wants to make America great again," Trump said. "If they don't have that feel and that attitude, they're not going to win the election." Looking back at Romney's defeat, he said a key factor was the "tons of conservatives who stayed home on election day" because "they just didn't feel that they had the incentive to go out and vote."

Trump's plan for incentivizing voters took dramatic form in a scene that may live forever in American political history. In mid-2015, Trump and wife Melania glided down an escalator into the marbled lobby at Trump Tower in New York. He announced his candidacy with a mix of scripted, made-for-TV pageantry and an improvised, ominous, anti-immigrant screed. "When Mexico sends its people, they're not sending their best," Trump said. "They're bringing drugs. They're bringing crime. They're rapists. And some, I assume, are good people."

Pundits and cable television were transfixed by the spectacle. Donald Trump—brash belligerent, and anti-immigrant—had seized the nation's attention. His rallies drew overflow crowds and TV ratings so robust that TV often aired the rallies live across the country. Pundits predicted he would flame out. They were certain that the public would recoil from the revelations of Trump's scandalous sex life, shadowy business ventures, crude assessments of women, and the crass insults he hurled at critics. But Trump was unapologetic and unsinkable.

Breitbart.com celebrated his nativist bombast. Trump proudly boasted that he had such ardent supporters that he could shoot someone on a busy street and not lose votes. "He's a very imperfect instrument," Bannon would tell PBS's Frontline. "But he's an armor-piercing shell." Said Republican pollster and messaging meister Frank Luntz, "People took a look at him and said, 'You know what? He really is different.'"[15]

Many Americans were primed for disruption, eager for the draining of the Washington swamp that Trump was offering. Some dared to endorse Trump's inclination to unbridled commentary that was widely denounced as racist, sexist or otherwise outrageous. "He says what I can't," they explained. But even President Obama observed that there was more behind the populist impulse than nativist bigotry and resentment and a furious determination to break something. In his 2016 State of the Union address, Obama acknowledged that because of globalization and automation "workers have less leverage for a raise, companies have less loyalty to their communities, and more and more wealth and income is concentrated at the very top." But Hillary Clinton scorned the working-class alienation at the heart of Trump's appeal. Two months before the 2016 election she issued a disdainful, imperious declaration. "You know, to just be grossly generalistic, you could put half of Trump's supporters into what I call the basket of deplorables," she said.[16] Clinton's hubristic disdain fueled the agitation of her foes. By the next morning, #BasketofDeplorables was trending on Twitter.

Nevertheless, Clinton remained the heavy favorite against Trump, who just three months before the election tapped Bannon to manage his campaign. The *New York Times* described Trump's move as "a defiant rejection of efforts by longtime Republican hands to wean him from the bombast and racially charged speech that helped propel him to the nomination but now threaten his candidacy by alienating the moderate voters who typically decide the presidency."[17] Bannon kept Trump defiantly on course even through the turbulence of the October surprise that sprang from Trump's on-camera boast of outrageously lewd behavior. The *Washington Post*, in a story amplified by a video on its website, reported that in 2005, when Trump was talking with the host of the "Access Hollywood." TV show, he had boasted that women were so enthralled by his celebrity that they allowed him to grope them. "You can do anything! Grab 'em by the pussy!" he said.[18]

Nearly every political wag and cable TV pundit was certain that Trump couldn't have done a better job of self-immolation if he had doused himself in gasoline and lit a match. But Bannon assured Trump that the story would not discourage his base. "I said, 'Listen, they don't care,'" Bannon told Frontline, the PBS documentary program. "They don't care about vulgarity or anything like that...They're losing their jobs. They're losing their country. They see their country going away from them. They don't have anything to pass down to the kids. That's what they care about."[19]

THE DRAMA OF DACA

As Trump took office in January of 2017, Bannon came to the White House as chief strategist. There he teamed up with Stephen Miller, an anti-immigrant zealot driven by the conviction that unchecked immigration was a dire threat to the country. Miller had been communications director for Sen. Jeff Sessions of Alabama. The two men shared a sense of alarm that the rules of the immigration system were routinely trampled by illegal immigrants and fraudsters angling for green cards and public benefits. As a senior adviser to President Trump, Miller became notorious for his obsession with immigration and his determination to contain it.

Miller was drawn magnetically to Trump's aggressive nativism. He said he felt a "jolt of electricity to my soul" when he saw Trump's 2015 announcement of his presidential candidacy "as though everything that I felt at the deepest levels of my heart were for now being expressed by a candidate for our nation's highest office before a watching world." Michelle Cottle of the *New York Times* called him "a force for darkness" who "seems to have rarely met an immigrant he didn't want to deport." According to *New Yorker* immigration reporter Jonathan Blitzer, Miller's tenure at the White House has made him "an Internet meme, a public scourge, and a catch-all symbol of the racism and malice of the current government."[20] Blitzer himself was an emblematic figure, a prototypical New York immigration reporter, with an approach to the story that combined an admirable empathy for the plight of the undocumented and a liberal ideologue's blindness to the concerns of restrictionists.*

Immediately after the Trump inauguration, Miller and Bannon were determined to make an aggressive start in fulfilling campaign promises for no-holds-barred enforcement. They worked feverishly to prepare a barrage of executive orders for Trump's signature. First came an order to penalize "sanctuary cities" that restricted their law enforcement agencies' cooperation with ICE. Then came an order to extend the 650 miles of border barrier that had already been

* A Columbia graduate and former translator for publishers in South America and Spain, Blitzer personifies the Upper West Side sensibility about immigration. His prose is fluid and graceful, but his reporting is narrow in its range and lopsided in its bias. It has widened the partisan divide of misunderstanding and disdain.

built under the authority of the Secure Fence Act of 2006. Bannon wanted the orders to be issued with such force and suddenness that they would induce shock and awe in the government agencies, especially among Obama-era holdovers who might want to obstruct them. But an order for a ban on travel from seven mostly-Muslim countries was implemented with such haste, indifference to process, and lack of preparation that it caused chaos at major airports. It also provoked spontaneous protests by anti-Trump activists who were itching for a fight.

Bannon welcomed the confrontation. According to *Fire and Fury*, a tell-all book of life inside the Trump White House, Bannon said the travel ban was implemented on a Friday "so the snowflakes would show up at the airports and riot" over the weekend. Bannon believed that such provocation "was the way to crush the liberals; make them crazy and drag them to the left."[21]

In a move that intensified the tumult, the administration cancelled Obama-era restrictions on ICE's authority to deport *non-criminal* illegal immigrants, that is, those who had not compounded their problematic status by committing serious crimes. White House press secretary Sean Spicer said Trump wanted to "take the shackles off." Trump, he said was signaling to ICE that: "You should do your mission and follow the law." Agents in New York, Chicago, Atlanta, San Antonio, and Los Angeles arrested more than 680 individuals. The agents targeted felons, gang members, and persons whose legal proceedings had ended with a court order for their removal. But there was collateral damage among more sympathetic people because when ICE encountered other illegal immigrants along the way, agents arrested them as well.

The *Washington Post* reported that the arrests "set off a wave of panic and protest in immigrant communities."[22] Thomas Homan, the hard-nosed career Border Patrol agent and investigator whom Trump had named as ICE's acting director, was emphatic in defending the agency's work. "If you're in this country illegally and you committed a crime by being in this country, you should be uncomfortable," he said at a congressional hearing. "You should look over your shoulder. You need to be worried."[23]

Amidst news reports of a White House beset with bickering, back-stabbing, and a chaotic Oval Office, Trump attacked the press for spreading "fake news." Staying in permanent campaign mode, he relished trips away from Washington for contact with crowds that packed arenas for the "Make America Great Again" rallies in states that would be key to his reelection. Trump hammered away at illegal immigrants, warning they were a criminal threat that must be confronted. "We are dismantling and destroying the bloodthirsty criminal gangs," he told supporters in Youngstown, Ohio. Savoring his role as enforcer-in-chief, he said, "I will just tell you this – we're not doing it in a politically correct fashion. We're doing it rough.... Our people are tougher and stronger and meaner and smarter than the gangs. One by one we're finding the illegal gang members, drug dealers, thieves, robbers, criminals and killers, and we're sending them the hell back home where they came from."[24]

At a rally in Harrisburg, Pa., Trump invoked a particularly sinister image. He read the lyrics of a song about a woman who was bitten by a venomous snake that she had sheltered. Reaching the moral of the story, Trump recited the snake's scolding words to the dying woman: "You knew damn well I was a snake before you took me in!" It was as an allegory about the threat of illegal immigrants, presented on Trump's 100th day as president.[25]

A STRUGGLE OVER DEFERRED ACTION

The hardline trio of Bannon, Miller, and Sessions worked to steer Trump away from other advisers—including first-daughter Ivanka and son-in-law Jared Kushner—who were eager to revive comprehensive immigration reform. The couple were especially concerned about the "Dreamers," the unauthorized immigrants who had arrived in the U.S. before age 16, usually in the company of their parents. After Republican immigration hawks thwarted legislation to put the Dreamers on a path to citizenship, President Obama in

2012 signed an executive order that gave them access to work permits and temporary protection from deportation. The protective policy was called Deferred Action for Childhood Arrivals (DACA). It was an election year initiative that, while problematic among legal scholars who debated its constitutionality, was morally compelling. The DACA recipients drew strong support in public opinion polls. But they received little sympathy from critics who contended that any "amnesty" would reward lawbreakers and motivate more people to come illegally.

In 2017 President Trump seemed eager to protect "the DACA kids," as he warmly called them, though many had been in the U.S. so long that they were in their 30s. "We are going to deal with DACA with heart," he said at his first press conference. After pointing to the challenge of persuading Congress to work with him, he said, "The DACA situation is a very, very—it's a very difficult thing for me. Because, you know, I love these kids. I love kids. I have kids and grandkids."[26]

WHITE HOUSE REALITY SHOW

At the end of Trump's first year in office *Fire and Fury* was a best-seller. It depicted the White House as a fever-swamp of dysfunction. It portrayed Trump as chronically unhinged, unfocused, and incapable of absorbing detail. He was a perpetually distracted chief executive who "could not really converse, not in the sense of sharing information, or of a balanced back-and-forth conversation. He neither particularly listened to what was said to him nor particularly considered what he said in response."[27]

In an attempt at damage control, Trump staged an event to demonstrate competence, reasonableness, and compassion. He convened a White House meeting to discuss DACA with congressional leaders. When he allowed the press corps to stay far longer than the customary few minutes, the scene played out like a spin-off of "The Apprentice," the NBC series that had made Trump a mega-celebrity. To the astonishment of everyone, Trump magnanimously declared not only that he was willing to approve any DACA agreement that Congress could reach but also that he was ready to work toward a deal for the comprehensive reform that was the Holy Grail of immigration policy-making. "If you want to take it that further step, I'll take the heat," Trump said magnanimously. "I don't care...I'll take the heat off both the Democrats and the Republicans. My whole life has been heat."[28]

Then came another plot twist, this one probably unintentional. Having thrilled everyone with the prospect of an historic deal, Trump proceeded to confound them with a string of contradictory statements about what should happen next. Uncertain how to characterize his position, the *New York Times* reported that Trump "appeared" to be open to negotiating a deal that might "flatly contradict the anti-immigration stance that charged his political rise."[29]

Before long the disjoined initiative crumbled under a barrage of criticism from the right that was led by Breitbart, where one headline blared, "IMMIGRATION SHOCK: AMNESTY DON SUGGESTS CITIZENSHIP FOR ILLEGAL ALIENS."[30] Rush Limbaugh, the talk radio guru who in 2018 celebrated his 30th year in syndication, was also chagrined. He warned that supporting an amnesty was "the only thing Donald Trump could do to possibly derail himself" from his base. Trump, in an Oval Office meeting with congressional Democrats, expressed vivid disapproval of a proposal for increased immigration from Haiti and Africa. "Why are we having all these people from shithole countries come here?"[31] he asked. Having just met with the Prime Minister of Norway, Trump said he preferred to have more immigration from that Nordic country.

Illinois Democratic Sen. Dick Durbin called the experience of negotiating with Trump "bizarre." The controversy diverted attention from an idea that deserved serious attention. Trump backed legislation sponsored by two Senate Republicans who proposed replacing the legal immigration system, which provides green cards mainly to extended families. The bill mirrored much of the Canadian system, which is designed to select immigrants who have educational and occupational backgrounds that would facilitate their integration into Canadian life. The system has helped Canada to build its middle class and minimize economic inequality and social stratification. It has had the secondary effect of building public support for immigration. "They can see it's managed, and that's an advantage," said Ravi Pendakur, a professor of public and international affairs at the University of Ottawa.[32]

A merit system for the selection of immigrants was included in the 2007 comprehensive immigration reform bill that failed in the U.S. Senate. But ethnic activists in the U.S. opposed it for reasons explained by Bill Ong Hing, a professor of law and Asian-American Studies at the University of California, Davis. Ong Hing called it an "attack on families." He said it "sends a wrong message to communities of color—Asians and Latinos—who rely on the family categories to complete family reunification and stabilize their families."[33]

ZERO TOLERANCE

The biggest immigration story of 2018 was the humanitarian and border-security crisis caused by the influx of hundreds of thousands of Central Americans, who streamed across the Texas border to seek asylum in the United States. The 2018 crisis was a reprise of the asylum drama that unfolded four years earlier, precipitating a response from the Obama administration that needs to be understood in order to evaluate the actions of the Trump administration.

Obama faced both political and humanitarian imperatives. The political imperative, tied to his effort to win passage of an immigration reform bill, was to demonstrate his commitment to managing the border and bringing order to the immigration process. The humanitarian imperative was to meet the immediate needs of asylum seekers, including parents with infants and young children.

The trade of smuggling families from Central America had burgeoned into a lucrative industry that earned hundreds of millions of dollars by guiding migrants through the Mexican gauntlet of corrupt immigration authorities and roadside checkpoints and into the

United States. The smugglers used radio advertisements and social media to spread the word of new opportunities. Central Americans who had grown up with harrowing stories of the dangers of illegal crossings, were learning that they could actually seek out the Border Patrol, ask for asylum, and be granted entry into the United States while their claims were adjudicated. Migration fever spread across Guatemala, Honduras, and El Salvador. Better hurry, the smugglers said, because Trump was unpredictable and the U.S. could decide at any moment to shut the door.

I traveled to the border in 2014, speaking with some of the migrants as they received food, clothing, and a warm welcome at a McAllen, Texas, shelter supervised by an inexhaustible nun named Norma Pimentel. Many of their stories were truly compelling. Patricia Umanzour, 32, told me why she and her husband decided to flee a San Salvador neighborhood that was overrun by gang violence and extortion. "We were watching CNN, and they were saying that the United States was giving opportunities to women with children," she said. "And since some neighbors of ours had come, we decided to try it."

Other stories involved not fear of persecution but yearning to escape poverty. Several single mothers told me they had been abandoned by the fathers of their children. All had family or friends in the U.S. who encouraged them to come and even lent them money for the trip. Such networks spread the word about free schools and government programs that provided a host of benefits. For many who fled the corruption and dysfunction of their homelands, the social welfare systems of the United States were a merciful safety net. The word spread fast. "It seems everyone I meet in Guatemala has family in the United States or is making their own plans to migrate," wrote an American essayist for a travel website.[34]

The crisis continued week after week, exhausting Border Patrol agents who took up the unfamiliar and demoralizing task of providing diapers for infants and shuttle service to the bus stations from which families would depart. The migrants traveled with orders to present themselves to an immigration court in their destination cities. Court dockets became so jammed with hundreds of thousands of cases that most cases couldn't be heard for months or years. At every level, the scale of the crisis was overwhelming.

In New York, Donald Trump was, as always, eager to criticize the work of President Obama. Trump suspected a plot to grow the Democrat base. "I mean, nobody can be that incompetent to allow what's happening to happen," he told Greta Van Susteren of Fox News. "So, it must be a concerted effort. There's no other way that you can think of it. And they come into the system and over a period of many years, they become Democrats and they vote for the Democrats."[35] Trump had yet to learn that U.S. law and international commitments obligated the Obama administration to allow asylum seekers to present their claims. At the opposite end of the political spectrum, immigration activists had yet to summon outrage over the chain-link fence holding areas that had been retrofitted in Border Patrol stations not designed to handle humanitarian emergencies of near-apocalyptic dimensions. During the Trump administration, they would be furious at the use of such "cages" and "dog kennels."

The 2014 crisis eventually eased, but only after the Obama administration launched a public information campaign to discourage the urge to emigrate. Radio advertisements somberly warned of the danger of borderland deserts and the treachery of smugglers. Roadside billboards showed a solitary man in a desolate landscape, haunted by regret that "I thought it would be easy for my child to get papers in El Norte.... It wasn't so." Vice President Joe Biden, after meeting with the presidents of Guatemala, El Salvador, and Honduras, warned that those pondering a trip to the U.S. "should be aware of what awaits them" as the U.S. stepped up its enforcement and removal operations. "It will not be open arms," Biden said. "We're going to hold hearings with our judges consistent with international law and American law, and we're going to send the vast majority of you back."[36]

Obama's former secretary of state, Hillary Clinton, made a similar comment that would intrude into her 2016 bid for the presidency. She said it was often necessary to return unaccompanied children to their home countries because, "We don't want to send a message that is contrary to our laws or will encourage more children to make that dangerous journey." When Clinton debated Sen. Bernie Sanders during the Democratic primary race, Sanders attacked her position as cold-hearted. "I said welcome those children into this country. Secretary Clinton said send them back," he said. Clinton tried to fend off the attack by pointing to Sanders' vote against 2007 legislation for comprehensive immigration reform, which he said would be harmful for American workers because it would allow the importation of large numbers of temporary workers. Maria Cardona, a Latina pundit and Clinton ally, wrote a column in which she said Sanders had received "praise from those on the right whose policies have made things harder for immigrants instead." Her essay for *U.S. News and World Report* was titled "Bernie is No Dream Candidate for Immigrants."[37]

In 2018, when the asylum crisis returned to the Texas border, President Donald Trump was infuriated that the Department of Homeland Security could not throttle an influx that became even larger than the 2014 version. In March of 2018, the Border Patrol arrested 40,000 unauthorized border crossers, most of whom were "family units" of at least one parent and a child. Some children came on their own. They were overwhelmingly Central Americans, following the routine of seeking out the Border Patrol and asking for asylum. As President Trump became increasingly upset, Attorney General Jeff Sessions announced a policy of "zero tolerance" intended to deter the influx. "If you are smuggling a child, then we will prosecute you," he said. Such a policy made it inevitable that the parents and children would be separated. Scott Schuchart, a senior adviser at the DHS Office for Civil Rights and Civil Liberties, objected. In a memorandum that was as anguished as it was angry, Schuchart protested, "Harm to children is being deliberately used for its deterrent effect." He soon resigned in protest.[38]

Soon, vivid recordings of children in federal custody sobbing and crying for their parents unleashed furious protests around the country. Trump and DHS Secretary Kirstjen Nielsen sought to deflect the criticism, blaming Congress for not tightening asylum laws in order to stem the tide. "It is the Democrats' fault for being weak and ineffective with Border Security and Crime," said Trump in a Tweet. "Tell them to start thinking about the people devastated by crime coming from illegal immigration. Change the laws!"

Protests exploded across the country. In Portland, Ore., a "Rally Against Zero Humanity" filled downtown streets. Elsewhere, thousands participated in "Families Belong Together" marches. Signs demanded "Deport Racism." Others, like the one that read "Cruelty = Kids in Cages," expressed the widespread outrage at the chain-link holding areas, which had walls that were 10 or 15 feet high. Protesters—acting either hyperbolically or hysterically, depending on one's point of view— described them as dog kennels. Others, expressing the widespread sense of disbelief and anguish, asked "What country is this?" In the face of such impassioned resistance, Trump retreated, ordering an end to family separation. Then came news reports that authorities had done such a poor job of administering the separation that they didn't know how to reunite some of the children with their parents.

In the weeks before the 2018 midterm elections, President Trump accused Democrats of encouraging the influx of thousands of asylum-seekers who clustered in "caravans" streaming toward the border. A vote for a Democrat was "a vote to let criminals and drugs pour into our country," he said.[39] The caravan became the lead story on "Fox and Friends," Trump's favorite morning television show, which every day demonstrated that Fox had effectively become the cable TV arm of the Trump White House. Over at MSNBC, which was the cable TV voice of the Democratic Party's anti-Trump resistance, the "Morning Joe" program frequently took the caravan story to the opposite extreme. One of its regular pundits, *New York Times* reporter Jeremy Peters, criticized Fox for parroting Trump by making the caravan "a story of an invading Central American army of ingrates who were coming to the United States to leech off our social services. And the humanitarian aspect of their trek up here was completely lost and ignored in much of the right-wing media."

Two weeks before the U.S. midterm elections, "Fox and Friends" began one morning with video of a teeming mass of humanity coupled with this ominous voice-over: "At this hour thousands upon thousands of illegal immigrants are now marching toward our southern border." Co-host Brian Kilmeade commented, "The average American says, as much as we feel for these people, we cannot be a social welfare program for every country in the world."[40] President Trump threatened to close the entire border. "This was my signature campaign issue," he told his advisers. "I have said many, many times on TV that they're not coming in. I'm going to stop them from coming in." When some Democrats made "Abolish ICE" a campaign battle cry, the White House was pleased. According to *New York Times* reporters Julie Hirschfeld Davis and Michael Shear, "Miller and Trump saw it as a gift. Polls showed that most voters, whether they backed the president's immigration policies or not, were opposed to the idea of getting rid of the federal immigration enforcement agency."[41]

The crisis at the border continued into 2019. When the Border Patrol made over 76,000 arrests in February, the acting chief of Customs and Border Protection said the system was at "the breaking point." But the arrest numbers continued to climb, reaching 109,000 in April and 144,000 in May. The smuggling of people from Guatemala, Honduras, and El Salvador was the most lucrative industry in Central America. Nick Miroff of the *Washington Post*, after examining investigators' reports on one smuggling operation, wrote that they "depict an upstart, highly profitable entrepreneurial operation that is designed to exploit dysfunction in the American immigration system and U.S. court rulings that mandate families be released from custody while their asylum claims are processed."[42]

NO CLIMATE FOR COMPROMISE

Immigration's substantive complexity and emotional fault lines have always made it one of the greatest challenges to our system of governance. Consensus is rare and compromise has been beyond the grasp of those who are willing to reach for it. This dysfunction is part of the legacy of IRCA.

In the widening gyre of the Trump-era immigration debate, the prospects for compromise have been consumed by the furies of partisanship and distrust. Both the Republican and Democrat bases have gravitated to the extremes, pressuring members of Congress to hold the partisan ground lest they face a primary challenge. The bipartisan 2013 "Gang of Eight" reform bill that the Senate adopted by a large margin probably could have passed the House and become law, had House speaker John Boehner allowed the bill to come up for a vote. But the threat of a revolt from immigration hawks in his caucus made him hesitate. And the defeat of Eric Cantor in the 2014 Republican primary delivered a knockout blow. A headline in *Politico* made the grim assessment: "Cantor loss kills immigration reform."[43]

The paralyzing partisanship isn't limited to the House of Representatives. The scarcity of common ground was the discouraging lesson of a 2019 hearing of the Senate Committee on Homeland Security and Governmental Affairs in April, as the border crisis continued.[44] One of the witnesses was Rodolfo Karisch, the chief agent of the Border Patrol's Rio Grande Valley Sector. "In my 30 years as an agent, I have never witnessed the conditions we are currently facing on the Southwest border," he said. He told the committee that over the previous three months, agents had apprehended some 192,000 "family units." He described fraudulent techniques used by smugglers to maximize their business. There were bogus families assembled by pairing adults with children who were not their own.

There were "recycled children," who were paired with one couple after another just long enough for the fake family to be processed and released. Then the process was repeated with another couple who had bought the family unification services of the smuggling rings.

The Republicans and Democrats on the committee made their comments from the trenches of their opposing battle lines. While Republicans saw an urgent need to stem an influx that had caused a national security crisis, the Democrats saw the crisis as one of human suffering.

Said committee chairman Ron Johnson, R-Wisc., "Our compassionate asylum system is being exploited – by economic migrants, drug cartels, human smugglers, and other bad actors – because we do not have the will and skill to fix it." Pointing to the multi-billion-dollar industry that enriched smugglers, Oklahoma Republican James Lankford called on Democrats to help tighten asylum rules that were a boon to smugglers who were making a fortune by exploiting the current system. "Our laws are incentivizing them," he said.

On the Democratic side, Sen. Jacky Rosen of Nevada invoked the troubled history of U.S. treatment of asylum seekers. "As the granddaughter of Jewish immigrants from Eastern Europe, I can't help but think about the time in the middle of the twentieth century when the U.S. used security concerns as an excuse to turn away thousands of refugees fleeing Europe," she said. Sen. Tom Carper of Delaware cited the Bible's call for kindness to strangers and urged attention to "the greatest commandment of all… the golden rule to treat everyone the way we want to be treated."

President Trump finally succeeded in stemming the asylum-seeking tide by persuading Mexico—using the carrot of a multi-billion-dollar aid package and the stick of threats to impose stiff tariffs on Mexican exports and even to shut down the border—to help stop the northward exodus. Mexico not only used its military to turn migrants back at its southern border. It also agreed to cooperate with the U.S. on a program that required the migrants to wait in Mexican border towns while their cases were processed in the U.S. But as press reports validated claims that Mexican criminals were preying upon the Central Americans, the "Remain in Mexico" program—mislabeled as the "Migration Protection Protocols" by the Trump administration—came under attack in the federal courts. From its base in San Francisco, the U.S. Court of Appeals for the Ninth Circuit ruled in early 2020 that the policy violated both U.S. and international law. But the court later allowed the Trump administration to maintain the policy until it was reviewed by the Supreme Court.

A FADING COMMITMENT TO E-VERIFY

The Trump administration's efforts to stop illegal immigration at the border and deport illegal immigrants have been firm and often draconian. Yet the president's commitment to worksite enforcement now appears as bogus as a fraudulent green card.

During his 2016 run for the presidency, Trump had pledged to implement "new immigration controls to boost wages and to ensure that open jobs are offered to American workers first."[45] In his speech to a cheering crowd in Phoenix two months before the election, he pledged full implementation of E-Verify, the computer-based verification system that allows employers to check workers' legal status against the documents they presented to prove they were authorized to work in the U.S. "We will ensure that E-Verify is used to the fullest extent possible," he said. Then he added a pledge to "work with Congress to strengthen and expand its use across the country."[46]

If Trump had delivered on that election-year promise, he would have taken an historic step toward repairing the fatal flaw of the Immigration Reform and Control Act. The need for a credible system to identify authorized workers has been apparent for decades. It was addressed by comprehensive immigration reform bills of 2007 and 2013, although critics on both occasions claimed that still better systems were needed. But a virtual wall around the American workplace would be far more effective in stopping illegal immigration than a wall across a border that stretches for nearly 2,000 miles of serpentine river valley, rugged mountain ranges, and forbidding desert. While the wall has certainly imposed order in once chaotic stretches adjacent to border towns, it is little more than an inconvenience for professional smugglers, whose job is to steer customers around impediments, both structural and human. It is as meaningless to a smuggler as the worker verification requirement is to an employer whose business plan includes cheap labor from workers who present phony documents. Congress has done such employers the great favor of making E-Verify voluntary in most instances.

But while Trump has maintained his passionate commitment to build the wall, his ardor for E-Verify has cooled. Indeed, there is good reason to suspect that it was never more than campaign rhetoric. The notoriously fickle president, who vowed to embrace E-Verify to protect American workers, built a business empire that ignored E-Verify in its own hiring practices. The *Washington Post* and *New York Times* have revealed that Trump resorts and golf courses hired numerous undocumented workers without submitting their documents to E-Verify. Only after those stories did the Trump Organization, as it is officially known, pledge to use the system. Trump went along grudgingly. He revealed his dislike of the system when he complained about the effectiveness of E-Verify during construction of his Trump International Hotel a few blocks from the White House. "It nearly killed me," he said, upset at losing access to the cheaper labor of unauthorized immigrants. "It was the worst, most expensive thing ever—a total mess....It's a disaster."[47]

The façade of Trump's pledge to implement E-Verify was still standing when his administration presented its budget for the 2020 fiscal year. Its title could have appeared on a poster for a Trump reelection rally: "A Budget for a Better America: Promises Kept, Taxpayers First." Its text could have been lifted from one of Trump's 2016 speeches. "The employment of illegal aliens by companies is a violation of the law, harms U.S. workers, and contributes to human smuggling, document fraud, identity theft, money laundering, and labor violations," it read. It described E-Verify as "a *critical* employment verification system. (Emphasis added.) Then it was even more emphatic, endorsing "mandatory, nationwide use of the E-Verify system."

Trump's façade collapsed in late 2019 with publication of his budget proposal for FY2021. Although the document retained the praise for E-Verify as a "critical" system, the proposal to make E-Verify mandatory was conspicuously absent. The *Washington Times* observed that the reversal "signals the White House's surrender on one of the best tools to shut down the jobs magnet that spurs illegal immigration." The newspaper went on to quote Jessica Vaughan, my colleague at the Center for Immigration Studies, who interpreted the course change as an effort to facilitate a new, business-friendly immigration reform proposal being developed by Jared Kushner. "It's a takeover of the president's immigration agenda by the special interests who benefit from illegal immigration," Vaughan said.[48]

The FY2021 budget was released near the end of a year in which Trump repeatedly proclaimed his determination to stop illegal immigration. He shut down the federal government in his dispute with Congress over border funding, declared a national emergency in order to direct funding to the wall, jettisoned a nominee to run ICE because he wanted to go in "a tougher direction," forced the resignation of DHS Secretary Kirstjen Nielsen after she refused to ignore asylum law, and threatened to close the border if Mexico did not stop the caravans flowing north to the U.S.

In a more contentious Republican environment, Trump's about-face might have been denounced as the sort of high-level betrayal he had promised to avenge on behalf of American workers. But the Republican Party had become the Party of Trump. And conservative media, especially Fox News and Breitbart, were loath to break partisan ranks. Moreover, unemployment rates reached historic lows, easing anxiety about unauthorized workers. So consternation over Trump's move was confined to restrictionists and others who understood that an effective system of worker verification was the best protection against future resentment and nativist turmoil. I asked Thomas Homan, a loyal supporter of Trump, what he thought of the retreat on E-Verify. "I'm perplexed," he said. "I don't know what to make of it."

To be fair to the president, it is important to point out that the division of ICE known as Homeland Security Investigations launched far more worksite cases in FY 2018 and 2019 than the Obama administration had in FY 2016, its final year in office. But the execution of worksite raids indicated that the Trump administration was far more interested in arresting workers than in punishing employers.

THE FACE OF ENFORCEMENT

Thomas Homan, with a boxer's face and a lineman's build, became the public face of immigration enforcement during the Trump administration. Trump had called him out of retirement to become the acting director at ICE. He had been a Border Patrol agent and later a special agent and supervisory agent within the old INS. After the creation of ICE in 2003, he continued his rise, becoming deputy associate director of enforcement within the division known as Enforcement and Removal Operations. In that capacity he was a central figure in the Obama administration's deportation effort. But he also chafed against Obama's efforts to limit deportation of illegal immigrants who had not committed serious crimes. Immigrant advocates regarded Homan as extreme, an enforcement zealot who even supported the "zero tolerance" policy that led to the trauma of family separation. Gabe Ortiz, an immigrant-rights activist and staff writer for The Daily Kos blog, called him "one of the most dangerous men in America." Norman Ornstein, one of Washington's most respected political commentators, condemned him as "an inhuman, sadistic monster." But in 2015, Homan's work was honored with the Presidential Rank Award, the highest honor for civil servants. He thought of himself as a cop's cop, steady in his commitment to personal integrity and the rule of law. He viewed illegal immigration as a destabilizing force that fomented a sense of impunity that often was accompanied by such crimes as counterfeiting, identity fraud, marriage fraud, and even drug trafficking. "We have to dispel this notion that you can violate the laws of this country and hideout, and that's okay," he said.

Homan had a role in two episodes that illustrated the explosive nature of the immigration debate at a time of embittered polarization. The first unfolded during the final weeks of the 2018 Democratic primary contest for New York's 14th Congressional District. The incumbent was Rep. Joseph Crowley, the fourth-ranking Democrat in the House of Representatives. He was so entrenched in his densely Democratic district that included parts of the Bronx and Queens and had a population that was half Latino that he hadn't faced a primary challenge since 2004. Crowley trusted in the polls that indicated he would easily turn back the challenge from a young, energetic but underfunded political novice named Alexandria Ocasio-Cortez. But a few weeks before election day he realized that Ocasio-Cortez, a member of the Democratic Socialists of America who called for guaranteed employment, a single-payer health care system, and the abolition of ICE, was a serious contender. Three weeks before the election, Crowley's late-blooming anxiety prodded him to pander. Invoking the Southern Poverty Law Center's "hate group" designation of the Center for Immigration Studies, Crowley called on Homan to cancel his planned appearance at the National Press Club with Jessica Vaughan of CIS. The interview went ahead. Crowley's congressional career soon came to an end. And Ocasio-Cortez's victory was seen as a sign of things to come in the Democratic Party. "She represents the future of our party," said Tom Perez, chairman of the Democratic National Committee.[49] CNN's Chris Cillizza said she "represents the beating heart of [the party's] liberal, activist wing."[50]

Homan's role in the second episode was more intense. It involved conflicting emotions that were more genuine than Crowley's transparent pandering. The drama played out in a Capitol Hill hearing room in mid-2019 after Homan had retired from ICE. As he sat at a witness table, he was confronted by Mexican-American Rep. Jesús Garcia, an Illinois Democrat, who had moved to the U.S. at the age of 10 after his father, a former bracero, obtained a green card. Garcia referred to reports of mistreatment of children, mentioning a boy who had died in federal custody, apparently after becoming sick on the journey from Guatemala. "Mr. Homan, I'm a father," Garcia said tersely. "Do you have children? How can you possibly allow this to happen under your watch? Do you not care?" Then Garcia answered his own question with an accusation. "Is it because these children do not look like children that are around you? I don't get it. Have you ever held a deceased child in your arms?"

Homan, sitting at the witness table, was enraged. "First of all, your comments are disgusting," he said, prompting Garcia to return the insult. Then Homan launched into a seething response. "I've served my country 34 years. And yes, I held a five-year-old boy in my arms in the back of that tractor trailer." He was describing the tragedy that he encountered in 2003, when he was called to Speedy Stop truck stop on U.S. 77 between McAllen and Houston. In the back of a tractor trailer, 19 unauthorized immigrants lay dead from suffocation because of the criminal negligence of the truck driver, who had ignored their banging on the trucks walls in temperatures that reached 173 degrees. "I held a five-year-old boy in my arms in the back of that tractor trailer," he said. "I knelt down and said a prayer for him because I knew what his last 30 minutes of his life was like. And I had a five-year-old son at the time." His faced was flushed with anger and he jabbed a finger toward Garcia. "For you to sit there and try to insult my integrity and my love for my country and for children, that's why this whole thing needs to be fixed! And you're the member of Congress. Fix it!" In an appearance the next day on "Fox and Friends," Homan said he had been so infuriated that he thought of "getting up and throwing that man a beating right there in the middle of the room."

A CONFLICT OF BACKGROUNDS AND VALUES

That incendiary exchange between the congressman and the cop laid bare emotions that often lie hidden just below the surface of immigration discussions before they combust into confrontations. Each man was defending the people and the cause with which he most closely identified. Garcia, whose hometown of Chicago had seen the migration of hundreds of thousands of Mexicans who came both legally and illegally since the 1920s, knew the pain suffered by families whose illegal status subjected them to deportation. His taunting implication that Homan was racist expressed a belief that is widespread among those whose greatest concern is the suffering of those for whom the undocumented are siblings, cousins, neighbors, or friends. They often see the rule of law as oppressive and racist. That is the world of Rep. Garcia. Thomas Homan is the son of a small-town policeman and became a small-town policeman himself before becoming a federal agent. His life was the law. He patrolled the nation's borders, investigated crimes connected to illegal immigration, and became the man in charge of deporting people who had violated the law, often in violent and damaging ways. "We arrest a lot of bad guys," he liked to say. "We prevent crimes." He had no patience for elected officials like Oakland Mayor Libby Schaaf, who in 2018 warned the public about impending ICE arrests. He said Schaaf wasn't any better than "a gang lookout." He saw enforcement as social glue in a turbulent and dangerous world. And those who didn't like the law, he said, should fix it.

WE NEED A GOVERNMENT THAT MANAGES IMMIGRATION

Of course, many people on opposing sides of the debate want to fix the law, and their ideas on what that means are many and varied. Our country badly needs political leaders to build a bridge of mutual concern and understanding. We need women and men who combine humanitarian decency with clear-eyed firmness, who can manage immigration in a way that is hard-headed but not hard-hearted.

We need those who will move us away from confrontation and toward reconciliation.

My ideal leaders would unite us behind a reform law that would be a more robust version of the Immigration Reform and Control Act of 1986. It would include a generous amnesty for established immigrants and firm enforcement, especially at the worksite, to stop future waves of illegal immigration. The enforcement provisions would be strong enough to prevent the worksite sham that IRCA allowed, strong enough to withstand the inevitable onslaught from those who benefit politically or financially from unchecked immigration.

The reform would rescue millions from the traumatic upheaval of deportation. But it would guarantee the rigorous worksite enforcement and strict accountability for employers, the lack of which has made restrictionists feel like Charlie Brown—unable to connect with Lucy's football. It would allow employers to import temporary workers at times of verified labor shortages. And it would establish a Canadian-style merit system that would replace extended family relationships as the principal criterion for selecting new immigrants.

In my ideal world, Congress would rally behind our president as she or he delivered a nationally televised speech, declaring that the newly enacted reform was essential to the preservation of our tradition as a nation of immigrants *and* a nation of laws and to sustain the blessings of an orderly society in which playing by the rules confirms our commitment to each other as Americans.

The president would address part of the speech explicitly to people around the world who are pondering illegal immigration to the United States, advising them firmly but amicably that the old disorder has been repudiated and the new order will make it impossible for them to establish lives here without legal permission. Scofflaw employers would be put on notice that the Department of Labor would henceforth be far more vigilant in enforcing wage and hour laws. Such a move, as immigration experts Nolan Rappaort and

Prakash Khatri have noted, would "herald a new era of enforcement of the laws already on the books against employers who are exploiting workers."†

THOUGHTS OF THEODORE WHITE

Of course, my fantasy of immigration reform is inevitably interrupted by ruminations about the complexity of the project. I think of the warning from Theodore White, whose insights into American politics and culture made him one of the most prominent journalists of the 20th century. Writing in 1984, White worried even then about the intensity of the immigration-driven demographic shift that was precipitated both by the 1965 immigration act and the increase in illegal immigration. "If the U.S. 'tips' ethnically as our big cities 'tip,' it may be impossible to pass any law that makes immigration just and orderly," White wrote. Perhaps he was anticipating the election of such ethnic advocates of immigration as Alexandria Ocasio-Cortez and Jesús Garcia, who have pushed the center of the Democratic Party well to the left.

A conundrum of Joe Biden's 2020 run for the presidency is that he needs to appeal to two powerful constituencies with conflicting views on immigration. There are the working class whites in such pivotal states as Pennsylvania, Michigan, and Ohio, who want immigration enforcement and whose concerns Biden expressed a 2019 debate among Democratic rivals. "If you cross the border illegally, you should be able to be sent back," he said. "It's a crime." But he also wants to reach the growing ranks of Latino voters in states like Florida, Colorado, and Arizona, who press for expansive immigration policies. Biden deferred to this group when he hailed immigration, illegal as well as legal, during a 2020 interview with Univision anchorman Jorge Ramos. "We stand up and act like it's a burden," he said. "It is not a burden. It's a gift."

---

† Both men are immigration attorneys. Rappaport has served as immigration counsel for the House Subcommittee on Immigration, Border Security, and Claims. He now writes a column for *The Hill*.

According to the *Washington Post,* Pennsylvania's Democratic Senator, Robert Casey, "urged Biden to emphasize the economic benefits of immigration while pledging to secure the southern border to keep drugs and criminals out." That would be a new version of the old diversionary tactic of sounding an alarm at the border while skipping past the issues of the worksite.

Biden faces the challenge of mobilizing—or at least not antagonizing—the party's activist wing, which wants to provide free health care and other assistance to unauthorized immigrants. They reject the ethos of the 1996 law signed by President Clinton that asserted a "compelling government interest to remove the incentive for illegal immigration provided by the availability of public benefits." Some activists want to decriminalize unauthorized border crossings. Some spoke of abolishing ICE. In asserting their resistance to Trump's draconian policies, they have pushed their party towards the extremes of the open-borders left.‡

The expansive, often utopian spirit on the left draws a stern rebuke from Reihan Salam, the son of Bangladeshi immigrants who wrote for the conservative *National Review,* and is now president of the Manhattan Institute. Salam argues that unless we carefully manage immigration, we may deepen divisions of class and race to the point that they will shatter civil society and plunge us into fratricidal violence. "High levels of low-skill immigration will make a middle-class melting pot impossible," he writes in a book provocatively titled *Melting Pot or Civil War? A Son of Immigrants Makes the Case Against Open Borders.*[51] David Frum made an equally incisive assessment when he said, "Choose well and you build a stronger, richer country for both newcomers and the long-settled. Choose badly and you aggravate inequality and inflame intergroup hostility."[52]

‡ One of Biden's campaign's advisers on immigration policy is Rep. Lucille Roybal-Allard, D-CA. A staunch advocate of the unauthorized, she is the daughter of the late Rep. Edward Roybal, who as we saw in Chapter One, led the opposition to worksite enforcement.

But on the other side of the ledger, extreme restrictionism of the kind that has caused the most conservative Republicans to obstruct votes on reform legislation is partially responsible for the dangerous gridlock of recent years. Most Americans, as public opinion polls show, are not just in favor of the amnesty-plus-enforcement approach; they crave the rationality, pragmatism, compassion, and firmness that a well-managed system could provide.

In his classic work about the history of conservatism, Russell Kirk wrote, "Conservatism never is more admirable than when it accepts changes that it disapproves, with good grace, for the sake of a general conciliation."[53] But President Trump has pushed the Republican Party in the opposite direction. Trump based his 2016 campaign on his understanding of legitimate populist grievances about illegal immigration. But then he inflamed and exploited those grievances, making our immigration politics more divided than ever before. When his disjointed effort to make a deal with Democrats in early 2018 prompted warnings that he would derail his prospects for a second term, he retreated, turtle-like-into his shell of anger and insult and pandering to his base.

In 2007, a decade before Trump became president, Nathan Glazer, the eminent sociologist and immigration scholar, noted that public opinion polls consistently showed support for limits on immigration. Then, pointing to the "disconnect" between what the people wanted and what their government had delivered, he warned that it "raises a problem for democracy whose resolution may well be very disturbing." He asked a question for which we now have a partial answer: "How long can what the majority claims it wants be ignored, and what are the consequences?"[54] Glazer seems to have anticipated the crisis that is now upon us as we wonder if our democracy can produce a government that can manage immigration.

Notes

CHAPTER 1

1. "The Real Immigration Bill," *Washington Post*, June 12, 1984.
2. "Bill to Curb Illegal Immigration: House Debate Reflects Diversity of Nation," *New York Times*, June 17, 1984, https://timesmachine.nytimes.com/timesmachine/1984/06/17/007468.html?pageNumber=21
3. Ibid.
4. *Fresno Republican*, March 17, 1913.
5. Quoted in Mark Reisler, *By the Sweat of Their Brow: Mexican Immigrant Labor in the United States, 1900–1940,* Westport, Greenwood Press, 1976, p. 129.
6. Ernesto Galarza, *Farm Workers and Agri-business in California, 1947–1960*, Notre Dame, Indiana: University of Notre Dame Press, 1977, p. 205.
7. Ibid. p. 82.
8. *New York Times*, August 9, 1951.
9. *McAllen Monitor*, "'Best We Can Expect: Comment on Labor Bill," February 6, 1952.
10. *New York Times*, "Brownell Tours 'Wetback' Border," August 16, 1953.
11. Ibid.
12. "Pauline Villegas, "65 Percent of Mexicans View U.S. Negatively, Survey Finds," *New York Times*, September 14, 2017, https://www.nytimes.com/2017/09/14/world/americas/mexico-us-survey.html.
13. "Why Didn't Collective Bargaining Transform California's Farm Labor Market?; A Promise Unfulfilled" Philip L. Martin, Center for Immigration Studies Backgrounder, January 2004, https://cis.org/Report/Why-Didnt-Collective-Bargaining-Transform-Californias-Farm-Labor-Market.
14. Sen. Mondale, Hearing before the Senate Subcommittee on Migratory Labor, "Migratory and Seasonal Farmworker Powerlessness," April 15, 1970, p. 4,548, http://archive.org/stream/migrantseasonalfb7unit/migrantseasonalfb7unit_djvu.txt.
15. Gilman testimony at House Immigration Subcommittee, June 10, 1971.
16. *U.S. News and World Report*, April 24, 1977.
17. *U.S. News and World Report*, July 4, 1977.
18. Jensen E. Branscombe, "Knights Riding the Border: The Ku Klux Klan and Security Along the U.S.-Mexico Border During the 1970s," in *Culture, Power, and Security: New Directions in the History of National and International Security*, edited by Mary Kathryn Barbier and Richard V. Damms, 2012, Newcastle upon Tyne, Cambridge Scholars Publishing.

19. Richard DeUriarte, "Communities Adjoin But Are a World Apart," *Phoenix Gazette*, March 14, 1993.
20. Lawrence H. Fuchs, "The corpse that would not die: The Immigration Reform and Control Act of 1986," *Revue Europeenne des Migrations Internationales*, Volume 6, No. 1, 1990, https://www.persee.fr/doc/remi_0765-0752_1990_num_6_1_1230.
21. Alan K. Simpson, *Right in the Old Gazoo: A Lifetime of Scrapping with the Press*, 1997, New York, William Morrow, p. 63.
22. David Gergen, "They Love You. Watch Out." *New York Times*, February 2, 1997.
23. President Johnson, Remarks at the Presentation of the 1964 Presidential Medal of Freedom Awards. September 14, 1964, http://www.presidency.ucsb.edu/ws/index.php?pid=26496.
24. SCIRP final report, "U.S. Immigration and the National Interest," Introduction by the Rev.Theodore Hesburgh.
25. Spencer Rich, "Commission on Immigration Recommends Criminal Penalties for Hiring Illegal Aliens", *Washington Post*, December 7, 1980.
26. Elizabeth Midgley, "Immigrants: Whose Huddled Masses?," *Atlantic Monthly*, April 1978.
27. Leonard W. Miller, Jerry L. Polinard, Roberg D. Wrinkle, "Attitudes Toward Undocumented Workers: The Mexican American Perspective," *Social Science Quarterly*, June 1, 1984; 65.2.
28. "Immigration Tangle,"*Washington Post*, December 16, 1980.
29. Jack Rosenthal, "Immigration and the Missing Nail," *New York Times*, March 1, 1981.
30. President Obama Announces the Presidential Medal of Freedom Recipients, March 10, 2014, https://obamawhitehouse.archives.gov/blog/2014/11/10/president-obama-announces-presidential-medal-freedom-recipients.
31. "Chicano! A History of the Mexican-American Civil Rights Movement" 1996, https://www.imdb.com/title/tt0321652/.
32. Edward Roybal, "Bill Wouldn't Provide Reforms Needed," column written for United Press International, *Daily Chronicle*, DeKalb, Ill., October 10, 1983.
33. *Washington Post*, "The Real Immigration Bill," June 12, 1984.
34. *New York Times*, "Hang on to Immigration Reform," July 27, 1984.
35. Author telephone interview with Simpson, April 23, 2009.
36. Alan K. Simpson, *Right in the Old Gazoo*, op. cit., p. 74.
37. Joint hearing between the Senate Judiciary Committee's Subcommittee on Immigration and Refugee Policy and the House Judiciary Committee's Subcommittee on Immigration, Refugees, and International Law, on the Final Report of the Select Commission on Immigration and Refugee Policy, 97th Congress, First Session, Washington, D.C., U.S. Govt. Printing Office, 1981, p. 245.
38. Ronald B. Taylor, "New Wave of Cheap Labor Seen," *Los Angeles Times*, October 22, 1985.
39. Harry Bernstein, "Growers Still Addicted to Foreign Workers," *Los Angeles Times*, October 2, 1985.

40. Julia Malone, "Growers' Influence Blossoms as Immigration Bill Takes Shape," *Christian Science Monitor*, September 19, 1985, https://www.csmonitor.com/1985/0919/agrate.html.
41. "Giving Immigration the Business," *New York Times*, September 22, 1985.
42. *The Washington Post*, "The Immigration Compromise", July 16, 1986.
43. Mary Thornton, "Immigration Bill Came from Morgue," *Washington Post*, October 11, 1986.
44. Bob Secter, "Immigration Bill Sent to President," *Los Angeles Times*, October 18, 1986.
45. Judy Wiessler, "Immigration bill: deja vu, yet different", *Houston Chronicle*, October 12, 1986.
46. "Debate Goes Back to Early '70s; Revision Became Idea That Would Not Die." *Los Angeles Times*, October 18, 1986.
47. Robert Pear, "House Approves Compromise Bill on Illegal Aliens," *New York Times*, October 16, 1986.
48. *The Economist*, September 28, 1985.
49. Philip Martin, *Promise Unfulfilled: Unions, Immigration and the Farmworkers*, Cornell University Press, 2003, p. 186.
50. Don Villarejo. "Environmental Effects of Living and Working in Agricultural Areas of California: Social and Economic Factors," 1990, *In Health Concerns of Living and Working in Agricultural California*. Report of a conference held at the University of California at Davis, Center for Occupational and Environmental Health.
51. Christopher Jencks, "Who Should Get In?" Part Two, *New York Review of Books*, December 20, 2001.
52. John Higham, October 1, 1993, statement to the U.S. Commission on Immigration Reform, See Kammer, "Historian John Higham's Widening Views on Modern Efforts to Limit Immigration," https://cis.org/Historian-John-Highams-Widening-Views-Modern-Efforts-Limit-Immigration#44. See also: U.S. Commission on Immigration Reform "Americanization and Integration of Immigrants."
53. Sullivan interview with Michael Krasny of KQED; see: https://cis.org/Kammer/Andrew-Sullivan-Discusses-Social-and-Political-Upheaval-US.

CHAPTER 2

1. Dianne Klein "Majority in State are Fed Up With Illegal Immigration," *Los Angeles Times*, September 19, 1993, https://www.latimes.com/archives/la-xpm-1993-09-19-mn-36919-story.html
2. Bill Keller, "Show Me Your Papers," *New York Times*, July 1, 2012, https://www.nytimes.com/2012/07/02/opinion/keller-show-me-your-papers.html
3. George I. Sanchez, *La Raza: The Forgotten Americans*, South Bend, University of Notre Dame Press, 1966, p. 9.
4. *The Washington Post*, "Harvest of Blame; Californians Turn on Illegal Immigrants," June 4, 1993.

5. George Ramos, "A House Divided Over Immigration," *Los Angeles Times*. September 27, 1993.
6. *The New York Times*, August 19, 2014, "Where We Came From and Where We Went, State by State, " August 19, 2014, https://www.nytimes.com/interactive/2014/08/13/upshot/where-people-in-each-state-were-born.html.
7. "California Takes Population Lead," *The New York Times*, September 1, 1964.
8. Robert Putnam, "E Pluribus Unum: Diversity and Community," *Scandinavian Political Studies*, v. 30, no. 2 (2007), p. 150.
9. Migration Policy Institute, Profile of the Unauthorized Population: California,https://www.migrationpolicy.org/data/unauthorized-immigrant-population/state/CA.
10. Jerry Kammer, "Border Patrol beefs up number of agents," The Arizona Republic, February 9, 1995.
11. Ibid.
12. Terry Goddard, "How to Fix a Broken Border," Immigration Policy Center, February, 2012.
13. Charlie LeDuff, "After the Crossing, Danger to Migrants Isn't Over," The New York Times, November 11, 2003.
14. Brian Ross, Richard Esposito, Asa Eslocker, "Kidnapping Capital of the U.S.A." ABC News, February 11, 2009, https://abcnews.go.com/Blotter/story?id=6848672&page=1.
15. Hugh Delios, "Cross-Border Traffic Ravages Desert Park," Chicago Tribune, August 19, 2003.
16. Jerry Kammer, "Strategic Negligence: How the Sierra Club's Distortions on Border and Immigration Policy Are Undermining Its Environmental Legacy," Center for Immigration Studies, October, 2009, http://cis.org/sierraclub.
17. Tom Clynes, "Arizona Park 'Most Dangerous' in U.S" National Geographic News, January 13, 2003, http://news.nationalgeographic.com/news/2003/01/0110_030113_organpipeclynes.html.
18. Jerry Kammer, "Illegal border crossers leave mark on land; Senate panel hears testimony of damage to reservation, refuge," San Diego Union Tribune, June 18, 2004, http://www.sandiegouniontribune.com/uniontrib/20040618/news_1n18border.html.
19. Tom Clynes, National Geographic News, op. cit.
20. Jerry Kammer, "Strategic Negligence," op. cit.
21. Ibid.
22. Author interview with Michael Hawkes.
23. Julie Cart, "In Border Battle, Land and Wildlife Are Casualties," Los Angeles Times, March 3, 2006.
24. Jimmy Breslin, The Short Sweet Dream of Eduardo Gutierrez, New York: Crown Publishers, 2002, p. 49.
25. Breslin at Barnes & Noble, March 26, 2002, http://www.c-span.org/video/?169466-1/book-discussion-short-sweet-dream-eduardo-gutierrez.
26. Jerry Kammer, "Arizona's Prop. 200 is Dividing a State," The San Diego Union Tribune, October 16, 2004.
27. Ibid.

28. Jerry Kammer, "Immigration Debate Likely to Intensify," The San Diego Union Tribune, November 22, 2004.
29. Jerry Kammer, "Desperate trek in desert: Enforcement pressure makes desolate Arizona border area a favorite." San Diego Union Tribune, September 7, 2004.
30. Emery P. Dalesio, Associated Press, "Census: N.C. Population Skyrockets," March 22, 2001.
31. E.J. Montini, "Fear of once again rousing sleeping giant in Arizona," The Arizona Republic, May 4, 2008.
32. John Judis, "The Border War," The New Republic, January 15, 2006.
33. Robert Robb, "GOP must condemn sweeps by Arpaio," The Arizona Republic, April 18, 2008.
34. Arizona Republic editorial, "The Issue: Arpaio's Roundups," April 1, 2008.
35. Ryan Gabrielson and Paul Giblin, "Reasonable Doubt: "Tribune Investigates Sheriff's Immigration Campaign. At What Cost?" East Valley Tribune, July 9, 2008.
36. Amy Chozik, "First Draft: Hillary Clinton Criticizes Sheriff Joe Arpaio, Immigration Proxy for Donald Trump," New York Times website, March 21, 2016, https://www.nytimes.com/politics/first-draft/2016/03/21/hillary-clinton-criticizes-sheriff-joe-arpaio-immigration-proxy-for-donald-trump/?_r=0.
37. Katie Mettler, "New sheriff in town to close Joe Arpaio's outdoor Tent City jail, of pink underwear fame," The Washington Post, April 5, 2017.

CHAPTER 3

1. Lawrence Downes, "One Hundred Hears of Multitude," *New York Times*, March 26, 2011, https://www.nytimes.com/2011/03/26/opinion/26sat4.html
2. Susan E. Tifft and Alex S. Jones, *The Trust: The Private and Powerful Family Behind The New York Times*, New York: Back Bay Books, 1999, p. 649.
3. *The Trust*, p. 651.
4. Sulzberger commencement address, May 21, 2006, https://www.c-span.org/video/?192696-1/suny-paltz-commencement-address.
5. "The Beltway Boys," Fox News, June 3, 2006.
6. Michael Wolff, "Panic on 43rd Street," *Vanity Fair*, September, 2006, https://www.vanityfair.com/culture/2006/09/wolff200609.
7. Vincent Carroll, "On Point: A Child Shall Lead Them," *Rocky Mountain News*, June 2, 2006.
8. The Immigration Deal," *New York Times*, May 20, 2007.
9. "Migrants Freedom Ride," *New York Times*, July 29, 2012.
10. Peter Beinart provides an excellent examination of this issue in *The Atlantic*'s July/August, 2017, issue: https://www.theatlantic.com/magazine/archive/2017/07/the-democrats-immigration-mistake/528678/.
11. Lawrence Downes, "Showdown in Arizona, Where Mariachis and Minutemen Collide," *The New York Times*, December 10, 2007.
12. Laurie Roberts, "Leadership Still Lacks in Migrant Fight," *Arizona Republic*, December 8, 2007.

13. Michael Kiefer, "Weekly Drama Persists; Signs, Shouting, Arrests," *Arizona Republic*, December 9, 2007.
14. "Why Won't Congress Act," *Arizona Republic*, December 6, 2006.
15. Daniel Okrent: "Is the New York Times a Liberal Newspaper?" *The New York Times*, July 25, 2004.
16. While editorials function as a statement of opinion and often of explicit bias, the strident bias of the *Times* editorial page has also infected its news reporting. One prominent example is the paper's coverage of the 2006 Duke lacrosse team, whose members were falsely accused of rape. In his book on the case, journalist Stuart Taylor wrote that the *Times*, other media, and activist groups seemed to "need to believe that those they classify as victims must be virtuous and those they classify as oppressors must be villains." Taylor's book, co-written by KC Johnson, is titled *Until Proven Innocent; Political Correctness and the Shameful Injustices of the Duke Lacrosse Rape Case*.
17. Lawrence Downes, "For Obama, Estranged in a Strange land, Aloha Had Its Limits," *The New York Times*, April 9, 2007.
18. Lawrence Downes, "Day Laborers, Silent and Despised, Find Their Voice," *The New York Times*, July 10, 2006.
19. Lawrence Downes, "Notes from the Immigration Battlefield," *The New York Times*, March 19, 2009.
20. Ibid.
21. "Immigrants, Criminalized," *New York Times*, November 26, 2009.
22. "Angry Arizona, Again," *New York Times*, February 27, 2011.
23. Kelefa Sanneh, "Raging Arizona; How a border state became a battleground," *The New Yorker*, May 28, 2012.
24. Sanneh, Live Chat: https://www.newyorker.com/books/ask-the-author/live-chat-kelefa-sanneh-on-arizona-immigration-politics.
25. Downes interview with Bill Moyers on "Moyers & Company," February 3, 2012.
26. "The Immigration Deal," *New York Times*, May 20, 2007.
27. David Brooks, "America's Admissions System," *The New York Times*, May 22, 2007.
28. Make a Bad Bill Better," *New York Times*, May 29, 2007.
29. Linda Qui "'Chain Migration' Has Become a Weaponized Phrase." *The New York Times*, January 26, 2018.
30. "We've Lost Control of Our Borders," *New York Times*, August 2, 1981.
31. "Guerrilla War on Immigration," *New York Times*, August 27, 1982.
32. "Time to Turn the Illegal Tide," *New York Times*, February 21, 1983.
33. "The Speaker and the Big Wink," *New York Times*, October 5, 1983.
34. "The Simpson-Nobody Bill," *New York Times*, May 25, 1984.
35. "The Cold Stove League," *New York Times*, June 16, 1982.
36. "The Last Place to Cut the Budget," *New York Times*, February 1, 1981.
37. "Immigration and the Missing Nail," *New York Times*, March 1, 1981.
38. Sam Roberts, "Jack Rosenthal, Times Journalist and Civic Leader, Is Dead at 82," *New York Times*, August 24, 2017.

39. Michael Lind, "Liberals Duck Immigration Debate," *The New York Times*, September 7, 1995.
40. Michael Lind at May 25, 2015 panel discussion: "The Progressive Argument for Reducing Immigration to the U.S." https://cis.org/Book-Discussion-Transcript-Progressive-Argument-Reducing-US-Immigration.
41. Jerry Kammer, "I'm a Liberal Who Thinks Immigration Must Be Restricted," *The New York Times*, January 16, 2020, https://www.nytimes.com/2020/01/16/opinion/immigration-democrats.html.

CHAPTER 4

1. John Tierney, "Social Scientist Sees Bias Within," *New York Times*," February 7, 2011.
2. Jason DeParle, *A Good Provider is One Who Leaves*, New York, Viking, 2019, p.234.
3. Carnegie grants database, description of grant to Pundit Productions, which, according to its IRS990 tax filings, did business as Capital News Connection https://www.carnegie.org/grants/grants-database/?q=Pundit+Productions&per_page=25&per_page=25#!/grants/grants-database/grant/29084.01/.
4. Elizabeth Wynne Johnson, "One in 10 U.S. Voters are New Legal Immigrants," https://web.archive.org/web/20101017082653/http://www.capitolnewsconnection.org/podcast/power-breakfast/new-american-voter-registration-report-released. The Immigration Policy Center provided a transcript: http://216.92.33.26/newsroom/clip/new-american-voter-registration-report-released.
5. https://www.americanimmigrationcouncil.org/sites/default/files/celebrate_america_2017_winners.pdf.
6. Capitol News Connection itself became the object of investigative reporting in late 2010. The Washington Post's Paul Fahri broke the story of an apparent conflict of interest stemming from the fact that CNC founder, executive director and bureau chief Melinda Wittstock, "is also the wife of the WAMU executive charged with determining which programs the station airs." Noting that WAMU paid CNC for its programs, Fahri reported that the WAMU platform had provided "a prestigious calling card for CNC in its efforts to market its programs to other public stations around the country." He said WAMU station executives were aware that Wittstock was married to WAMU's Mark McDonald. It also quoted McDonald as saying he did not take part in decisions involving CNC. The Post did not note something that CNC reported in its tax filings as a non-profit: that CNC also paid consulting fees to a media company that McDonald ran apart from his work on WAMU. In the aftermath of the Post's story, WAMU severed its ties with CNC. Then the Corporation for Public Broadcasting, under financial pressures of its own, decided not to renew its grant to CNC. Shortly thereafter, in the summer of 2011, CNC went out of business.
7. Promotional video with Melinda Wittstock, https://www.youtube.com/watch?v=4Wt9AD74j9s.

8. Daniel Samuels, "Philanthropical Correctness," *The New Republic*, September 18, 1995.
9. Carnegie description of a $5 million grant to The Freedoms Fund, https://www.carnegie.org/media/filer_public/95/a8/95a8b3eb-dedc-424c-b7db-d23f377efcc3/ccny_annualreport_2013.pdf.
10. Joyce Baldwin, "The Reform Movement Rebuilds" Carnegie Reporter, Fall, 2008.
11. Carnegie grants database: https://www.carnegie.org/grants/grants-database/?q=%22faster+and+edgier%22&per_page=25&per_page=25#!/grants/grants-database/grant/32124.01/.
12. Carnegie grants database: https://www.carnegie.org/grants/grants-database/?q=%22immigrants+advocate+for+their+needs%22&per_page=25&per_page=25#!/grants/grants-database/grant/23176.03.
13. https://www.carnegie.org/grants/grants-database/?q=%22bring+its+unique+libertarian%22&per_page=25&per_page=25#!/grants/grants-database/grant/46070.0/.
14. Ford description of its goals and rationales: https://www.homelandsecuritygrants.info/GrantDetails.aspx?gid=25859.
15. Darren Walker, "Philanthropy in a Complex World," Ford Foundation blog, May 15, 2014, https://www.fordfoundation.org/ideas/equals-change-blog/posts/philanthropy-in-a-complex-world/
16. Caroline Preston, "Bring Odd Bedfellows Together to Promote Social Change, Foundations Urged," *Chronicle of Philanthropy*, April 25, 2010, https://philanthropy.com/article/Bring-Odd-Bedfellows-Together/191267.
17. Montini column in the *Arizona Republic*, May 4, 2008.
18. Connie Bruck, "The World According to Soros," *The New Yorker*, January 23, 1995.
19. Paloma Esquivel, "Redondo Beach day laborer ordinance is ruled unconstitutional," *Los Angeles Times*, September 20, 2011.
20. Prerna Lal, "Herndon City Council Revisits Discriminatory Day Laborer Restrictions," NDLON, January 24, 2011, http://ndlon.org/en/component/content/category/77-news?layout=blog&start=370.
21. Michelle Fei, "Secure Communities and the U.S. Immigrant Rights Movement: Lessons from New York State." https://nacla.org/blog/2012/7/11/secure-communities-and-us-immigrant-rights-movement-lessons-new-york-state
22. 2012 grant to Reform Immigration for America, http://www.atlanticphilanthropies.org/grants/reform-immigration-for-america-rifa. Reform Immigration for America is a program of the Center for Community Change.
23. http://www.atlanticphilanthropies.org/grants/core-support-617.
24. Paul Krugman, "North of the Border," *New York Times*, March 27, 2006, https://www.nytimes.com/2006/03/27/opinion/north-of-the-border.html.

CHAPTER 5

1. Nicholas Kulish, "Dr. John Tanton, Quiet Catalyst in Anti-Immigration Drive," New York Times, July 18, 2019, https://www.nytimes.com/2019/07/18/us/john-tanton-dead.html
2. George Orwell, *1984*.
3. Rebecca Bowman Woods, "Speakers Urge pre-Synod Immigration Gathering to Organize for Change," *Worldwide Faith News*, June 26, 2009, https://archive.wfn.org/2009/06/msg00165.html.
4. Western States Center, https://www.westernstatescenter.org.
5. Jonathan Tilove, "Father of Anti-Immigration Movement Awaits History's Judgment," *Newhouse News Service*, April 19, 2006.
6. Paul Ehrlich, *The Population Bomb*, New York, Sierra Club/Ballantine, 1970, p. 132.
7. Alexander Cockburn, "A Big Green Bomb Aimed at Immigration," *Los Angeles Times*, October 2, 1997.
8. FAIR ad in the *Chicago Tribune*, March 19, 1981.
9. S.I. Hayakawa speech, August 13, 1982, https://www.usenglish.org/legislation/hayakawa-speech.
10. Andy Hall, "'English' Advocate Assailed, Proposition Foes Call Memo Racist," *Arizona Republic*, October 9, 1988.
11. James Crawford, "Anti-Immigrant Bias of U.S. English Revealed," *Palm Beach Post*, October 27, 1988.
12. Larry Lopez, "Head of U.S. English Group Steps Down amid resignations of Chavez, Cronkite," *Arizona Daily Star*, October 18, 1988.
13. Earl Shorris, *Latinos: A Biography of the People*, New York, Norton, 2001, p. 228.
14. Sam Quinones, "Neither Here Nor There," book review, *Los Angeles Times*, January 13, 2002.
15. Ashley Pettus, "End of the Melting Pot? The new wave of immigrants presents new challenges," *Harvard Magazine*, May-June, 2007.
16. Christopher Hayes, "Keeping America Empty," *In These Times*, April 24, 2006.
17. Lori Montgomery, "A Doctor Takes Aim at Abraham: Anger Over Senator's pro-Immigrant Stance Spurs Possible Campaign," *Detroit Free Press*, March 14, 1997.
18. SPLC press release, "New SPLC Report: Nation's Most Prominent Anti-Immigration Group Has History of Hate, Extremism," December 11, 2007.
19. Howard Kurtz, "Washington Times Clips Its Right Wing," *Washington Post*, October 19, 1995.
20. Vdare blog, "The Tale Of John Tanton: CIS` Krikorian, Kammer Make Fatal Concessions To SPLC," April 7, 2010, https://vdare.com/articles/the-tale-of-john-tanton-cis-krikorian-kammer-make-fatal-concessions-to-splc.
21. *The Washington Post*, "FAIR Leader Fights for Immigration Curbs," November 29,1983.
22. Jason DeParle, "The Anti-Immigration Crusader," *New York Times*, April 17, 2011.
23. Steven Camarota and Leon Kolankiewicz, "Immigration to the United States and Worldwide Greenhouse Gas

Emissions," Center for Immigration Studies, https://cis.org/Immigration-United-States-and-WorldWide-Greenhouse-Gas-Emissions-0.

24. Caitlin Flanagan, "How Late-Night Comedy Fueled the Rise of Trump," *The Atlantic*, May 2017.

CHAPTER 6

1. Dees quoted in John Egerton, "Poverty Palace: How the Southern Poverty Law Center got rich fighting the Klan," *The Progressive* magazine, July 1988.
2. Mark Pulliam, "The Southern Poverty law Center's Demagogic Bullying," *City Journal* July 31, 2017
3. Ken Silverstein, "The Church of Morris Dees; How the Southern Poverty Law Center profits from intolerance," *Harper's*, November 2000.
4. The Center for Responsive Politics, OpenSecrets.org, https://www.opensecrets.org/revolving/rev_summary.php?id=70566.
5. Bernie Sanders, Congressional Record, May 22, 2007, Volume 153, Pt. 10, p. 13419.
6. Andres Oppenheimer, "Time to hit back against anti-Latino bigotry," *Miami Herald,* July 22, 2007.
7. David Schimke, "Why Words Can Hurt You," Utne Reader, December 2009. https://www.utne.com/politics/how-hate-speech-can-hurt-you-intelligence-report.
8. Open Society Institute Memorandum by Ann Beeson, Nancy Change, and Raquiba LaBrie, "U.S. Models for Combating Xenophobia and Intolerance," January 12, 2011.
9. Hagedorn Foundation, "Local & National Immigration Grants," http://hagedornfoundation.org/assets/downloads/Imm-Grants.pdf.
10. Janet Murguia on "Lou Dobbs Tonight," CNN, February 4, 2008.
11. Mary Ann Akers, The Sleuth, "New Immigration Ads Stir the Melting Pot," *Washington Post,* September 9, 2008, http://voices.washingtonpost.com/sleuth/2008/09/new_immigration_ads_stir_the_m.html.
12. https://web.archive.org/web/20081106054336/http://www.wecanstopthehate.org/allies/.
13. Spencer Hsu, "Immigration, Health Debates Cross Paths, Activists on Both Sides Step Up Efforts," *The Washington Post*, September 15, 2009.
14. Jonathan Roos, "Radio show on immigration spurs dispute," *Des Moines Register*, December 20, 2007.
15. Eunice Moscoso, "Immigration Reduction Groups Frustrated," Cox News Service, August 7, 2008.
16. Carmen Duarte, "Debunking the crime myth about migrants," *Arizona Daily Star*, September 22, 2008.
17. Michael Cass, "English-first backer tied to alleged hate groups," *The Tennesseean*, August 19, 2008.
18. "Hate groups targeting Latinos," *San Jose Mercury News*, March 10, 2008.
19. David Crary, "Report links anti-immigrant sentiment to rise in hate groups," The Associated Press State & Local Wire, March 10, 2008.

20. Morris Dees, *A Lawyer's Journey: The Morris Dees Story*, (Chicago. American Bar Association, 2001) p. 79, (Originally published as *A Season for Justice*, 1991).
21. Ibid. p. 136.
22. John Egerton, "Poverty Palace: How the Southern Poverty Law Center got rich fighting the Klan," *The Progressive* magazine, July 1988.
23. Nieman Foundation panel discussion on covering nonprofit organizations, May 1999, http://niemanwatchdog.org/index.cfm?fuseaction=about.Panel%20 Discussion:%20Nonprofit%20Organizations%20May%2099.
24. Dan Morse, "A Complex Man, Opportunist or Crusader," *Montgomery Advertiser*, February 14, 1994.
25. Ibid.
26. Editorial, "Misplaced Focus: Little Poverty at Poverty Law Center," *Montgomery Advertiser*, February 16, 1994.
27. Dan Morse and Greg Jaffe, "Charity of Riches: Critics question $52 million reserve, tactics of wealthiest civil rights group," *Montgomery Advertiser*, February 13, 1994.
28. John Egerton, op.cit.
29. Marlon Manuel, "Neo-Nazis next target of lawyer who broke Klan," Cox News, March 4, 1999.
30. Ibid.
31. Ken Silverstein, "'Hate,' Immigration, and the Southern Poverty Law Center," *Harper's* blog, March 22, 2010, https://harpers.org/blog/2010/03/hate-immigration-and-the-southern-poverty-law-center/.
32. Raymond Schroth, "Morris Dees and HBO documentary receive negative assessment," *National Catholic Reporter*, October 13, 2000.
33. JoAnn Wypijewski, "You Can't Get There From Here," *The Nation*, February 8, 2001.
34. J.M. Berger, "The Hate List," Foreign Policy, March 12, 2013, http://foreignpolicy.com/2013/03/12/the-hate-list/.
35. Joel Rose, "Mark Krikorian, Who Urges Cutting Immigration, Gains Relevance in Trump Era," National Public Radio, April 10, 2017, https://www.npr.org/2017/04/10/523311475/mark-krikorian-who-urges-cutting-immigration-gains-relevance-in-trump-era.
36. NPR Ethics Handbook, http://ethics.npr.org/category/a1-accuracy/.
37. Ben Schreckinger, "Has a Civil Rights Stalwart Lost Its Way," *Politico Magazine*, July/August 2017.
38. Carl M. Cannon, "The Hate Group that Inspired the Middlebury Melee," *Real Clear Politics*, March 19, 2017.

CHAPTER 7

1. Harry Bernstein, "Stopping Flood of Illegal Immigrants," *Los Angeles Times*, June 9, 1992
2. Gloria Skurzynski, Sweat *and Blood: A History of U.S. Labor Unions*, Minneapolis, Twenty-first Century Books, 2009, p.67.

3. John Higham, *Strangers in the Land: Patterns of American Nativism, 18601–1925*, New Brunswick, Rutgers University Press, 1955, p. 303.
4. Ibid, p. 291.
5. Transcript of joint hearings before the Subcommittee on Immigration and Refugee Policy of the Senate Committee on the Judiciary and Subcommittee on Immigration, Refugees, and International Law of the House Committee on the Judiciary., May 5, 6, and 7, 1981, https://archive.org/details/finalreportofsel1981unit.
6. Robert Pear, "Bill on Aliens a Divisive Issue for Democrats," *New York Times*, April 22, 1984.
7. Harry Bernstein, "Illegal Alien Law is Here to Stay," *Los Angeles Times*, July 17, 1990.
8. *Not Your Father's Union Movement: Inside the AFL-CIO*, edited by Jo-Ann Mort, Verso (an imprint of New Left Books) New York, NY, 1998, p. 88.
9. Ibid., p 96.
10. Cited by Eduardo Porter, "Here Illegally, Working Hard and Paying Taxes," *New York Times*, June 19, 2006.
11. AFL-CIO statement cited by Alex Aleinikoff, "Illegal Employers," *The American Prospect*, December 19, 2001.
12. Frank Swoboda, "Unions Reverse on Illegal Aliens," *The Washington Post*, February 17, 2000.
13. Editorial, "Hasty Call for Amnesty," *The New York Times*, February 22, 2000.
14. Bruce Bartlett, *Wrong on Race: The Democratic Party's Buried Past*, New York, Palgrave MacMillan, 2008, p. 190.
15. Diana Marrero, "Unions' opposition to guest workers helped kill immigration bill," Gannett News Service, July 3, 2007.
16. AFL-CIO Now, "Richard Trumka Comments on Donald Trump's Racist Campaign," https://www.youtube.com/watch?v=ortKx3sr-rE.
17. C-SPAN, "The Immigration Debate in 2000," September 23, 2000.
18. National Immigration Forum panel, "The Immigration Debate in 2000," February 23, 2000, https://www.c-span.org/video/?155594-1/immigration-debate-2000&start=623.
19. Cited by Alex Aleinikoff, "Illegal Employers," *American Prospect*, December 4, 2000.
20. Ibid.
21. James Goldsborough, "Out of Control Immigration," *Foreign Affairs*, September/October 2000.
22. Patrick Buchanan, "GOP Weak on NAFTA, Immigrants, Quotas," *Augusta Chronicle*, February 3, 1999.
23. Louis Uchitelle," INS is Looking the Other Way as Illegal Immigrants Fill Jobs," *The New York Times*, March 9, 2000, https://www.nytimes.com/2000/03/09/business/ins-is-looking-the-other-way-as-illegal-immigrants-fill-jobs.html.
24. Harry Bernstein, "Economic Recovery Hasn't Helped the Average Worker," *Los Angeles Times*, July 16, 1986.
25. Jon Thurber, "Harry Bernstein, 83; Veteran Labor Reporter for The Times." *Los Angeles Times*, May 4, 2006.

26. Harry Bernstein, "Stopping Flood of Illegal Immigrants," *Los Angeles Times*, June 9, 1992.
27. Harry Bernstein, "A New Card Could Help Border Control," *Los Angeles Times*, January 3, 1995.
28. Bernstein, June 9, 1992, op.cit.
29. Harry Bernstein, "A New Card Could Help Border Control," *Los Angeles Times*, January 3, 1995.
30. Harry Bernstein, June 9, 1992, op.cit..
31. Jeff Cohen and Norman Solomon, "Media Don't Break a Sweat to Cover Organized Labor," *Seattle Times*, September 5, 1994.
32. Mickey Kaus. *The End of Equality*," New York, 1992, Basic Books, p. 27.
33. Janelle Brown, "For Mickey Kaus, Winning Isn't the Point," *New York Times*, June 4, 2010.
34. Peter Skerry, "Opposing immigration wasn't always racist," *Boston Globe*, April 15, 2017, https://www.bostonglobe.com/ideas/2017/04/15/opposing-immigration-wasn-always-racist/ZToPxnulS41s95cP53PdHM/story.html.

CHAPTER 8

1. Nathan Glazer, "America's Open Door," *Harvard Magazine*, January, 2000. https://harvardmagazine.com/2000/01/americas-open-door.html
2. Washington Watch with Roland Martin, https://www.youtube.com/watch?v=c-D4Eu4a3Fk
3. Earl Ofari Hutchinson, *The Latino Challenge to Black America*, Los Angeles, Middle Passage Press, 2007, pp. 160–161.
4. Robert Lopez, "L.A. March Against Prop. 187 Draws 70,000," *Los Angeles Times*, October 17, 1994.
5. Joe Hicks, "Amnesty Decree Would Hurt Blacks," *Orlando Sentinel*, August 22, 2014.
6. Politico Staff, "Transcript: Donald Trump's full remarks in Des Moines, Iowa," August 27, 2016, https://www.politico.com/story/2016/08/full-text-trump-227472
7. Van Jones, on ABC's This Week, March 6, 2016, See: Tim Hains, "Van Jones Much More Afraid of Donald Trump as Republican Nominee," Real Clear Politics, March 7, 2016, https://www.realclearpolitics.com/video/2016/03/07/van_jones_much_more_afraid_of_donald_trump_as_republican_nominee.html.
8. Patrick Ruffini, "Black Voters Aren't Turning Out for the Post-Obama Democratic Party," FiveThirtyEight, May 30, 2017, https://fivethirtyeight.com/features/black-voters-arent-turning-out-for-the-post-obama-democratic-party/.
9. Jacquelyne Jackson, "Illegal Aliens: Big Threat to Black Workers," *Ebony*, April 1979.
10. In 2013, Smithfield Foods was bought by a Chinese company, Shuanghui Group, for $4.72 billion. Shuanghui Group later became known as WH Group.
11. "Charlotte: A Welcome Denied," Woodrow Wilson International Center for Scholars, 2008, p. 1, https://www.wilsoncenter.org/publication/charlotte-welcome-denied.

12. "An Interview with Frank Morris," Center for Immigration Studies, June 25, 2013, https://cis.org/Interview-Frank-Morris.
13. *The Messenger*, Volume 7, pp. 261 and 275, July 1925.
14. Associated Press, "Illegal Aliens Hurt Wages, Working Conditions," *Los Angeles Times*, March 18, 1988.
15. Borjas's views were an echo of those eight decades earlier of historian Arthur Schlesinger, Sr., who wrote: "The swarming of foreigners into the great industries occurred at considerable cost to the native working men, for the latter struggled in vain for higher wages or better conditions as long as the employers could command the services of an inexhaustible supply of foreign laborers. Thus, the new immigration has made it easier for the few to amass enormous fortunes at the expense of the many and has helped to create in this country for the first time yawning inequalities of wealth." Schlesinger's observations were published in 1922 in *New Viewpoints in American History*.
16. George Borjas, *Heaven's Door: Immigration Policy and the American Economy*, Princeton, Princeton University Press, 1999, p. 13.
17. Kevin F. McCarthy and Georges Vernez, "Immigration in a Changing Economy," Rand National Defense Research Institute, 1998, https://www.rand.org/content/dam/rand/pubs/monograph_reports/2007/MR854.1.pdf.
18. William Julius Wilson, *When Work disappears: The World of the New Urban Poor*, New York, Knopf, 1996, p. 144.
19. Pew also reported: "Despite these concerns, however, blacks in the general public are more supportive than whites of permitting illegal immigrants to stay in the U.S. About half (47%) say they should be allowed to stay, while an identical percentage...believe illegal immigrants should be required to leave the U.S. In contrast, whites by a 59% -33% margin say that illegals should be required to return home."
20. "Illegal Immigration Issues," Hearing before the Subcommittee on Immigration and Claims of the House Judiciary Committee, June 10, 1999.
21. Vaughn Greene, statement to the Select Committee on Immigration and Refugee Policy, Los Angeles, February 5, 1980. In Fuchs archives at Brandeis University.
22. Lawrence Fuchs, "The Reactions of Black Americans to Immigration," chapter in *Immigration Reconsidered: History, Sociology, and Politics*," edited by Virginia Yans-McLaughlin, Oxford University Press, 1990, p. 301.
23. *The Washington Post*, "The Real Immigration Bill," June 12, 1984.
24. Jim Boren, "Jackson Pushes Onward Despite Primary Outlook," *Sacramento Bee*, June 5, 1984.
25. Fuchs, "The Reactions of Black Americans to Immigration," op.cit.
26. "Good Immigrant Bill," *The New York Times*, October 9, 1984.
27. Sen. Mondale, Hearing before the Senate Subcommittee on Migratory Labor, "Migratory and Seasonal Farmworker Powerlessness," April 15, 1970, p. 4,548.
28. *Los Angeles Times*, "Mondale Not Aggressive on Immigration Bill, Jackson Charges," June 17, 1984.
29. Joe Rosato, "Ballot Boycotted by 37 Hispanics," *Sacramento Bee*, July 19, 1984.

30. "The Death of a Humane Idea, *NewYork Times*, October 18, 1984.
31. General Accounting Office, "Immigration Reform: Employer Sanctions and the Question of Discrimination," March 1999, https://www.gao.gov/assets/150/148824.pdf.
32. Jack Miles, "Blacks vs. Browns," *The Atlantic*, October 1992, https://www.theatlantic.com/magazine/archive/1992/10/blacks-vs-browns/306655/.
33. Michael Fix, 1991, *The Paper Curtain: Employer Sanctions' implementation, Impact, and Reform*, Washington, Urban Institute Press, p.1.
34. Yzaguirre quoted in *The Paper Curtain*, op.cit., p. 289.
35. John L. Mitchell, "It's time to reach outside formerly 'safe' districts, veteran lawmaker Dymally and others say," *Los Angeles Times*, August 4, 2006.
36. George Borjas testimony at "Making Immigration Work for American Minorities, Hearing Before the Subcommittee on Immigration Policy and Enforcement," Committee on the Judiciary, March 1, 2011.
37. John M. Broder, "A Black-Latino Coalition Emerges in Los Angeles," *New York Times*, April 24, 2005.
38. Morris comments, July 14, 2013, at rally in Washington, D.C. See Roberto Suro, *Strangers Among Us: Latino Lives in a Changing America, New York, Knopf, 1998*, pp. 258–260.
39. Michelle Cottle, "Black American Leadership Alliance D.C. Anti-Immigration Rally Wilts," Daily Beast, July 16, 2013, https://www.thedailybeast.com/black-american-leadership-alliance-dc-anti-immigration-rally-wilts.
40. Peggy Noonan, "Slow Down and Absorb," *Wall Street Journal*, May 26, 2007.

CHAPTER 9

1. Edward O. Wilson, The Diversity of Life (Second edition), Norton, New York, 1999, p. 328.
2. Nan Robertson, "Earth Day, Like Mother's, Pulls Capital Together," *New York Times*, April 23, 1970.
3. National Environmental Policy Act, Title 1, "Congressional Declaration of National Environmental Policy," https://www.aphis.usda.gov/wcm/connect/aphis_content_library/sa_resources/sa_laws_and_regulations/environmental_protection/statutes/environmental_policy_title1
4. Population and the American Future," The Report of the Commission on Population Growth and the American Future, July 18, 1969, http://www.population-security.org/rockefeller/001_population_growth_and_the_american_future.htm.
5. Judy Kunofsky, "History of Sierra Club and the Population-Immigration Connection," Sierrans for U.S. Population Stabilization." November 20, 1997, https://www.susps.org/history/jkmemo.html.
6. Judy Kunofsky, "Sierra Club Population Report, Spring, 1989," https://www.susps.org/history/popreport1989.html.
7. While the debate over immigration's environmental consequences was most intense at the Sierra Club, it reverberated throughout the environmental movement. For an excellent analysis of this broader debate, see: Leon Kolankiewicz and Roy Beck, *Forsaking Fundamentals: The Environmental*

Establishment Abandons U.S. Population Stabilization, Washington, Center for Immigration Studies, 2001.

8. Marty Durlin, "The Shot Heard Round the West," *High Country News*, July 8, 2010.
9. Ibid. See also, "A Place at the Table," in *A Hammer in Their Hands: A Documentary History of Technology and the African-American Experience*," Cambridge, MIT Press, 2005, p. 360.
10. William Branigin, "Immigration Policy Dispute Rocks Sierra Club," *Washington Post*, March 7, 1998.
11. Leslie Aldridge Westoff, "Should we Pull up the Gangplank?" *New York Times Magazine*, September 16, 1973.
12. Pope letter to the editor, *The New York Times*, December 27, 1992.
13. Sierra Club Environmental Policy, adopted September 18–19, 1993, https://www.sierraclub.org/policy/environmental-justice.
14. Isabel Alegria, "Population Growth Also an American Issue," All Things Considered, September 13, 1994.
15. Cathi Tactaquin, "The 'Greening of Hate' and the Sierra Club Referendum," http://web.archive.org/web/19980206005229/http://www.nnirr.org/background/greening.html.
16. Sierra Club board vote at its quarterly meeting in Washington, D.C. See: https://vault.sierraclub.org/planet/199605/clubbeat.asp.
17. Jenny Coyle, "Population Activists Do it at Zoos, Rock Concerts, Fairs," The Planet newsletter, December, 1997, http://vault.sierraclub.org/planet/199712/activist.asp.
18. www.igc.org/peg/ February, 1998. The statement reads: "The Political Ecology Group is a multi-racial, volunteer based organization working for environmental justice in the San Francisco area…PEG builds alliances to confront environmental destruction, racism, sexism, homophobia and corporate power."
19. Quoted in Jim Motavalli, "Balancing Act," *E Magazine*, Volume 11, Issue 6; December 31, 2000.
20. Dave Foreman, "Progressive Cornucopianism,." *Wild Duck Review*, Winter 1998.
21. William Wong, "Environmentalists and Immigration," *San Francisco Examiner*, March 11, 1998.
22. Ben Zuckerman, "Cut Immigration, Save the Environment," *Los Angeles Times*, March 15, 1998.
23. E.O. Wilson, *The Diversity of Life*, New York, Norton, 1999, p. 328.
24. Ibid.
25. Paul Rogers, "Immigration Question Tears at Environmentalists," *San Jose Mercury News*, April 12, 1998.
26. Josette Shiner, "New Citizens or Green Space," *Chicago Sun Times*, April 26, 1998.
27. Frank Clifford, "Immigration Vote Divides Sierra Club," *Los Angeles Times*, March 16, 1998.

28. Ben Zuckerman, "Immigration and the Sierra Club: Did the Fuss Matter?" Center for Immigration Studies, August 1, 1998, https://cis.org/Report/Immigration-and-Sierra-Club-Did-Fuss-Matter.
29. Associated Press, "Rights Activists Seek Humane Treatment for All Immigrants," *The* [Salinas] *Californian*, June 6, 1998.
30. Glen Martin, "Sierra Club Pioneer Quits Board, Brower Says Group Has 'No Sense of Urgency' Over Environmental Issues." *San Francisco Chronicle*, May 19, 2000.
31. James Ricci, "The Sierra Club and the Immigration Freight Train," *Los Angeles Times*, June 9, 2002.
32. Felicity Barringer, "Bitter Division For Sierra Club On Immigration," *New York Times*, March 16, 2004, https://www.nytimes.com/2004/03/16/us/bitter-division-for-sierra-club-on-immigration.html.
33. Ibid.
34. Michelle Nijhuis, "Immigration Controversy Engulfs Sierra Club Board Election," *Grist*, March 2, 2004, https://grist.org/article/nijhuis-sierra/.
35. Southern Poverty Law Center, "Morris Dees' Sierra Club Candidate Statement Seeks Tolerance," January 22, 2004, https://www.splcenter.org/news/2004/01/22/morris-dees-sierra-club-candidate-statement-seeks-tolerance.
36. Zuckerman interview with author.
37. Ben Adler, "Sierra Club Votes for Its Future," *The Nation*, April 14, 2004, https://www.thenation.com/article/sierra-club-votes-its-future/.
38. Drusha Mayhue, Ouside Interests Push to Hijack Sierra Club," *Delta Sierran* (Louisiana), Jan/Feb 2004
39. Felicity Barringer, op. cit.
40. John Leo, "A Really Ugly Shade of Green," *U.S. News & World Report*, April 5, 2004.
41. Felicity Barringer, op. cit.
42. Sierrans for U.S. Population Stabilization, "SUSPS Analysis of Results," in "Sierra Club Yearly Election Results," https://www.susps.org/info/election_results.html.
43. Jim Motavalli, "The Numbers Game: Myths, truths, and Half-Truths About Human Population Growth and he Environment," *E Magazine*, January, 2004.
44. Kenneth R. Weiss, "2 Candidates Fault Sierra Club Finances," *Los Angeles Times*, March 13, 2004.
45. Ibid.
46. Kenneth R. Weiss, "The Man Behind the Land," *Los Angeles Times*, October 27, 2004.
47. Richard Lamm, "For Sale: The Policies of the Sierra Club," *The Social Contract*, Fall 2006, https://www.thesocialcontract.com/artman2/publish/tsc_17_01/tsc_17_01_lamm_sierra.shtml.
48. Author interview with Lamm, December 12, 2014.
49. Weiss, "The Man Behind the Land," op. cit. Drusha Mayhue, Ouside Interests Push to Hijack Sierra Club," *Delta Sierran* (Louisiana), Jan/Feb 2004

PART 3 INTRODUCTION

1. President Reagan's signing statement, November 6, 1986 http://www.presidency.ucsb.edu/ws/?pid=36699
2. Office of the Inspector General, Dept. of Justice, https://oig.justice.gov/reports/INS/e9608/i9608p1.htm
3. Select Commission on Immigration and Refugee Policy, "U.S Immigration Policy and the National Interest," March, 1981, p. 60
4. David A. Martin, "Eight Myths About Immigration Enforcement," New York University Journal of Legislation and Public Policy, 10 (2006-2007): 525, 544
5. Katherine McIntire Peters," "A House Divided," *Government Executive* magazine, November 1, 1998
6. Author interview with retired INS agent

CHAPTER 10

1. INS Commissioner Alan Nelson, press conference, October 8, 1987, https://www.c-span.org/video/?849-1/new-immigration-law.
2. Author interview with Schroeder.
3. Zita Arocha, "INS tries a new approach," *Washington Post*, August 23, 1987.
4. Mary Ann Galante, "Sting of New Immigration Law Felt in a Labor-Short County: Hotels/Owners Could Be Forced to Lure Workers With Higher Wages," *Los Angeles Times*, October 18, 1987.
5. Eric Schine, "Sanctions Fail to Cut Alien Jobs; Threat of Penalties Ignored in Hiring of Illegal Workers," *Los Angeles Times*, May 2, 1988, https://www.latimes.com/archives/la-xpm-1988-05-02-mn-1454-story.html.
6. Michael Bigelow, "The Immigration Dilemma: Survey Raises Doubts About U.S. Law's Effectiveness." *San Francisco Chronicle*, July 5, 1989.
7. INS 1990 *Yearbook of Immigration Statistics*, p. 163.
8. Julie Brossy, "Aliens Entering Without Papers Show Sharp Rise," *San Diego Tribune*, March 12, 1990.
9. Robert Bach and Doris Meissner, "Employment and Immigration Reform: Employer Sanctions Four Years Later," in *The Paper Curtain*, Michael Fix editor, Washington, The Urban Institute Press, 1991, p. 298.
10. Interview with author, December 2016
11. Michael Fix and Paul Hill, "Implementing Sanctions: Reports from the Field," in *The Paper Curtain*, op, cit., p. 78.
12. Kim I. Mills, "Immigration Law Poorly Enforced, Congressman Says," Associated Press, March 21, 1989.
13. Author interview with Shaw, February 2017.
14. Roberto Suro, "Migrants' False Claiims: Fraud on a Huge Scale," *New York Times*, November 12, 1989, https://www.nytimes.com/1989/11/12/us/migrants-false-claims-fraud-on-a-huge-scale.html.
15. Eric Schlosser, "In the Strawberry Fields," *The Atlantic*, November 1995.
16. Philip Martin, "Hired Farm Workers," *Choices: The Magazine of Food, Farm, and Resource Issues*, Vol. 27, No 2, 2nd Quarter 2012.
17. Author interview with Shaw, February, 2017.

18. Author interview with Lucero, January, 2017.
19. Author interview with Moon, October, 2016.
20. Dan Cadman, "Lessons Learned by an Insider in the 30 Years Since IRCA," blog post, Center for Immigration Studies, October 26, 2016, http://cis.org/cadman/insiders-look-back-30-years-irca.
21. Author interview with Yates, January 2017.
22. John M Crewdson, "U.S. Immigration Service Hampered by Corruption," *New York Times*, January 13, 1980.
23. Email from McGraw to author, February 2, 2017.
24. Collins Foods International, Inc., Petitioner, v. U.S. Immigration and Naturalization Service, Respondent, 948 F.2d 549 (9th Cir. 1991), http://law.justia.com/cases/federal/appellate-courts/F2/948/549/287247/.
25. "Illegal Aliens: Significant Obstacles to Reducing Unauthorized Alien Employment Exist," United States General Accounting Office, April 1999, http://www.gao.gov/assets/230/227062.pdf.
26. Demetrios A. Papademetriou, B. Lindsay Lowell, and Deborah A. Cobb-Clark, "Employer Sanctions: Expectations and Early Outcomes," *The Paper Curtain*, op. cit., p 228.
27. Michael Fix, at news conference sponsored by the Urban Institute and the Rand Corporation, March 15, 1990, https://www.c-span.org/video/?11502-1/immigration-policy-employer-sanctions.
28. Dan Freedman, "Lack of Standardization Blamed for INS Inequities," *San Antonio Light*, March 25, 1991.
29. Ibid.
30. Bill McAllister, "Parting Shots at 'Totally Disorganized' INS," *Washington Post*, October 18, 1989.
31. Pamela J. Podger, "Border Patrol to Quit Valley?" *Fresno Bee*, July 15, 1991.
32. Author interview with Bednarz, March 2013.
33. General Accounting Office, "Immigration Reform: Employer Sanctions and the Question of Discrimination," March 1990, http://www.gao.gov/assets/150/148824.pdf.
34. Senate Judiciary Committee hearing, "The GAO Report on Employer Sanctions and Discrimination," March 20 and April 20, 1990, Transcript: https://catalog.hathitrust.org/Record/009874610; video: https://www.c-span.org/video/?11998-1/employment-discrimination-immigrants.
35. Ibid.
36. Yzaguirre quoted in Bach and Meissner, in *The Paper Chase*, op. cit., p. 289.
37. Cecilia Muñoz, "Unfinished Business: The Immigration Reform and Control Act of 1986," Policy Analysis Center, Office of Research, Advocacy and Legislation of the National Council of La Raza, 1990, p. 54, https://cis.org/sites/cis.org/files/articles/2013/NCLR.pdf.
38. Associated Press, "Deportation 'Flaw' Assailed," *St. Louis Post Dispatch*, April 16, 1990; and Charlotte Grimes, "McNary Is Challenged on Illegal Immigrants," *St. Louis Post Dispatch*, April 21, 1990.

CHAPTER 11

1. Justin Wm. Moyer, "The forgotten story of how refugees almost ended Bill Clinton's Career,"*Washington Post*, November 17, 2015, https://www.washingtonpost.com/news/morning-mix/wp/2015/11/17/the-forgotten-story-of-how-refugees-almost-ended-bill-clintons-career/?utm_term=.2d79a2a0ebe7.
2. Tim Weiner, "Pleas for Asylum Inundate System for Immigration," *New York Times*, April 25, 1993, http://www.nytimes.com/1993/04/25/nyregion/pleas-for-asylum-inundate-system-for-immigration.html.
3. Hearing of the Subcommittee on Immigration and Claims of the House Judiciary Committee, "Immigration and Naturalization Service's Interior Enforcement Strategy", July 1, 1999, p. 108, http://commdocs.house.gov/committees/judiciary/hju63127.000/hju63127_0f.htm.
4. William Branigin, "Immigration Fraud Schemes Proliferating Inside U.S." *Washington Post*, May 19, 1997, https://www.washingtonpost.com/archive/politics/1997/05/19/immigration-fraud-schemes-proliferating-inside-us/013fe2e3-3e1c-4877-bc1c-b337c3677d77/?utm_term=.e71ce8d36c91.
5. Roberto Suro, "California Border Crackdown Vowed; With the Administration Under Fire, Reno Promises a New Effort," *The Washington* Post, September 18, 1994.
6. Jeffrey Passel, "U.S. Immigration: Numbers, Trends, and Outlook." Pew Hispanic Center Report, March 26, 2007, pp. 12–13.
7. Laura Mecoy, "Despite 187, Fake ID Sales Booming: Proposition Has Done Little to Slow Flow of Counterfeit Documents," *Sacramento Bee*, December 12, 1994.
8. Paul Feldman, "INS Breaks Up Ring that Makes Fake I.D.s," *Los Angeles Times*, January 4, 1995.
9. Philip Martin, "INS Evaluates Gatekeeper, SouthPAW," *Migration News*, October 1995, Volume 2, Number 10, https://migration.ucdavis.edu/mn/more.php?id=767.
10. U. S. Commission on Immigration Reform," U.S. Immigration Policy: Restoring Credibility," p. 14.
11. William Douglas, "Panel: Check Immigrants at Jobs," *Newsday*, August 4, 1994.
12. Marcus Stern, "Illegal Immigration Bill Weakened by Unlikely Alliance," Copley News Service, November 4. 1995.
13. Paolo Pereznieto, "The Case of Mexico's 1995 Peso Crisis And Argentina's 2002 Convertibility Crisis," UNICEF, https://www.unicef.org/socialpolicy/files/Impact_of_Econ_Shocks_Mexico_and_Argentina(3).pdf.
14. Gilbert Klein, "Cost of illegal immigration is high", *Richmond Times-Dispatch*, April 17, 1994.
15. Feinstein statement on the Senate floor, May 1, 1996. It can be seen at approximately the 3:44:00 mark on this video: https://www.c-span.org/video/?71567-1/senate-session&start=13454.
16. Mary Beth Rogers, *Barbara Jordan: An American Hero*, New York: Bantam Books, 1998, p. 325.
17. Pew Research Center, "Key Findings About U.S. Immigrants" May 3, 2017, http://www.pewresearch.org/fact-tank/2017/05/03/key-findings-about-u-s-immigrants/.

18. Patrick J. McDonnell, "INS to Get Tough With Employers," *Los Angeles Times*, May 7, 1995.
19. Author interview with Bargerhuff, March, 2017.
20. Author interview with Fischer, February 2017.
21. INS Internal document, "PROPOSED OPERATION SOUTHPAW PHASE II," provided by confidential source who participated in the operation.
22. Immigration and Naturalization Service, "Worksite Enforcement: Reducing the Job Magnet," https://babel.hathitrust.org/cgi/pt?id=uc1.31210024789362;view=1up;seq=1.
23. Video of INS raid in Dalton, Georgia, available at U.S. Citizenship & Immigration Services History Library, Washington, D.C.
24. Sandra Sanchez, "Heat Being Turned Up on Illegal Immigrants: Some Believe Politics Behind Increased Raids," *USA Today*, September 29, 1995.
25. Interview with Fischer, op.cit.
26. Jordan testimony before the U.S. Senate Committee on the Judiciary Subcommittee on Immigration and Refugee Affairs, August, 3, 1994.
27. Robert Pear, "Clinton Embraces a Proposal to Cut Immigration by a Third," *New York Times*, June 8, 1995.
28. Conyers, Congressional Record, March 20, 1996, pH2497.
29. Frank: Congressional Record, March 20, 1996, pH2498.
30. Senate Judiciary Subcommittee on Immigration, Immigration and Naturalization Service Oversight," October 2, 1996, p. 40, https://www.loc.gov/law/find/hearings/pdf/00139299097.pdf.
31. Ibid. p 32.
32. Ibid.
33. Micah Bump, Andy Schoenholtz, Susan Martin, and B. Lindsay Lowell, "Controlling Irregular Immigration: The Challenge of Worksite Enforcement," Institute for the Study of International Migration, September 2007, https://isim.georgetown.edu/sites/isim/files/files/upload/Lowell%20and%20Martin%20Controlling_irregular_migration.pdf.
34. Michael Kranish, "Clinton Policy Shift Followed Asian-American Fund-Raiser," *Boston Globe*, January 16, 1997.
35. Richard T. Cooper, "How DNC Got Caught in a Donor Dilemma," *Los Angeles Times*, December 23, 1996.
36. Edward Walsh and Lena H. Sun, "Panel Examines Hiring of Huang at Commerce," *Washington Post*, July 17, 1997.
37. Meissner press briefing, October 29, 1996, https://www.c-span.org/video/?76334-1/fiscal-year-1996-deportations.
38. Statement on the Executive Order on Illegal Immigration, February. 13, 1996, http://www.presidency.ucsb.edu/ws/?pid=52396.
39. Kevin Johnson "Deportation of illegals is up 62% over 1996," *USA Today*, October 31, 1997.
40. Jules Witcover, "Dole Launches Ariz. Campaign in Buchanan's Wake," *Baltimore Sun*, February 25 1996.
41. Gregory R. Jones "INS Raids," *Macon Telegraph*, May 14, 1998.

42. Marcus Stern, "A Semi-Tough Policy on Illegal Workers," *Washington Post*, July 5, 1998.
43. Author interview with Szafnicki, November, 2016.
44. Martin, "Eight Myths About Immigration Enforcement," op.cit.
45. Author interview with Martin, February, 2017.
46. 1996 Senate Judiciary Immigration Subcommittee hearing, op. cit., p 6.
47. Ibid., p. 9.
48. DOJ Office of the Inspector General, Inspections Report: https://oig.justice.gov/reports/INS/e9608/i9608p2.htm.
49. Paul Hutchinson, "INS raid reveals labor woes U.S. workers don't want low-paying jobs," *Denver Post*, March 23, 1997, https://extras.denverpost.com/immi/immi7.htm.
50. Ibid.
51. Lars-Erik Nelson, "Congress Won't risk Alienating Big Business," *New York Daily News*, September 30, 1996.
52. Chishti at hearing of the House Judiciary Subcommittee on Immigration and Claims, "Immigration and Naturalization Service's Interior Enforcement Strategy," July 1, 1999, page 209, http://commdocs.house.gov/committees/judiciary/hju63127.000/hju63127_0f.htm.
53. Senate Judiciary Immigration Subcommittee, oversight hearing, Oct. 2, 1996, op. cit., p. 26.
54. Jerry Kammer "Illegals on Job Being Ignored: Border Patrol Buildup No Help at Work Sites," *Arizona Republic*, November 30, 1998.
55. Quoted by Sen. Alan Simpson in his opening statement of Senate Judiciary Immigration Subcommittee hearing, October 2, 1996, op. cit., p. 2, https://www.loc.gov/law/find/hearings/pdf/00139299097.pdf.
56. Richard Stana of GAO, statement at the hearing of the Subcommittee on Immigration and Claims of the House Judiciary Committee, "Immigration and Naturalization Service's Interior Enforcement Strategy", July 1, 1999, p. 50.
57. "INS: Fewer Workplace Raids," *Migration News*, April 1999, https://migration.ucdavis.edu/mn/more.php?id=1767.
58. Ana Aca, Diego Bunuel and Maria A. Morales, "Brutal INS Raid Angers Public; Justice Department Set to Investigate," *Miami Herald*, April 25, 1998.
59. Luisa Yanez, "INS Raids Flower Company. Congressman Asks Reno to Investigate 'Thug-Like' Operation," *South Florida Sun-Sentinel*, April 26, 1998.
60. Ana Aca, Diego Bunuel, and Maria A. Morales, op. cit.
61. Fiscal Year 1998 Fourth Quarter Performance Review, Interior Enforcement, December 18, 1998.
62. Robert Bach, "Mexican Immigration and the American State," *International Migration Review*, Vol. 12, No. 4, Special Issue (Winter 1978), pp. 536–558.
63. Bach and Meissner, "Employment and Immigration Reform: Employer Sanctions Four Years Later," *The Paper Curtain*, op. cit., pp. 281–302.
64. House Judiciary Subcommittee on Immigration and Claims, "Designations of Temporary Protected Status and Fraud in Prior Amnesty Programs," March 4,

1999, pp. 57–63, https://babel.hathitrust.org/cgi/pt?id=pur1.32754071749794;view=1up;seq=3.

65. Ned Glascock and Craig Whitlock, "Law vs. Reality," *News and Observer*, November 30, 1998. (In the interest of clarity and context, this excerpt is more complete than the one inserted into the hearing record.)
66. Interview with Veysey,Jan. 18, 2017 (approx.).
67. Interview with Bednarz, March 2013.
68. Kevin Phillips, Arrogant Capital: Washington, *Wall Street, and the Frustration of American Politics*, Boston, Little, Brown, 1994, p. xv.
69. Robert J. Samuelson, "Build a Fence—and Amnesty," *Washington Post*, March 8, 2006.
70. Michael Hedges, Scripps Howard News Service, "Chasing Immigrants No Long Priority. Agency's New Policy On Illegal Residents Raises Concerns in Congress," *Milwaukee Journal Sentinel*, March 6, 1999.
71. Bach and Meissner, op. cit., p. 298
72. William Branigin, "INS Shifts 'Interior' Strategy to Target Criminal Aliens, *Washington Post*, March 15, 1999
73. House Subcommittee on Immigration and Claims, "Immigration and Naturalization Service's Interior Enforcement Strategy," July 1, 1999, p.9. http://commdocs.house.gov/committees/judiciary/hju63127.000/hju63127_0f.htm.
74. Ibid., p.31.
75. Laurie P. Cohen, "Meatpacker Taps Mexican Labor Force, Thanks to Help from INS Program," *Wall Street Journal*, October 15, 1998.
76. House hearing, July 1, 1999, p. 134.
77. Ibid., p 119.
78. Eric Schlosser, *Fast Food Nation*, Boston, Houghton Mifflin, 2001.
79. Interview with author, DATE??.
80. Rural Migration News, July 1999, Volume 5, Number 3, http://migration.ucdavis.edu/rmn/more.php?id=377_0_2_0.
81. Leslie Reed, "Task Force Rips Vanguard Recommendations Include Amnesty for Immigrant Workers," *Omaha World Herald*, October 16, 2000.
82. Table 60, 2000 Statistical Yearbook of the Immigration and Naturalization Service, https://www.dhs.gov/xlibrary/assets/statistics/yearbook/2000/Yearbook2000.pdf.
83. Meissner on C-SPAN's Washington Journal, March 29, 2007, HTTPS://WWW.C-SPAN.ORG/VIDEO/?197729-2/1986-IMMIGRATION-LAW.
84. "Doris Meissner on Immigration Bills," C-SPAN, April 3, 2013, https://www.c-span.org/video/?311879-5/doris-meissner-immigration-bills.
85. Ibid., at 30:17.
86. Hearing of the Senate Subcommittee on Immigration and Refugee Policy, "The Knowing Employment of Illegal Immigrants," September 30, 1981, p. 5.
87. Ibid., p. 194.
88. Nancy Cleeland, "Unionizing Is Catch-22 for Illegal Immigrants, *Los Angeles Times*, January 16, 2000.

89. Frank Swoboda, "Unions Reverse on Illegal Aliens," *The Washington Post*, February 17, 2000.
90. Louis Uchitelle, "I.N.S. Is Looking the Other Way As Illegal Immigrants Fill Jobs," *New York Times*, March 9, 2000.
91. Alex Aleinikoff, "Illegal Employers," *The American Prospect*, December 19, 2001, https://prospect.org/features/illegal-employers/.
92. James Goldsborough, "Out of Control Immigration," *Foreign Affairs*, September/October 2000.
93. Jared Bernstein, *Crunch: Why Do I Feel So Squeezed? (And Other Unsolved Economic Mysteries)*, Berrett-Koehler Publishers, 2008, p. 157.

CHAPTER 12

1. Carla Marinucci, "Reaching Out to State's Latinos, Bush Distances Himself From Pete Wilson," *Houston Chronicle*, April 8, 2000.
2. Republican Party Platform of 1996, August 12, 1996, http://www.presidency.ucsb.edu/ws/?pid=2584.
3. "A weak choice. INS needs more than a political appointee," *San Diego Union Tribune*, May 1, 2001.
4. *9/11 and Terrorist Travel, A Staff Report of the National Commission on Terrorist Attacks Upon the United States*, Hillsboro Press, Franklin, Tenn., 2004, p. 101, https://govinfo.library.unt.edu/911/staff_statements/911_TerrTrav_Monograph.pdf.
5. Ibid. p. 94.
6. Belinda I. Reyes, Hans P. Johnson, Richard Van Swearingen, "Holding the Line? The Effect of the Recent Border Build-up on Unauthorized Immigration," Public Policy Institute of California, July 2002, https://www.ppic.org/publication/holding-the-line-the-effect-of-recent-border-build-up-on-unauthorized-immigration/.
7. Philip Wrona, "U.S. Immigration and Naturalization Service: Dysfunctional Not by Design," Naval Postgraduate School master's thesis, March 2007, https://apps.dtic.mil/dtic/tr/fulltext/u2/a467713.pdf.Philip Wrona, "U.S. Immigration and Customs Enforcement: Dysfunctional Not by Design," Naval Post Graduate School thesis, Monterey, CA; 2007,
8. Congressional Research Service, "Immigration Enforcement Within the United States," August 6, 2006, p. 40, https://fas.org/sgp/crs/misc/RL33351.pdf.
9. Government Accountability Office, "Immigration Enforcement: Weaknesses Hinder Employment Verification and Worksite Enforcement Efforts," August, 2005, p, 32, http://www.gao.gov/new.items/d05813.pdf.
10. Government Accountability Office, "Immigration Enforcement: Challenges to Implementing the INS Interior Enforcement Strategy," p. 3, http://www.gao.gov/assets/110/109419.pdf.
11. National Drug Intelligence Center, "Washington/Baltimore High Intensity Drug Trafficking Area Drug Market Analysis," June 2007, https://www.justice.gov/archive/ndic/pubs23/23834/strateg.htm.
12. Stephanie Hanes, "More than two dozen illegal aliens with sex offense records arrested," *Baltimore Sun*, August 19, 2004.

13. "Immigration Enforcement Within the United States," op. cit., p. 41, Table One.
14. Jerry Kammer, "Immigration Plan's assumption on Unskilled Workers Contested," *San Diego Union Tribune*, March 31, 2005.
15. Jerry Kammer, Kerry, Bush Mix Messages on Immigration," *San Diego Union* Tribune, October 31, 2004.
16. Laura Frank, "Crackdown on illegals 38 Commerce City workers arrested, part of national investigation," *Rocky Mountain News*, April 21, 2006. Also: Department of Justice press release, June 2, 2010, https://www.justice.gov/archive/usao/txs/1News/Releases/2010%20June/060210%20IFCO%20Systems_print.htm
17. Center for Immigration Studies, "The 2006 Swift Raids: Assessing the Impact of Immigration Enforcement Actions at Six Facilities," http://cis.org/2006SwiftRaids.
18. CQ Transcripts Wire, "President Bush Addresses U.S. Chamber of Commerce on Immigration," *The Washington Post*, June 1, 2006, http://www.washingtonpost.com/wp-dyn/content/article/2006/06/01/AR2006060100814.html.
19. Spencer S. Hsu and Kari Lyderson, "Illegal Hiring is Rarely Penalized," *Washington Post*, June 19, 2006.
20. Silvestre Reyes on C-SPAN's Washington Journal, August 17, 2006, https://www.c-span.org/video/?193847-4/immigration-policy.
21. Karen Lee Ziner, "Bianco workers allege violations," *Providence Journal*, March 20, 2007. See also: Associated Press, "Fines issued for New Bedford factory targeted in immigration raid," July 6, 2007. See Also: *The Washington Post* editorial, "Raid shows need for immigration policy," March 20, 2007.
22. Sen. Kennedy press release, "New Bedford Immigration Raid Devastation Reminiscent of Hurricane Katrina," US Federal News, March 13, 2007.
23. Carol Rose and Christopher Ott, "Immigration raid was just one of many," *Boston Globe*, March 26, 2007.
24. Jerry Seper, "Chertoff defends ICE raid on illegals. Rejects complaint from Kennedy," *Washington Times*, March 22, 2007.
25. Hearing of the Senate Subcommittee on Immigration, Border Security, and Citizenship, "Immigration Enforcement at the Workplace: Learning From the Mistakes of 1986," June 19, 2006, https://babel.hathitrust.org/cgi/pt?id=pst.000066754251;view=1up;seq=5.
26. C-SPAN, Washington Journal, May 29, 2007, HTTPS://WWW.C-SPAN.ORG/VIDEO/?197729-2/1986-IMMIGRATION-LAW.
27. Author interview with Baker, November 2016.
28. Gladwin Hill, "3 U.S. Officials Accuse Farmers of Forcing Illicit Mexican Labor," *New York Times*, August 9, 1951.
29. Robert L. Bach, *Latin Journey: Cuban and Mexican Immigrants in the United States*," Berkeley, University of California Press, 1985, pp. 14–15.
30. Stana testimony at hearing of House Homeland Security Subcommittee on Border and Maritime Security, "A Study in Contrasts: House and Senate Approaches to Border Security," July 23, 2013, https://homeland.house.gov/files/documents/Testimony%20Stana.pdf.

CHAPTER 13

1. Barack Obama, *The Audacity of Hope: Thoughts on Reclaiming the American Dream*, New York, Three Rivers Press, 2006, p.260.
2. Ibid., p. 263.
3. "Obama Addresses the National Council of La Raza," transcript, *Washington Post*, July 15, 2008, http://www.washingtonpost.com/wp-dyn/content/article/2008/07/15/AR2008071501138.html.
4. Stephen Dinan, "Illegals Raid Dismays Obama Voters," *Washington Times*, February 26, 2009.
5. Elise Fialkowski and Kate Kalmykov, "Immigration compliance vital to avoid fines, criminal sanctions," *Nation's Restaurant News*, December 14, 2009.
6. Figures provided by ICE Western Region Communications Office.
7. Statement of Laurie E. Ekstrand, GAO, before the House Subcommittee on International Law, Immigration and Refugees, September 21, 1994, http://archive.gao.gov/t2pbat2/152558.pdf.
8. Erin Kelly, "U.S. to Expand Workplace Immigration Audits," Gannett News Service, November 19, 2009.
9. Lamar Smith, Hearing of the House Subcommittee on Immigration and Border Security, "E-Verify Program Benefits," February 27, 2013.
10. Morton on C-SPAN, Washington Journal, August 8, 2010, https://www.c-span.org/video/?294964-5/us-deportation-policy&start=1259.
11. Brendan Sasso, "Obama: Deportation Statistics 'deceptive'" *The Hill*, September 28, 2011.
12. Brian Bennett, "High deportation figures are misleading," *Los Angeles Times*, April 1, 2014, https://www.latimes.com/nation/la-na-obama-deportations-20140402-story.html.
13. Peter Wallsten, "From Fierce Activist to White House Defender," *Washington Post*, November 10, 2011. See also, David Nakamura, "White House Immigration Adviser Cecilia Muñoz is Taking the Heat for Obama," *The Washington Post*, September 8, 2014.
14. William Douglas, "Panel: Check Immigrants at Jobs," *Newsday*, August 4, 1994.
15. http://nation.foxnews.com/illegal-immigration/2011/09/14/white-house-compares-illegal-immigration-jaywalking.
16. "Cecilia Muñoz: 'Even Broken Laws Have to be Enforced,'" *Frontline*, October 11, 2011, http://www.pbs.org/wgbh/frontline/article/cecilia-Muñoz-even-broken-laws-have-to-be-enforced/.
17. Peter Wallsten, "Activists say Obama aide Cecilia Muñoz has 'turned her back' on fellow Hispanics," *The Washington Post*, November 9, 2011, https://www.washingtonpost.com/politics/activists-say-obama-aide-cecilia-Muñoz-has-turned-her-back-on-fellow-hispanics/2011/11/09/gIQAnTFp6M_story.html.
18. Univision newscast, April 12, 2011; See also: CIS blog, "Univision Does It Again," April 13, 2011, http://cis.org/kammer/Univision-Does-It-Again.
19. Andrew Joseph, "Immigration-reform advocate to lead Domestic Policy Council," *Government Executive*, http://www.govexec.com/oversight/2012/01/immigration-reform-advocate-to-lead-domestic-policy-council/35800/.

20. States News Service, "Remarks by the President on Comprehensive Immigration Reform in El Paso, Texas," May 10, 2011.
21. Charles Krauthammer, "Obama's amnesty-by-fiat—naked lawlessness." *Washington Post*, June 21, 2012. https://www.washingtonpost.com/opinions/charles-krauthammer-obamas-amnesty-by-fiat—naked-lawlessness/2012/06/21/gJQAa5PltV_story.html.
22. Chris Cillizza, "Three sentences on immigration that will haunt Republicans in 2016," *Washington Post*, July 1, 2014, https://www.washingtonpost.com/news/the-fix/wp/2014/07/01/three-sentences-on-immigration-that-will-haunt-republicans-in-2016/?utm_term=.bf7e0b573841.
23. EFE World News Service, "Latino leader calls Obama 'deporter-in-chief,'" March 5, 2014.
24. Dan Nowicki, "Little Hope Remains for Reform One Year After 'Gang of 8' Bill," *Arizona Republic*, June 25, 2013.
25. Adam Nagourney, "Upbeat Schumer Battles Poor Polls, Low Turnouts and His Image", *New York Times*, May 16, 1998.
26. Michael Grynbaum, "Senator, Senator, Make Me a Match: For Staff, Schumer Is Cupid", *New York Times*, August 17, 2012.
27. Judy Wiessler, "Immigration Bill: déjà vu, yet different", *Houston Chronicle*, October 12, 1986.
28. Meredith Shiner, "Portman Quietly Positions Himself, but for What" *Roll Call*, March 11, 2013.
29. See the Portman-Schumer exchanges in *Congressional Record*, June 26, 2013, pp. S5246-S5251.
30. *New York Times*, "Guerrilla War on Immigration," August 27, 1982.

EPILOGUE

1. David Frum, "If Liberals Won't Enforce Borders, Fascists Will." *The Atlantic*, April 2019, https://www.theatlantic.com/magazine/archive/2019/04/david-frum-how-much-immigration-is-too-much/583252/
2. "Transcript: Donald Trump at the G.O.P. Convention," *New York Times*, July 22, 2016, https://www.nytimes.com/2016/07/22/us/politics/trump-transcript-rnc-address.html.
3. Nolan D. McCaskill, "Trump promises wall and massive deportation program," *Politico*, August 31, 2016, https://www.politico.com/story/2016/08/donald-trump-immigration-address-arizona-227612.
4. Kevin Robillard, "Trump: 'Self-deportation' cost votes," *Politico*, November 26, 2012, https://www.politico.com/story/2012/11/trump-romneys-crazy-policy-of-self-deportation-cost-votes-084238.
5. Jennifer Rubin, "GOP autopsy goes bold," *The Washington Post*, March 18, 2013, https://www.washingtonpost.com/blogs/right-turn/wp/2013/03/18/gop-autopsy-report-goes-bold/.
6. On the Issues: Republican Party on Immigration, https://www.ontheissues.org/Celeb/Republican_Party_Immigration.htm, https://politicalwire.com/2016/03/04/flashback-quote-of-the-day-26/.

7. Kyle Cheney, "Trump kills GOP autopsy," *Politico*, March 4, 2016, https://www.politico.com/story/2016/03/donald-trump-gop-party-reform-220222.
8. Cleve R. Wootson, "Seth Meyers invited Trump to be a guest on his show. Trump wanted an apology first," *Washington Post*, May 8, 2018, https://www.washingtonpost.com/news/arts-and-entertainment/wp/2018/05/08/seth-meyers-invited-trump-to-be-a-guest-on-his-show-trump-wanted-an-apology-first/.
9. Joshua Geen, *Devil's Bargain*, New York, Penguin Press, 2017, p. 109.
10. Katie Glueck, "Trump bashes Rove's $400M 'failure,'" Politico Now blog, March 15, 2013.
11. Matt Pearce, "Andrew Breitbart warned conservatives about Trump, but he never saw this coming," *Los Angeles Times*, March 18, 2016, https://www.latimes.com/nation/politics/la-na-breitbart-rise-fall-20160318-story.html.
12. Katherine Krueger,"How Breitbart Went from 'Trump's Personal Pravda' to Running His Campaign," *Talking Points Memo*, August 17, 2016, https://talkingpointsmemo.com/news/steve-bannon-trump-breitbart-love-affair.
13. Kristina Peterson and Janet Hook, "Eric Cantor Loses to Tea Party's Dave Brat in Virginia Primary," *Wall Street Journal*, June 10, 2014, https://www.wsj.com/articles/no-2-house-republican-eric-cantor-defeated-in-virginia-primary-upset-1402445714.
14. Mathew Boyle, "DONALD TRUMP: CANTOR'S DEFEAT SHOWS 'EVERYBODY' IN CONGRESS IS VULNERBLE IF THEY SUPPORT AMNESTY," Breitbart.com, June 10, 2014, https://www.breitbart.com/politics/2014/06/12/donald-trump-cantor-s-defeat-shows-everybody-in-congress-is-vulnerable-if-they-support-amnesty/.
15. Frontline, "Trump's Road to the White House," https://www.pbs.org/wgbh/frontline/film/trumps-road-to-the-white-house/transcript/.
16. Amy Chozik, "Hillary Clinton Calls Many Trump Backers 'Deplorables,' and G.O.P Pounces," *New York Times*, September 10, 2016, https://abcnews.go.com/Politics/clinton-regrets-grossly-generalistic-statement-trump-supporters/story?id=41999384.
17. Jonathan Martin, Jim Rutenberg, Maggie Habeman,"Donald Trump Appoints Media Firebrand to Run Campaign," *The New York Times*, August 17, 2016, https://www.nytimes.com/2016/08/18/us/politics/donald-trump-stephen-bannon-paul-manafort.html.
18. David A. Fahrenthold, "Trump recorded having extremely lewd conversation about women in 2005," *Washington Post*, October 8, 2016, https://www.washingtonpost.com/politics/trump-recorded-having-extremely-lewd-conversation-about-women-in-2005/2016/10/07/3b9ce776-8cb4-11e6-bf8a-3d26847eeed4_story.html.
19. Frontline "America's Great Divide: From Obama to Trump," https://www.pbs.org/wgbh/frontline/film/americas-great-divide-from-obama-to-trump/transcript/.
20. Jonathan Blitzer, "How Stephen Miller Manipulates Donald Trump to Further His Immigration Obsession," *The New Yorker*, March 2, 2020.

21. Michael Wolff, *Fire and Fury: Inside the Trump White House*, New York, Henry Holt and Company, 2018, p. 65.
22. Abigail Hauslohner and Sandhya Somashekhar, "Immigration authorities arrested 680 people in raids last week," *The Washington Post*, February 13, 2017, https://www.washingtonpost.com/national/immigration-authorities-arrested-680-people-in-raids-last-week/2017/02/13/3659da74-f232-11e6-8d72-263470bf0401_story.html.
23. Stephen Dinan, "No apologies: ICE chief says illegal immigrants should live in fear of deportation," *Washington Times*, June 13, 2017, https://www.washingtontimes.com/news/2017/jun/13/thomas-homan-ice-chief-says-illegal-immigrants-sho/.
24. Paul Bedard, "Trump endorses immigration reform, says he's 'liberating cities'with arrests," *Washington Examiner*, July 26, 2017, https://www.washingtonexaminer.com/trump-endorses-immigration-reform-says-hes-liberating-cities-with-arrests.
25. MSNBC "On his 100th day, Donald Trump remembers 'The Snake,'" http://www.msnbc.com/rachel-maddow-show/his-100th-day-donald-trump-remembers-the-snake.
26. David A. Graham, "One Way to Get Through to Trump? Children," *The Atlantic*, April 11, 2018, https://www.theatlantic.com/politics/archive/2018/04/trump-children/557633/.
27. Michael Wolf, *Fire and Fury*, op. cit., p. 71.
28. Julie Hirschfeld Davis and Sheryl Gay Stolberg, "Trump Appears to Endorse Path to Citizenship for Millions of Immigrants," *The New York Times*, January 9, 2018, https://www.nytimes.com/2018/01/09/us/politics/trump-daca-immigration.html.
29. Ibid.
30. The headline was subsequently changed to "Trump Says He's Open to U.S. Citizenship for DACA Illegal Aliens," Breitbart.com, January 24, 2018, https://www.breitbart.com/politics/2018/01/24/trump-says-hes-open-to-u-s-citizenship-for-daca-illegal-aliens/. See an image of the original headline at https://twitter.com/thehill/status/956370312349745152.
31. Daily Beast, "Trump Wants Fewer Immigrants from Sh*thole Countries, More Norwegians," January 11, 2018, https://www.thedailybeast.com/trump-wants-less-shthole-immigrants-more-norwegians.
32. Catherine Porter "Canada's Immigration System, Lauded by Trump, is More Complex than Advertised," *The New York Times*, March 2, 2017.
33. Bill Ong Hing, testimony to the House Subcommittee on Immigration, Citizenship, Refugees, Border Security, and International Law, May 8, 2007, https://www.aila.org/File/Related/07050860d.pdf.
34. Meg Brauckmann, "Conversations on war and migration in Quetzaltenango," Matador Network, May 15, 2013, https//matadornetwork.com/notebook/conversations-on-war-and-migration-in-quetzaltenango/.
35. Fox News, "Trump: Illegal immigration crisis is 'concerted effort' by Pres Obama to bring more migrant children into the system because they become

Democrats, vote Democrat," https://www.foxnews.com/transcript/trump-illegal-immigration-crisis-is-concerted-effort-by-pres-obama-to-bring-more-migrant-children-into-the-system-because-they-become-democrats-vote-democrat.

36. White House Office of the President, "Remarks to the Press with Q&A by Vice President Joe Biden in Guatemala, June 20, 2014, https://obamawhitehouse.archives.gov/the-press-office/2014/06/20/remarks-press-qa-vice-president-joe-biden-guatemala.
37. Maria Cardona, "Bernie is No Dream Candidate for Immigrants," *U.S. News and World Report*, February 19, 2016, https://www.usnews.com/opinion/articles/2016-02-19/in-nevada-bernie-sanders-immigration-record-is-a-nightmare.
38. Julie Hirschfeld Davis and Michael D. Shear, *Border Wars: Inside Trump's Assault on Immigration*, New York, Simon & Schuster, 2019, p. 260.
39. Matt Viser and Josh Dawsey, "In the closing days of the election, Trump turns to his favorite weapon: Immigration," *The Washington Post*, October 27, 2018, https://www.washingtonpost.com/politics/in-the-closing-days-of-the-election-trump-turns-to-his-favorite-weapon-immigration/2018/10/25/7c42fa44-d79f-11e8-83a2-d1c3da28d6b6_story.html.
40. Jerry Kammer, "MSNBC and Fox Mix Reporting with Electioneering," Center for Immigration Studies Blog, October 24, 2018, https://cis.org/Kammer/MSNBC-and-Fox-Mix-Reporting-Electioneering.
41. Davis and Shear, *Border Wars*, op. cit., p. 325.
42. Nick Miroff, "The Conveyor Belt," *The Washington Post*, March 15, 2019, https://www.washingtonpost.com/national/the-conveyor-belt-us-officials-say-massive-smuggling-effort-is-speeding-immigrants-to—and-across—the-southern-border/2019/03/15/940bf860-4022-11e9-a0d3-1210e58a94cf_story.html.
43. Seung Min Kim, "Cantor loss kills immigration reform," *Politico*, June 10, 2014, https://www.politico.com/story/2014/06/2014-virginia-primary-eric-cantor-loss-immigration-reform-107697.
44. Senate Committee on Homeland Security and Governmental Affairs, Hearing on Unprecedented Migration at the U.S. Southern Border: Perspectives from the Frontline, https://www.hsgac.senate.gov/hearings/unprecedented-migration-at-the-us-southern-border-perspectives-from-the-frontline. See also, Kammer blog, "Hearing Describes Border Chaos, but No Sign that Congress Can Fix It," April 10, 2019, https://cis.org/Kammer/Hearing-Describes-Border-Chaos-No-Sign-Congress-Can-Fix-It.
45. *Politico*, "Full Text: Donald Trump Speech in Arizona," August 31, 2016, https://www.politico.com/story/2016/08/donald-trump-immigration-address-transcript-227614.
46. Ibid.
47. Julie Hirschfeld Davis and Michael D. Shear, *Border Wars*, op. cit., p. 281.
48. Stephen Dinan, "Trump's retreat on E-Verify called special interest takeover of immigration agenda," *Washington Times*, February 12, 2020.

49. The Bill Press Show, July 3, 2018. Cited by States News Service, "Meet Alexandria Ocasio Cortez, the Minimaduro," August 17, 2018.
50. CNN, July 18, 2018; also cited by States News Service, August 17, 2018.
51. Reihan Salam, *Melting Pot or Civil War?: A Son of Immigrants Makes the Case Against Open Borders*, New York, Sentinel, 2018, pp. 27–28.
52. David Frum, "If Liberals Won't Enforce Borders, Fascists Will," The Atlantic, April 2019.
53. Russell Kirk, *The Conservative Mind, from Burke to Santayana*, Chicago, Henry Regnery Company, 1953, p. 42.
54. Nathan Glazer, "Concluding Observations," in *Debating Immigration*, Carol Swain, ed., New York, Cambridge University Press, 2007, p. 259.

INDEX

Note: Organizations which have been restructured as well as renamed (example: INS) will be listed under their legacy title. "n" in a page number refers to the Notes section at the end of the book.

NUMBERS

A

B

C

E

G

H

I

O

T

U

V

W

Y

Z

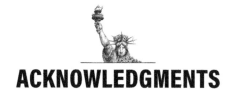

ACKNOWLEDGMENTS

I am grateful to many people for their help, going back to 1986, when I began learning about immigration. I'm especially grateful to Bill Waters, my editor at the Arizona Republic and to George Condon and Marcus Stern at the Copley News Service. My wife Marie's love and encouragement were a constant source of motivation. Mark Krikorian's support for protracted research was indispensable. Charles and Lynn DuBois, Lenore Devore, Claire Gray, Hilary Hinzmann, Sally Heffentreyer, Amos and Casey Goodall, and Lynn Petnick provided valuable suggestions or editing. I am grateful to the undocumented immigrants who told me their stories, some of whom became friends, especially Luis from Chiapas, Mexico and Miguel from Aguilares, El Salvador. And I am grateful to the many employees of the federal government, especially the agents of the INS and DHS, who helped me understand the long unraveling of the 1986 immigration reform legislation that is the centerpiece of this book. I want to thank some friends, especially Ben Johnson and Jose Lopez Zamorano, who didn't let our disagreements destroy our friendship. Finally, my thanks to the remarkably talented Michael Ramirez, who created the art for the book's cover, and to David Wogahn, who did a wonderful job managing the book's publication.

ABOUT THE AUTHOR

Jerry Kammer, a native of Baltimore and a graduate of Notre Dame, began his reporting career in 1974 with the *Navajo Times*. As a reporter for the *Arizona Republic*, he won the Robert F. Kennedy Journalism Award for reporting on the lives of workers at Mexican border factories known as maquiladoras. For reporting on the financial empire of Phoenix financier Charles H. Keating Jr., the central figure of the national savings and loan scandal, Kammer received the Gerald Loeb Award for business reporting and the National Headliner Award for investigative reporting. In 2006 he received a Pulitzer for reporting in the *San Diego Union-Tribune* that helped expose the bribery scandal whose central figure was Rep. Randy "Duke" Cunningham. During the 1990s and 2000s he traveled widely to report on immigration. He earned an M.A. in American Studies from the University of New Mexico and was a Nieman journalism fellow at Harvard. A senior research fellow at the Center for Immigration Studies, he lives in State College, Pa., with his wife, Marie Hardin.

Made in the USA
Monee, IL
06 July 2020

35959559R00233